SpeedPro Series

HOW TO POWER TUNE
ROVER
V8
ENGINES

FOR ROAD & TRACK

DES HAMMILL

VELOCE PUBLISHING
THE PUBLISHER OF FINE AUTOMOTIVE BOOKS

Also from Veloce –

SpeedPro Series
4-Cylinder Engine - How to Blueprint & Build a Short Block for High Performance by Des Hammill
Alfa Romeo Twin Cam Engines - How to Power Tune by Jim Kartalamakis
BMC 998cc A-Series Engine - How to Power Tune by Des Hammill
BMC/Rover 1275cc A-Series Engines - How to Power Tune by Des Hammill
Camshafts - How to Choose & Time them for Maximum Power by Des Hammill
Cylinder Heads - How to Build, Modify & Power Tune Updated & Revised Edition by Peter Burgess
Distributor-type Ignition Systems - How to Build & Power Tune by Des Hammill
Fast Road Car - How to Plan and Build New Edition by Daniel Stapleton
Ford SOHC 'Pinto' & Sierra Cosworth DOHC Engines - How to Power Tune Updated & Enlarged Edition by Des Hammill
Ford V8 - How to Power Tune Small Block Engines by Des Hammill
Harley-Davidson Evolution Engines - How to Build & Power Tune by Des Hammill
Holley Carburetors - How to Build & Power Tune New Edition by Des Hammill
Jaguar XK Engines - How to Power Tune New Edition by Des Hammill
MG Midget & Austin-Healey Sprite - How to Power Tune Updated Edition by Daniel Stapleton
MGB 4-Cylinder Engine - How to Power Tune by Peter Burgess
MGB - How to Give your MGB V8 Power Updated & Revised Edition by Roger Williams
MGB, MGC & MGB V8 - How to Improve by Roger Williams
Mini Engines - How to Power Tune on a Small Budget 2nd Edition by Des Hammill
Motorsport - Getting Started in by SS Collins
Nitrous Oxide Systems - How to Build & Power Tune by Trevor Langfield
Rover V8 Engines - How to Power Tune by Des Hammill
Sportscar/Kitcar Suspension & Brakes - How to Build & Modify Enlarged & Updated 2nd Edition by Des Hammill
SU Carburettors - How to Build & Modify for High Performance by Des Hammill
Suzuki 4WD for Serious Offroad Action - Modifying by John Richardson
Tiger Avon Sportscar - How to Build Your Own Updated & Revised 2nd Edition by Jim Dudley
TR2, 3 & TR4 - How to Improve by Roger Williams
TR5, 250 & TR6 - How to Improve by Roger Williams
V8 Engine - How to Build a Short Block for High Performance by Des Hammill
Volkswagen Beetle Suspension, Brakes & Chassis - How to Modify for High Performance by James Hale
Volkswagen Bus Suspension, Brakes & Chassis - How to Modify for High Performance by James Hale
Weber DCOE, & Dellorto DHLA Carburetors - How to Build & Power Tune 3rd Edition by Des Hammill

Those were the days ... Series
Alpine Trials & Rallies 1910-1973 by Martin Pfundner
Austerity Motoring by Malcolm Bobbitt
Brighton National Speed Trials by Tony Gardiner
British Police Cars by Nick Walker
Crystal Palace by SS Collins
Dune Buggy Phenomenon by James Hale
More Dune Buggies by James Hale
Motor Racing at Brands Hatch in the Seventies by Chas Parker
Motor Racing at Goodwood in the Sixties by Tony Gardiner
Three Wheelers by Malcolm Bobbitt

Enthusiast's Restoration Manual Series
Citroën 2CV - How to Restore by Lindsay Porter
Classic Car Body Work - How to Restore by Martin Thaddeus
Classic Cars - How to Paint by Martin Thaddeus
Reliant Regal, How to Restore by Elvis Payne
Triumph TR2/3/3A - How to Restore by Roger Williams
Triumph TR4/4A - How to Restore by Roger Williams
Triumph TR5/250 & 6 - How to Restore by Roger Williams
Triumph TR7/8 - How to Restore by Roger Williams
Volkswagen Beetle - How to Restore by Jim Tyler

Essential Buyer's Guide Series
Alfa GT Buyer's Guide by Keith Booker
Alfa Romeo Giulia Spider Buyer's Guide by Keith Booker
Jaguar E-Type Buyer's Guide
Porsche 928 Buyer's Guide by David Hemmings
VW Beetle Buyer's Guide by Ken Cservenka & Richard Copping

Auto Graphics Series
Fiat & Abarth by Andrea & David Sparrow
Jaguar MkII by Andrea & David Sparrow
Lambretta LI by Andrea & David Sparrow

General
AC Two-litre Saloons & Buckland Sportscars by Leo Archibald
Alfa Romeo Berlinas (Saloons/Sedans) by John Tipler
Alfa Romeo Giulia Coupé GT & GTA by John Tipler
Alfa Tipo 33 Development, Racing & Chassis History by Ed McDonough
Anatomy of the Works Minis by Brian Moylan
Armstrong-Siddeley by Bill Smith
Autodrome by SS Collins & Gavin Ireland
Automotive A-Z, Lane's Dictionary of Automotive Terms by Keith Lane
Automotive Mascots by David Kay & Lynda Springate
Bentley Continental, Corniche and Azure by Martin Bennett
BMC's Competition Department Secrets by Stuart Turner, Phillip Young, Peter Browning, Marcus Chambers
BMW 5-Series by Marc Cranswick
BMW Z-Cars by James Taylor

British 250cc Racing Motorcycles by Chris Pereira
British Cars, The Complete Catalogue of, 1895-1975 by Culshaw & Horrobin
Bugatti Type 40 by Barrie Price
Bugatti 46/50 Updated Edition by Barrie Price
Bugatti 57 2nd Edition by Barrie Price
Caravans, The Illustrated History 1919-1959 by Andrew Jenkinson
Caravans, The Illustrated History from 1960 by Andrew Jenkinson
Chrysler 300 - America's Most Powerful Car 2nd Edition by Robert Ackerson
Citroën DS by Malcolm Bobbitt
Cobra - The Real Thing! by Trevor Legate
Cortina - Ford's Bestseller by Graham Robson
Coventry Climax Racing Engines by Des Hammill
Daimler SP250 'Dart' by Brian Long
Datsun 240, 260 & 280Z by Brian Long
Dune Buggy Files by James Hale
Dune Buggy Handbook by James Hale
Fiat & Abarth 124 Spider & Coupé by John Tipler
Fiat & Abarth 500 & 600 2nd edition by Malcolm Bobbitt
Ford F100/F150 Pick-up 1948-1996 by Robert Ackerson
Ford F150 1997-2005 by Robert Ackerson
Ford GT40 by Trevor Legate
Ford Model Y by Sam Roberts
Funky Mopeds by Richard Skelton
Honda NSX Supercar by Brian Long
Jaguar, The Rise of by Barrie Price
Jaguar XJ-S by Brian Long
Jeep CJ by Robert Ackerson
Jeep Wrangler by Robert Ackerson
Karmann-Ghia Coupé & Convertible by Malcolm Bobbitt
Land Rover, The Half-Ton Military by Mark Cook
Lea-Francis Story, The by Barrie Price
Lexus Story, The by Brian Long
Lola - The Illustrated History (1957-1977) by John Starkey
Lola - All The Sports Racing & Single-Seater Racing Cars 1978-1997 by John Starkey
Lola T70 - The Racing History & Individual Chassis Record 3rd Edition by John Starkey
Lotus 49 by Michael Oliver
Marketingmobiles, The Wonderful Wacky World of, by James Hale
Mazda MX-5/Miata 1.6 Enthusiast's Workshop Manual by Rod Grainger & Pete Shoemark
Mazda MX-5/Miata 1.8 Enthusiast's Workshop Manual by Rod Grainger & Pete Shoemark
Mazda MX-5 (& Eunos Roadster) - The World's Favourite Sportscar by Brian Long
Mazda MX-5 Miata Roadster by Brian Long
MGA by John Price Williams
MGB & MGB GT - Expert Guide (Auto-Doc Series) by Roger Williams
Micro Caravans by Andrew Jenkinson
Mini Cooper - The Real Thing! by John Tipler
Mitsubishi Lancer Evo by Brian Long
Motor Racing Reflections by Anthony Carter
Motorhomes, The Illustrated History by Andrew Jenkinson
Motorsport in colour, 1950s by Martyn Wainwright
MR2 - Toyota's mid-engined Sports Car by Brian Long
Nissan 300ZX & 350Z - The Z-Car Story by Brian Long
Pass Your Theory & Practical Driving Tests by Clive Gibson & Gavin Hoole
Pontiac Firebird by Marc Cranswick
Porsche Boxster by Brian Long
Porsche 356 by Brian Long
Porsche 911 Carrera by Tony Corlett
Porsche 911R, RS & RSR, 4th Edition by John Starkey
Porsche 911 - The Definitive History 1963-1971 by Brian Long
Porsche 911 - The Definitive History 1971-1977 by Brian Long
Porsche 911 - The Definitive History 1977-1987 by Brian Long
Porsche 911 - The Definitive History 1987-1997 by Brian Long
Porsche 911 - The Definitive History 1997-2004 by Brian Long
Porsche 911SC 'Super Carrera' by Adrian Streather
Porsche 914 & 914-6 by Brian Long
Porsche 924 by Brian Long
Porsche 933 'King of Porsche' by Adrian Streather
Porsche 944 by Brian Long
RAC Rally Action! by Tony Gardiner
Rolls-Royce Silver Shadow/Bentley T Series Corniche & Camargue Revised & Enlarged Edition by Malcolm Bobbitt
Rolls-Royce Silver Spirit, Silver Spur & Bentley Mulsanne 2nd Edition by Malcolm Bobbitt
Rolls-Royce Silver Wraith, Dawn & Cloud/Bentley MkVI, R & S Series by Martyn Nutland
RX-7 - Mazda's Rotary Engine Sportscar (Updated & Revised New Edition) by Brian Long
Singer Story: Cars, Commercial Vehicles, Bicycles & Motorcycles by Kevin Atkinson
Subaru Impreza by Brian Long
Taxi! The Story of the 'London' Taxicab by Malcolm Bobbitt
Triumph Motorcycles & the Meriden Factory by Hughie Hancox
Triumph Speed Twin & Thunderbird Bible by Harry Woolridge
Triumph Tiger Cub Bible by Mike Estall
Triumph Trophy Bible by Harry Woolridge
Triumph TR6 by William Kimberley
Turner's Triumphs, Edward Turner & his Triumph Motorcycles by Jeff Clew
Velocette Motorcycles - MSS to Thruxton Updated & Revised Edition by Rod Burris
Volkswagen Bus or Van to Camper, How to Convert by Lindsay Porter
Volkswagens of the World by Simon Glen
VW Beetle Cabriolet by Malcolm Bobbitt
VW Beetle - The Car of the 20th Century by Richard Copping
VW Bus, Camper, Van, Pickup by Malcolm Bobbitt
VW - The air-cooled era by Richard Copping
Works Rally Mechanic by Brian Moylan

First published in 2005. Veloce Publishing Ltd., 33 Trinity Street, Dorchester DT1 1TT, England. Fax 01305 268864. E-mail: info@veloce.co.uk Web: www.veloce.co.uk
ISBN 1-903706-17-3/UPC 6-36847-00217-6

Readers with ideas for automotive books, or books on other transport or related hobby subjects, are invited to write to the editorial director of Veloce Publishing at the above address.

British Library Cataloguing in Publication Data -
A catalogue record for this book is available from the British Library.
Typesetting, design and page make-up all by Veloce on Apple Mac.
Printed in Spain.

Contents

Using this book
  & Essential information **7**
Introduction **9**
Buick & Oldsmobile engines 10
Rover engines 12
TVR Tuscan engines 12
Leyland P76 engines 12

Chapter 1: Cylinder block, liners,
  pistons & timing chain **14**
Cylinder block types. 14
Type 1: 1967 to 1980 3.5in bore P5,
  P6, Range Rover and early SD1 blocks . 15
Type 2: June 1973 to December 1980
  Australian-made Leyland P76 engine
  (4.4 litre) 16
Type 3: 1980 to 1993 3.5in bore
  uprated 'stiff' block 16
Type 4: October 1989 to December 1993
  3.9 litre engines 17
Type 5 & 6: January 1994 onward 3.9 &
  4.2 litre 'interim' engines 18
Type 7: September 1994 onward 4.0 &
  4.6 litre '38A' block engines 20
Type 8: 1995, 1997/1998 3.5 litre 'service'
  engine blocks 22
Quick reference block identification 23
Which cylinder block to use?. 23
Wildcat modified blocks 26
Water loss problems caused by block
  cracking 29

Symptoms 30
Repairing cracked blocks 31
Standard blocks 32
Two bolt main cap blocks 32
Two bolt main cap problems 33
Stud & nut kits for two bolt main caps . . . 37
Camshaft bearings (all blocks) 39
Timing chain (all blocks). 40
Engine block requirements for
  high performance 41
Fitting a camshaft thrust plate to
  pre-1994 engine blocks 41
Teflon-faced 'thrust bolt' 43
Oversized cylinder liners for
  3500cc blocks. 44
Standard cast pistons 45
Standard piston sizes. 46
Hypoeutectic, eutectic &
  hypereutectic cast pistons 46
Forged pistons 47
Bore wear 47
Summary 48
Cylinder bore preparation 48
Cylinder head fixings 50

Chapter 2: Cylinder head
  identification **51**
Identification. 51
Buick heads 51
Original Rover 3.5 litre heads. 51
First change: SD1 & Range Rover

heads 1976 on. 51
Second change: 1982 on 53
Third change: 1982 on 53
Fourth change: 1993 on 53
Fifth change: 1994 on. 54
Early heads & unleaded fuel 55
Valves 56
Valve spring & valve spring retainers. 56
Standard inlet & exhaust ports 56

Chapter 3: Distributor, front cover &
  oil pump identification **57**
Distributors 57
Car distributors 57
4X4 & commercial vehicle distributors 58
Front covers 58
Type 1 & 2 58
Type 3 58
Type 4 59
Types 5 & 6 59
Type 7 59
Type 8 60
Gear-driven oil pumps 60
Water pumps 60
Camshaft skew gears. 61
Buick versus Rover skew gears 61
Adjustable oil pressure (crank-driven oil
  pump-type front covers). 61

Chapter 4: Distributors &
  ignition timing **62**

SPEEDPRO SERIES

Lucas distributors 62
Repair 63
Mechanical advance system 63
Changing static advance setting 63
Changing the rate of advance 63
Vacuum advance system 64
Racing engines 64
Vacuum advance on racing engines 64
Mallory distributors 65
Repairing 65
How dual points work 65
Dual points reliability 66
Adjustable mechanical advance 66
Changing amount of static advance 66
Changing rate of ignition advance 66
Road cars 67
Racing 67
Conclusion 67
True TDC 67
Degree marking the crankshaft
    pulley rim 67
Ignition advance 68
Stroboscope ignition timing 68
Too much compression 69
Standard sparkplug leads (wires) 69
Sparkplug lead location 69
Condenser 69
Further reading 69

Chapter 5: Rocker arms, rockershaft
    & pushrods 71
Rocker arm geometry 71
Rockershaft height 72
Roller rockers 73
Hydraulic lifter preload 73
Shorter pushrods 74
Standard rocker arms 74
Standard rocker arms & shaft
    with high lift camshaft 75

Chapter 6: Camshafts &
    valve springs 77
Camshafts with standard valve lift 77
Camshaft choice 78
Standard camshafts 78
Regrinds 78
Aftermarket camshafts 78
Valve springs & retainers 79
Hydraulic lifters 79
Using old lifters 80
Common problems 80
Camshafts for 'Group A' racing 81
Summary 81
Increasing valve lift above standard 81
Early cylinder heads 82
1976-1993 cylinder heads 82
1993 on cylinder heads 83
Valve springs for high performance
    applications 85

Standard single valve springs 85
Aftermarket valve springs 85
Which aftermarket camshaft? 87
The consequences of higher valve lift 88
High performance aftermarket camshafts . . 88
'Smooth idle' camshafts 88
'Rough idle' camshafts 89
270-280 degree camshafts 90
280-290 degree camshafts 90
Long duration (295-305 degrees plus) . . . 91
Alternative profiles & phasings 91
Summary 91

Chapter 7: Balance 92
Original factory engine balance 92
Engine balance for high performance 93

Chapter 8: Lubrication 95
Low oil pressure 95
Improving oil systems of
    non-crank-driven oil pump engines 96
Increasing oil pressure 96
Oil pump 97
Pressure relief valve 99
Extra oiling of the distributor &
    camshaft skew gears 100
Camshaft bearing modification 100
Dual oil feed to the centre three
    main bearings 100
360 degree main bearing oiling 101
Crankshaft bearing clearances 101
Lifter to lifter bore fit 102
Adjustable oil pressure relief valve:
    crank-driven oil pumps 102
Improved main & big end bearing
    oiling (all engines with standard
    crankshaft oilways) 102
260-270 degree main bearing oiling 102
Altering standard bottom main
    bearing shells 103
Big end bearing oiling improvement
    summary 104
Radiusing crankshaft oilways 104
Restricting rockershaft oil feed
    (all engines) 104
Wet sump (oil pan) 105
Crankcase ventilation 107

Chapter 9: J.E. Developments & other
    specialists 108
J.E. Developments 108
Cylinder blocks 108
Crankshafts 109
Connecting rods 110
Special capacities for racing
    applications 111
Other racing engine capacities 112
Cylinder heads 112
Valve set 1 112

Valve set 2 112
Valve set 3 112
Valve set 4 113
Valve springs 114
Camshafts 115
Valve train 116
Engine balance 118
Ignition systems 119
Induction systems 119
Optimum fuel mixture settings 120
Fuel 120
Exhaust systems 121
Other specialists 121

Chapter 10: Wildcat Engineering . . . 122
Wildcat Engineering 122
Connecting rods 123
Crankshafts 124
Maximum bore (up to 6000cc) Rover V8
    competition engines 124
Crankshaft dampers 126
Turbo block 126
Cylinder heads 127
High performance cylinder heads 128
Stage 1 cylinder heads 130
Stage 2 cylinder heads 130
Inlet manifolds 132
Fuel injection throttle bodies 133
Dry sump system 133
Steel flywheels 134
Wildcat engine example 134

Chapter 11: Cylinder head
    modifications 136
Which heads? 136
Modifications 137
Preparation 137
Valve guides 137
Minor porting 137
Valve seats 138
Refacing 140
Fully modified cylinder heads 140

Chapter 12: SU carburettors 148
Setting up 148
1) Float levels 148
2) Needle heights 149
3) Main jet heights 149
4) Idle adjustment screws 149
5) Balance 149
6) Idle mixture 149
7) Synchronising butterflies 150
Fuel pressure 150
Emission control poppet valves 150
Crankcase breather 150
Air cleaners & ram pipes 150
Changing & modifying needles 151
Standard needles 153
Needle tuning 154

Modifications for racing 155

Chapter 13: Holley carburettors . . . 156
390-CFM vacuum secondary with
   automatic choke. 156
Setting up 156
1) Float levels. 156
2) Idle adjustment screw 156
3) Accelerator pump 157
4) Idle adjustment screws 157
5) Metering block. 157
390-CFM mechanical secondary
   ('double pumper') four barrel 158
Tips (all Holley carburettors) 158
1) Float levels. 158
2) Fuel pressure. 158
3) Backfiring through the carburettor 158
4) Fuel spillage. 158
5) Gaskets 158
6) Butterfly opening. 159
7) Fuel filter 159
8) Accelerator pump 159
Summary. 159
Air filters 159
Fuel filters. 160
Fuel pumps. 160

Chapter 14: Inlet manifolds. 161
Inlet manifolds for Holley carburettors . . 161
180 degree manifolds 162
Low rise. 162
High rise 162
Aftermarket 180 degree manifolds 163
360 degree manifold 163
Summary. 164
Other downdraught carburettor
   options/adaptors. 164
Standard & aftermarket inlet
   manifolds for SU carburettors 164

**Chapter 15: Fuel injection & engine
   management systems 166**
L-Jetronic 4CU fuel injection system
   (USA & Australian types 1974-1990):
   overview 166

L-Jetronic 4CU fuel injection system
   (UK type 1983 to 1990): overview 167
L-Jetronic 4CU fuel injection system:
   operation. 168
ECU (electronic/engine control unit) 168
Airflow meter. 168
Airflow meter: setting 169
Throttle body potentiometer 170
Throttle body potentiometer: setting. . . . 170
Fuel delivery control 170
Fuel supply system 171
Cold start controls. 172
Lambda sensors 172
Ignition system 172
L-Jetronic 4CU fuel injection system:
   early methods of modification for
   high performance 173
Airflow meter: altering setting 173
Fuel pressure: increasing 174
Temperature feedback: altering. 174
Conclusion 174
L-Jetronic 4CU fuel injection system:
   current methods of modification for
   high performance 174
Injectors. 174
ECU upgrade. 175
Airflow meter 176
Rising rate fuel pressure regulator 176
4.2 litre upgrade 177
Twin plenum L-Jetronic 4CU fuel
   injection system. 178
Twin plenum L-Jetronic 4CU fuel
   injection system: twin airflow meters . . 179
L-Jetronic 13CU and 14CU electronic
   fuel injection system: overview 179
L-Jetronic 14CUX electronic
   fuel injection system: overview 180
Injectors. 180
ECU. 180
Airflow meter 181
GEMS 8 integrated engine
   management system: overview 182
GEMS 8: methods of modification
   for high performance 184
GEMS 8: ignition system 186

Bosch Motronic ML.2.1 engine
   management system: overview 187
HT (High Tension) lead/wire
   requirements (all systems) 187
Catalytic converters (all systems) 187

Chapter 16: Exhaust system 189
Original exhaust manifolds 189
Tubular exhaust manifolds (headers) . . . 190
4 into 1 190
4 into 2 into 1. 192
Pipe dimensions 193
Pipe dimensions 194
Sealing exhaust manifolds. 194

Chapter 17: Cooling system 195
Kit cars 196
Radiator. 196
Thermostat 196
Fan. 196
Pipework 196
Racing cars. 197
Optimum temperature range. 197
Radiator. 197
Restrictor plate 197
Selecting & fitting a radiator 197
Radiator caps & header tanks 197
Water pump speed. 199
Swapping pulleys 200
Other options 200

Chapter 18: Flywheel & clutch 201
Flywheel 201
J.E. Developments' dry sump
   system flywheel. 201
Clutch 202

Chapter 19: Rolling road dyno. 203
Chart A 206
Chart B 206
Conversion chart 207

Index 213

Veloce SpeedPro books -

ISBN 1 903706 76 9

ISBN 1 903706 91 2

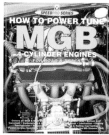
ISBN 1 903706 77 7

ISBN 1 903706 78 5

ISBN 1 901295 73 7

ISBN 1 903706 75 0

ISBN 1 901295 62 1

ISBN 1 874105 70 7

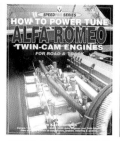
ISBN 1 903706 60 2

ISBN 1 903706 92 0

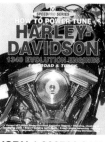
ISBN 1 903706 94 7

ISBN 1 901295 26 5

ISBN 1 901295 07 9

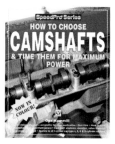
ISBN 1 903706 59 9

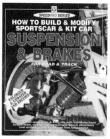
ISBN 1 903706 73 4

ISBN 1 904788 78-5

ISBN 1 901295 76 1

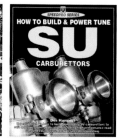
ISBN 1 903706 98 X

ISBN 1 903706 99 8

ISBN 1 84584 005 4

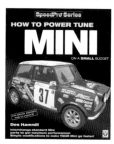
ISBN 1-904788-84-X

ISBN 1-904788-22-X

ISBN 1 903706 17 3

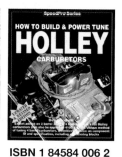
ISBN 1 84584 006 2

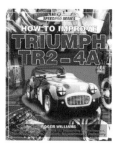
ISBN 1 903706 80 7

ISBN 1 903706 68 8

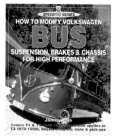
ISBN 1 903706 14 9

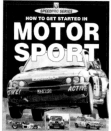
ISBN 1 903706 70 X

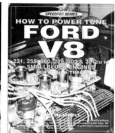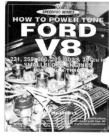
ISBN 1 903706 72 6

- more on the way!

Using this book & Essential information

USING THIS BOOK

Throughout this book the text assumes that you, or your contractor, will have a workshop manual specific to your engine to follow for complete detail on dismantling, reassembly, adjustment procedure, clearances, torque figures, etc. This book's default is the standard manufacturer's specification for your engine type so, if a procedure is not described, a measurement not given, a torque figure ignored, you can assume that the standard manufacturer's procedure or specification for your engine should be used.

It is essential to read the whole book before you start work or give instructions to your contractor. This is because a modification or change in specification in one area can cause the need for changes in other areas; you might also be inspired by a particular aspect of J. E. Developments' or Wildcat's approach to tuning these engines. Get the whole picture so that you can finalize specification and component requirements as far as possible *before* any work begins.

For those requiring more information on building techniques and blueprinting, Des Hammill's *How to Blueprint & Build a V8 Shortblock for High-Performance* (also from Veloce Publishing) is essential reading.

ESSENTIAL INFORMATION

This book contains information on practical procedures; however, this information is intended only for those with the qualifications, experience, tools and facilities to carry out the work in safety and with appropriately high levels of skill. Whenever working on a car or component, remember that your personal safety must **ALWAYS** be your **FIRST** consideration. The publisher, author, editors and retailer of this book cannot accept any responsibility for personal injury or mechanical damage which results from using this book, even if caused by errors or omissions in the information given. If this disclaimer is unacceptable to you, please return the pristine book to your retailer who will refund the purchase price.

In the text of this book "**Warning!**" means that a procedure could cause personal injury and "**Caution!**" that there is danger of mechanical damage if appropriate care is not taken. However, be aware that we cannot foresee every possibility of danger in every circumstance.

Please note that changing component specification by modification is likely to void warranties and also to absolve manufacturers from any responsibility in the event of component failure and the consequences of such failure.

Increasing the engine's power will place additional stress on engine components and on the car's complete driveline: this may reduce service life and increase the frequency of breakdown. An increase in engine power, and therefore the vehicle's performance, will mean that your vehicle's braking and suspension systems will need to be kept in perfect condition and uprated as appropriate. It is also usually necessary to inform the vehicle's insurers of any changes to the vehicle's specification.

The importance of cleaning a component thoroughly before working on it cannot be overstressed. Always keep your working area and tools as clean as possible. Whatever specialist cleaning fluid or other chemicals you use, be sure to follow - completely - manufacturer's instructions and if you are using petrol (gasoline) or paraffin (kerosene) to clean parts, take every precaution necessary to protect your body and to avoid all risk of fire.

Introduction

This book aims to be the definitive guide to making a Rover V8 engine produce more power with reliability.

Most readers who are going to rebuild an engine, or have one rebuilt for them, will specify as many standard replacement parts as possible to keep the cost down. In this scenario engine revs must be limited to 5800rpm so that reliability is ensured, otherwise hydraulic lifter 'pump up', and the prospect of valve spring retainer failure (the later sintered ones of SD1 and later engines), looms. Replacement of later standard sintered valve spring retainers with aftermarket high strength ones lifts the maximum safe rpm to 6000rpm: the standard type cast aluminium pistons then become the weakest link.

Excellent power is available from these engines for a reasonable overall cost provided time, effort and money is spent in the right places:

many people waste money when building Rover V8 high performance engines. This book is designed to ensure that readers get maximum performance value for their money.

The general recommendation is not to rev any standard short block engine assembly-equipped Rover V8 over 6000rpm; instead aim at having the widest possible spread of usable power/torque within this rpm limitation. Don't 'over cam' such an engine under any circumstances. Choose componentry which ensures that power is still being developed at 6000rpm but still gives useful power as low down in the rpm range as possible. It's quite feasible to have optimum 'pulling power' available from 2000rpm with all of these engines with the power surge going right through and strongly to the safe limit of 6000rpm. Get it right and you'll achieve excellent performance given the standard componentry's

mechanical strength limitations. 6000rpm should not be considered a low limit.

Very large budgets – and the requirement for high revving racing engine applications (7000-7500rpm) – are rare in relation to the total number of Rover V8 engines being rebuilt with higher performance in mind. Even so, this book also covers Rover V8 engines which are going to be built for high rpm, maximum power applications.

There is a wide variety of increased engine capacities on offer from a range of Rover V8 engine specialists: in fact, over 20 different sizes. These engines use a range of bore sizes in conjunction with about ten different crankshaft strokes. Some of the capacity differences are really quite minor (e.g. 0.020in/ 0.5mm to 0.060in/1.5mm overbores). Engine capacities of up to 6000cc are available using specially cast, standard type cylinder blocks and long throw crankshafts with special connecting rods and pistons.

Aftermarket cylinder heads are available from the likes of Wildcat Engineering, as are special 360 degree, single plane inlet manifolds (single four barrel Holley carburettor), or pairs of inlet manifolds for downdraught Webers or Dellortos, as well as electronic fuel injection with individual throttle bodies.

You can still buy pretty much any standard component for these engines, also a huge range of aftermarket tuning parts. Rover V8 engine specialists are gearing up for the future so that services can be continued as per normal now that the engine is out of production. These engines and parts for them are going to be around for a very long time yet ...

Buick & Oldsmobile engines

At the time of these engines' introduction, by General Motor's Buick and Oldsmobile car divisions, to power 1961 compact cars, no other similar capacity V8 engine was available. The Buick 215ci engines were fitted into Buick Specials and Pontiac Tempests (2 years) and the Oldsmobile 215ci engines were fitted to the F-85. These cars were available in late 1960, even though they were 1961 models.

The original, all aluminium, 3.5 litre Buick V8 has stood the test of time, in original production form from 1960-1963 and then from 1967 in Rover guise. Had it not been for Rover taking over the engine, it would have finished in its 3.5 litre aluminium form at the end of 1963. Oldsmobile stopped production of this engine in 1963 and discontinued

using this series of engine altogether.

Best estimates put Oldsmobile production at around 250,000 units; Buick at around 500,000 units.

Buick, however, made increased capacity derivatives of the 215 cubic inch engine into the 1980s after stopping production of the original all aluminium engine in 1963. The smaller than usual V8 capacity engine phase for compact cars was over. These lightweight engines had proved much more expensive to build than the traditional all cast iron units. Although there had been no significant production or in-service problems, Buick engineers rejected the idea of enlarging the 3.5 inch bores of the original aluminium unit as too difficult and expensive and initially made a larger capacity (300ci/4918cc) derivative using a cast iron block but still with aluminium cylinder heads for the first year of production (1964). After that they fitted cast iron cylinder heads only. The 300 cubic inch engine had a bore size of 3.750in and a stroke of 3.400in, and had 2.500in/63.5mm diameter main bearings but retained the original 2.000in/50.80mm diameter big end size. The block deck height was increased by 0.5 inch.

Buick made 340ci (5569cc) and then 350ci (5752cc) capacity engines, based on the original 215ci design, until the mid-1980s.

There's more than one so-called 'Rover V8-engined' racing car around today using larger capacity, cast iron Buick short block assemblies!

The crankshafts of the 300 cubic inch Buick engines were later used in small numbers (a few hundred) as stroker cranks for Rover V8 engines in England. This wasn't

a straightforward 'drop-in fit' swap, but was quite possible with a little bit of remachining.

The later, and larger again, 340 and 350 cubic inch engines had 3.750in and 3.800in diameter bores respectively, and the same very long crankshaft strokes at 3.850in/97.5mm with a 3.000in/76.20mm diameter main bearing journal size, although retaining the 2.000in/50.80mm diameter big end journal size. The camshafts of these engines were phased so that the big ends of the connecting rods missed the camshaft lobes! Cylinder heads varied in their port configurations, and two types of cast iron cylinder head were used over the years.

Buick V8 engine sizes (after the 215ci) –
4.9 litres (4918cc) – 3.750in/95.2mm bore by 3.400in/86.36mm stroke
5.57 litres (5569cc) – 3.750in/95.2mm bore by 3.850in/97.80mm stroke
5.75 litres (5752cc) – 3.800in/96.5mm bore by 3.850in/97.80mm stroke

Buick switched from aluminium to cast iron blocks because it wanted to increase the bore size of the engine. The company achieved the required 0.25in bore increase quite easily within the original dimensions of the block by going to cast iron, which allowed it to maintain adequate bore wall thickness.

Buick engineers, with their vast V8 engine experience, knew what was possible in terms of developing this engine. The decision to change to a cast iron block was dictated by the need for increased capacity to satisfy customers demanding more powerful engines. At a stroke, the cast iron block cut costs and improved the unit's integrity when it came to larger capacities.

Rover engineers took a different approach, deciding that enlarged bores could be accommodated within cast iron sleeves in the alloy block. This decision would lead to reliability problems in the future due to variations in the amount of aluminium surrounding the liners. The switch to cast iron by Buick engineers also removed the expansion problem between the main caps and block registers which led to fretting. In service there were no 'bottom end' reliability problems with these later, all cast iron Buick derivatives of the original all aluminium engine.

In the early 1960s the very well respected Traco race engine preparation facility in the USA started modifying Oldsmobile F85 engines, and sold them under the name of Traco-Oldsmobiles. They certainly took the modification of these engines (using the original Oldsmobile F85 blocks and cylinder heads) to the logical conclusion and made engines with a range of capacities including 4.2, 4.4 and 5 litres. Traco did not use the Buick blocks for these engines as they were cast slightly differently, and were not as strong as Olds blocks. Equipped with 48mm IDA downdraught Weber carburettors and all of the other usual gear this company used on the engines it prepared, Traco-Oldsmobile engines performed exceptionally well.

Note that Traco fitted a ¼ inch thick steel plate across the bottom of the sump rails of the blocks it prepared for racing purposes. Specially made long studs passed

through holes drilled in this plate, then through the main caps and into the block. The studs were very close fitting in the holes in the plate and the main caps. When everything was bolted together, the main caps and the sides of the block (extended skirts) were connected very rigidly through this plate in this plane. Therefore, expansion and possible main cap movement was reduced to an absolute minimum. This modification didn't ultimately stop the fretting, but it took a lot longer for the block to become unserviceable. Traco also fitted crankshaft dampers, precisely tuned to the power and torque outputs of its engines, in order to damp the torsional vibration as much as possible, and thereby reduce the effects of torsional vibration on the block componentry.

There was another application of the Olds block in 1965. Repco Engineering in Australia used these blocks as the basis for the Repco Brabham 3.0 Formula One and 2.5 litre Tasman Series single overhead camshaft engines. The 3.0 F1 engines were used very successfully when Jack Brabham won the Championship in 1966 and Denis Hulme in 1967. The 3.0 litre engines used the standard 3.5in bore in conjunction with a specially made single plane crankshaft with a 2.375in stroke, while the 2.5 litre engines used a 3.340in bore in conjunction with a specially made single plane crankshaft with a 2.165in stroke.

The Rover V8 engine was definitely a derivative of the Buick block as opposed to the Oldsmobile unit. The 215ci Oldsmobile cylinder heads are quite different to the 215ci Buick heads; Rover heads are just

like the Buick items. The Oldsmobile F85 block was sand-cast, although the holes for the liners were machined and the liners pressed into the block Rover style. Oldsmobile heads had 18 stud retention and the block was made accordingly, the rocker shaft being secured by four of the head studs. The Buick block, on the other hand, had its liners fitted in the mould and the aluminium of the block cast around them (this process is called 'cast in liners'). Buick blocks had 14 stud cylinder head retention; although bosses for the 'missing' studs are cast into the block they cannot be used. These bosses could not be drilled and tapped to take extra studs because the water jacket went into them! The Buick block was diecast with a sand-cast crankcase area making it a 'semi' (part metal moulding and part sand casting), much the same as the Rover V8 block. The early Rover V8 block has 14 stud head retention like the Buick.

There are good reasons why the Buick and Oldsmobile engines are different to do with the fact that the engine was originally designed by 'General Motors Engineering Staff' in 1958. This was a group of General Motors engineers that did the design work for most of the General Motors powertrains and then passed their designs on to the various divisions of the company, any of which might decide to use a particular design. In this case both Buick and Oldsmobile decided to use the same basic engine design for the new compact cars they were planning. The Buick engine plant was in Flint, while the Oldsmobile engine plant was in Lansing, about 40 miles away, with little communication, if any, between the two. The engineers of each division developed the basic design to suit themselves and quite independently of the other ...

Rover engines

In order of capacity –
3.5 litres (3528cc) - 3.500in/ 88.90mm bore by 2.800in/71.12mm stroke
3.9 litres (3947cc) - 3.702in/ 94.04mm bore by 2.800in/71.12mm stroke
4.0 litres (3947cc) - 3.702in/ 94.04mm bore by 2.800in/71.12mm stroke
4.2 litres (4275cc) - 3.702in/ 94.04mm bore by 3.030in/77.00mm stroke
4.6 litres (4553cc) - 3.702in/ 94.04mm bore by 3.220in/82.00mm stroke

There were also a few special engines made for some motorsport applications. Early TR8 sports cars used for rallying had smaller pistons and liners to get the engines right on the 3500cc capacity limit (3499.9cc) as the standard 3.5 Rover V8 engine's capacity is actually 3528cc.

3.5, 3.9, 4.2 and 4.45 litre Rover V8 30A block engines are all 'small journal' crankshaft engines. The earlier 3.9 30A block engine and later 4.0 litre 38A block engines are actually the same capacity (same bore and stroke), and the listed capacity difference is really only to differentiate one engine design from the other.

Note the reference to 30A and 38A with regard to types of block. 30A are early small main bearing crankshaft journal blocks while 38A are later large main bearing crankshaft journal blocks.

The major difference between 3.5, 3.9, 4.2, 4.45 litre engines

and the 1994 and on 4.0 and 4.6 litre units is actually in the short assemblies. The 1994 and on 4.0 and 4.6 standard production engines have 'large journal' crankshafts compared to earlier standard production engines, (2.500in/63.50mm for the mains and 2.185in/55.50mm for the big ends of 'large journal' crankshafts; 2.299in/58.40mm for the mains and 2.000in/50.80mm for the big ends of 'small journal' crankshafts).

The connecting rods of 4.0 and 4.6 litre cross-bolted block engines differ from the earlier 3.5 and 3.9 litre connecting rods. The 4.0 and 4.6 litre engines also have different length connecting rods from each other. The pistons are of the same basic design for each engine with the compression ratios being varied by the depth of the dish in the tops of the pistons. Smaller dish 4.0 litre engine pistons fit 4.6 litre engines too.

Rover codenamed the later 'large journal' V8 blocks 'Pegasus' and all of these later standard blocks have cross-bolted, four bolt main caps. Once the 'Pegasus' engine was in production it was referred to as '38A'. The 4.0 and 4.6 litre 38A engine blocks are virtually identical to the last production blocks made. Thee later engines (January 1994 on) are also known by the name 'Serpentine' – this is to do with the convoluted single belt drive system and the counter rotating water pump employed on the 'interim' or 'intermediate' 3.9 and 4.2 litre engines.

Rover V8 cylinder block production peaked in the 1980s at 1420 blocks per week with cylinder heads at 2900 per week at the Bruhle-owned 'West Yorkshire

Foundry.' The original 3.5 litre engine was available in some Land Rovers as late as 2002, the engines coming from the 'service' engine stock made in the mid-1990s. The 4.0 and 4.6 litre engine production stopped in 2004.

TVR Tuscan engines

Engine size –
4.45 litres (4445cc) - 3.702in/ 94.04mm bore by 3.150in/80.00mm stroke
The TVR Tuscan engine was modified with Rover's approval. The crankshaft castings that had been made for the proposed Rover V8 diesel engine (code named 'Iceberg') were used for the TVR unit. While this diesel engine was tested, it never went into production. The standard production 4.2 litre Rover V8 and the TVR Tuscan engine did however use the 'Iceberg' crankshaft casting to get longer crankshaft strokes. As a result of this association with the Rover V8 diesel engine project, the 4.2 litre production engine and the original 4.45 litre TVR Tuscan engines, are commonly quoted as having 'Iceberg' crankshafts.

Leyland P76 engines

4.4 litres (4414cc) - 3.500in/ 88.90mm bore by 3.500in/88.90mm stroke
Another early variant of the Rover V8 was made by British Leyland in Australia in the 1970s. This engine was called the 'P76' and had a 3.500in/88.90mm bore and a 3.500in/88.90mm stroke. There were some differences in these Australian-made engines compared to the 3.5 litre Rover V8, some minor but others quite significant. For example, they had a 10 bolt

P76 type pressed steel rocker arms and pair-shared aluminium bridge.

cylinder head pattern which really amounted to nothing more than not including the lower head studs (a feature which is now standard on all 4.0 and 4.6 litre 38A production blocks). The distance from the centre of the crankshaft axis to the block deck was 0.690in/17.5mm (taller than the Rover V8). The crankshaft had 2.550in/64.80mm diameter main bearing journals, but retained the 2.000in/50.80mm diameter big end journal diameter. The rear flange of the crankshaft was larger and the flywheel/flexplate bolt holes were on a different pitch circle diameter. The connecting rods were 6.25in/158.8mm long (big end bearing centre to little end bearing centre).

Twin SUs were not used on the P76, instead the inlet manifold had a twin barrel downdraught carburettor. The inlet manifold was exclusive to this engine via wider placement of the cylinder heads due to the higher block decks.

One clear difference in the P76 cylinder heads is the pressed steel rockers and the absence of a rocker shaft. The rockers were paired and linked with a frame with two bolts used to fasten the two rockers to the cylinder head.

Many people used these Australian P76 engines for racing applications, and one notable modifier, not long after introduction of the Leyland P76 car, was John McCormack who modified P76 engines for use in Formula A racing. These engines were equipped with four 48mm IDA downdraught Weber carburettors, and went very well, producing 400bhp at 6500rpm and 370 foot pounds of torque. In the mid-1970s John McCormack even made his own cylinder heads in conjunction with Repco Engineering. These engines were eventually enlarged to 5000cc and faced the then all-conquering 5000cc small block Traco-Chevrolet V8, Al Bartz-Chevrolet V8 and Repco Holden V8 engines of the day in competition: a daunting task if ever there was one ...

Repco also experimented with 4.2 litre single plane crankshaft Rover V8 engine derivatives. These performed well enough, despite the massive vibration problem caused by the crankshaft design, coupled with the weight of internal engine componentry.

Chapter 1
Cylinder block, liners, pistons & timing chain

CYLINDER BLOCK TYPES

There are two standard (stock) bore size blocks; one of 3.500in/88.9mm bore, and one of 3.702in/94.0mm bore.

There are eight main versions of the production cylinder block when the various block castings, main bearing, crankshaft main bearing sizes and main cap types are taken into consideration. In each case, the later blocks are the better ones although not all later blocks are perfect (reliable).

The identification of all Rover V8 blocks is easy once you know exactly what to look for. In the first instance, all blocks have a number and letter coding stamped on them which allows identification if you have a factory code listing. The number/letter code is stamped on the lower edge of one of the block decks (that's the block deck on

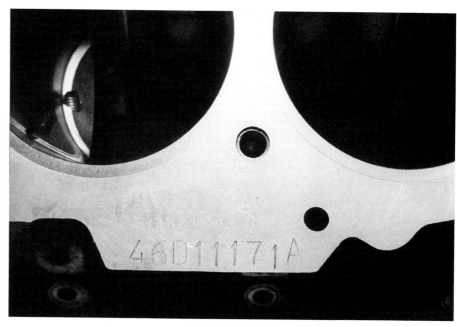

Number and letter code stamped on the block deck.

your right when you are standing in front of the block). Consult a Land Rover/Range Rover or a Rover V8 engine specialist if you want to find out exactly what vehicle your engine came from.

14

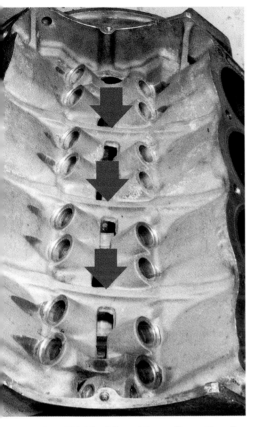

Close up of early 3.5 litre engine's main cap end.

Register height as machined in the block: "A" is 0.200in/5.0mm.

Type 1: 1967 to 1980 3.5in bore P5, P6, Range Rover and early SD1 blocks

The first series of cylinder blocks were made from late 1967 until 1980. These 3.500in bore blocks with 14 head bolts are easily and unmistakably recognisable via the fact that the three strengthening ribs in the valley of the block are quite thin (see accompanying photo) compared to all later blocks.

The register which the main caps locate in is machined 0.200in/5.00mm into the block. The main cap, however, is of such a design

1967-1980 block has thin section valley ribs (arrowed).

Early main cap.

You don't need to know the code details to accurately categorise a Rover V8 engine block or cylinder head. There is the visual identification method which, once you know the differences between the blocks, makes any block quite easy to categorise/identify within minutes.

Early two bolt main caps fitted into a 1967-1980 block: note registers.

that only a narrow band actually contacts the block register. Band width is just 0.090in/2.2mm.

Valley rib thickness and the shape of the main caps are the two easiest ways of positive and quick identification of these early blocks. The design of these two bolt main caps is unique to these early blocks.

Type 2: June 1973 to December 1980 Australian-made Leyland P76 engine (4.4 Litre)

This 3.500in bore block is a tall deck, large main bearing journal diameter item made in Australia between June 1973 and December 1980. These blocks are quite easy to distinguish from all other 3.500in bore blocks because of their distinctive features.

They have main bearing journal diameters of 2.550in/64.77mm, this feature being incorporated into

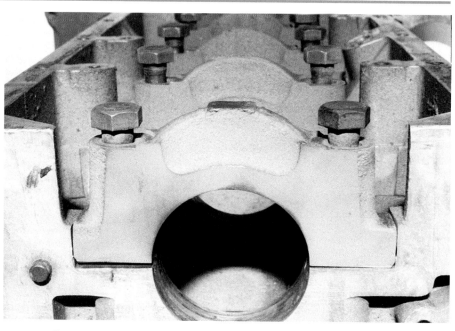

Two bolt main caps as found on all 1980-1993 3.500 inch bore blocks.

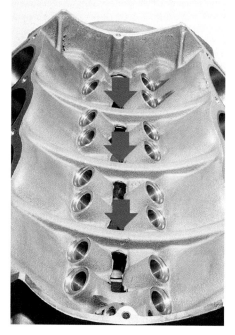

1980 on Rover V8 'stiff' block with thick valley ribs.

Close-up of an uprated engine block's main cap end.

the design to increase the journal overlap for the 3.500in/88.90mm stroke crankshaft. The crankpin big end journal diameter size is 2.000in/50.80mm, which is the same as the

3500cc Rover V8 engine.

This engine also features 10 bolt cylinder head retention (as used by Rover from January 1994 on with the introduction of the 'interim' 3.9 & 4.2 litre engines).

The block height is 9.500in, which is 0.540in taller than the 8.960in of the Rover 3500cc V8 engine block.

The P76 block is an easy block to identify after a few measurements have been taken.

Type 3: 1980 to 1993 3.5in bore uprated 'stiff' block

1980 saw the introduction of the stiffer 3.500in bore block with its thicker section ribs across the valley of the block (see photos).

These blocks are cast slightly differently to earlier blocks in a few places to increase overall strength.

All Rover V8 engine blocks from 1980 onwards had valley ribs of exactly the same thickness.

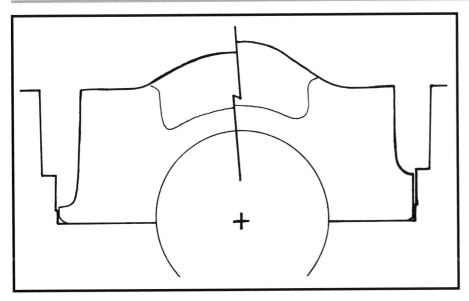

The end of the main cap on the left is as per the early engines (1967-1980), while that on the right is as per later engines (1980 to April 1994).

3.9 litre engine block as made before January 1994 (no cross-bolting bosses cast into the side).

The 3.9 block has 14 stud cylinder head retention.

On these 3.500in bore uprated blocks, the main bearing register height (machined into the block) stayed the same as the early blocks at 0.200in/5.0mm, but the main cap design was changed and the ends of the caps were much taller (0.650in/16.5mm compared to 0.250in/6.3mm). The contact area of the ends of the caps and the block was, however, increased only by about 0.015in/0.4mm in height, even though the ends of the main caps are more than twice the size of the originals.

Type 4: October 1989 to December 1993 3.9 litre engines

The end of 1989 (October) saw the introduction of the 3.9 litre engine for the Range Rover; this was the first of the large bore block engines. The bore was taken out to 3.702in/94.0mm (a 0.202in/5.0mm increase in bore size).

This block had more ribbing on the outside and the block cores were different from those of earlier blocks to accommodate the new bore size. The main caps of these blocks were the same as those used on the 3.5 litre engines.

The 3.9 litre engine block was used to make the 4.2 litre engine as fitted to the LSE Range Rover engine, the capacity increase coming from a longer crankshaft stroke.

The 4.2 litre engine was introduced because the 3.9 litre engine – in low compression form – was not performing well and US customers were complaining about the lack of power.

The 4.2 litre engine has a 3.702in/94.0mm bore by a 3.034in/77.0mm stroke crankshaft and a 8.9:1 compression ratio to suit 87

The main caps look like this on pre-January 1994 3.9 & 4.2 litre engine blocks.

AKI (Anti-Knock Index) US fuel which has a 91 RON and an 83 MON rating. This engine used the same connecting rods as the 3.9, but different pistons with a shorter gudgeon pin to crown height.

Type 5 & 6 : January 1994 onward 3.9 & 4.2 litre 'interim' engines

The 3.9 and 4.2 litre 'interim' or 'intermediate' engines (referred to as 'interim' engines from here on), were first introduced in January 1994. This was a time of major change for the Rover V8 engine with many improvements being made. These

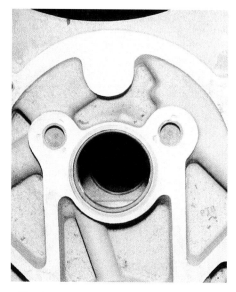

The front of all blocks to December 1993 had a camshaft thrust surface only (no drilled and tapped holes).

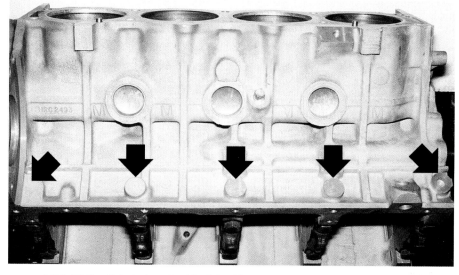

3.9 & 4.2 litre 'interim' engine block had bosses cast into it to allow for future cross-bolting of the main caps (bosses are arrowed).

two engines used the same new '38A'-type block casting. The block casting was slightly different from the previous 3.9 & 4.2 litre units in that five bosses per side were now incorporated into the block; the main cap registers were machined differently; the sides of the blocks

now had more and different ribbing. These bosses would later be used for cross-bolting the main caps of the 4.0 & 4.6 litre engines when they came out in October 1994 (essentially the same block).

Both 'interim' engines had crank-driven oil pumps, but retained the use of a camshaft-driven distributor, like all previous Rover V8 engines, and had a new 'serpentine' drivebelt system.

On these engines the crankshaft nose (sometimes referred to as the 'snout') was the same length as on all previous engines, but the key/keyway was longer. An early 3.5, 3.9 or 4.2 litre engine's crankshaft key was long enough to drive the new crank-driven oil pump, but was

not sufficiently long to also engage an 'interim' engine's crankshaft damper keyway.

The camshaft was now held in place by a thrust plate, whereas before, rearward axial thrust (generated by camshaft lobe taper against the lifter bases) was all that

Two new threaded drillings are needed to allow the mounting of the 'interim' type camshaft thrust system (two drilled and tapped holes arrowed).

3.9 & 4.2 litre 'interim' engine's camshaft thrust plate system.

kept the camshaft in the block. The 'interim' engine's camshaft thrust plate assembly can be installed onto any pre-'interim' Rover V8 engine block by drilling and tapping two holes into the block, while the early camshaft's flange is turned down to suit plus 0.002-0.003in/0.05-0.07mm endfloat (lash) clearance. This is now a very common modification.

Note that all 3.5 litre Rover V8 engines and all 3.9 and 4.2 litre engines, including the 'interim' 3.9 and 4.2 litre engines, have what we now call 'short nose' crankshafts. These crankshafts were retrospectively named 'short nose' after the introduction of the 4.0 & 4.6 litre engines in October 1994 which had a 'long nose' crankshaft by comparison.

Any early short nose pre-'interim' engine's crankshaft can have the keyway remachined to take an 'interim' engine's key and then be able to use the crank-driven oil pump, distributor, front cover and an

'interim' engine's crankshaft damper. Removal of the original oiling system on any 3.5 and pre-'interim' 3.9 and 4.2 and its replacement with

Short-nosed (2.75 inch/70mm) crankshaft of an 'interim' 3.9/4.2 litre engine with the 60mm long Woodruff key slot shown.

the 'interim' crank-driven oil pump system/distributor drive system is an extremely good move on the basis of efficiency and reliability, especially

for racing purposes.

The 'interim' engines can be quite confusing when it comes to identification of some components. For example, all of these blocks were the same casting as the later 4.0 and 4.6 litre '38A' block engines (introduced in September of 1994), with the bosses cast into the sides of the block for cross-bolting of the main caps. However, early versions of the 3.9 & 4.2 litre 'interim' engines (January 1994 to April 1994) had main caps that were the same as the earlier two bolt pre-interim 3.9 and 4.2 litre engines and the blocks were drilled for 14 bolt cylinder head fixing, even though the cylinder heads fitted to these engines had only ten bolt holes. This factor defines the 5th type of cylinder block option for the Rover V8, and the first of the two 'interim' type blocks. It's only a slight variation but it's significant enough to list as a type.

Later 'interim' 3.9 & 4.2 litre engines (April 1994-October 1998

This April 1994 on 'interim' engine block is the '38A'-type which has provision for main cap side bolts and has the '38A' four bolt main caps, but they're still only fitted with two vertical bolts.

3.9 litre engine, and April 1994-April 1996 4.2 litre engine) had the main caps that you'd find in the '38A' block 4.0 and 4.6 litre engines as introduced in October 1994 for HSE 4.0 & 4.6 Range Rovers, but the blocks and main caps were not drilled for cross-bolting. They remained two bolt main cap blocks. These later 'interim' engine blocks are cross-bolted blocks which have not been drilled and tapped appropriately for cross-bolting. Consequently, they can be drilled and tapped to become cross-bolted '38A'-type blocks. These later 'interim' engine blocks constitute the 6th type of Rover V8 engine block.

What remains different about these 'interim' 3.9 & 4.2 litre blocks is the fact that the main bearing tunnels are machined to suit 'small journal' crankshafts

Stretch bolt as used for head retention 1994 to 2004. The substitution of studs and nuts is recommended when rebuilding.

(2.000in/50.80mm big end journals and 2.300in/58.40mm main bearing journals) whereas **all** later 38A 4.0 and 4.6 litre engines are machined to suit the later 'large journal', long nose/snout crankshafts (2.185in/55.50mm big end journals and 2.500in/63.50mm main bearing journals).

Note that the early 'interim' 3.9 & 4.2 litre engine blocks (January 1994-April 1994) were drilled and tapped to suit 14 cylinder head bolt retention, like all previous 3.5, 3.9 & 4.2 litre engines, but were factory-fitted with 28cc volume combustion chamber, 10 bolt cylinder heads, composite head gaskets, and used stretch bolts for head retention (ie: the four extra retention bolt holes were drilled and tapped in the blocks, but were not used).

The introduction of the 'interim' 3.9 & 4.2 litre engines brought the 38A block casting, the change to 28cc combustion chamber cylinder heads, composite head gaskets, 10 bolt cylinder head retention and the change to stretch bolts.

From April 1994 on, all 3.9 and 4.2 litre 'interim' blocks were drilled and tapped for 10 bolt cylinder head retention. As a consequence, the vast majority of 'interim' blocks have 10 bolt holes in each of the two block decks, and large main caps of

the same design as the 4.0 & 4.6 litre '38A' engines.

Note that the crankshaft dampers of the 3.9 and 4.2 litre 'interim' engines do not interchange with those of the earlier 3.5, 3.9 and 4.2 litre engines. They are specific to the 'interim' engine conversion because of the crank-driven oil pump arrangement.

3.9 and 4.2 litre 'interim' engines are mainly fitted with the 14CUX electronic fuel injection system and require a distributor (unlike the 4.0 & 4.6 litre engines which are fitted with engine management systems – 1994 to 2004 – and are distributorless).

All 'interim' 3.9 & 4.2 litre and 4.0 & 4.6 litre engines use a 'serpentine' drivebelt (one belt to drive all accessories), although the systems are not identical because the distributor has to be cleared on the 'interim' engine, meaning that the belt is further forward on these engines by about 1in/25mm compared to the 4.0 & 4.6 litre engines.

Note that the 3.9 litre 'interim' engine was last fitted in October of 1998 with the introduction of the Discovery II, while the 4.2 litre 'interim' engine was last fitted in April of 1996 when the last of the trickle of LSE Range Rovers being made left the assembly line.

Type 7: September 1994 onward 4.0 & 4.6 litre '38A' block engines

With the introduction of the '38A' (as opposed to the earlier '30A') block for the new 4.0 & 4.6 litre engines in September 1994 in the Series II Range Rover, the block decks were all drilled and tapped for ten bolt cylinder head retention. The 4.0

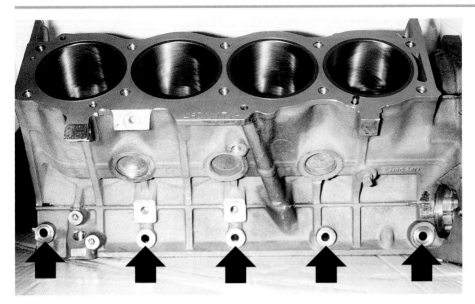

Substantial four bolt main caps of the '38A' block. Cross-bolted main bearing caps are a very distinguishing – and important – feature.

4.0 & 4.6 litre '38A' engine blocks of September 1994 on have the five bolt holes (arrowed) on each side necessary for cross-bolting the main bearing caps.

& 4.6 litre engine cylinder heads have 28cc combustion chambers, composite head gaskets and use stretch head retaining bolts. It's quite easy to identify 4.0 & 4.6 litre blocks because they have the prefix numbers "40" and "46" stamped on the block deck. "40" stands for 4.0 litre, and "46" stands for 4.6 litre.

The crankshafts featured larger 2.500in/63.5mm main bearing and 2.185in/55.50mm big end/crankpin journal diameters compared to earlier 3.5, 3.9 and 4.2 litre engines.

The noses or snouts of all 4.0 and 4.6 litre engine crankshafts are longer than those of all other engines at 90mm (earlier ones being 70mm long). The longer nose incorporated into the design of these later crankshafts gives better support to the crankshaft damper because earlier pre-serpentine engines (the poly-vee ones), had problems with the crankshaft pulleys coming loose. This crank nose length is easy to check with a vernier caliper or ruler.

Main bearing tunnel bore

4.0 and 4.6 litre engines, later 'interim' 3.9 and 4.2 litre engines and 1995, 1997/1998 3.5 litre engines have main caps that look like this. Only the 4.0 and 4.6 litre blocks are cross-bolted. All of these engines use a '38A' block casting.

diameters are 2.665in/67.577mm (bearing shells removed).

Cross-bolted main caps, 10 bolt cylinder head drillings and larger main bearing sizes mean it's not difficult to identify a 4.0 or 4.6 litre '38A' engine block.

Note that the 'interim' 3.9 litre engine and the later 4.0 litre engines have exactly the same bore and stroke but they're not identical engines. The 3.9 litre engine's block features two bolt main cap retention, smaller crankshaft journal sizes, original style connecting rods and

The '38A' cross-bolted block register has only one recess.

pistons. The 4.0 litre engine has the new larger main caps with four bolt retention, larger crankshaft journal sizes, all new connecting rods and pistons, and a longer nose on the crankshaft.

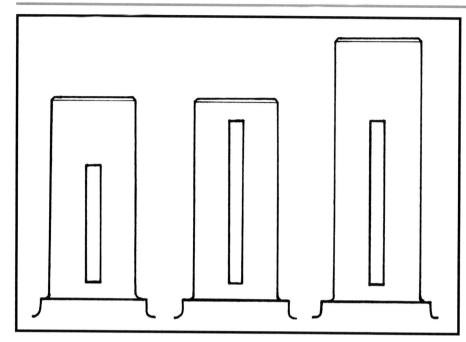

1967 to December 1993 short nose crankshaft with the short key which is 35mm long (left). 'Interim' 3.9 & 4.2 litre engine's short nose crankshaft with the long key, which is 60mm long (centre). 4.0 & 4.6 litre engine's long nose crankshaft with the long key which is 60mm long (right).

The key fitted to the nose of the 'interim' 3.9 & 4.2 litre engine's crankshaft, and that of the 4.0 and 4.6 litre engine's is the same. It's only the length of the nose itself that's different and, as a consequence, there have been two crankshaft nose key/keyway sizes and nose lengths used on Rover V8 crankshafts. Smaller/shorter keys from 1967 to January 1994; larger/longer keys from January 1994 on for 3.9, 4.2 interim engines and 4.0 and 4.6 litre engines. Noses of the short nose crankshafts are 70mm long and the 4.0 & 4.6 litre long nose 90mm long.

Type 8: 1995, 1997/1998 3.5 litre 'service' engine blocks

Although mass production of the 3.5 litre engine ended in late 1993, 3.5 litre engines continued to be available for supply to the military services, for the V8 90, 110 and 130 Land Rovers, for Freight Rovers and LDV commercial vehicles.

In 1995, a large batch of 3.5 litre 'service' engines was made which used the later '38A'-type block casting and four bolt-type main caps, though the block and main caps were not drilled to make them cross-bolted. Instead, they used only two vertical bolts, the same as the September 1994 on 3.9 & 4.2 litre engines. These later 'service' engine blocks and main caps can be drilled to create proper cross-bolted blocks, something which makes these particular 3.5 litre (3.500in bore) engine blocks potentially the best of the bunch.

The crankshafts of these later 3.5 litre engines are the same as all earlier 3.5 litre engine cranks (ie; short nose and with 2.300in/58.40mm main bearing journals).

The main bearing tunnel bores are 2.4911in/63.274mm: the same as all previous 3.5 litre engines.

These 'service engines' were not fitted with the crank-driven oil pumps and retained the early style oil pump/distributor system of all earlier 3.5 litre engines.

The crankshaft noses of these engines can be remachined to take the longer key of the 'interim' engine to allow the fitting of an 'interim' crank driven oil pump and crankshaft damper.

These 3.500in bore '38A' blocks are all drilled & tapped for 10 bolt, as opposed to 14 bolt, cylinder head retention, making them very easy to identify against all other 3.500in bore, small main bearing diameter crankshaft-equipped blocks. These engines were all fitted with the later 10 bolt drilled cylinder heads (the same as found on all 3.9 & 4.2 'interim' engines and all 4.0 and 4.6 litre engines) with 28cc combustion chambers, composite head gaskets and stretch cylinder head retaining bolts.

Rover attempted to build another sizeable batch of 3.5 litre engines in 1997/1998 but ran out of parts. As a consequence many of the very last 3.5 litre engines made were not completed by Rover and these part built engines were sold off to Rover V8 specialist companies.

Caution! – Anyone involved with racing a 3.500in bore block needs to use one of these 'service' blocks with the cross-bolting work completed for guaranteed bottom end reliability, but there is still a problem with these blocks and it is to do with the cylinder liners coming loose. Rover machined the blocks with a 360 degree ridge for the liners to sit on, however, on average the

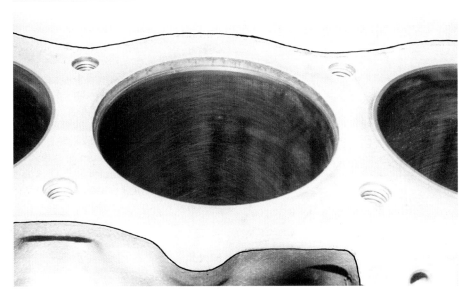

This is what happens to one, or more, liners in the 1995, 1997/1998 3.5 litre blocks: they drop downwards in the block, below the deck.

liners are often about 0.100in/2.5mm shy of this positive stop position. These 'service' blocks don't crack behind the liners, but the liners do come loose in the block and drop down: just about all of these blocks seem to have this problem.

Anyone who is intending to use one of these 'service' engines is advised to have flanged liners fitted to the block from the outset. Using the block as it comes from the factory is just too risky.

Anyone who is going to rebuild a 3.5 litre 'service engine' for road going use needs only to have the fit of the liners in the block checked by a Rover V8 engine specialist rebuilding company/business. This is done by heating the block to 100 degrees C and seeing if the liners can be moved up out of the block. Pressure can be applied to the base of each liner through the crankcase of the block via a specially altered, ¾in wide, flat chisel that fits in neatly under the base of the liner. If a liner can be tapped and moved as little as

0.002in/0.05mm then it's no good. The liners have to 'sound' right, as in solid, (indicating that they are fitted firmly in the block) when the base of the liner is tapped to try and move it up in the block. The temperature of 100 degrees C is above what the engine operates at in use.

QUICK REFERENCE BLOCK IDENTIFICATION

Type 1 – 3.5 litre, 3.5in bore, 1967-1980 block – two bolt main caps, thin-ended main caps, three 'thin' strengthening ribs in the valley of the block, 14 bolt head stud head fixing.

Type 2 – 4.4 litre, 3.5in bore, 1973-1980 Australian Leyland P76 block – unique tall deck block (9½in/241.3mm), 10 bolt cylinder head fixing – larger main bearings than all other 3.500in bore blocks.

Type 3 – 3.5 litre, 3.5in bore, 1980-1993 uprated block – larger two bolt main caps, thick-ended main caps – three thick strengthening ribs in the valley of the block, 14 bolt cylinder head fixing. All blocks have the same

strengthening ribs from here on.

Type 4 – 3.9 litre, 3.702in bore, 1989-December 1993, and 4.2 litre 1992-December 1993 blocks – same main caps as uprated 3.5 litre engine blocks – 14 bolt cylinder head fixing.

Type 5 – 3.9 & 4.2 litre '38A'-type 'interim' blocks, 3.702in bore, January 1994-April 1994 'interim' engines – camshaft retaining plate, early style main caps, 14 drilled & tapped cylinder head bolt holes.

Type 6 - 3.9 & 4.2 litre '38A'-type 'interim' blocks, 3.9 litre, 3.702in bore, April 1994-October 1998 and 4.2 litre April 1994-April 1996 – camshaft retaining plate, large cross-bolted '38A'-type main caps (only the two vertical bolts drilled & tapped), 10 drilled & tapped cylinder head bolt holes.

Type 7 – 4.0 & 4.6 litre '38A' blocks, 3.702in bore, September 1994-2004 – four bolt, cross-bolted main caps, 10 bolt cylinder head fixing, large main bearings, camshaft retaining plate.

Type 8 – 3.5 litre, 3.5in bore, 1995, 1997/1998 – 'service' blocks, 10 bolt cylinder head fixing, large cross-bolted '38A'-type main caps (only the two vertical bolts drilled & tapped).

WHICH CYLINDER BLOCK TO USE?

There are three distinct basic cylinder block options for Rover V8 engines.

The first option is the earlier standard two bolt main cap production block (1967 to December 1993) in 3.500in/88.9mm bore form (3.5 litre engine block), in 3.702in/94.0mm bore form (3.9 and 4.2 litre engine blocks) and the 'interim' 3.9 and 4.2 litre blocks made between January 1994 and April 1994. The

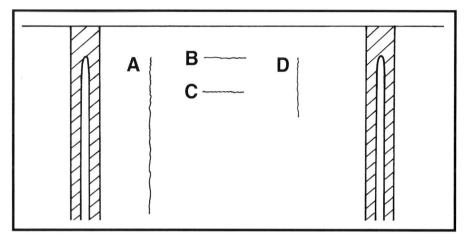

Cross-sectional view of a block bore with the liner removed, Commonly found cracks are shown at 'A', 'B', 'C' and 'D', the most frequent being that shown at 'C'. The block deck thickness is about 0.400in/10mm, cracks never appear at a higher point than 'B'. The cracks at 'B' and 'C' are frequently adjacent to a cylinder head bolt hole. This diagram shows a uniform ⅛in/3mm of wall thickness.

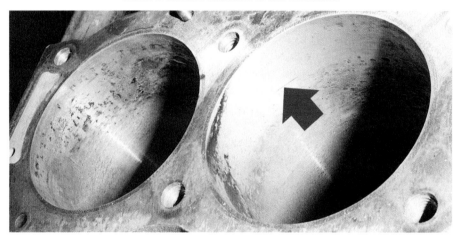

The liners have been removed from this block to expose the crack (arrowed) in the block wall. This is where a crack is most commonly found in 3.9, 4.2, 4.0 and 4.6 litre cylinder blocks.

by the factory in October 1994 to supersede the earlier block which had several problems, all of which showed up in general road use. The factory should have been aware of these problems – in some instances, for twenty years. The problems would have come to its attention through feedback from main dealers and car owners.

The 38A block incorporates several significant improvements –
1 – All cylinder liners theoretically sit on a full 360 degree shoulder machined at the base of each bore.
2 – 10 bolt cylinder head location (as opposed to 14) and composite head gaskets (as opposed to shim-type) and stretch bolts are used.
3 – Original skew gear driven oil pump system replaced by a crank driven oil pump. The new oil pump has 25% more volume capacity and can also easily maintain 50psi of oil pressure (and this oil pressure can be increased substantially: 8 to 10psi per thousand rpm used, for example).
4 – Main bearing cap location improved by cross-bolting ('X-bolting') all five main caps (four bolts per main cap). The skirts of the block are tied to the main cap by bolts to eliminate all movement.

38A blocks have, however, not been without problems. A recurring, and now fairly common problem on a lot of them, is cracking behind the liners, much the same as the earlier 3.9 and 4.2 litre blocks did.

3.5 litre aluminium blocks (including the later 90, 110, 130 Land Rover V8 engines) never had a behind the liners cracking problem because the problem only manifested itself after the bore size was changed from 3.500in/88.9mm to 3.702in/94.0mm, and the effective

limitation of all of these blocks being the main cap to block fretting problem that they are all prone to.

The second option is the 'interim' 3.9 and 4.2 litre engines made after April 1994 and the 3.5 litre engines made in 1995, 1997/1998. These engines have provision to enable them to become cross-bolted blocks like the 4.0 and 4.6 litre engines of October 1994 on. Also included in this option are the

1995, 1997/1998 3.5 litre 'service' blocks as they can become proper cross-bolted blocks. The cross-bolting aspect of all of these later blocks meaning that the main cap to block fretting problem is eliminated.

The third option is the later 4.0 and 4.6 litre cross-bolted four bolt main cap block which has a 3.702in/94.0mm bore (same basic block for both engine capacities). This block, known as the '38A', was introduced

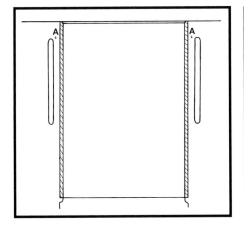

Standard 3.5 litre block which has a 3.500 inch diameter bore size. The liner has approximately 0.220in/5.5mm aluminium wall thickness between it and the water passages between adjacent cylinders where the letters 'A' are placed.

Diagram shows the effect of 'core shift'. The aluminium wall thickness behind the liner is thinnest at 'A' and 'C' at 2.1 to 2.2mm. Such a block will crack at 'A' and 'C', not at 'B' or 'D'.

material thickness behind the liner reduced as a consequence. The original 3.500in/88.9mm bore 3.5 litre engines had 0.088in/2.2mm wall thickness liners and a minimum nominal 0.220in/5.5mm wall thickness in the aluminium casting which surrounded the liner. This is a very reasonable minimum amount of aluminium material to have around a liner. The gap between the cylinders for water to pass through is nominally 0.140in/3.5mm (that's at the top of the waterway between the adjacent bores just under the block's deck). Even though there was always an amount of 'core shift' when these blocks were cast, the amount of aluminium wall thickness still remained well within reason.

When the bore size was increased to 3.702in/94.0mm to make the 3.9 litre engine in 1989, the core was altered to increase the wall thickness of the aluminium surrounding the liner by just 0.040in/1.0mm so the aluminium wall thickness was effectively reduced from that of the earlier 3.5

litre engine block. This meant that if there was a slight 'core shift' in the moulding of the block, the aluminium on one side of every bore could end up being quite thin.

With the advent of the 3.9 litre engine, the water passage width between the bores remained much the same, although the passage was made shorter and the tapering of the core reversed, thus reducing the amount of aluminium around the top of the liner. So, whereas with the 3.5 litre blocks, the hole bored in the block to take the liner was a nominal 3.672in/93.25mm in diameter, the equivalent for the 3.9 block was a nominal 3.880in/98.6m (a considerable difference for an almost identical casting to stand and meaning not enough 'parent metal' was left in the casting into which the liner was fitted).

If a block was cast perfectly, the thickness of aluminium surrounding the cast iron cylinder liner would be uniform and not less than 0.120in/3.0mm – except for the slight thinning between adjacent cylinders – this applies to 3.9 litre blocks made between 1989 and 1993, 3.9 litre 'interim' blocks made between

1994 and 1998, 4.2 litre blocks made between 1992 and 1993, 4.2 litre 'interim' blocks made between 1994 and 1996, or the 4.0 and 4.6 litre blocks made from 1994 and on.

However, the casting of cylinder blocks cannot be completely accurate and the controlling of the core positioning within the mould before the metal is poured is only as

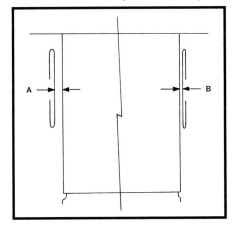

Comparison of aluminium wall thickness of 3.5 litre blocks (A) and 3.9, 4.2, 4.0 and 4.6 litre blocks (B).

good as it is possible to get it within the framework of the technique used to make these blocks.

In 1993, the factory, which was

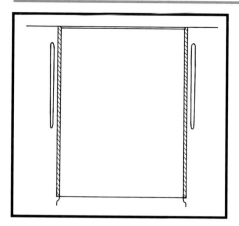

Standard 3.9 litre block which has a 3.702in/94.0mm diameter bore. The liners have varying amounts of wall thickness between them and the water passageways between adjacent cylinders. Wall thickness ranges from 0.085in to 0.120in/2.1mm to 3.0mm.

aware of the block wall thickness problem, started ultrasonic testing – by hand – of wall thickness of all engine blocks, and recording what each block's wall thickness was. The operator of this equipment would check all bores and write on the valley wall of the block (where the pushrods and lifters are) with a black indelible ink pen what the minimum wall thickness of the aluminium was. The sort of numbers seen on blocks would be 2.1, 2.2, 2.3, 2.4, 2.5, 2.6, 2.7, 2.8, 2.9 and 3.0.

In 1993 the core and the block mould were altered to reduce the amount of 'core shift' possible so that the block wall thickness would be more uniform. It's not all that easy to maintain high accuracy with a sand-casting at the best of times, let alone to the strict 0.020in/0.5mm to 0.040in/1.0mm tolerances required from the foundry from this point on.

After 1997 the blocks were all ultrasonically checked by machine and were each given one of three grades: blue, yellow and red. Blue being the thinnest walled at a

minimum of 0.088in/2.2mm, yellow at 0.100in/2.5mm and red at 0.112in/2.8mm. The way to identify what grade of block you have is to look in the valley of the block and see what colour the daub of paint on the side wall is.

Caution! – Note that daubs of paint (blue, for example) are also used externally on these engines in other places such as the timing cover, but they're nothing to do with this block grading business.

The improved ultrasonic testing meant that no blocks were allowed out of the plant which had less than the minimum (0.085in/2.1mm) amount of aluminium wall thickness between adjacent cylinders. The best of the blocks, those which are uniformly cast, can have as much as 0.120in/3.0mm of wall thickness between adjacent cylinders. These blocks were still graded red even though they might well exceed the minimum requirement for aluminium wall thickness.

With the advent of the X-bolted 38A blocks in 1994, 4.0 litre engines would use blocks with 2.1, 2.2, 2.3, 2.4 to 2.5mm of minimum wall thickness. The 4.6 litre engines were made using 2.5, 2.6, 2.7, 2.8, 2.9 and 3.0mm minimum wall thickness blocks.

After 1997/8 the 4.6 litre engines were made using red-graded blocks (and yellow when the factory ran out of red) but never blue-graded blocks. The 4.0 litre engines were made using blue-graded blocks (and some yellow-graded blocks if there were no blue blocks available). Only the yellow-graded blocks could be either engine size if the engine was a genuine Rover assembled unit.

Note that readers need to be aware of the fact that it wasn't

only Rover which assembled and sold new Rover V8 engines. Other specialist businesses built up new engines and, as a consequence, all manner of engine capacities have been found with blue-graded blocks. If you find a 4.6 litre engine with a blue grade block which is cracked, the engine wasn't necessarily assembled by Rover.

Caution! – You really do need to be aware of the block grading system by colour code and if you are not sure, for any reason, what block you have, it needs to be ultrasonically tested by someone who has the right equipment. Many engine reconditioning businesses do have this sort of gear. There is no point building up an engine based on, in this sense, a substandard block.

On inspection in the early years (pre-1994) some blocks were found to have as little as 0.048in-0.060in/1.2mm-1.5mm in places of aluminium wall thickness between adjacent liners. Consequently, a mountain of blocks was scrapped by Rover after they failed pressure testing.

Wildcat modified blocks
Shortly after the introduction of the 3.9 litre engine in 1989, this block cracking problem became evident to Wildcat Engineering when they fitted oversized liners (up 0.080in/2.0mm on a 3.9 litre engine's standard bore diameter). The standard 3.9 litre block was factory bored to 3.878in/98.5mm for the liners and to increase the bore size to 3.780in/96.0mm Wildcat Engineering further bored the liner holes to 3.8975in/9.98mm. It then fitted liners which were of 3.900in/99.05mm outside diameter giving an

interference fit of 0.0025in/0.065mm and with a nominal 3.790in/96.0mm inside diameter (actual cylinder bore diameter). The wall thickness of the liner was 0.060in/1.5mm.

After the engine had been built and run on the dyno for some time the closed cooling system became pressurised when the engine was on wide open throttle and under load. The engine was partially stripped (heads off) and a stain mark was seen going across the gasket line of one cylinder. Consequently the top of the liner was found to be 0.002-0.003in/0.051-0.076mm below the deck of the block. The engine was then fully stripped down and that particular liner removed. The aluminium of the block behind the liner between the two cylinders, where the wall thickness of the water jacket is the thinnest, was found to be cracked lengthwise (a 2in/50mm long crack a good 0.031in wide) and that part of the wall was quite distorted. The wall thickness of the block in this area after being bored oversize by Wildcat Engineering was down to about 0.060in/1.5mm.

When the aluminium wall cracked, the interference fit holding the liner in place was lost, or at least reduced considerably, and the cylinder pressure of 1000psi plus under wide open throttle was then able to get behind the loose liner and escape into the water jacket through the crack: this block was only good for scrap.

Wildcat Engineering's solution to this problem in 1989 was to buy in flanged cylinder liners and fit them in a special way. Another block was prepared in much the same way as the original 3.9 litre block with regard to the liner hole diameters, but the tops of these holes were

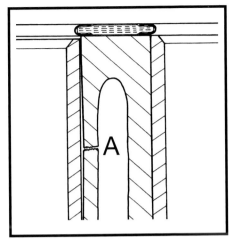

The aluminium wall cracks, allowing coolant through the crack, up behind the (dropped) liner and into the combustion space. Note that the liner's interference fit has been lost because of the distortion of the aluminium wall, but it'll only drop if it was not fully seated on original installation.

counterbored to a depth of 0.200in/5.0mm using a counterboring tool set to cut an outside diameter of 4.136in/105.03mm. The new liners had flanged tops which were machined to 4.134in/104.98mm outside diameter (giving 0.002in/0.05mm clearance when assembled between the outer diameter of the flange and the counterbore in the block) and the ridge of the flange was 0.210in/5.25mm thick. The length of the liner from the underside of the flange to the bottom was 0.020in/0.5mm shorter than the overall length of the bored hole in the block so that there was no possibility of the base of the liner bottoming out.

This block was ultrasonically

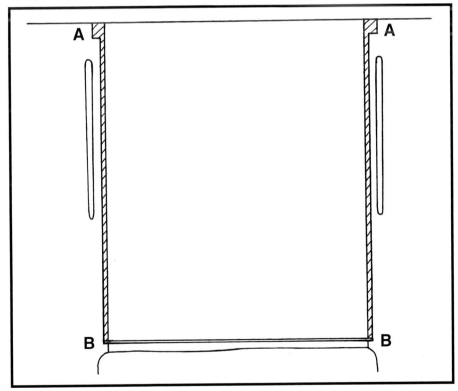

Wildcat Engineering flanged liner as fitted into a red-grade block. Flange is at 'A' and 'A' at the block deck. The gap at 'B' and 'B' is filled with silicone sealer. The wall thickness between the water passageways and the liners is uniform via boring each liner hole to suit the as-cast passageways of the particular block.

tested before it was machined to accept the larger than standard diameter liners to make sure that there would be a minimum wall thickness of 0.088in/2.2mm between adjacent cylinders after machining. This required 'offsetting' some of the bore centres to obtain as uniform as possible aluminium material around the cylinders.

The block was heated to 100 degrees C/212F and the liners, which were at ambient temperature, were fitted into the block, but not so far in that the flanges of the liners seated on the counterbore. The flanged liners were hand fitted into the block so that they were all about 0.080in/2.0mm proud of the fully seated position (judged by eye). The block was then allowed to cool completely before silicone sealer was finger smeared into the gap (of about 0.100in/2.5mm) between the bottom of the liner and the block. With all eight liners treated with silicone sealer in this manner, the sealer was allowed to cure for 30 minutes. Then the block was placed in a 50 ton garage press and the liners individually pressed into the fully seated position (the bottom edge of each flange of each liner making contact with the bottom of the counterbore). The surplus partially cured silicone sealer that was squeezed out when each liner was pressed into the fully seated position, was cut away with a razor blade after it had fully cured. After fitting the flanged liners the block's two decks were machined to true them as well as remove the excess material on the top edge of each liner's flange.

The advantages of fitting flanged liners, and in this manner, are threefold –

1. The cylinder head gasket now rests on the top of the flanged liner which provides a 0.25in/6.3mm wide band of cast iron liner in the vital flame ring area of the cylinder head gasket (as opposed to the flame ring being partially on the aluminium of the block and partially on the cast iron of the liner. This gives a much more reliable cylinder head gasket seal.

2. The silicone at the bottom of the liner acts as an 'O' ring and seals the joint between the bottom edge of the liner and the aluminium of the block. If a block does crack behind the liner in service, coolant can not leak into the crankcase because the silicone sealer is sealing the base of the liner and the flange is sealing the top of the liner.

3. There is also no possibility of the liner dropping down as the flange prevents downward movement.

The aluminium wall thickness around the liners is not uniform on 3.9 and 4.2 litre blocks or later 38A X-bolted 4.0 or 4.6 litre blocks. It reduces (by design) between the adjacent cylinders. That means that the two middle cylinders of each bank of cylinders have two thin walls on either side and the two end cylinders have one thin wall. This has been done to ensure that there is sufficient waterway between all cylinders and 360 degree coolant flow around each cylinder bore.

In summary, Wildcat Engineering's successful solution to the block cracking problem is to fit flanged liners to thick wall, red factory graded, X-bolted cylinder blocks only. This rework of a block involves mounting a used block on one of Wildcat's three large jig boring machines and removing the eight original cast iron liners by machining

them away. Or, if a new block is to be used, Wildcat will use a standard block which it buys in semi-finished form (no liners fitted, but otherwise fully machined) from Rover or uses one of its own strengthened blocks which it has cast.

Note that any Rover V8 block, which is sound, or even cracked, can have flanged liners fitted to it to prevent liner problems or as a remedy for an already cracked block.

If the block is going to retain the standard 94.0mm diameter bore size, each liner hole is bored oversize by 0.030in/0.75mm to clean it up so that it has a diameter of 3.870in/98.30mm. This overboring is done to remove any distortion that may be present but mainly to suit pre-finished liner dimensions. The outside diameter of the flanged liner is 3.8735in/98.38mm to give an interference fit of 0.003-0.0035in/0.76-0.89mm which is not as tight as Rover uses (up to 0.007in/0.175mm). Wildcat Engineering considers the factory interference fit amounts to be a bit to much, and reduces it accordingly. The top of this liner hole is then counterbored with a recess which is exactly 0.160in/4.0mm deep by 4.104in/104.25mm in diameter.

If the block is going to have a 3.780in/96.0mm bore size, the interference fit of the liners is reduced slightly to 0.0025-0.003in/0.063-0.075mm. The block is bored out to 3.8975in/98.947mm to suit the 3.900in/99.05mm outside diameter of the liner. The counterbore is machined to 4.134in/104.98mm and to a depth of 0.200in/5.0mm to accommodate the flange of the liner.

The seemingly odd choice of boring out the aluminium of

Flanged liner as used by Wildcat Engineering.

the blocks to 3.870in/98.3mm for 94mm diameter bore liners, and 3.900in/99.05mm diameter for the 96mm diameter bore size is done for expediency because the liners are supplied cylindrically ground to these sizes. The liners are essentially off the shelf production items.

Because Wildcat only uses red-graded blocks this overboring to suit pre-manufactured liners has not proved to be a problem. The minimum block wall thickness of one of its 94mm flange linered blocks is 0.097in/2.4mm and on a 96mm flange linered block 0.093in/2.3mm.

The S.G. (spheroidal graphite) iron liners Wildcat buys have inside diameters undersized by approximately 0.020in/0.50mm so need to be bored to the correct size after fitment. After the cylinders have

been bored, the bores are machine honed (the type of honing the bores receive depending on the type of piston rings going to be used). Most engines are going to be fitted with forged pistons and that means 0.001in/0.025mm of piston to bore clearance perin of bore diameter which results in an overall amount of piston to bore clearance of 0.004in/0.1mm.

If hypereutectic KB pistons are going to be used, the piston to bore clearance is halved so the total amount of piston to bore clearance is 0.002in/0.5mm. Each bore is sized exactly to suit the individual piston that is going to run in it. To achieve this, the set of pistons to be used must be on hand for Wildcat Engineering staff to measure so that they can finish machine each bore to suit each piston.

Note that, as a matter of course, aftermarket studs and nuts are used for cylinder head retention: **not** standard bolts/stretch bolts.

All of the foregoing is very precise: it has to be if the work is to be successful and the engine reliable enough for racing. In fact, Wildcat Engineering reports no block failures in well over ten years during which time numerous blocks have been reworked in this manner by the company.

WATER LOSS PROBLEMS CAUSED BY BLOCK CRACKING

This is a common problem with 3.9 and 4.2 litre blocks, a massive number of 4.0 litre blocks and quite a lot of 4.6 litre blocks. The 3.9 & 4.2 litre engines seem to suffer block cracking - behind the liners - of the rear two cylinders (cylinders 6 and 8) more than any others. In the long

term, approximately 25% of 3.9 and 4.2 litre engines suffer from block cracking. The cracking problem was carried over to the '38A' engines, as fitted into HSE Range Rovers, and when it comes to the 4.0 litre engine blocks approximately 80% suffer cracks. Approximately 15% of 4.6 litre engine blocks crack.

The high failure rate arose largely because of the cooling system used on HSE Range Rover, specifically top radiator hose failures. To reduce harmful emissions these engines were designed to run much hotter than all previous Rover V8s. On these engines coolant was circulated around the engine and heater only until the thermostat started to open at 82 degrees C (179.6F). Coolant would then be able to flow through the radiator too, and the temperature would ultimately be maintained at 96 degrees C (204.8F). Had it not been for this higher running temperature, the failure rate would have been much the same as that of the previous 3.9 & 4.2 litre engines, which still isn't good.

There's no doubt that there is a weakness in the big bore blocks in standard road car applications. However, John Eales of J.E. Developments says that he's only had one or two liner failures in the hundreds of racing engines that he's built, and doesn't consider the reported failure problem to be an issue in his sphere of activity. The difference is brought about largely by making sure that the coolant temperature is kept to between 75 and 80 degrees C (167 and 176F) under **all** circumstances. Also, John uses all new componentry of known quality and stretch bolts are not used on his engines, but rather studs and nuts.

The actual problem with the HSE Range Rover engines comprises several factors: the high 96 degree C rating of the thermostat, the small radiator, the positioning of the thermostat in the cooling system and, very importantly, the height the top radiator hose goes to above the height (air trap) of the radiator inlet, before it drops down to connect to the inlet. At the very least, the installation should have had a larger aluminium radiator of crossflow design and a top radiator hose that gradually inclined from the engine to the water inlet at the top of the radiator.

A further factor which affected all Rover V8 engines from January 1994 and on (serpentine belt upgrade), was the premature failure of the water pump bearings. Admittedly, all water pumps fail at some stage, but the Rover ones don't last as long as you might reasonably expect (**Caution!** – replacement at 45,000miles/75,000 km is recommended to avoid failure). If the water pump bearings fail, the coolant is usually lost in the gross overheating that follows (so is the power steering!) This all adds up to another opportunity to seriously overheat the engine and crack the block.

These same engines used in the other Range Rover & Land Rover products have a different radiator (a very large crossflow one), a different thermostat rating (80 degrees C/176F) and a different thermostat positioning: consequently they didn't suffer anything like the failure rate of Range Rover units (although still unacceptably high for a mass production vehicle).

The failure rate of the top hose between 1994-1999 was of massive proportions, with many engines losing virtually all of their coolant on each occasion. On the third occasion - if not sooner - with a 4.0 litre engine the engine would often start an ongoing coolant loss problem due to the fact that the block was now cracked. When such an engine was stripped down one or two liners would be found to be loose, especially the liners of cylinders 6 & 8. The 4.6 litre engines would fare a lot better in the same situation because of the greater thickness of aluminium behind the liners: nevertheless, they, too, can only stand so many complete water losses before failure. Frequently 4.6 litre engines would only require head gaskets after the third or fourth massive overheating.

The top hose was altered three times in the first five years of production; the third upgrade finally stopping the problem for good. The proportion of 38A blocks that have suffered cracking is in the region of 50% with the percentage likely to increase as time goes on. This whole situation means that suspect blocks are everywhere; however, flange linering blocks does mean that the overall situation is not too bad, even if the solution is a bit expensive.

Symptoms

If your engine has been overheated, the loss of water problem may not come as a surprise to you, but if you are not aware of past overheating incidents, the coolant loss problem can seem a complete mystery. The mystery stems from the fact that water is not found in the engine oil (making it go a milky colour). Unfortunately, once started, the situation will continue to deteriorate until the header tank has to be refilled every day and, at this point, most owners take the car to a garage which will often (commonly and wrongly) diagnose blown cylinder head gaskets. With the cylinder heads off the engine at least one piston crown will usually be seen to be 'washed' (clean, without carbon build-up), which is actually a clear indication that water is getting into that cylinder. The head gaskets will frequently look to be in perfect condition (they very likely will be) and will not show any signs of blowing.

In many instances garages fit new head gaskets and give the car back to the customer but, in a very short space of time, it becomes obvious that the water loss continues. The problem has not been solved by replacing the gaskets because they were not the fault; blown head gaskets **can** lead to coolant loss, but this will be indicated by the cooling system becoming over-pressurised.

Any Rover V8 engine with a water loss problem needs to be carefully inspected with the cylinder heads off. Look for 'washed' piston crowns, there could be more than one, but normally it's just one. Close inspection of the top of the liner of the affected cylinder, or cylinders, will reveal whether or not the liner has dropped down a little, or not. If the block is cracked behind the liner, the liner will usually be found to have dropped by between 0.005 and 0.015in/0.125-0.4mm. The liner isn't always dropped, but most times it is. What's happened here is that the aluminium of the block surrounding the liner cracks and distorts at the thinnest point, which is between adjacent cylinders, then the liner is no longer held as firmly in place as it was and is able to drop down by whatever gap there is between its bottom and the base edge machined into the block. If there is no gap, then the liner can't drop down but it can still be a loose fit in the block and it can still leak coolant into the combustion space.

The reason for the possible gap at the base of the liner is to do with what happened when the liners were fitted into the block at the factory. When the liners (at room temperature) were fitted into the blocks (which had been heated to 145-150 degrees C/293-302F), the liners sit on the machined edge at the bottom of each bore hole in the block. As the heat of the block transfers to the liners, the liners have a tendency to lift up a little so that they no longer rest on the bottom edge register of the block. Rover did not press the liners after they have been fitted to make sure that each and every liner has bottomed out.

In normal circumstances the liner lifting phenomenon in blocks wouldn't matter, but it does matter if the material of the block behind the liner cracks. If the bases of the liners sat directly on the machined edge at the bottom of the block, they wouldn't be able to drop even if they were 'loose' in the block: although this wouldn't prevent coolant from getting into the cylinder, of course. With the aluminium of the block cracked, the engine up to temperature and the coolant under pressure, the coolant leaks through the crack in the aluminium of the block and behind the liner. The coolant is eventually able to pass up the back of the liner, across the top of the liner and into the cylinder.

Caution! – Be aware that the coolant leakage problem can get so bad that when the engine is cranked

for the first time in the day it won't turn over because a cylinder is full of water.

Note that the coolant leaks into the cylinder after the engine has been switched off because it is still hot and therefore the coolant is under pressure for a considerable amount of time. An engine block in this condition is, of course, beyond further service by this stage: replacement or repair is the only solution.

Another indication of a block problem is a knocking noise when the engine is first started. Not all blocks crack behind the liner, but any block can still can have a liner or two become loose. What happens here is that, when the engine is cold, the liner is loose in the block and goes up and down in the available space until it gets warm enough to lock in the block through expansion. The whole engine has to come to bits for repair. The solution is to fit a new liner or liners having checked all of them for firmness of location at 100 degrees C (212F).

Seemingly, there is no end to the possible/probable liner problems with standard Rover V8 engine blocks ...

Repairing cracked blocks

Engine reconditioners are now universally flange-linering cracked blocks as a method of repair. New blocks are not cheap, and what's more, fitting a new block is no guarantee that the new block, in turn, might not also end up cracked, especially if the one you get is a blue graded block. This factor could mean that in a few years' time you'll be back in exactly the same position ...

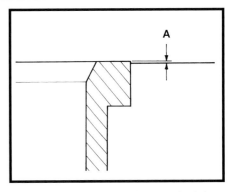

The top of the flanged liner can be left 0.05mm/0.002in proud of the block deck as shown at 'A'.

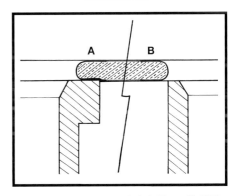

If the flanged liners are left 0.05mm/0.002in proud of the block deck, the top of the liner applies extra comression to the flame ring of the gasket as shown at 'A'. The standard arrangment is shown at 'B'.

The option being followed nowadays is to flange-liner the existing cracked block rather than buying new. While it's expensive to have done, the failure rate after having all eight liners replaced is zero. What engine reconditioners tend to do is plane the decks of the block 0.002-0.004in/0.05-0.1mm to clean them up, bore the block out to take the flanged liners, fit the liners and then machine the tops of the flanged liners down so that they are 0.002in/0.05mm proud of the block deck. Leaving the liners a little proud applies a bit more pressure to the composite gasket.

Sometimes the main bearing

tunnels may have to be align-honed to correct misalignment/block bend, but not usually. In many respects reconditioning a cracked block in this manner makes it better than new. In fact, it can be said with certainty that, if the factory had fitted flanged liners in the first place, none of the bore reliability problems with the 3.702in/94.00mm bore blocks would have happened. The factory must have known about the efficacy of flanged liners, but baulked at the cost of installing them.

STANDARD BLOCKS

Caution! – Anyone building a 3.702in/94.0mm bore, or larger bore, Rover V8 for racing ideally needs to use a X-bolted late model block which has been ultrasonically tested to make sure that it has a uniform 0.120in/3.0mm of aluminium wall thickness behind the original liners and then has had flanged liners fitted. This will result in trouble-free service and, while, perhaps, costing a bit more initially, will prove good value for money. The fact that all large bore 38A blocks are cross-bolted means that there is no main cap movement (fretting) which resulted in the chronic bottom end reliability problems of the earlier two-bolt-type blocks.

All 3.5, 3.9 and 4.2, and the later 4.0 and 4.6 factory-built blocks, always had the liners fitted to them in the following manner. The blocks were all machined to specific diameters to take the appropriate liners. The liners were machined to specific outside and inside diameters which meant that (with block and liners at room temperature) the liners couldn't be fitted into the block. The liners were made 0.0055in/0.115mm to 0.007in/0.175mm larger than the

holes which they would fit into in the block.

At the factory, the blocks were heated up to 140-145 degrees centigrade in an oven (had to be this hot to expand the block enough to get the liners in easily). When the block was removed from the oven, the liners, which were at room temperature, were simply slipped into the bored holes in the block. With the liners in the block, the heat from the block transferred to the liners (took about 20 to 30 seconds), the block contracted and the liners became firmly fixed in the block. This method of retention (the fact that the liner is of a larger diameter than the bored hole it is fitted into) is termed 'interference fit.' Once the liners were fitted, the cylinders were bored and honed to finished size.

Note that the main bearing tunnels were machined and sized after the liners had been shrunk into the block.

Blocks with a daub of red paint or numbers in the range 2.8, 2.9 or 3.0 written on them are clearly the most desirable (4.6 litre ones).

Note that the use of aftermarket studs & nuts for cylinder head retention is highly recommended for **any** Rover V8 engine.

TWO BOLT MAIN CAP BLOCKS

Despite the potential problems, a significant proportion of Rover V8 engine re-builders will be intending to use the original earlier two bolt main cap stock block because they have one already or because they're cheaper than later blocks. This position might change over time as more second-hand X-bolted '38A' blocks become available at lower prices.

Always compare the cost of rebuilding a two bolt block against the price of an all new 38A red-graded short block assembly: the difference can be small depending on how extensive the rebuild of the two bolt block needs to be. New short blocks are available for reasonable cost when all things are taken into consideration. Having an all new short assembly as the basis for your engine can be cost effective and considerably less trouble in the long run. Some Rover V8 specialist companies now actively stock brand new short block assemblies because they no longer consider reconditioning the old two bolt block as worthwhile. A lot of money can be spent and still the engine could fail.

Two bolt main cap blocks can be successfully rebuilt and used for most applications and there are things that can be done to reduce the likelihood of block problems occurring (although 3500cc blocks don't usually suffer the behind liner cracking, they did have liners coming loose in the very early days).

A two bolt main cap block can be made very reliable for long term use provided the potential problems are fully understood, it is thoroughly inspected to ascertain it is sound before any reconditioning work is undertaken, and then changes are made to reduce the likelihood of problems occurring in service.

Caution! – The critical factors are as follows:

Any two bolt 3.9 or 4.2 litre engine block needs to have the tops of the cylinder liners checked to ensure that they're still flush with the top of the block decks. If a liner is lower than the deck, the block may have or develop the cracking behind the liner coolant leakage problem.

All 3.9 and 4.2 litre blocks must be pressure tested to check for the water leak/cracking behind the liners problem. **Caution!** – There's no point whatsoever in using a cracked block unless you are prepared to have it fitted with flanged liners. Many Rover V8 specialists have geared up to carry out this check and it's not all that expensive to have them do it. The block will either leak around the top of a liner or it won't.

All 3.5, 3.9 and 4.2 litre two bolt main cap blocks are prone to 'bottom end' problems that need to be checked before any money is spent on the block. The problems are: 1) cracking in the threaded holes in the block that the bolts of the three centre main caps screw into and, in particular, those of the 4th main cap (back from the front of the engine); 2) fretting of the aluminium surfaces to which the centre three main caps are clamped; 3) the main caps being a loose fit in the machined registers of the block. The 1st and 5th main caps are not normally affected by the cracking problem, although it is not impossible to find some that are.

When standard two bolt Rover V8 engine blocks are stripped down, most Rover V8 engine specialist rebuilding companies report that about 50% of the blocks are consigned to scrap because of cracking within a main cap bolt hole, or holes, main cap to block register fretting (the 'black death'). In most instances, these two bolt blocks have never been stripped before and have only seen service in standard production road going cars ...

This is quite a significant point and clearly means that all two bolt main cap blocks have a problem in this area. This potential problem

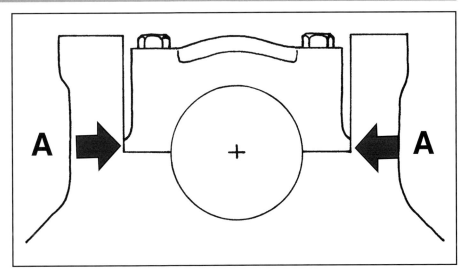

Two bolt main caps fitted into the block register. The main caps are an interference fit into the block register at 'A' and 'A.'

was present until the introduction of the X-bolted four bolt main block in 1994 at which point problems with the 'bottom end' of the engine block ceased to exist.

Two bolt main cap problems

The Rover V8 has a factor that sets it apart from other conventional V8 engines, and that factor is that the Rover V8 has a block and main caps made out of different material (aluminium alloy for the block and cast iron for the main caps). Virtually all American-made production passenger car V8 engines of the same era had cast iron blocks and main caps (same expansion rates for the two components). The Rover V8 engine block is different in this one aspect and herein lies a part of the problem.

With the block and main caps at ambient temperature, the ends of the main bearing caps are a 'snap-in fit' (interference fit) in the block registers. This means that the length of each cap is larger than the

block register aperture that they fit into. It's not by much, of course, otherwise the cap would never fit in. The aperture (block register) is on average 0.0007in/0.018mm to 0.001in/0.025mm smaller than the main bearing cap that it is going to fit into it. To get the main caps to fit into the machined register in the block, force is required (copper hammer and an angled tap!). If the main caps simply fall into place in the block, the correct fit has been lost and the block is not usable.

Caution! – The fitting of the main bearing caps into Rover V8 engine blocks is a critical business: the block can be ruined irretrievably in about five minutes through the incorrect handling and fitting of the main caps. The procedure is fully explained in great detail in the Veloce SpeedPro Series book on V8 short block rebuilding: *How To Blueprint & Build a V8 Short Block for High-Performance*. This book covers all aspects of general V8 short block preparation for high performance applications and should be used in

Early Rover V8 block's register edge (arrowed) which the main cap butts up against. It's this vertical face which is prone to damage by careless fitting of the main caps into the block.

Early Rover V8 block's front main cap which had the shallow depth registers.

conjunction with the details specific to the Rover V8 engine described in this book. When one of these Rover V8 engines is rebuilt correctly using good serviceable parts and not allowed to overheat, it usually gives trouble-free service for a very long time.

The inherent problem of cap to register fit does not normally occur until the engine gets hot (95-100 degrees C). Aluminium has a coefficient of linear expansion nearly twice that of cast iron so, for every degree of temperature change, the cast iron of the main bearing caps only expands or contracts half the amount of aluminium register. The higher the temperature the block gets to, the greater the size disparity between these two components. This unequal expansion/contraction

is what can cause the problem of the main caps 'losing' their correct fit in the register and subsequently it can be the start of the fretting problem.

With the engine up to a high operating temperature (eg: 95 degrees C) the aluminium block will have expanded, possibly to the point where there is no longer the required 'snap-in fit' needed for the solid location of the main caps. In fact, there are plenty of scenarios that explain why some blocks crack through the main webs and others don't: a faulty radiator being but one.

This is why the fitting of a new radiator, a 77 degrees C thermostat – so that he engine runs at 80 degrees C – is recommended. Also recommended is the fitting of an accurate water temperature gauge in a prominent position so you'll register it and slow down or stop if the engine temperature gets too high.

Some blocks will have been factory machined so that the main cap to register fit is better than other blocks (slightly tighter by 0.0002in/0.0051mm). This means that some blocks are going to maintain the correct 'snap-in fit' (interference fit) better than other blocks for the same operating temperature. If the correct fit is maintained between the block and main caps at all times, the main caps are not able to move at all and there won't be any fretting of the aluminium of the block.

The later increase in the height of the main cap register contact area and the block register by Rover had little or no curative effect, although it did improve the reliability of the register in the sense that it was more difficult to damage it during fitting (the main cap tended to get straightened up before bottoming

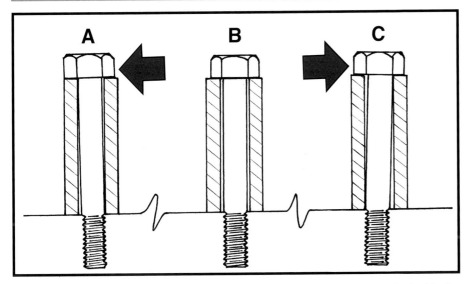

Three sectional side on views of the main cap bolt, the main cap movement in the block situation and the effect of the latter on the securing bolts (exaggerated for clarity). The main cap shown in the backwards position at A, the standard bolted down position at B and the forward position is at C. It's this sort of movement that breaks the block casting.

Fretting has caused the shiny wear patches on the main cap register shown here.

out on its matching surfaces).

With the block up to a higher temperature than normal (over 80 degrees C), the effective 'snap-in fit' (interference fit) starts to be lost through differential expansion. When the main caps are effectively 'loose' in the block they're able to move backwards and forwards when there is high loading of the engine despite the massive clamping power of the two main cap bolts. When a cap is not securely held in its block register loading is imposed on the retaining bolts and therefore on the threaded holes in the block which eventually causes the casting to crack through the bolt holes.

Note that it's not just alloy block to cast iron main cap blocks that suffer from fretting. Cast iron blocks with cast iron main caps fret if the main cap is not firmly located in a register. An example of this is the four bolt main cap small block Chevrolet block which has register location for the main caps. These blocks are notorious for losing the register fit and suffering from main cap base surface to matching block surface fretting. **Caution!** – any block which does not have its main caps firmly located will fret!

Fretting between the main caps and the block is caused by torsional vibration and loosely located main caps allowing relative movement.

When the harder cast iron surface of the main cap moves around in relation to the aluminium block surface to which it is clamped, the aluminium of the block surface will start fretting. This involves the eventual transferring of aluminium from the block to the surface of the main cap. This fretting action eventually leads to a wearing down of the aluminium surface that the main cap is clamped against which, in effect, loosens the clamping action of the main bearing bolts making the situation progressively worse. This scenario is commonly called 'the black death.' Blocks which have suffered minor fretting can be repaired by having all five registers machined deeper into the block (up to 0.005in/0.120mm) and the block align-honed, but it's seldom done because of the expense.

Clearly any two bolt Rover V8 block that is going to be rebuilt has to be very thoroughly checked for the main cap fretting problem. **Caution!** – Don't be tempted to use a block with loose main cap to register fit, or which shows signs of fretting (actual loss of material as opposed to discolouration of the aluminium surface) under any circumstances.

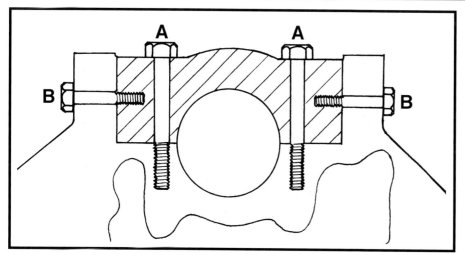

Diagram shows the principle involved in tying in the skirts of the block to the sides of the main cap (shaded) by the two bolts as arrowed at B and B. The two bolts are in tension for this purpose. These two bolts are also technically in shear when taking the loading that the two main bolts arrowed at A and A take (double function).

The 'problem' main caps are the 2nd, 3rd and 4th (predominantly the 4th) counting back from the front of the engine. On some Rover V8 engine blocks, the vicinity of the 4th main cap back will have a part of the block cracked right around to the oil gallery hole that feeds the main bearing ...

The solution for when deep skirt blocks fail in this manner has been common knowledge for decades. Coventry Climax, for example, strengthened its large capacity FPF four cylinder in-line racing engines for 1959/60 by redesigning the aluminium block and using cross-bolted steel main caps (four extra bolts per cap). The later Coventry Climax FWMV-V8 1.5 litre Formula One engine of 1961-1965 had cross-bolted main caps from day one.

This design principle involves having two bolts or studs clamping the main cap to the block much the same as in most engine blocks (these two bolts being in tension). A further two bolts go in through the side/skirt of the block and into

the main cap holding the cap in the block, these two bolts being in shear. This main cap retaining design can only be used on what are termed 'deep skirt' blocks. The resulting cross-bolting of the block and main caps makes for a very rigid structure as the sides/skirts of the block are firmly clamped to the main cap and the material cannot expand away from the cap.

Caution! – For anyone using a correctly rebuilt two bolt main cap block – in any situation – there are certain things that can be done to help prevent the main bearing cap fretting problem occurring. The first is to ensure that the cooling system is able to keep the coolant temperature down to 80 degrees C (176F) maximum under ALL circumstances. Doing this will limit the amount of block expansion that can take place and reduce the possibility of the block expanding so much that the main caps are no longer firmly held in place in the block registers. A suitably sized radiator (capacity and surface area)

with good air ducting and airflow through the radiator and a lower temperature opening thermostat is required to do this.

Note that Traco fitted a steel plate across the bottom of the sump rails of the blocks it prepared. When everything was bolted together, the main caps and the sides of the block (skirts) were connected more rigidly (expansion reduced to the minimum possible). This modification didn't stop the fretting in high load situations, but it took a lot longer for the block to become unserviceable through fretting. Traco also fitted crankshaft dampers which were tuned to damp torsional vibration as much as possible, and so reduce the effects of torsional vibration on the block componentry.

Keeping the coolant temperature to 80 degrees C (176F) maximum under **all** circumstances, even if not using an oil cooler, will usually be enough to keep the block expansion to a minimum.

For kit car owners, etc, fitting a large, high speed, manually or thermostatically controlled, electric fan in front of the radiator may be necessary to enable this sort of temperature control. Fitting an adequately sized radiator with plenty of air flowing through it is really the key to getting this aspect of engine cooling right.

Caution! – For racing use and in addition to an absolutely efficient water cooling system that can maintain the 75-80 degrees C (167-176F) maximum coolant temperature under **all** circumstances, an oil cooling system of some description **must** also be used.

Note that maximum power is produced by any Rover V8 when its coolant temperature is maintained at

CYLINDER BLOCK, LINERS, PISTONS & TIMING CHAIN

an optimum 75 degrees C (167F). On the other hand, if the temperature is allowed to rise to, say, 100 degrees C (212F), the engine power drops off by 10%. Controlling the engine's coolant temperature is clearly critical for power production as well as limiting block expansion. Aim to keep the water temperature at 75 degrees C (167F).

Note that Lucas fuel injection systems don't switch off the last stage of fuel enrichment during warm up until 80 degrees C/176F is reached, which is why for so-equipped engines the running temperature will have to be set at 80 degrees C if excessive fuel use is to be avoided. All carburettor-equipped engines can be set to run at 75 degrees C (167F) and the fitting of a 72 degree C/161 degree F thermostat will do this.

Stud & nut kits for two bolt main caps

Fitting a stud and nut kit is a very good idea, but it's not the complete solution to the problem of main cap movement (it can help). What a stud and nut kit does is allow better clamping power for a similar amount of torque applied to the nuts. Winding the coarse thread of the bolts into the threads in the block while torquing the bolts is a major extra loading in itself and one this alloy block can do without, especially on a frequent basis, such as on a racing engine which comes apart often for maintenance. The well known fastener company ARP makes stud and nut main cap kits for these two bolt main cap engines and they are available from most Rover V8 engine specialists. The studs are fitted into the block with 5ft.lb/7Nm of torque.

Stud and nut kits are effective because of their clamping power – mechanical advantage – the difference between a fine thread and a coarse thread (UNF as opposed to UNC). They do not solve the problem of cap movement.

Caution! – The studs should be fitted into the block after the caps have been 'snapped' into position. This is to avoid the possibility of 'shaving' or 'bruising' the aluminium block register edge through the cap not being able to be fitted into the block register in the correct manner (angled before being 'snapped in'). If the studs are fitted into the block first, the cap must go down into the register more or less square and this is just not the right way to install a main cap, especially into aluminium which is quite soft. The ends of the main cap and the surfaces of the block registers should be smeared with oil before the main caps are 'snapped' into position.

In the first instance a stud should be wound down into each and every one of the threads as tapped into the block just to make sure that each thread is clear and sized to suit the new studs. Most will be but they all need to be checked to make sure. The studs must also go right down to the end of the thread. Next, with all studs removed, the caps are all fitted into their respective registers and then the studs fitted to see if they can be wound – using fingers only – into the block.

The studs must easily start in the threads of the block, with no force being required at that point, or when you continue winding the threads into the block. Any binding of the stud indicates interference with the drilled hole in the cap, or

that the cap is not aligned with the two threaded holes in the block. The cap can be removed and repositioned on the block again to effect better alignment. The use of a torch can sometimes be useful in checking to see how good the basic alignment of the cap is in relation to the threaded holes in the block.

If the studs cannot be screwed into the block in the described manner, the holes in the main caps will have to be individually eased until they do. This can usually be accomplished by holding the offending main cap in an engineer's vice (fitted with jaw protectors) and hand filing the hole to effectively elongate it to gain sufficient stud clearance. Removing just sufficient material from each cap for minimal clearance being the requirement. An engine reconditioner or Rover V8 engine rebuilding specialist should be consulted if you have any doubts about doing this sort of work yourself as it must be done properly. The recommended torque for the nuts of the ARP stud and nut set is 70-90ft.lb/95-122Nm, but check the manufacturer's instructions.

Be aware that fitting a stud and nut kit brings another factor into the equation: the increased clamping power causes the bearing tunnel to distort (the diameter of the main bearings with the cap fitted to the block without the bearing shell inserts fitted). Fitting a stud and nut kit to a Rover block and torquing the nuts to 70ft.lb/95Nm results, on average, in about 0.0005in/0.013mm of main bearing tunnel diameter distortion (ovality) which, while not being good, is generally considered to be acceptable if not as good as perfectly round. Torquing the nuts to 90ft.lb/122Nm can result in 0.0007in/

0.017mm to 0.001in/0.025mm of tunnel diameter distortion (diameter reduction and ovality): this is getting a bit too much.

Caution! – When main bearing stud and nut kits are fitted to a Rover block, the main bearing tunnels should be align-honed to remove any consequent distortion to the tunnel diameters. Many engine reconditioners have suitable equipment and most Rover V8 specialist businesses will too. Most professional engine builders who use ARP stud and nut kits tend to use 75ft.lb/102Nm of torque on the nuts.

Main bearing tunnel bore diameter is measured using an inside micrometer. These dimensions need to be measured by someone experienced with doing this sort of work, such as an engine reconditioner/engine machine shop/Rover V8 engine specialist. The figures must be completely accurate.

For early two bolt 3.5 and 3.9 litre blocks (or what are called 'small diameter' main bearing journal blocks), the factory specified tolerances for main bearing bore sizes are 2.4911in/63.274mm to 2.4916in/63.287mm. That's a 0.001in/0.025mm allowance between the smallest and the largest factory-machined diameters. The 2.4911in diameter is 'bottom size' and the 2.4916in/63.287mm is 'top size'. If your block measures up at say 2.4929in/63.320mm (0.0013in/0.033mm over 'top size'), for example, the main bearing tunnel bore diameter is too large and the main bearing shell inserts will not have enough crush (the clamping pressure applied to the shells by the bearing cap) for reliability. The block will need to be remachined by an engine reconditioner/engine machine

shop/Rover V8 engine specialist.

Align-honing the main bearing journals means fitting all of the main caps (without bearing shells) into the block with the studs and nuts fitted and torqued to the designated amount and then machining the tunnels to 'bottom factory size' (if possible). **Caution!** – If you decide to use the minimum ARP recommended torque value of 70ft.lb/95Nm, the nuts must always subsequently be torqued up to this same amount. Similarly, if you decide to torque the nuts to 90ft.lb/122Nm you must always subsequently use 90 foot pounds. The higher the torque used the higher the clamping power and the greater distortion of the tunnel bore to be cured by having the block align-honed. Another aspect of chosen torque is that the threads still 'pull up' in the block and the greater the torque used the greater the amount of 'pull up'.

The ideal bearing tunnel diameters are 'bottom size': that's 2.4911in/63.274mm diameter. This diameter will allow for the largest amount of bearing crush when the bearing shell inserts are fitted into the block.

Caution! – Failure to correct bearing crush is what leads to engine failure through the main bearing shells spinning in the block. This can lead to a catastrophic big end failure resulting in a completely ruined engine. If the main bearing tunnel bore diameter size is not correct the engine's reliability is suspect from this point on ...

Some Rover V8 specialists have had special main bearing cap retaining studs made which utilise the maximum amount of thread possible in the block. This means as

Aftermarket ARP studs, nuts and washers.

much as 1.5in/38mm of stud thread in the block as opposed to the lesser amount achieved by ARP studs.

J.E. Developments, for example, has studs made which have the maximum possible amount of thread length (0.375in/10mm more than an ARP stud) as well as having a conical point on the bottom of the stud. This conical point ensures that the studs are held square in the threaded hole (perfect alignment), the stud bottoms out on the conical point and not on the end of the thread where it meets the parallel section of the stud. The extra length of thread on these studs, while technically unnecessary on the basis of strength, does tend to reduce 'pull up' of the threads in the block and spreads the thread loading in the casting as much as it is possible to do, as well as anchoring the stud in the block better. Even though using extra long threads might be regarded as overkill, there's little doubt that it is the better thing to do. The stud threads, by means of the conical point arrangement, are pre-tensioned against the underside of the thread, and such studs sit dead straight in the block. **Caution!** – The studs are torqued into the block to 5ft.Ib/7Nm, and **no more**.

J.E. Developments torques the stud nuts to 75-80ft.Ib/102-112Nm and always align-hone the main bearing tunnel bores to bottom factory size to remove tunnel diameter distortion and achieve the maximum factory recommended bearing crush. J.E. Developments says its overall system is still not perfect, and certainly not as good as the later cross-bolted mains, but as good as the standard two bolt system can ever be made.

Note that align-honing is the recognised method of correction (ovality and undersize) of main

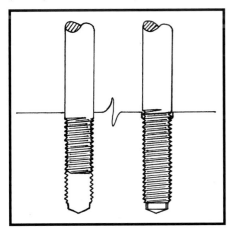

ARP-type stud on the left. The 'run-out' of the rolled thread form effectively bottoms out on the counterbored recess in the block deck machined by the factory. Thread length/thread engagement is the same as the standard bolt. J.E. Developments-type stud on the right has a conical pointed end and 0.375in/10mm more thread length. The conical point centres on the bottom of the drilled hole and positions the stud vertically.

bearing and connecting rod tunnel bore diameters. The process relies on the fact that to make a diameter smaller than it currently is, a small amount of material can be removed from the base of the main or connecting rod cap which reduces the effective diameter in that plane. The diameter across the block cannot be reduced and this could mean that the diameter at the part-line could remain oversized by a few ten-thousandths of an inch (0.0001-0.0002in/0.0025-0.0051mm): this is not cause for concern. Up to 0.005in/0.127mm can be removed to clean up and restore a fretted block surface, but most engineers do not like doing this because it moves the centre line of the crankshaft axis and, if a timing chain is being used, non-removable slack is being built into the system. The cost of this block register remachining, line-boring and align-honing work makes the cost of a cross-bolted block an attractive alternative.

For studs and nuts to be reasonably effective in locating the main caps, so that the caps are solidly located by the studs once the block is up to operating temperature, they would have to be a precision fit in the main caps. This is just not possible as Rover originally machined the caps for bolt retention. The reality of the situation is that on average one in five studs cannot be easily fitted into the main caps and block, instead the main cap holes have to be 'eased' to provide stud clearance.

Note that standard bolts fitted to 4.0 and 4.6 litre cross-bolted blocks are suitable for all applications, including racing.

CAMSHAFT BEARINGS (ALL BLOCKS)

The camshaft bearings wear in these engines at much the same rate as other V8 engines of similar design: the complete set will need to be replaced in any block which has done 75,000 miles/120,500km or more. Lower mileage blocks which have not had frequent oil changes will also need to have the camshaft bearings changed. Camshaft bearings predominantly wear on their lower side through the loading imposed on the cam by the valve springs.

Camshaft bearing replacement work is best carried out by an engine reconditioner who is familiar with this particular engine, or a Rover V8 engine specialist concern. They'll have the right tools and equipment (the excellent Eaton camshaft bearing removal and installation tool, for example) and be able to change the camshaft bearings in around 45 minutes.

Many engine reconditioners are reluctant to change the camshaft bearings on these Rover engines because they've heard that the camshaft bearings are non-serviceable. This is not true at all, even though the factory lists the camshaft bearings as being non-serviceable. What is true is that the factory installed semi-finished camshaft bearings in the blocks and then line bored the bearing bores to finished size. The inference taken is that no one outside the factory can possibly get the alignment of the camshaft bearings accurate enough when fitting pre-finished camshaft bearings.

The reason the factory fitted semi-finished bearings into the blocks and then line bored the camshaft bearing bore using diamond tipped tools, is that it used equipment that installs all of the camshaft bearings in one operation. During this procedure,

Set of pre-finished camshaft bearings.

there is some risk of damaging the bearing surfaces when the installing mandrels are retracted. The factory engineers decided that to preclude any possibility of camshaft bearing bore damage through the installation process, they'd fit semi-finished bearings and finish sizing them afterwards.

The camshaft bearing tunnels machined in the block are perfectly in-line and diameter sized so, as a consequence, it's very acceptable to fit pre-finished replacement camshaft bearings. The camshaft will be able to rotate freely provided the replacement camshaft bearings have been installed correctly. **Caution!** – Replacement camshaft bearings must be fitted using installation equipment that does not damage the bearing surfaces. It only takes a small amount of burring of the edges of a bearing, or two, and the camshaft will not turn freely.

Engine reconditioning companies which replace camshaft bearings on a regular basis, always use special equipment to do this exacting work (eg: they make correct fitting removal and installation mandrels specifically to suit the Rover V8 engine, or use the special installing tools made by Eaton or K-Line).

Whenever camshaft bearings are being replaced, take the camshaft with you when you take the block to the engine reconditioner. After the camshaft bearings have been fitted, the reconditioner will be able to check that the camshaft fits into the block and rotates freely. **Caution!** – Make sure that the camshaft is able to be turned freely, by hand, before taking the block away!

Caution! – Not to replace worn camshaft bearings is folly. The 'it'll go another time' syndrome is just not good enough for a professional rebuild. The solution, if necessary, is to send the block away to an experienced firm which can do the work correctly. Any fettling of pre-fitted bushes once they have been installed should be minimal.

Caution! – An engine destined for the race track should have new camshaft bearings fitted to it as a matter of course unless the block has done exceptionally low miles. With high pressure valve springs fitted, coupled with high lift and an aggressive camshaft lobe action, the camshaft bearing loading is increased significantly over standard and a faster rate of wear is inevitable: if the camshaft bearings are marginal, an expensive engine failure could be on the way ...

Note that worn camshaft bearings are a potential major cause of oil pressure loss as well as not supporting the camshaft properly!

TIMING CHAIN (ALL BLOCKS)

Caution! – The standard Morse-type timing chain is totally unsuitable for any high-performance application. The rate of wear is too high, which results in retarded ignition and camshaft timing. In years gone by this type of chain was used very successfully in NASCAR racing, but the timing chain only had to last for 500 miles, after which it went in the bin; and that's the point, they were not in the engines for long. Although ignition timing can be re-adjusted in about five minutes, camshaft timing cannot. The progressive retardation of camshaft timing caused by chain stretch results in a gradual reduction in engine power and efficiency.

Be aware that it's not impossible for a Morse timing chain to wear (stretch) so much that the camshaft timing is retarded by 10 degrees, or even more. In extreme cases a tooth, or two, of the camshaft sprocket may break off.

One advantage of the Morse chain is its low cost in power absorption, but this is outweighed by the design's short span reliability caused by a fast rate of wear.

The solution to the timing chain problem is to fit a relatively inexpensive aftermarket duplex timing chain set. While not perfect, a duplex chain will hold the ignition and cam timing settings quite accurately for a considerable amount of use. There are several chain and sprocket sets on the market, the steel sprocket ones being more durable than the cast iron sprocket ones. Piper Cams sell duplex timing chain sets and the very well known 'Cloyes True Roller' is available at Rover V8 specialists. Caution! – Don't even consider replacing the standard equipment Morse timing chain and sprocket set with another new set: they're acceptable for standard use only.

Standard Morse-type timing chain which is very loose.

Duplex timing chain set complete with multi-indexing bottom sprocket for quick camshaft timing changes.

ENGINE BLOCK REQUIREMENTS FOR HIGH PERFORMANCE
Fitting a camshaft thrust plate to pre-1994 engine blocks

The standard pre-1994 Rover V8 engine block does not have a camshaft thrust plate (unlike many other American designed V8 engines) although common for GM designs. Camshaft thrust plates prevent the camshaft from being able to move forward in the block by effectively trapping the camshaft in a set position in the block with minimum endfloat (lash).

The camshaft in the Rover V8 generates rearward thrust through the shape of the camshaft lobes. Each camshaft lobe is tapered (lobe surface not parallel with cam axis) and this, combined with the position in the block of each lifter (slightly in front of each lobe) and the convex shape of the lifter bases, keeps the camshaft in position. That's the theory at least. The camshaft generates its own rearward axial thrust and the movement is checked by a flange that is in contact with the front face of the block.

This lack of camshaft axial movement control is quite unacceptable for any engine let alone a performance oriented engine which will rev higher than standard units. This is because the camshaft can move forward in the block and movement of up to ¼in/6mm is entirely possible depending on the chain wear and compliance. The camshaft is able to move backwards and forwards in the block when the engine is running and this can be the cause of abnormal camshaft drive gear wear, distributor driven gear wear, abnormal lifter base wear, camshaft lobe wear and camshaft and ignition timing fluctuations. One

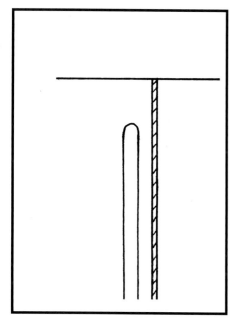

The convex lifter bases are positioned in relation to the camshaft lobes in the manner shown in this diagram. This factor creates rearward thrust so that, theoretically, the camshaft is always trying to move backwards in the block.

Pre-1994 3.5, 3.9 and 4.2 litre engine camshaft flange.

solution is to fit a camshaft thrust plate which will limit the fore and aft movement of the camshaft within the block to 0.003 to 0.005in/0.0762-0.127mm.

Fitting a 1994 on an 'interim' engine's ring plate/thrust plate, as made by Rover, is really an uprating procedure that should be considered a mandatory improvement for any engine, not just for performance oriented engines. Two holes have to be drilled and tapped in the block to secure the ring plate to the block. The camshaft has to be machined down to fit the ring plate/thrust plate, but this is a minor task.

The camshaft's flange is turned down to suit the ring plate recess and to allow for 0.003-0.005in endfloat. The ring plate is fitted over the camshaft and the hole positions spotted through the ring plate onto

'Interim' (3.9 and 4.2 litre of 1994 and later) engine camshaft flange is shaped to suit the thrust plate used on these engines.

the block: it's not a complicated procedure. **Caution!** – Care must be taken to ensure that the holes drilled, do not go into the oil gallery!

When the Rover V8 engine

became distributorless, the camshaft location method changed again. The camshaft has a groove machined into it and a C-shaped thrust plate is used to locate the camshaft axially.

Outside flat face of camshaft thrust plate.

Inside face of camshaft thrust plate.

Teflon-faced 'thrust bolt'

There is a much cheaper alternative than the camshaft thrust plate modification to prevent undue forward movement of the camshaft, it's called a 'thrust bolt'. This Teflon headed bolt screws into the front of the camshaft in place of the original securing bolt. The Teflon headed surface of the replacement bolt is positioned close to the inside of the cast aluminium timing chain cover (aim for 0.010in/0.254mm) and locked in position with a locknut. The flat portion of the Teflon thrust surface comes into contact with the underside of the timing chain cover when the camshaft moves forward. Because the camshaft turns at half

engine speed, there's plenty of oil around the inside of the timing cover and there isn't all that much axial load pushing the camshaft forward anyway, the Teflon thrust face generally wears very well.

Rover has sold a Teflon 'thrust bolt' under part number 'STC 3620 K' since 1996. This item is intended to stop camshaft knock on standard engines which don't have a ring plate/thrust plate fitted to them as standard (all pre-January 1994 blocks). The knock occurs at low engine speed on standard engines. The Rover thrust bolt has an Imperial thread to suit the early-style camshaft.

Before the Rover manufactured product became readily available, Rover V8 specialists used to make their own thrust bolts by turning a recess into the head of an imperial or metric bolt and machining a piece of Teflon to suit the recess. Until the advent of the 'interim' engine with its thrust plate, this is how most racing engines had their camshaft endfloat controlled.

Note that the Rover thrust bolt and its accompanying spacer will not generally allow the timing chain cover to fit on to the block and have the required 0.010in/0.250mm of endfloat/end clearance. The parts in combination are made to work in a 'top tolerance' situation, but most engines are not like this so an amount of material will have to be removed from the spacer washer to obtain the correct end float (turn the excess material off in a lathe). Small amounts of material (0.005in/0.125mm at a time) are removed from the spacer until the camshaft is able to be turned freely with the timing cover fitted, meaning the clearance will then be between

0.005-0.010in/0.125-0.250mm. It takes a few goes to get this right. If too much is taken off, a new spacer will have to be made to the right thickness. This situation is caused by production tolerances. Rover clearly states in its service bulletin that the clearance must be checked

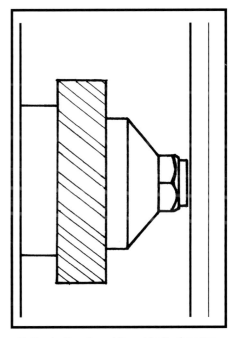

Teflon button-faced thrust bolt, showing small gap between button and inside of front cover.

and adjusted as necessary to create the correct running clearance (endfloat).

One disadvantage with the thrust bolts available today is that they are only available from Rover with an imperial thread. This is, of course, the standard original thread, but the problem is that the UK aftermarket camshaft companies, like Piper Cams and Kent Cams, for instance, usually tap their camshafts with a metric thread. This means that a Rover manufactured Teflon thrust button is limited to use on imperial threaded camshafts.

However, having a metric thrust bolt made is not a difficult task. Wildcat Engineering & J.E. Developments, for example, have always made their own thrust bolts (imperial or metric) and will supply anyone to order with whichever one they want.

The Teflon 'button' does have a service life which means that as the Teflon wears away the clearance and camshaft movement will increase. If used in conjunction with a brand new camshaft and lifters, expect the Teflon to remain on size for a long time (50,000 miles/80,000km or more in a road going engine before the bolt needs to be readjusted or, possibly, replaced).

If a thrust bolt is used in a racing engine, expect to have to readjust the bolt's endfloat (make a new spacer or shim the spacer) when the engine is stripped down for a rebuild, or to replace the Teflon thrust bolt entirely if the Teflon shows gross signs of wear.

The adjustment of the thrust bolt by machining material from the spacer is a little bit 'hit and miss' but anything between a minimum clearance of 0.005-0.010in/0.125-0.25mm is fine.

Thrust bolts are readily available from Rover/Land Rover dealerships, Rover V8 engine specialists and some camshaft manufacturers. This solution to controlling camshaft endfloat is not to be regarded as being as good as fitting a thrust plate (because of the Teflon wearing away), but there's no doubt that it is a simple and effective solution with a reasonable 'life.'

OVERSIZED CYLINDER LINERS FOR 3500CC BLOCKS

All 3500cc blocks in good

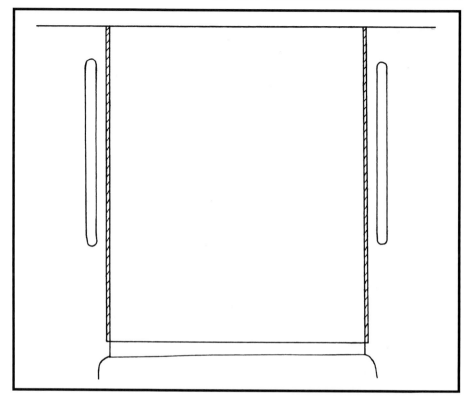

A thin-walled liner in a 3.5 litre block which safely converts it to 3.9 litres.

serviceable condition can be very successfully bored out to take larger liners and pistons to increase the capacity of the engine. That means an increase in bore size from 3.500in/88.9mm to 3.702in/94.0mm, making a 3.5 litre engine into a 3.9 litre engine.

In light of the problems the standard large bore factory machined blocks have had since 1988, the question has to be "how is it possible for automotive reconditioners to do this correctly when it is a known fact that the amount of aluminium in the earlier blocks is less than in the later cast blocks and there is a likelihood of core shift?" The answer lies with the wall thickness of the new liners that engine reconditioners and Rover V8 engine specialists use.

Engine reconditioners who have geared themselves up to do this work on a semi-production basis use the following method. The original cast iron liners are bored out to remove them, then the aluminium of the block bored out to a nominal diameter of 3.808in/96.70mm. The bottom of the liner recess is machined so that the bottoms of the new liners will sit on a 360 degree step (much the same as that of the later X-bolted '38A' blocks). The liners that they use in are 3.813in/96.80mm in diameter: 0.004-0.005in/0.1-0.125mm larger than the new bores in the block. These new liners are then 'shrink fitted' into the block (much the same as the factory originally did) by heating the blocks to 145-150 degrees C/325-334F. The liners are at room temperature when they are hand fitted into place in the hot blocks. After the block has fully cooled its decks are machined to true them up and also to remove the small amount of protruding liner.

The 0.004-0.005in/0.10-0.125mm 'interference fit' of the liners in the block is strictly controlled and each individual block/liner combination accurately measured so that all liners are held in the block by the correct specified amount of interference fit. Oversized liners are held in stock by companies that do this work so that if a block liner bore happens to be a 'thou,' or two, over the specified size, they have the option of rectifying the problem by fitting an oversized liner.

The liner bores are then bored and honed to finished size, which is 3.702in/94.00mm precisely.

Readers contemplating the purchase of a new liner kit should be aware that removing the old liners, boring the cylinder block to new dimensions and fitting the new liners is all very exacting work and very time consuming. The project needs to be discussed with the engine reconditioner/engine machine shop which is actually going to do the work for you before you go ahead and buy the kit.

The essence of fitting new liners successfully is the use of thin walled liners (made from top quality, high strength material) which enable as much aluminium material as possible to be left in the block to support the new liners, and making sure that fit between the liners and the block is perfect. No over boring of these liners is possible. The wall thickness of the finished liner in these blocks is a nominal 0.055in/1.40mm, whereas that of a standard Rover 3.9 litre liner is 0.091in/2.30mm.

Blocks with new liners machined to the exact standards as described earlier are available on an exchange basis provided your own block is fit for further use, outright purchase if it isn't, from RPI Engineering, for example. You can also have your own block relinered if you prefer, but you'll have to wait for it to be done. You do need to balance the cost of having this done, in total, against the cost of a later X-bolted block.

Caution! – All of this liner work could be wasted if the main caps are able to fret leading to their failure. In many respects it's a case of spending money on a block that could ultimately fail through another factor. The main bearing tunnels might also need to be align-honed, although they don't usually. If the crankshaft does not turn as freely as expected, main bearing tunnel mis-alignment could be the problem! It is fixable.

STANDARD CAST PISTONS

Using standard parts in one of these engines means limiting the rpm because the standard parts are only so strong. The standard parts likely to fail first in the short block assembly are the cast aluminium pistons. There were two early designs of standard pistons for the early 3.5 litre engines and one later design. The later design of piston is the only one available these days and, luckily, it's also the best design. If a Rover V8 engine is used for racing purposes with the later standard cast replacement pistons fitted, the rpm limit is 6000rpm and this is without serious risk of piston failure.

The later standard '38A'-type cast piston can be used for up

to 6500rpm reliably for a limited amount of time in racing situations, but there is some consequent risk of piston failure (although many racers get away with it entirely). Such an engine must have regular piston changes to prevent breakage. While the standard later-type cast pistons are capable of being run to 6500rpm, they should not be expected to remain in one piece for thousands of miles, year in year out, while receiving this sort of treatment, such as in a racing class that requires the use of standard cast pistons. One or two seasons of racing or 1000 racing miles is the maximum life.

If you're using a 3.5 litre engine for racing purposes where the use of standard-type cast pistons is required, you'll need to invest in a set of Omega cast replacement pistons as they are stronger than the original equipment fitted pistons.

Occasional use up to, but not exceeding 6000rpm, can be tolerated over many tens of thousands of road miles, but this is very different to a racing environment where the engine is being revved to 6500rpm before every gear change and accelerated under full loading.

In the case of the Rover V8, engines used for racing are likely to be revving between 4000 to 6000rpm most of the time with rpm dropping below 4000rpm on occasion and going up to 6500rpm fairly frequently. The regularity of the piston changing intervals can be decided by two methods. The first is to replace pistons and rings after each racing season when most engines get rebuilt. On average this will mean that the pistons will have done no more than 500-1000 racing miles. In this situation the pistons are not usually in the engine long enough to develop cracks or wear in the usual places, unless the engine has been repeatedly and excessively over-revved. New replacement pistons and ring sets are not terribly expensive (check around as there is considerable variation) which means that this method of ensuring reasonable piston reliability is not an outrageous suggestion. The second method is to replace the pistons when they have worn in certain places such as the top ring groove.

Caution! – with new rings fitted a 0.0025in/0.067mm feeler gauge must not be able to be inserted into the gap. The skirt of the piston must not have worn more than 0.001inch from when new and first installed in the engine (measure and record the piston sizes before installing them in the engine). This could mean that the engine has done two or three seasons of racing or 2000 racing miles (3000km). The inspection and measuring of the pistons at the end of each racing season when the engine is stripped down for maintenance is the time when a decision to replace or not is taken. If the rings get replaced the pistons must also be replaced.

Caution! – Using any standard later design-type cast pistons in an engine being used for racing carries some risk of breakage in service. The risk is a reasonably small one if the foregoing replacement procedure is followed. Nevertheless, cast aluminium pistons will fail from time to time for a variety of reasons, so there's no guarantee against failure. If this risk is unacceptable to you, forged pistons are required or the 6000rpm limit must be strictly adhered to. Fitting a rev-limiter to racing engines equipped with cast pistons is pretty much mandatory.

Caution! – Note that any cast piston will very likely fail if a valve or valves contact its crown in an over revving situation. Help to avoid this by fitting an electronic rev-limiter but be aware that a rev-limiter will not stop over revving during a down shifting gearchange which goes a bit wrong. If this happens and the engine suffers bent valves and clear valve indentations in the top of the pistons, replace the pistons before running the engine again, otherwise you could lose the engine as the pistons are likely to fracture/fail.

Use a piston to bore clearance of 0.0026inch to 0.0028in/0.0676 to 0.072mm for all stock-type cast original equipment or aftermarket replacement cast alloy pistons. More clearance than this is not required for cast aluminium pistons. Having too much clearance (0.004-0.005in/0.1-0.125mm, for example) leads to other problems, although piston seizing is not one of them.

Note that Rover lists standard piston to bore clearances of 0.0007in/0.017mm to 0.0013in/0.032mm. While this is ideal for standard road use it is not ideal at 0.0013in/0.032mm top tolerance for a high-performance orientated engine. The maximum factory listed size is just too tight, and seizure is possible.

STANDARD PISTON SIZES

There is quite a wide range of cast aluminium (and forged aluminium) pistons available for the Rover V8 engine. The standard engines were all fitted with cast aluminium pistons made by Hepolite, and pistons have been available from the original manufacturer in the following standard and oversize sizes –

3.5 Rover/Hepolite 8.25:1 compression – std, plus 0.020inch
3.5 Rover/Hepolite 8.3:1 compression – std, plus 0.020inch
3.5 Rover/Hepolite 9.25:1 compression – std, plus 0.020inch
3.5 Rover/Hepolite 9.35:1 compression – std, plus 0.020inch
3.5 Rover/Hepolite 9.75:1 compression – std, plus 0.020inch
3.5 Rover/Hepolite 10.25:1 compression – std, plus 0.020inch
3.5 Hepolite/Wellworthy 8.13:1 compression – std, plus 0.020, 0.040inch
3.5 Hepolite/Wellworthy 9.35:1 compression – std, plus 0.020, 0.040inch
3.5 Omega (cast flat topped 10.25:1 compression) plus 0.020inch only
3.9 Rover/Hepolite 8.3:1 compression – std, plus 0.020inch
3.9 Rover/Hepolite 9.35:1 compression – std, plus 0.020inch
4.2 Rover/Hepolite 8.7:1 compression – std only
4.0 Rover/Hepolite 8.3:1 compression – std only
4.0 Rover/Hepolite 9.35:1 compression – std only
4.6 Rover/Hepolite 8.3:1 compression – std only
4.6 Rover/Hepolite 9.35:1 compression – std only

HYPOEUTECTIC, EUTECTIC & HYPEREUTECTIC CAST PISTONS

These are aftermarket pistons with higher than standard strength. Such pistons are available from the likes of Wildcat Engineering for quite a few Rover V8 engine applications/bore sizes. Wildcat uses Australian-made ACL pistons bought in semi-finished, which do not have an oil return slot (meaning that the piston skirt is tied directly to the piston crown).

No claim is made that these pistons are the equivalent of forged pistons strengthwise, but they are most definitely stronger than standard cast pistons. Their unique feature, which is an advantage on the basis of piston ring stability, is their requirement for very close piston to bore clearances, such as 0.0015-0.0018in/0.038-0.046mm (a factor of the stability of the particular aluminium material used). These pistons require larger than normal compression ring gaps to prevent the ends of the rings 'butting' in use. Consider these pistons to be between the standard castings and forgings in terms of strength.

Caution! – it is essential to follow the manufacturer's piston to bore clearance and ring end gap recommendations. Increasing piston to bore clearance and/or not having enough compression ring end gap because both tolerances seem too small, can lead to engine failure. The requirements of these pistons are a little bit different to what most people are used to, but that isn't a reason not to follow the manufacturer's advice.

The terms 'hypoeutectic', 'eutectic' and 'hypereutectic' denote various saturation levels of silicon in the aluminium of the piston material. The nominal level of the point of saturation of silicon is 13%. A piston which is listed as having this exact amount of silicon is termed 'eutectic'. If a piston has less than a nominal 13% silicon saturation it is referred to as 'hypoeutectic' and if it has more it's referred to as 'hypereutectic'. This type of piston is now quite common as original equipment. Ford in the USA has been using these sorts of pistons

in some of its V8 engines for over a decade. The latest use of these pistons in Ford engines sees them fitted with one steel compression ring, a three piece oil scraper ring and with 0.001in/0.025mm piston to bore clearance. The technology is proven.

FORGED PISTONS

There's no doubt that for all out racing purposes forged pistons are required: they have proven, over the last 45 years, to have the durability required for this activity. There are plenty of forged piston manufacturers, such as Omega, Arias, JE, Ross and Diamond, to name but a few. Most forged piston manufacturers will make pistons of the size and configuration you require, and many offer a 3-4 week delivery service. Many include an extra two pistons and gudgeon pins in the deal, and will keep your individual piston specifications on file for future reference.

There's quite a range of piston size requirements for the Rover V8 when all of the bore, stroke and connecting rod length permutations are taken into consideration, meaning that sometimes the only way to get a suitable piston set is to get them made by a custom piston manufacturer. Ross and Diamond offers quick services.

Usual piston to bore clearances are 0.001in/0.025mm per 1in/25mm of piston diameter. Therefore, a 3.500in/89mm bore engine requires 0.0035in/0.0889mm clearance, while a 3.702in/94mm bore engine requires 0.0037in/0.0939mm (and no extra clearance, unless it's a special application such as a supercharged/turbocharged application where it is known that more heat than usual

will be being put into the pistons).
Caution! – Excessive piston to bore clearances are unnecessary and can be the cause of abnormal bore wear characteristics.

Note that the diameter of all modern pistons is measured at the very bottom of the skirts and at 90 degrees to the gudgeon pin axis only. This is because piston skirts are oval with the maximum diameter at 90 degrees to the gudgeon pin axis; they also taper outwards from just under the oil control ring down to the lowest point of the skirt.

BORE WEAR

One of the very good aspects of the Rover V8 engine block is its very low bore wear over a high mileage. The bore wear could be as low as 0.002in on an engine that has covered 100,000 miles or more. Even so, this amount of bore wear is really too much for a high performance engine. The only acceptable bore is one which is on size (perfectly round and parallel) with no perceptible wear of any description. This means that any engine which has covered 50,000 to 75,000 miles plus will need to be re-bored even though the bores will not be worn very much.

There is no substitute for having an engine which has perfectly round parallel bores fitted with brand new pistons and rings. All the bores must have an optimum and identical amount of piston to bore clearance with an ideal hone pattern on the bore walls.

Realistically, this means fitting new oversized pistons to virtually any engine block. Pistons are seldom still 'on size' (as new) if they have been in a road going engine that has done more than 50,000 miles. The piston skirts wear and so do the top ring grooves. On top of this is the factor of fatigue.

The cost of replacing pistons and reboring a block is not high, so, for high performance use, it's not an unrealistic suggestion to rebore a block and fit new pistons and rings, even if there's only 0.002in/0.05mm bore wear and 0.0015in/0.039mm piston skirt wear. These not unrealistic wear figures would mean that an engine that once had 0.0013in/0.032mm piston to bore clearance could now have 0.0048in/0.117mm wear clearance (through wear) at the top of the bore and still have the original 0.0013in/ 0.032mm piston to bore clearance at the bottom of the bore.

Summary

Don't consider using a block with worn bores and old pistons with new rings fitted to them if you want top engine performance. Old pistons are much more prone to failure than new pistons (running-in period excepted). If the block's bore wear is minimal at 0.0015in/0.040mm, for instance, the bores can be parallel machine honed which will end up giving 0.0028in/ 0.072mm piston to bore clearance (ideal). If the engine has 0.0013in/ 0.032mm piston to bore clearance and has 0.0015in/0.039mm of wear at the top of the bore, the wear can be cleaned up by parallel honing the bores: the result will be an 'on size' correctly clearanced bore. Any more wear than the slight amounts mentioned requires a rebore to the very next oversize to restore the situation.

CYLINDER BORE PREPARATION

With the cylinder bores on size, perfectly round and parallel, and with the correct piston to bore clearance, the next factor that has to be taken into consideration is the honing pattern and surface finish on the bore walls. All bores in all rebored engines are finish honed. Alternatively, if the bores are still on size (don't need a re-bore), re-honed to create good ring seating. The thoroughness of the cylinder honing is vital for correct piston ring seating and effective sealing, and also relates to how long the effective seal between the bore wall contact edge of the ring and the bore wall lasts. Getting this part of the rebuild correct can pay real dividends.

Accepted standard measurements of piston ring sealing within the motor industry can be directly related to a 'leak down' test. This test checks the rate of compressed air 'leakage' past the rings. Leak down testing equipment is readily available for reasonable money and is a requirement for anyone who is racing one of these engines. With this equipment available, the condition of the rings can be monitored as the engine is used and when the percentage of leakage is too high, the engine rebuilt to restore the piston ring sealing. This is a certain method of making sure that this aspect of the engine's mechanical integrity is a known quantity.

If you have an engine which has a leak down rate of 1% to 2% consider the engine to have absolutely excellent piston ring sealing. 2% to 5% is very good. 4% to 7% is still good. An engine that has been conventionally honed and run for just 30 minutes, or so, will often have a leak down reading of around 15%. Expect this reading to improve after further running of the engine to 7% to 10% which is still an entirely acceptable figure, but on the low side of being good. Anything beyond 10% after a reasonable running-in phase is cause for concern and is not going to allow the production of optimum engine power.

Various ring sets are available for the Rover V8 with the standard late model piston rings sets being excellent, reasonably priced and readily available. Other top quality rings sets are available for the Rover V8 such as the American made 'Total Seal' gapless ring sets. These ring sets are available for most piston sizes, but not all, and cost more than standard conventional ring sets. Any set of rings can be fitted into bores which have been 'plateau honed' which will result in better than normal ring seating and sealing. However, correct running-in procedures are critical.

For a racing engine, the cylinder bores can be treated a bit differently, especially if the engine is going to be run-in on an engine dyno: in fact only if the engine is going to be run in on a dyno. The reason being that the special cylinder hone treatment means that it is very easy to end up 'glazing' the bores and then the rings will never seat properly, the only solution being to replace them!

The normal method of honing cylinder bores means honing each cylinder, preferably using mechanical honing equipment, so that the cylinders are all finished with 45 degree cross hatch pattern. Experienced engine reconditioning engineers can hand hone cylinders as well as any machine, but the trend these days is to use a machine which guarantees the end result. Normally the honing stones used would be 280 grit, which is the industry wide accepted standard grade of grit.

What can be done in addition, after this basic honing process, is to change the 280 grit honing stone for a 500 grit one, then 'corking shoes' or 'finishing shoes' as they are sometimes known, which smooth off the rough top edges of the grooves created by the 280 grit hone. This process is called 'plateau honing'. The British engine reconditioning machine tool company Delapena, for example, markets alternative interchangeable honing stones for its hones. Other companies which make honing stones/corking shoes for this honing process are Sunnen and K-line. It's a well-known and respected process. Many race engine preparation workshops buy plateau honing equipment and go to the trouble of preparing the bores in this manner as they want their racing engines to have the best possible piston ring sealing in order to develop maximum power for their customers.

A common practice nowadays is to assemble an engine with penetrating oil (CRC or WD40) sprayed on the bores, pistons and rings (no regular oil at all applied to these components). Using this method, ring seating is quick and almost guaranteed.

With the engine built, fitted on to the engine dyno and ready for testing the engine is started. The oil used initially for the running-in process is a good quality 15/50 or 20/50 motor oil with no additives whatsoever, or a 'running-in oil' as marketed by Castrol, Millers or Morris, for example. **Caution!** – Irrespective of how quickly the engine is put under loading with a

friction modified or a synthetic oil in it, the bores will glaze, so such lubricants **must not be used** initially under any circumstances. The use of a specially made running-in oil is recommended if you have the choice. Failing this start with a good quality 15/50 or 20/50 motor oil (Kendall, Valvoline, etc) and stay with it. Synthetics can be used after the rings have proven to be fully seated (after 2000 miles/3000km for road engines; 3-4 race meetings for racing engines).

The procedure for running-in an engine which has had its bores plateau honed is to fire up the engine and within 30 seconds of doing this have at least 50 pounds of dyno loading on the engine with the engine revving at 2000-2500rpm and the throttle quarter open. This may seem a bit harsh, but it's the only way to prevent bore glazing and to start the ring bedding-in process. The oil will have been preheated so that warm oil is circulating through the engine. What this dyno loading does is cause the engine to generate substantial combustion pressure which forces the piston rings to rub quite firmly against the bore wall surface.

This dyno procedure is quite a different situation from an engine which is turning 2000-2500rpm with no dyno loading and with virtually no throttle opening. In this situation the engine is revving at the same rpm, but, with no serious combustion generated cylinder pressure acting behind the rings, they're not being forced outwards against bore walls. This is when the bore walls become glazed as the rings are just lightly rubbing up and down in the bore and, once glazed, the bores remain glazed because the situation is only

reversible by replacing the rings and re-honing the bores (full strip down).

Mechanics have been known to try bedding-in rings which are in this state by administering Ajax or Vim scouring powder to the induction system, while the engine is running. The abrasive action of the powder can do the trick, but this method is not guaranteed.

Unless requested, race engine preparation workshops do not normally 'plateau hone' cylinder bores unless they are going to run the engines in themselves on a dyno before sending them to the customer. This is because few engine owners have an engine dyno to run-in the engine in the specified manner. If it's done incorrectly the engine will burn oil from day one (and lots of it) and will not produce top engine power.

The benefits of plateau honing a cylinder block and running the engine in the correct manner are leak down test readings of between 1% and 2%, even with conventional Rover factory-made piston rings fitted. If Total Seal gapless rings are fitted to such an engine the likely result is a 1% leak down test reading, or less (zero), which is simply excellent. The other factor here is that it is quite possible for the rings to 'hold' this efficiency for up to 20 hours of racing use. The instant a leak down test shows that the piston ring sealing efficiency is reducing (percentage of leakage increasing), the engine should be rebuilt to avoid any possibility of bore damage and to restore full performance.

With first class ring sealing the difference in overall engine efficiency is noticeable and cannot be ignored. An example is off the turn under full throttle at around maximum torque. With the engine generating maximum cylinder pressures, the better the ring seal, the more the pressure is pushing the piston down as opposed to leaking past it and into the crankcase!

The following clearances are the general clearance requirements necessary for high-performance work with engine reliability within the mechanical limitations of standard componentry (eg: standard replacement cast pistons, connecting rods and crankshaft). Optimum clearances will make for a smoother running, more willing and a more reliable engine.

Piston to bore clearance 0.0026in to 0.0028in/0.063 to 0.072mm

Main bearing clearance 0.002in to 0.0022in/0.05 to 0.056mm

Big end bearing clearance 0.0018in to 0.002in/0.046 to 0.05mm

Connecting rod side clearance 0.008in to 0.010in/0.2 to 0.25mm

Crankshaft endfloat 0.002-0.004in/0.5 to 0.1mm.

CYLINDER HEAD FIXINGS

It is highly recommended that for cylinder head retention **all** Rover V8 engines be fitted with aftermarket studs and nuts, as opposed to the standard bolts/stretch bolts.

While there's no definite link between the cracking behind the liners problem and bolt fixings, the fact that a very high proportion of cracks are found adjacent to the bolt holes is cause for concern and indicates that the tensioning action of bolts could be having some affect.

As a matter of course, specialists like John Eales and Ian Richardson use studs and nuts for head retention and they've noticed a lack of cracking in this area of blocks so equipped.

Chapter 2
Cylinder head identification

IDENTIFICATION

The cylinder heads of these engines have not had any major design changes made to them since they were introduced by Rover in 1967. However, there have been several minor changes made over the years: valve sizes, combustion chamber volume, sparkplug thread lengths, valve springs, valve spring retainers, valve seat inserts. Luckily, it's not overly complicated to identify the sequence of events and categorise the various cylinder head types.

Buick heads

The Buick 215 engines of 1960-1963 had single valve springs, sintered valve spring retainers and collets (keepers/split locks) which were very similar to the later SD1 ones of 1976 on, but the valve springs were wound the opposite way and had a higher coil bind height. The Buick 215 engine also had short reach sparkplugs. The Buick and early Rover V8 engine cylinder heads are virtually the same.

Original Rover 3.5 litre heads

The original 3.5 litre P5, P6, MGB V8 and early Range Rover cylinder heads have 1.500in/38.0mm diameter headed inlet valves and 1.312in/33.3mm headed exhaust valves, and cast iron/mehanite valve seat inserts.

The combustion chamber volume is a nominal 36cc.

Dual valve springs are fitted, which are 1.300in/33.0mm in outside diameter of the outer valve spring and 0.680in in inside diameter of the inner valve spring. The two valve springs are wound the same way and there is a collective clearance of 0.075in/1.9mm between the two springs when in situ. The valve spring retainers on these heads are turned out of high tensile steel and were of 1.345in/34.1mm diameter. The spot-facing/recess for these springs machined into the cylinder head is 1.250in/31.8mm in outside diameter and 0.840in/21.3mm inside diameter and is a single depth spot-facing which is, on average, 0.125in/3.2mm deep.

The sparkplugs used are 'short reach' ones, with a thread length of 0.5in/12.5mm (dating any Rover V8 cylinder head which has them to between 1967-1976).

The cylinder heads have 14 bolt retention.

There were no valve guide stem seals, of any description, fitted to these cylinder heads.

First change: SD1 & Range Rover heads 1976 on

With the introduction of the SD1 cars in 1976, the inlet valve heads were increased to 1.575in/40.0mm in diameter and the exhaust valve heads to 1.350in/34.3mm in diameter. The valve seat inserts were increased to match.

The valve springs were now singles and 1.225in/31.1mm in outside diameter and, as a consequence, the valve springs do not interchange between cylinder heads as the spot facing machining is different on each cylinder head. The early dual valve springs will not fit into these later cylinder heads, although the later single valve springs will fit the early cylinder heads provided 16 steel valve spring bases are specially made to suit the head as there isn't any proper base location for the valve springs otherwise. The valve spring retainers to suit the new single valve springs were of steel up until 1980, at which point they changed to sintered material, which is less strong. Sintered valve spring retainers were used from this point on until the end of the production run of the engine.

Note that the first two factory made steel valve spring retainers have not been available from Rover for many years and the identical ones made by replacement part suppliers are all but gone, most Rover V8 engine specialists not having any new sets in stock. However, aftermarket camshaft manufacturers supply similar retainers for use with their valve springs.

Sparkplugs became 'long reach' with a thread length of 0.75in/19mm, making these 1976 on cylinder heads very easy to distinguish from the early ones. The inlet valve guides were now fitted with a flat rubber washer type oil seal.

1967-1976: P5, P6 and early Range Rover 3.5 litre combustion chamber shape. 1.5in diameter inlet valves and 1.312in exhausts.

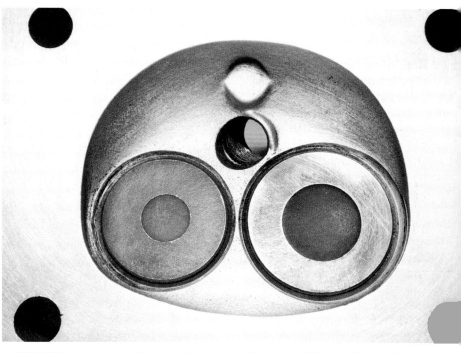

1976-2004 basic combustion chamber shape with larger 1.570 inch diameter inlet and exhaust valves and long reach sparkplugs. Note that the combustion chamber was made shallower from January 1994 and stayed that way until the end of production.

Second change: 1982 on

In 1982 the valve seat inserts were changed from close grain cast iron/mechanite to the exceptionally hard wearing copper/bronze ones made by Brico. These later valve seats are suitable for use with unleaded fuel and remained the standard fitting from this point on. Copper/bronze is a vastly superior material to the earlier cast iron in terms of wear resistance. Even after long term use with unleaded fuel, the valve seats will remain in good condition and, more or less, as machined by the factory. However, exhaust valves will need to be reground more often than you might think if absolutely perfect seating is to be maintained. This is because the contact surface of the valve which contacts the valve seat insert will slowly deteriorate showing signs of minor wear/pitting usually at between 50,000 and 80,000 miles/120,000km.

Third change: 1982 on

While the 3.5 litre Vitesse engines introduced in 1982 only were fitted with waisted stem inlet valves, these inlet valves became standard in all engines from the introduction of the 3.9 litre engine in October 1989 and on and all subsequent Rover V8 engines.

Fourth change: 1993 on

On the later 3.9 and 4.2 engines of 1993 on, and **all** subsequent engines, the inlet and exhaust valve guides were fitted with neoprene valve stem oil seals which are a 'press on' fit to the top of the valve guide. The tops of the relevant valve guides are machined differently to accommodate these seals. These later valve stem oil seals are

Pre-1994 showing three of the four drilled bosses for the bottom row of head retaining bolts (14 bolt retention).

This photo shows the same bosses, this time undrilled, for post 1994 heads (10 bolt retention).

excellent, and far superior to the earlier arrangement, making these 1993 and later cylinder heads better than any of the earlier ones on the basis of limiting the amount of oil that can pass down the guides. All production engines from 1993 and on featured this arrangement.

Note that all cylinder heads made until December 1993, with the exception of the Australian made P76 engine, have 14 bolt cylinder head retention. The Australian made 10 bolt cylinder heads don't have the small notches (fuel injection nozzle notches) in the inlet port entries like all later 10 bolt Rover V8 cylinder heads made after January 1994.

Fifth change: 1994 on
With the introduction of the 'interim' 3.9 & 4.2 litre engine in January 1994, several changes were made at the same time. The combustion chamber volume was reduced from the nominal 36cc of all previous cylinder heads to a nominal 28cc, cylinder head retention became 10 bolt instead of 14 bolt (with the non use of the bottom row of four bolts), and the cylinder head gasket changed from a shim one to a composite one.

The cylinder head casting was exactly the same as the previous ones, but was machined down an extra 0.040in/1.0mm on the cylinder head gasket matching face. This machined face is the datum point from which all other dimensions are taken for subsequent machining, the change ultimately only results in shallower combustion chambers (28cc volume) with no other effective changes to the cylinder head. These cylinder heads are quite easy to recognise because the valves are recessed whereas in all earlier cylinder heads, they are not. The difference is subtle, but it's there if you look closely.

The main way of quickly identifying a 28cc combustion chamber cylinder head is via the fact that it will have 10 cylinder head retention bolt holes and small notches in the top of the inlet port entries to suit the fuel injection nozzles.

The combustion chamber

The 28cc combustion chamber has recessed (0.040inch/1.00mm) inlet and exhaust valves. The flat head surfaces of the valves are virtually level with the combustion chamber surface.

capacity was reduced because of the change from shim steel head gaskets to composite ones. The shim gaskets are, on average, 0.020in/0.50mm thick while the composite ones are approximately 0.050in/1.25mm thick. Making the combustion chambers shallower compensated for the increased thickness of the cylinder head gaskets. With the use of the composite cylinder head gaskets and 28cc combustion chamber volume cylinder heads, the compression ratio remained the same as it was before. The reason for the change to composite head gaskets and 10 cylinder head retention was to provide better combustion sealing.

The other change in January 1994 was the use of 'use one time' stretch bolts for head retention. These bolts are easy to recognise

Stretch bolt as used from January 1994 on. Best replaced by studs and nuts.

by their flanged heads ('washer' and bolt head all in one piece) as opposed to all 1967 to the end of 1994 bolts which have separate washers.

Caution! – These stretch bolts must be renewed whenever the head is removed and refitted.

The original 3.5 litre 'service engines' of 1995, and the later run of partially completed 'service engines' in 1997/1998, also used the January

1994 on 28cc combustion chamber volume cylinder heads, composite cylinder head gaskets and stretch bolts (10 bolt pattern).

EARLY HEADS & UNLEADED FUEL

Note that early cylinder heads which have cast iron valve seats (cylinder heads made between 1967-1982) can only be successfully used with the unleaded fuel available now if an approved lead substitute additive is mixed with the fuel. Failure to use a fuel additive will result in valve seat recession (VSR).

For high performance use, replacing the exhaust valves of 50,000 miles/80,000km plus engine is very good practise. As a general rule, old well used exhaust valves are more prone to dropping heads than new ones (though it has to be said that the Rover V8 is not particularly prone to this malady).

As cylinder heads made prior to 1982 are not really suitable for use with unleaded fuel, Rover V8 engine specialists and engine reconditioning companies can replace the exhaust valve seats with hardened steel ones (Well-Tite, for example). This is the only way of guaranteeing that there will be no valve seat recession when straight unleaded fuel is used.

In this process, the original 'soft' exhaust valve seats are removed (bored away) and the new hardened type ones fitted by heating the cylinder heads to 110 degrees C/230F while freezing the valve seat inserts in liquid nitrogen. With the cylinder head expanded and the inserts contracted, the inserts are able to be pushed into the recesses machined in the cylinder heads. This fitting method ensures that the aluminium of the cylinder head is not 'shaved' as the valve seat insert is pushed into place, damage which would result in a poorly fitted insert which could come out in service ...

When the cylinder head and the inserts have returned to ambient temperature there will be an effective 0.005-0.006in/0.127-0.152mm interference fit between the valve seat inserts and the cylinder heads. Provided the machined recess in the cylinder head is perfect (parallel and a smooth surface finish), the sides of the valve seat inserts parallel and the inserts fully seated without undue force, it is extemely unlikely they'll ever come out.

With the cost of older cylinder heads being virtually zero, the expense of having them converted (after crack testing/pressure testing) for unleaded fuel and reconditioned (new valve guides/K-Line valve guide inserts fitted, valve seats re-cut and a gasket face skim) is now an economic proposition. The fact that this whole operation can be geared up for on a semi-production basis means that the cost of having them fully reconditioned is reasonable (RPI Engineering, for example, does this).

If you have a good pair of early small valve cylinder heads, for example, and want to use them as they are, you should not think that any engine that you build up will be vastly inferior in performance level to an engine fitted with newer cylinder heads. The earlier small valve cylinder heads (1967-1976) are still good heads and will flow a sufficient amount of gas for any road going 3.5 litre engine. They do, of course, need to be in a good serviceable condition which means no worn valve guides, pitted or misshapen valve seats, nor valve seats that are too wide or have old and weak valve springs fitted

to them (check the pressures). In many instances a pair of low mileage cylinder heads will only need to have the valve seats re-cut, the gasket surfaces skimmed and the valves ground or renewed to be put into service. If unleaded fuel is going to be used, an approved additive will of course have to be mixed with the fuel or LRP used, unless hardened valve seats are retro-fitted.

Caution! – LRP fuel (Lead Replacement Fuel). If you live in the UK LRP is still available at the time of writing, although it's gradually being phased out. This fuel will prevent valve seat recession from happening except in the severest of applications. UK readers using LRP need to be aware of the fact that there is a limit to the effectiveness of LRP in preventing valve seat recession in heavy duty/high performance applications. LRP is **not** equivalent to the last of the tetraethyl leaded fuel made by the large petrol (gasoline) companies (0.149gm of tetraethyl lead per litre) which was phased out in 2000. That fuel had the maximum allowance of tetraethyl lead allowable under British Standard 4040 and gave very good valve seat protection. LRP gives minimum valve seat protection, it's more equivalent to older, cheaper fuel mixes which had 0.050gm of tetraethyl lead per litre (the minimum amount allowed under the BS4040).

Anyone using a Rover V8 with the older early cylinder heads for towing, where the engine is under a constant loading with a wide throttle opening, needs to use unleaded fuel with something like TetraBOOST (web: tetraboost.com/email: tetraboost@aol.com/'phone UK 020 8870 9933), for example, mixed in. LRP is 95 octane (RON) premium unleaded fuel with potassium added at a rate of 8 parts per million.

VALVES

The valve stem diameters and lengths of all Rover V8 valves are the same, as are the collet (keeper/split lock) groove shape and position. There have been two inlet and two exhaust head diameter sizes. Waisted inlet valve stems were used for 3.5 litre Vitesse engines and then universally adopted in September 1988 for all engines; as a consequence there have been two exhaust valves and three inlet valve types.

VALVE SPRING & VALVE SPRING RETAINERS

The early engines (1967-1976) had dual valve springs and steel valve spring retainers that suited dual springs. The SD1/Range Rover engines of 1976 on had single valve springs and steel valve spring retainers to suit the new single valve

Early steel valve spring retainers to suit dual valve springs as used 1967-1976.

springs. These first two valve spring retainers are very strong and are even suitable for racing purposes.

Later SD1 engines, 1980 on, had sintered material valve spring retainers that suited the same single valve spring arrangement. **Caution!** – These valve spring retainers are **not** suitable for use above 5800rpm.

Valve springs and their retainers are companion sets and those of P5, P6, MGB V8 and early Range Rovers **do not** interchange with later engines.

STANDARD INLET & EXHAUST PORTS

The inlet and exhaust ports of the early Rover V8 engines (1967-1976) were very near to being the same as those of the original Buick 215 engine. One thing the Buick cylinder heads did have, compared to the Rover V8 heads, were fully machined combustion chambers, whereas all Rover ones are as cast.

Subtle porting changes were made over the years to Rover V8 cylinder heads. These changes were of a minor nature, such as the small cutout on each inlet port opening to suit the fuel injection system, and there have been slight increases in the sizes of some areas of the inlet and exhaust ports.

The later the cylinder heads, the better the castings on the basis of general neatness and quality of finish.

Chapter 3
Distributor, front cover & oil pump identification

These three components of the Rover V8 engine are inextricably linked to each other because of the various types of front cover/timing chain cover (referred to as a 'front cover' from here on) to which they are fitted. While outwardly it might seem quite simple to identify all front covers, distributors and oil pumps, in fact it's anything but simple ...

The identification of some of the early componentry is less relevant these days as engines are being modernised, irrespective of when they were made, or what they were originally equipped with as standard. There were eight types of front cover for these engines between 1967-2004, incorporating three different distributor drives, two different capacity gear type oil pumps, two different drives for these oil pumps, two types of oil pump, four different water pump positions, two types of water pump (one clockwise rotating,

the other anti-clockwise), 3 basic water pumps (about 20 water pump variants when all of the flanges for bolting on water pump pulleys and fans is taken into consideration) and four oil filters! The following explains the sequence of events:

DISTRIBUTORS

All Rover V8 engines made between 1967 and October 1994 had Lucas distributors of various types fitted (Lucas 35 D8, 35 DEM, 35 DM8 & 35 DLM8).

From October 1994 on this all changed. The engines that retained the use of a Lucas distributor after this date were all of the 3.5 litre 'service' units, all 'interim' 3.9 & 4.2 litre Range Rover Classic engines, and virtually all 'interim' 3.9 litre Land Rover Discovery engines (except the last few that went to North America, which were fitted with GEMS 8).

In October 1994, when the

4.0 & 4.6 litre 38A engines were introduced, they all came fitted with the GEMS 8, distributorless, engine management system. The engine management system that followed GEMS 8 in 2000 for all 4.0 & 4.6 litre 'Thor' engines was the Bosch Motronic ML. 2.1 which was also distributorless.

Car distributors

Lucas originally supplied single and dual point-type distributors, coded 35 D8, to Rover for fitting into P5 & P6 car engines (1967-1976). With the introduction of the SD1 car in 1976, contact breaker points-type ignition systems were no longer used.

Distributors are referred to as 'early' or 'late', the change point being at the change of oil pump drive type in 1976 for **all** 3.5 litre engines. The 'early' distributors are compatible with the early 'short gear'-type oil pumps used until

1976, while the 'late' distributors are compatible with the later 'long gear'-type oil pumps of 1976 onward.

Note that all EFI (electronic fuel injection) Rover V8 engines, starting in 1977, have 'electronic' (contact breakerless) distributors fitted: never contact breaker points-type distributors.

The Lucas 'Opus' 35 DE8 electronic distributor was used in conjunction with a new oil pump drive on the end of the spindle. This distributor was followed, in 1982, by an improved version called '35 DM8' and, in 1985, the '35 DLM8' - which was used until the end of SD1 car production in 1987. The 35 DM8 distributor had the ignition module mounted separate from the distributor body, while the 35 DLM8 had it mounted on the side of the distributor body, making recognition of each type easy on SD1 engines.

4x4 & commercial vehicle distributors

The 3.5 litre Range Rover engines used the original contact breaker points-type Lucas 35 D8 distributors from 1970-1981, as did the 3.5 litre V8 Military SIII Land Rover of 1972 on.

The new 'long gear'-type oil pump, and different drive system, was used from 1976, phased in over about three months.

From 1981 until mid-1984 all twin carburettor Range Rover and Land Rover SIII Stage 1 V8 engines were fitted with Lucas 35 D8 'sliding point', single contact breaker, distributors.

After mid-1984 all engines were fitted with Lucas 35 DM8 electronic distributors.

At the end of 1985 (October) the first engines fitted with the Lucas

4CU EFI system were available in Range Rovers (as an option), and these engines retained 35 DM8 'electronic' (contact breakerless) distributors.

EFI became standard for Range Rovers in December 1986, the last Zenith carburettors being fitted to the Range Rover V8s in November 1986. 3.5 litre V8 Land Rovers, Freight-Rover Sherpas, Freight-Rovers, LDVs and Defenders all retained the use of carburettors.

In October 1987 the first engine fitted with the Lucas 'hot wire' 14 CUX EFI system became available, it used the Lucas 35 DLM8 electronic distributor. The Lucas 35 DLM8 electronic distributors (1987-1993) can have either of two types of ignition module fitted to them (two or three pin). The two pin module is the earlier type (1985-1991); the three pin module was used from 1992-1993. Either module can be used on **any** Lucas 35 DLM8 distributor which is designed to have the nodule bolted to the side of it (1985 to December 1993). The link leads are module specific so, if you change the module, you'll need to use the appropriate link lead.

The Discovery I, introduced in 1989, used a 3.5 litre EFI V8 engine and the same distributor.

In January 1994, Rover introduced the 3.9 & 4.2 litre 'interim' engines which used a **new** version of the 35 DLM8 electronic distributor. This distributor had a remotely mounted ignition module, and no provision to mount a module on its side. This change was made at this late stage because of the high failure rate of distributor-mounted modules (1987-1993) caused by exposure to excessive heat. Remote ignition modules were now mounted on the

bulkhead, next to the ignition coil, and are different to the previous 35 DLM8 modules in that they have fixing points to make them suitable for bulkhead mounting. Despite the different mountings, the remote-type ignition module is a three pin-type which uses the same technology inside as earlier modules. There is a further difference between the **new** version of the 35 DLM8 electronic distributor and all previous 35 DLM8s: this later unit has no oil pump drive at the bottom of the spindle because the engines used a crank driven oil pump from this point onward.

FRONT COVERS
Type 1 & 2

The P5, P6 saloon engines of 1967-1976, and the Range Rover engines of 1970-1976, both had front covers which had small capacity gear-type oil pumps; These covers used a 'toothed' drive contact breaker points-type distributor, but they were not the same as each other. The Range Rover engine's front cover had the water pump positioned higher to give a more suitable fan placement in relation to the radiator. This accounts for the first two types of front covers, the first and second types of water pump and the first type of distributor (although there were two slightly different versions of the same type of distributor: one single point, the other a dual point unit.

Type 3

With the introduction of the SD1 car in 1976, the front cover of both the SD1 and the Range Rover engine got a large capacity oil pump (longer gears). A corresponding change at this time was that the distributor

SD1-type front cover with it's external oil pump.

Types 5 & 6

The 'interim' 3.9 and 4.2 litre engines, as fitted to Classic Range Rovers, retained the use of a conventional distributor for the entire production run. However, the Lucas distributors for these engines had no oil pump drive on the end of the spindle (oil pump was crank driven) and were, as a consequence, the fourth type of distributor.

The last of the 3.9 litre 'interim' engines, that went to the USA in Discovery Is, were slightly different to earlier 3.9 litre 'interim' engines, in that they were fitted with Lucas GEMS-8 engine management

Rear view of an 'interim' front cover.

was fitted with a 'slot' drive instead of a 'tooth' drive and a 'flexible' or 'wobbly' drive incorporated at the bottom of the distributor spindle to connect to the oil pump spindle. This distributor type constitutes the second type and was an electronic ignition unit as opposed to a contact breaker points-type. The water pump position for the SD1 engine was the same as that for the previous P5 and P6 engines. This third front cover remained for the SD1 car production run of 1976-1987.

Type 4

With the changeover to the large capacity gear-type oil pump on the Range Rover in 1976, the water pump position remained as per the original Range Rover. This fourth front cover remained in production on all subsequent 3.5, 3.9 and 4.2 Range Rover engines until the 'interim' engine was introduced in January 1994. Distributors from 1976 onward used the 'slot' drive system, the same as the SD1 engines, but retained the use of contact breaker points exclusively until mid-1984: this constitutes the third type of distributor.

Front on view of an 'interim' front cover (distributor and crank-driven oil pump).

systems. The front cover on these particular engines was not machined to take a distributor. The water pump on all 'interim' engine front covers was now positioned in a similar place to that of the P5, P6 and SD1 engines, and not higher like all previous Range Rover engines. This

accounts for the fifth and sixth type of front cover.

Type 7

The front cover fitted to 4.0 and 4.6 litre 38A engines, as fitted to the HSE Range Rovers, has no provision whatsoever for a distributor. The water pump on all 4.0 and 4.6 litre engines is positioned in exactly the same place in relation to the crankshaft as the 'interim' engine's, but it's closer to the cylinder block. This was because there was no distributor to clear and recessing the water pump meant that the engine could be made shorter. This accounts for the seventh type of front cover. The water pump used on the 3.9 and 4.2 litre 'interim' engines and the 4.0 and 4.6 litre engines is the same.

Another significant distinguishing feature of the 4.0 and 4.6 litre 38A engines is that the 'serpentine' belt is driven off the damper's rim, which has poly-vee belt drive grooving machined into it. The 'interim' engines, by

Front on view of a 4.0-4.6 litre front cover.

Rear view of a 4.0-4.6 litre 38A, HSE-type front cover (distributorless and crank-driven oil pump).

comparison, all have a separate poly-vee type pulley bolted on to the front of the damper, which drives all of the accessories. The 'serpentine' belt drive arrangement was used on all 'interim' 3.9 and 4.2 and 4.0 and 4.6 litre 38A engines, meaning that the water pumps of these engines are all contra rotating compared to all other Rover V8 engines.

From October 1994 the 38A 4.0 and 4.6 litre engines fitted to HSE Range Rovers became distributorless via their exclusive use of the Lucas GEMS-8 engine management system. Any 1994-2000 distributorless Rover V8 can, however, be fitted with a distributor ignition system by fitting the 'interim' front cover and related componentry (including the camshaft and camshaft skew gear, etc).

Type 8

The later 4.0 and 4.6 litre 'Thor' engines of 2000-2004 have a slightly different oil pick up system to earlier engines. These engines have a separate steel oil pick up pipe that is affixed to the front cover and runs to the rear of the engine enclosed in either a pressed steel or cast aluminium sump (oil pan) reservoir. This accounts for the eighth type of front cover. These engines can still have the 'interim' engine's front cover retro-fitted (the block still has the usual oil gallery drilled in it from the pick up to the oil pump.

GEAR-DRIVEN OIL PUMPS

The oil pump aspect of 'early' front covers (types 1 and 2) made between 1967-1976, revolves around the fact that they had a short gear chamber and 'short' oil pump gears (0.875in/22.20mm long), a slot drive in the oil pump spindle, and used a distributor which had a tooth drive on the end of the spindle.

Note that there are 'long gear' conversions available from Rover V8 specialists for early engines. This means that you can have oil pump gears the same length as the later SD1 engine's and onward, **but** retain the drive system, and therefore distributor, of the early engines. The conversion kit comes with two gears, a spacer plate and a gasket. The basis for this conversion is the 340-350ci Buick engines which had this length of gears while retaining the slot drive of the original Buick 215ci engine/Rover V8 engine.

From 1976 on, a front cover was used which had a long gear chamber, 'long' oil pump gears (1.045in/26.60mm) and a tooth drive on the oil pump spindle. This cover used a distributor which had a slot drive on the end of the spindle. These covers are termed 'late' and were initially fitted to all SD1 car engines, then phased in over a few months on Range Rovers. These 'late' front covers remained in production until 1987 for the SD1 and until December 1993 for Range Rover Discovery engines. They were also fitted to the 3.5 litre 'service' engines produced in 1995 and 1997/1998. This was done to maintain parts uniformity for the military services.

Both types of front cover, oil pump type and related drive distributor are directly interchangeable **as complete units** and will fit **any** Rover V8 engine.

WATER PUMPS

There were three water pump types used on Rover V8 engines from 1967-2004. P5, P6 and SD1 engines (1967-1987) all used one basic water pump casting/configuration and impellor, but there were three different versions of the same water pump in terms of drive pulley fitting and viscous fan coupling fitting.

The Range Rover of 1970-1993 and Discovery of 1989 to 1993 used one basic water pump casting/configuration and impellor, but there were about 15 different versions of this water pump in order to accommodate the various drive pulley fittings and viscous fan coupling fittings used until 1986. After 1986 another basic pump casting/configuration and impellor was used on Range Rovers. Between January 1994 and 2004 the 'interim' and 4.0 and 4.6 litre 38A engines all used one water pump configuration which was similar to the previous type.

If you want to replace a Range Rover water pump, you need to positively identify which type it is before ordering a replacement. Parts suppliers might require your old water pump, or a photo of it, to positively identify the particular unit if it's a Range Rover one and you're obtaining a replacement pump by mail order.

CAMSHAFT SKEW GEARS

There is a difference (different parts) between the pre-SD1 (1976 on) camshaft skew gears and later camshaft skew gears. The difference is to do with the key and keyway fitting of the gear on the camshaft, not a difference in the gear tooth form or the gear diameter. All Rover-made camshaft skew gears, and all distributor skew gears share the same respective tooth form.

Buick versus Rover skew gears

There can be a slight discrepancy between Rover-made and Buick-made distributor and camshaft skew gear tooth forms. **Caution!** – To avoid any possibility of abnormal wear, **don't** use Rover and Buick items in combination.

ADJUSTABLE OIL PRESSURE (CRANK-DRIVEN OIL PUMP-TYPE FRONT COVERS)

The crank-driven oil pumps maintain between 45 and 50psi/31 and 35kPa of oil pressure. This can be adjusted (increased) for racing purposes. Wildcat Engineering makes an adjustable oil pressure relief valve which uses dual springs. By this means the maximum oil pressure can be adjusted with a screwdriver once the locking nut has been undone. To obtain one of these systems you can send your existing front cover to Wildcat which will convert it, or you can buy an already converted front cover outright. Note that, at the time of writing, replacement oil pump gears are not available in sets on their own, you have to buy the whole front cover assembly to get new gears.

Chapter 4
Distributors & ignition timing

LUCAS DISTRIBUTORS
Early distributors had single or dual contact breaker points with vacuum advance. While these distributors were efficient they will all have had extensive use by now and will be exhibiting the usual shaft and bush wear. Such wear will cause the engine firing to become erratic as revs rise and the shaft starts gyrating within its bushes.

Any perceptible sideways movement of the distributor shaft is not acceptable for any high performance application, especially a high rpm one. Rather than have the existing distributor rebushed, go to a wrecking yard or a Rover V8 specialist for a replacement without any play between shaft and bush. Distributor bodies can be rebushed, but the shaft may still be worn and so may the cam. Although replacing the bush will often reduce the amount of play by 50%, replacing

the worn shaft and the bush of an older points type distributor is seldom considered cost effective given the keen price of brand new aftermarket high performance distributors.

Of the two early versions of the Lucas distributor, the twin point is the better one to have because of its better electrical efficiency at anything above 5000rpm. The later 'sliding point' single points distributors, as used in Range Rovers from 1981-1984, have longer lasting points.

Electronic conversion kits are readily available for the 35 D8 distributors from companies such as Lumenition under its part number C FK114 PMA50 CEK150. For details of Lumenition, visit the website at <http://www.lumenition.com>.

The 35 DE8, 35 DM8 & 35 DLM8 Lucas electronic (without contact breakers) distributors

can all be fitted with Lumenition conversions. The cost of repairing a Lucas electronic distributor can be quite high, depending on how much work is involved in the rebuild. The spark intensity of a standard Lucas electronic distributor is quite sufficient for any application, including racing use up to 7000rpm, and many engine builders stay with the Lucas distributor for all applications. The Lumenition conversion kits for the 35 DE8, 35 DM8 & 35 DLM8 distributors are part numbers C FK110, PMA150 and CEK150.

Make sure that you quote the Lucas distributor type when ordering a Lumenition conversion kit so that you get the right pickup. The basic electronics in the two kits are identical, but the attachment of the pickup in a contact breaker points-type and an electronic distributor is different!

Repair

Most readers will find that their skills and available facilities will limit the repairs and modifications that they can make to any of these distributors. Most of the 'repair' work will be making sure that all of the components used are serviceable, such as the distributor cap, points, condenser, rotor arm, electronic module, vacuum advance canister, coil, ignition leads and sparkplugs. The spark intensity can be checked at the end of each sparkplug lead (wire) by using a tester, such as a Snap-On MT 2700 inductive pickup tool or a Gunson 'Flashtest'. The module will need to be checked by an auto-electrician/automotive parts supplier for uniform output.

Mechanical advance system

All Lucas distributors fitted to Rover V8s have a mechanical advance mechanism which automatically advances the ignition timing via the centrifugal action of two interlinked bob-weights. These bob-weights are located inside the distributor, under the contact breaker points baseplate or electronic pickup plate. As the distributor shaft rotates, the advance mechanism's bob-weights move outwards from their at rest position. This movement rotates the eight-sided cam in relation to the distributor shaft, a process which advances the ignition timing.

The mechanical advance mechanism (or 'centrifugal advance' mechanism as it is sometimes known) has a built-in limit as to how much advance can be provided. The maximum amount of centrifugal advance is preset by the factory and is not designed to be altered.

Most Rover V8 distributors

have a maximum 11 degrees of mechanical advance built in, which equates to 22 degrees of crankshaft advance (the crankshaft turns at twice the speed of the camshaft). Ignition advance is always measured in crankshaft degrees: never in actual distributor degrees because it's more convenient and logical to relate the firing point to the crankshaft position and hence to the piston crown position.

Another aspect of the mechanical advance mechanism is the rate at which the ignition timing advances from the static/idle speed setting. The rate of the advance is controlled by two small springs which control the movement of the bob-weights. A standard Rover V8 will idle at about 800rpm and, at this speed, the mechanical advance will not be operating because the advance springs are strong enough to prevent movement of the bob-weights. The springs allow the advance to start at about 1000rpm and full advance will be achieved at about 4500rpm.

Changing static advance setting

The factory static/idle speed advance settings range from 2 to 6 degrees BTDC, which is very low. Most engines will respond to the advance being increased to between 10 and 16 degrees, depending on the engine's capacity and its state of tune.

Take a standard SD1 3.5 engine fitted with a Lucas 35 DEM distributor as an example. If this is set with the standard recommended static/idle speed advance of 6 degrees before top dead centre (BTDC) and it has the usual 22 degrees of mechanical advance

built into these distributors, then there is going to be 28 degrees of total advance registering at about 4500rpm and above.

A significant improvement can be made to the performance by simply advancing the ignition timing so that there is 12 to 14 degrees of static/idle speed advance and, hence, 34 to 36 degrees of total advance. Not only will the engine perform much better, it will have a lower fuel consumption during normal running. The only drawback is that the engine will be less tolerant to labouring in a high gear without 'pinking' ('pinging'). This is no problem for most of us who would naturally change down a gear anyway. Heavy cars with automatic transmission might not be able to stand 14 degrees of static timing, but 12 degrees should be acceptable.

Remember! – always disconnect the vacuum advance pipe whenever ignition timing is being measured by a stroboscope.

Changing the rate of advance

Changing the stronger advance spring of the two for a weaker one will allow the mechanical advance mechanism to advance quicker, which usually equates to quicker engine acceleration. A suitable light spring is the lighter spring of the two fitted to the X-Flow (1300cc/1600cc 'Kent' engine from the 60s and 70s) Ford Motorcraft distributor which will reduce the point of total advance to 3300-3500rpm (as opposed to the standard 4500rpm). The rpm point can be quickly and easily checked with a stroboscopic ignition timing light once the crankshaft pulley/damper has had the appropriate extra timing marks added to it.

Check with a stroboscope the rpm point of maximum mechanical advance with the two standard springs fitted, then carry out an acceleration test over a measured distance against the clock. Replace the stronger standard Lucas spring with the weaker of the X-Flow Ford distributor's springs. Check again with a stroboscope the rpm point of maximum ignition advance and then repeat the acceleration test of the car. Compare the results.

A whole series of similar tests needs to be carried out using a range of springs which are progressively weaker than the standard stronger spring in order to identify the optimum rpm point of maximum mechanical advance. You should be looking at a range from the standard 4500rpm down to 2750rpm, in 250rpm steps. There are many advance springs from other types/makes of distributors that can be tried, as well as those from other Lucas Rover V8 distributors.

Vacuum advance system

The vacuum advance mechanism is designed to advance the ignition timing under low load conditions in order to save fuel, which is why all road going engines have them fitted. An engine doesn't create any significant manifold vacuum when the throttles are wide open and the engine is accelerating. An engine does create manifold vacuum when the engine isn't under high loads, such as when cruising along with the accelerator pedal just into its travel. Under such conditions the fuel consumption is improved significantly by the vacuum advance system.

The amount of vacuum advance can be anything from 1 to 15 degrees in addition to the mechanical advance, resulting in up to 35-50 degrees of total advance. The advance mechanism is activated when there is between about 3-4in Hg and 15in Hg of vacuum in the manifold.

If you are concerned about fuel economy, it can be checked quite easily and with extreme accuracy. If you think your engine is running with too much advance under cruise conditions, fill the fuel tank to the brim and then test the car over a piece of motorway (freeway), driving the car as you normally do there and back over about 20 miles/32km. Fill the car's fuel tank to the brim again, noting the precise distance covered and the amount of fuel used. Reduce the static ignition timing 5 degrees and repeat the test, then compare the results. A series of such tests may be necessary to find the optimum advance setting for the best economy with acceptable performance, and it's possible this might involve limiting the vacuum advance by modifying the distributor to limit the travel.

An engine used on the road without a vacuum advance will use on average about 10% more fuel for no gain in engine performance. It's worth checking the vacuum advance mechanism twice a year to make sure it's functioning correctly, with no leaks. Vacuum canisters have rubber diaphragms that do perish over time, so a new canister should be fitted whenever a distributor is being rebuilt. Any sudden loss in fuel economy should always send you straight to the vacuum advance mechanism. Start by checking the vacuum tube for leaks and then

check the diaphragm to make sure that engine vacuum is translating into movement of the contact breaker points baseplate. With the distributor cap off, disconnect the vacuum pipe from the engine and suck as hard as you can on the vacuum pipe. This is usually enough to detect either a leak in the diaphragm or see movement in the points plate/pick up plate. If you can't see any movement, something is wrong.

Caution! – Some Lucas distributors are specifically designed for use with SU or Zenith carburettors. If you're using one of these in conjunction with another type of carburettor and inlet manifold, then be careful. The Lucas distributor's vacuum advance is calibrated to accept vacuum from a specific position within the carburettor, which is much less than inlet manifold vacuum. The result will be the distributor on maximum vacuum advance at idle and the engine likely to be misfiring at idle.

Racing engines

Any Lucas distributor can be altered to suit any Rover V8 in any state of tune and to match anything else on the market. Many race engine builders use little else because the Lucas distributor has proved to be very reliable to 7000rpm and beyond. The only shortcoming is that the amount of mechanical advance cannot be altered easily, and not everybody is able to do it. The alternatives follow!

VACUUM ADVANCE ON RACING ENGINES

On racing engines the vacuum advance mechanism serves no useful purpose because the engine spends most of its life on full throttle. **Caution!** – The vacuum advance should be removed from a racing engine's distributor in case the mechanism fails and remains in the fully advanced position. In these circumstances the engine could end up running with 10-15 degrees of excessive total advance and catastrophic engine damage is highly likely.

When an original equipment Lucas distributor is going to be used for racing, the advance plate will need to be permanently fixed in the non-advanced position. This is usually done by spot brazing or mig welding the two plates together in the non-vacuum advanced position. The vacuum canister is removed from the distributor body and, if applicable, the slot covered by a plate made out of 16-gauge aluminium to keep out dirt. This plate can be held in place using the redundant screws and screw holes in the body of the distributor that held the vacuum canister in place. **Caution!** – Don't forget to block the vacuum take-off point on the manifold or carburettor.

MALLORY DISTRIBUTORS

A very popular alternative to the standard Lucas distributor is the US-made Mallory distributor. Mallory has been making electrical equipment for decades, and it's of excellent quality and represents good value for money. The website www.mrgasket.com lists the whole range of Mallory ignition equipment for the Rover V8. Mallory makes several distributors for the Buick/Oldsmobile 215ci V8 from the early 1960s and they're listed below with their part numbers (P/N) –

P/N 2564301 – Dual Point distributor (no vacuum advance)
P/N 2664301 – Dual Point distributor (with mechanical tachometer drive)
P/N 2764301 – Dual Point distributor (with vacuum advance)
P/N 3764301 – Unilite Electronic distributor (no vacuum advance)
P/N 3864301 – Unilite Electronic distributor (with a tachometer drive)
P/N 4764301 – Unilite Electronic distributor (with vacuum advance)
P/N 5064301 – Magnetic Breakerless distributor (no vacuum advance)
P/N 5764301 – Magnetic Breakerless distributor (with vacuum advance)

These are all 'drop in' fits for pre-1976 Rover oil pumps/front covers. Most Rover V8 specialist companies buy these Buick/Oldsmobile distributors because they're cheaper than those made specifically for the Rover with straight spade or tooth drives. They will also fit the later 1976-1993 front covers, with some slight alteration, so that they only have to stock one series of this distributor.

The distributors intended for the Buick/Oldsmobile engine have a long shaft with the end machined with a 'spade' or 'tooth' drive to suit any early-type oil/pump front cover. This means that it can be used on any 1976-1993 front cover by cutting the shaft to the correct length and then drilling and reaming a new hole in the shaft **Caution!** – a jig is required to ensure the gear is positioned correctly. All that's required then is a post 1976 Rover distributor flexible ('wobble') drive.

These same distributors will also fit all 'interim' front covers without

any modification. They're all fitted with drive gears which can be used with the 'early' and 'interim' engine camshaft gears.

The use of a Mallory dual points distributor should include the company's Promaster ignition coil (P/N 28720) or the Voltmaster Mark II ignition coil (was P/N 28675), which are the recommended companions for these types of distributors. These two coils are compatible with contact breaker points type distributors because they are high voltage, but not high energy like those used with electronic distributors. The dual points distributors are not designed to carry high current. If necessary use Mallory's ballast resistor (P/N 700) with both of these coils, and the company's plated copper core 'Super Wire' high tension leads for the distributor. Note that the Mallory non-points type distributors use a high energy Promaster ignition coil listed under P/N 29440 or P/N29216.

Repairing

Generally, It's better to buy a brand new distributor just to ensure that everything is in perfect condition rather than buy a second-hand one and rebuild it. If you buy a second-hand item or your original distributor gets damaged and you do want to rebuild it, Mallory sells a very comprehensive rebuild kit.

How dual points work

The 'dual points' system has two sets of points, one set opens the low tension circuit and the other set closes the circuit within 2 or 3 degrees of distributor rotation. Single points systems open and close within 10 or 12 degrees of distributor rotation. The benefit of the dual points system is that it allows the coil more time to build up its voltage before the next ignition firing. The Mallory 'dual points' distributor is one of the best contact breaker points type ignition systems available, and is ideally suited for use on the Rover V8 up to 7000rpm. Use at high rpm relies on the points, condenser, cap, HT leads (wires), rotor and coil being in perfect condition.

Dual points reliability

For those who prefer to stay with technology that they understand and can fix themselves, rather than use electronic distributors, 'dual point' ignition systems are very cost effective and efficient. After all, the world used contact breaker points systems for 75 years. They are very reliable if the points used are Mallory or of equivalent quality, and the condenser is of the correct capacity and in a good serviceable condition.

The contact breaker points are the Achilles heel of this type of distributor, as everybody knows, and they will wear out eventually. In most racing use substantial wear will take quite a while because of the low mileage covered in a racing season. It's unlikely that the points will even need adjusting within 2000 racing miles let alone need to be replaced. Points life on a road going engine will be very good, in fact vastly superior to most conventional points systems. Mallory contact breaker point sets are top quality, which is why they're relatively expensive.

Adjustable mechanical advance

A near unique feature of many Mallory distributors is their adjustable mechanical advance

mechanism, and it's a big part of their attraction. Other distributors require permanent modifications to alter the mechanical advance, involving specialist facilities. The Mallory distributor enables the optimum static/idle advance and the optimum total advance to be established in testing, after which a simple adjustment sets the exact amount of mechanical advance that's required.

For example, if your engine requires 16 degrees of static/idle advance and 34 crankshaft degrees of total advance, 18 crankshaft degrees advance will need to be built into the distributor. If your standard Lucas distributor has 22 degrees of mechanical advance built in, then you're going to have to compromise somewhere. There are three options: set the distributor for 34 degrees of total advance and run 12 degrees of static/idle advance, set the distributor for 16 degrees of static/idle advance and run 38 degrees of total advance, or set the distributor with a split around the optimum timing point such as 14 degrees of static/idle advance and 36 degrees of total advance. The engine will run well, but not quite as well as when everything is optimised, as it can be with a Mallory distributor.

Changing amount of static advance

On YL models the mechanical advance is altered by first removing the contact breaker points baseplate from the distributor body. With the plate out, the length of the two slots is checked using the plastic 'key' that Mallory supplies with all new distributors. Both slots should always be exactly the same length. Each flat of the key has numbers

adjacent to it that are the crankshaft degrees of advance. The advance is changed by altering the slot length. Undo each securing screw in turn and position the plastic key in the slot with the appropriate flat in contact with the end of the slot and the moveable stop, then tighten the securing screw. Set the other slot in exactly the same way. Both of the securing screws must be tight. Finally re-check each slot length with the key just to make sure that it's set correctly. It's as simple as that!

Changing rate of ignition advance

The Mallory range of distributors frequently have the right rate of advance built into them by the factory. On average they're set to be fully advanced at 2700rpm, but if this is too quick the advance springs can be changed for stronger ones to reduce the rate of advance. All Mallory rebuild kits come with a full range of advance springs, or the springs can be bought in a separate pack. Other aftermarket advance springs can also be used. Stronger advance springs can be used in any combination, allowing any advance rate to be built into a distributor up to, but not exceeding, 4000rpm. Generally, the ignition needs to be fully advanced between 2700-4000rpm. Reducing the full advance point to below 2700rpm is possible, but it's not recommended because it usually tends to make the engine 'knock' or 'kick back' under acceleration. It's not unknown for engines to run perfectly acceptably with the ignition fully advanced by 2500rpm, but this is the absolute earliest that should be set.

The ignition should advance from the static/idle position to the totally advanced position at a rate that causes the engine to accelerate as quickly as possible, but not so quickly that the engine hesitates or 'pinks' ('pings'). This ideal setting is quite easy to achieve through straightforward acceleration testing. Start with the ignition set to be totally advanced at 3750rpm and test the vehicle's acceleration rate over a set distance. Then reduce the total setting down to, say, 3500rpm and repeat the test, continuing downward in 200-250rpm steps until the optimum advance for the particular engine is reached. It's best to start high and go down to avoid damaging the engine.

Once the total advance has been set in this way the engine will give its best overall performance. Setting the advance in this way takes time, but it only has to be done once and it can mean the difference between optimum street performance and even winning or losing races. It's always the simple things that make one car's performance stand out from another similar car, and, clearly, it often has nothing to do with money.

Road cars

Vacuum advance is required for all road-going engines to provide good fuel economy. All of the appropriate Mallory distributors have this feature as an option.

Racing

At race meetings, always have on hand two spare sets of genuine Mallory points, a distributor cap and a rotor. While Mallory parts are top quality, failure is always possible through the rigours of racing and it's best to be prepared for the worst. Points, caps and rotors do fail from

time to time and getting replacement parts might prove difficult when you need them in a desperate hurry.

Conclusion

Chose with confidence from the Mallory range of distributors with the full knowledge that they do exactly as claimed by this well respected manufacturer. Any Lucas distributor can without doubt be altered to suit any Rover V8 engine's state of tune; it's just that it usually involves some fairly difficult modification to achieve an optimum result. When you buy a new Mallory distributor every single component is new and all the required tuning/timing alterations are via simple built-in adjustments. This all adds up to making the Mallory distributor a very reasonably priced and user-friendly piece of equipment.

TRUE TDC

Top dead centre (known as TDC) **must** be checked to make sure that the crankshaft pulley (damper) markings are **absolutely accurate**. This is a critical datum for the engine and it's ignition system: don't assume that Rover got it right.

There are several ways of checking TDC accurately, but an ideal time is when the cylinder heads are off because a dial test indicator can then be positioned over the crown of number 1 piston. Turning the crankshaft clockwise, the piston is brought slowly up to the top of the bore and stopped the instant that the dial needle reaches its peak. The dial is then zeroed, the crankshaft turned back about a half a turn and then brought slowly back up to TDC. As soon as the needle gets to the zero, stop rotating the crankshaft and mark the damper in relation to

the pointer. Continue rotating the crankshaft slowly until the needle just starts to move, and stop rotating the crankshaft. Mark this second position of the damper in relation to the pointer. The midway point between the two marks you have just made on the pulley rim is true TDC.

There are other ways of checking TDC when the engine is assembled: you can use a probe down through the sparkplug hole of number 1 cylinder or an old sparkplug with an extension welded on the end of it to act as a dead stop. In the latter case, rotate the crank in both directions until the piston is stopped by the device and mark the crankshaft pulley: TDC is the mid point between both marked positions. Clearly it isn't as easy to check TDC with the cylinder heads in place, but it's still possible and necessary.

DEGREE MARKING THE CRANKSHAFT PULLEY RIM

Once TDC has been accurately established and marked on the crankshaft pulley, the remainder of the timing markings can be placed on the pulley rim using TDC as the datum. These additional marks should include static/idle and total advance. The following list includes all the degree marks required to cater for all known advance regimes relevant to the Rover V8.
3.5 litre – 10, 12, 14, 16, 18, 34, 36, 38, 40 degrees BTDC
3.9 litre – 10, 12, 14, 16, 18, 32, 34, 36, 38 degrees BTDC
4.2 litre – 10, 12, 14, 16, 18, 30, 32, 34, 36 degrees BTDC
4.5 litre – 10, 12, 14, 16, 18, 28, 30, 32, 34 degrees BTDC

It's also a good idea to add the camshaft full lift inlet timing point to help in any camshaft timing. If your camshaft is full lift timed at 108 degrees after top dead centre (ATDC) for example, the damper should be clearly marked at 108 degrees ATDC, and so should 104, 106, 110 & 112 degree ATDC to assist in checking and adjusting.

IGNITION ADVANCE

While each individual engine will need to be tested to establish the amount of total advance that produces maximum torque and maximum bhp, the following settings will be suitable for 98% of engines.

The static/idle advance for all engines will vary between 10 and 16 degrees BTDC, with the smaller engines requiring slightly more than the larger ones. For example, 3.5 litre engines are likely to require 14-16 degrees, while 4.5 litre and larger engines are likely to require 10-12 degrees. You'll need to experiment a bit here and find the least amount of advance that causes the engine to idle as smoothly as possible with the highest rpm. For example, if 14 & 16 degrees of advance produce equal idle smoothness, but there is no increase in engine rpm between 14 & 16 degrees, then set it at 14 degrees.

As a guide, the chart below sets out the total mechanical advance that can be used on the various capacity engines and that will be correct for 98% of them -
3.5 litre – 36 degrees of total advance.
3.9 litre – 34 degrees of total advance.
4.2 litre – 30 degrees of total advance.

4.5 litre, or more – 28 degrees of total advance.

To set the absolute optimum total advance for your individual engine will mean having it dyno-tested on a rolling road. Before setting the ignition advance the air/fuel ratio needs to be checked to make sure that it's not too lean or rich, noting that this is not the final setting. The air/fuel ratio at maximum torque and maximum rpm should be in the range 12.5:1 to 11.8:1, which translates into 0.85 Lambda or 5.0% CO.

Next take a power reading with the engine set at the suggested total advance for the engine capacity (eg: 36 degrees for a 3.5 litre unit). This result will give you a baseline reading. Now the total advance can be increased by 1 degree and the engine tested again. If the maximum torque increases, increase the ignition advance by 1 more degree, and continue until peak torque is achieved. Any adjustment to the suggested total advance figure is likely to be slight.

Maximum torque is produced at maximum volumetric efficiency, which means maximum cylinder filling. If too much ignition advance is used the engine will 'knock'. If your engine's compression ratio is too high it will not cope with the suggested total advance, and either the octane rating of the fuel will have to be increased or the compression ratio will have to be reduced.

Mechanical conditions aside, obtaining the correct air/fuel ratio and the correct amount of total advance are inextricably linked to achieving the maximum torque and the maximum power possible for any engine. Once the amount of total advance has been finalised the

mixture will very likely need to be altered slightly to achieve maximum torque and maximum power.

STROBOSCOPE IGNITION TIMING

It's important to always use a stroboscopic ignition timing light when setting the ignition timing, which means having a clearly marked crankshaft damper with the correct range of degree markings for the particular engine.

It is essential to check the total advance as well as the static/idle timing. A huge number of people spend a lot of time setting the standard static/idle advance, while giving little thought to the total advance requirements of their engine. This can mean losing anywhere between 10-100bhp on a Rover V8, all for the sake of a little bit of preparation work and something as simple as undoing the distributor's securing bolt and altering its position.

In fact, total advance figures have rarely been published by car/engine manufacturers over the years, which is a pity because the lack of this information has caused a massive amount of confusion and loss of achievable power.

The optimum total advance ignition timing figures available today have come from race engine builders who have extensively dyno tested these engines in the quest to obtain maximum power.

When you look at the very conservative nature of recommended standard ignition timing settings you could be forgiven for wondering what the engineers were thinking of when they were calibrating these engines in their laboratories. Well, it's all quite easy to explain. Engine manufacturers have to produce engines that do everything that might be required of them by all manner of drivers. This could mean having to go up a hill in top gear with the engine labouring away and about to stop, which is something most of us would never ever do. The engines leave the factory being able to cater for an unbelievably wide range of abuse. Electronics have changed this to a degree because they can adapt to a given situation but a mechanical advance distributor can't cope with the wide range of operating conditions in the same way that an engine management system can.

When you set your engine to the type of ignition regime listed in this book you are individualising your engine's ignition system for optimum performance without compromise. This means the engine might not be able to cope too well with outrageous situations such as gross labouring under extremely high loadings. If you are not prepared to accept this limitation, you should stay with the standard ignition settings.

Important! – The vacuum advance tube must always be removed from the distributor when a stroboscope is used to identify and set the idle speed and total advance settings. Failure to do this will usually lead to an engine running with too much advance when under load and this causes a loss of engine performance.

TOO MUCH COMPRESSION

If an engine has too much compression ratio (CR) for the octane rating of the fuel being used it will not be able to use the correct amount of ignition advance. The correct solution is to reduce the compression ratio, but many people don't do this and reduce the ignition advance just enough to prevent 'pinking' ('pinging'). Engine efficiency is lost when this compromise is made. It's better to have slightly less compression ratio and be able to use full throttle under all circumstances than it is to have an engine that is slightly over compressed and have to use reduced throttle to avoid 'pinking'. A huge number of engines are over compressed in relation to the octane of the fuel that is available. The amount of compression to be used needs to be sorted out **before** the engine is rebuilt. We all tend to want to use as high a compression ratio as possible and with good reason, but you do need to be mindful of the limitations.

As a guide, 9.25:1 compression ratio is the maximum possible for use with 91-93 RON octane fuel, 9.75:1 is the maximum possible for use with 95 RON octane fuel and 10.5:1 is the maximum possible with 98 + RON octane fuel (a super unleaded fuel such as Shell Optimax in the UK). Racing engines will usually stand 12.5:1 compression ratio using 98 + RON octane super unleaded fuel with or without an additive such as TetraBOOST, but this is the limit.

STANDARD SPARKPLUG LEADS (WIRES)

The standard Lucas suppression sparkplug leads are of excellent quality and can be used with confidence, knowing that they will perform as required. Leads on any racing engine should only be used for 1 year.

As a general rule the lower the resistance in the sparkplug leads the better, and 5-10kOhms of resistance is generally acceptable.

J.E. Developments racing engines frequently use standard suppression ignition leads and rev to 7000rpm without problems.

Massive loss of potential power can occur if every aspect of the ignition system is not operating at peak efficiency.

Sparkplug lead location

There was a change made by the factory to the position of the sparkplug leads on the distributor cap from 1987 onwards. At this point they all moved around the cap by one position to reduce the possibility of 'cross firing' between cylinders 5 & 7.

CONDENSER

It used to be common practice to replace the condenser whenever the points were replaced, when in fact the old condenser was frequently better than it's replacement! When the points are replaced, always check to see if the deterioration of the two contact faces looks to be much the same. If it does, don't replace the condenser. If on the other hand one contact looks to be much worse for wear than the other, to the extent that one point looks to have a rough looking hollow in it while the other has a rough looking raised section on it, replace the condenser as it isn't working as it should. Don't replace a condenser unless it needs to be replaced.

FURTHER READING

For those seeking in depth information on optimising and modifying ignition systems *How to Build & Power Tune Distributor*

Type Ignition Systems by Des Hammill is recommended reading. One of the SpeedPro series, the book covers, in detail, the methods of marking crankshaft pulleys and altering distributors for improved performance and much else on the important subject of ignition systems.

Chapter 5
Rocker arms, rocker shaft & pushrods

The standard rocker assembly was designed by GM to ensure that the rocker arm's position, its arc of travel, and the contact of the rocker foot with the tip of the valve stem, are all geometrically correct. Any increase in valve lift above the standard 0.390in/9.9mm causes the rocker geometry to 'move' past its optimum, as little as an extra 0.010-0.020in/0.25-0.5mm making a difference.

As the cam lobe rotates and lifts the valve, the radiused contact pad on the rocker arm, which is pressing on the tip of the valve stem, moves progressively from one side of the stem tip to the other in a wiping action. Any movement beyond the design limit takes the rocker pad towards edge contact with the tip of the valve stem (abnormal contact).

In theory, there's no latitude to increase the valve lift beyond standard without compromising

rocker geometry although, in practice, 0.400-0.410in/10.1-10.4mm is possible and acceptable.

It's fair to say that standard rockershaft assemblies, with packing shims under them, have been used with medium/maximum lift hydraulic camshafts (0.450-0.470in/11.3-12.0mm lift) for years without problems. However, these engines would perform better with optimum rocker geometry.

ROCKER ARM GEOMETRY

If the valve lift is to be increased above standard, then a compromise of rocker arm geometry will be necessary. The key point here is to avoid overloading the valve rocker and valve stem, this means ensuring that the rocker arm contact pad is still in its geometrically correct position on the valve stem tip at its new maximum lift (this is the position

Standard rocker arm position when the valve is seated. The rocker arm contact pad is near to the rockershaft side of the valve stem. The point of contact by the rocker pad onto the tip of the valve stem is about 0.040in/1.0mm in from the edge of the valve stem closest to the rockershaft.

of maximum load for the rocker arm and valve stem).

Minimum loading is achieved by lowering the rockershaft by the same amount that the valve

Standard rocker arm position after the rocker arm has gone through its arc of travel and is at maximum standard lift (0.390in/9.9mm). The rocker arm's contact pad has travelled across the tip of the valve stem during the valve lifting process and is now on the other side of the tip of the valve stem, away from the rockershaft. The point of contact is now about 0.040in/1.0mm from the opposite edge of the valve stem. Any further valve lift takes the rocker arm contact pad into edge contact with the tip of the valve stem. Ultimately, it will draw back across the tip of the valve stem with extreme edge contact between the rocker arm contact pad and the tip of the valve stem. There are definite limits as to how much mismatch can be allowed.

lift is increased above standard, either by removing metal from the base of the rockershaft pedestals or from the pedestal bosses on the cylinder head. **Caution!** – The cylinder head bosses or underside of the rockershaft pillars will need to be **accurately** machined using a turret-milling machine (Bridgeport, or similar). This sort of machine tool is quite common and relatively easy to find at precision engineering workshops and many engine reconditioners.

A complication is that the camshaft, say an aftermarket item with 0.470in/12.0mm lift, is being used in conjunction with rockershafts that have already been

packed up by, say, 0.030in/0.75mm to set the hydraulic lifter preloading to the minimum of 0.020in/0.5mm. In these circumstances a standard rockershaft could be working 0.100in/2.5mm over the maximum design criteria. An engine with this set up will give the impression of running quite well, but the rocker arms will be imposing a lot of side loading onto the valve stems. This leads to a high wear rate of valve stems and valve guides, and harsh operation of the valve train. Ultimately, this affects the reliability of the engine, and adversely affects the power output of the engine.

Rockershaft height

The following list gives the amounts of metal to remove from the cylinder head rockershaft mounting bosses, or the underside of the rockershaft pillars, when increased lift camshafts are used.

Caution! – The maximum amount that it is recommended be removed is 0.060in/1.5mm. This is because the rocker arm can only be positioned so high above its standard position when the valves are at zero lift before there is edge contact between the rocker arm contact pad and the tip of the valve stem. Admittedly, the edge contact doesn't matter quite so much in this position (compared to the full lift) because the valve spring tension is less, and the loadings are at their lowest. As it happens, the majority of non-standard lift hydraulic camshafts fall are in a range with a maximum lift of 0.470in/12.0mm, with few above this. As a consequence, the following table caters for this maximum amount of lift. Few camshafts and valve trains actually deliver their advertised full valve

The rocker arm's contact pad can clearly be seen to be right on the edge of the tip of the valve stem. This will occur if, for example, a 0.470in/11.95mm lift camshaft is used with a rockershaft that has been packed up by 0.030in/0.75mm.

After a rockershaft has been height adjusted the rocker arm's point of contact with the top of the valve stem moves closer to the edge of the stem (rockershaft side).

lifts, so the table below has been adjusted to suit the usual advertised valve lift values:

0.430in/10.90mm lift: remove 0.20in/0.50mm from pillar/boss
0.440in/11.15mm lift: remove 0.030in/0.75mm from pillar/boss
0.450in/11.40mm lift: remove 0.040in/1.0mm from pillar/boss
0.460in/11.65mm lift: remove, 0.050in/1.25mm from pillar/boss
0.470in/11.90mm lift: remove 0.060in/1.50mm from pillar/boss

The preferred method is to remove material from the cylinder head bosses, this is because it's easier than removing precisely the same amount (within 0.001in/ 0.025mm) from the undersides of each of the rockershaft pillars. Although, if no more than 0.030in/ 0.75mm is going to be removed, then it's quite acceptable to remove it from the pillars. Taking material off the cylinder heads means that they must be removed from the engine and stripped so that they can be placed on a milling machine for the machining operation.

Roller rockers

An alternative to the complexity of altering rocker shaft height is to use roller rockers. Relative simplicity is the reason that many tuners go down the expensive route of roller rockers assemblies.

Caution! – Unfortunately, the simple operation of bolting on a set of roller rocker arms and the associated rockershaft assemblies doesn't always solve all the problems in one go. Roller rocker set ups **must** still have their geometry checked and, if necessary, adjusted.

Usually roller rocker set ups are extremely reliable and do exactly as their makers claim. Price limits their popularity; however, they are justifiably expensive because of the number of precision machined components they include.

When set (height adjusted correctly) roller rockers concentrate their roller lift contact to within about 1-1.5mm/0.040-0.60in either side of the centre of the tip of the valve stem. The roller moves from one side of the top of the valve stem to the other in a single progressive motion. It starts to roll across the valve tip as soon as the valve starts to lift, reaching the other side as the valve lift gets to its maximum. The rolling action **must** continue from the start of valve lift to the finish, and only one basic height position will allow this to happen correctly.

HYDRAULIC LIFTER PRELOAD

The industry standard preload distance for this type and design of hydraulic lifter is between 0.020-0.030in/0.5-0.75mm. This is the distance (from its maximum height) that the plunger is down inside the lifter body when it's up against the retaining circlip.

When a standard engine is assembled, the average amount the pushrod causes the lifter plunger to move down inside the lifter body is about 0.030-0.060in/0.75-1.5mm.

A minimum of 0.020in/0.5mm is the optimum, especially when hydraulic lifter camshafts with standard hydraulic lifters are fitted into engines revving to high, say 5800, rpm. Having the lifter preload set at its minimum also reduces the potential for hydraulic lifter pump up to a minimum.

Setting the lifter preload to its minimum is often achieved by packing the rockershaft assemblies away from the cylinder heads, and shim sets of varying thickness are available from aftermarket sources for this purpose. However, doing this will upset rocker geometry which won't necessarily lead to rocker gear reliability problems, but will compound the problem of rocker arm geometry when higher lift camshafts are fitted.

Shimming the pillars is certainly not the correct thing to do to obtain minimum lifter preload and is, at best, a quick fix, although not a good one because of the adverse

Roller on the left is shown in the zero valve lift position. That on the right is shown in the full valve lift position.

affect on rocker geometry.

If racing quality 'anti pump' lifters are being fitted to the engine, such as Iskenderian 'Superlifters' (as well as new valve springs), the position of the plunger in the lifter really doesn't matter too much. Anywhere between 0.020-0.060in/0.5-1.5mm is okay for engine speeds up to 6500rpm. Iskenderian recommends that its lifters be set with a minimum of 0.020in/0.5mm of preload when they're used in high revving engines (6500-7500rpm). **Caution!** – In all cases it's important to check that the plunger is not near to bottoming out. It's an unlikely occurrence, but is possible if the cylinder heads and block deck have been planed by more than just 'clean up' amounts, perhaps in an effort to increase the engine's compression ratio. Iskenderian 'Superlifters' or anti-pump-up lifters are simply excellent, if not unbeatable.

SHORTER PUSHRODS

Unless the engine is going to be built to production specification with standard hydraulic lifters and limited to 5000rpm, then shorter pushrods will probably have to be used. The need for shorter pushrods is a consequence of the rockershaft height adjustments made to cope with increased valve lift and setting the hydraulic lifter preload. There are several possible options for obtaining correct length pushrods, irrespective of what has been changed on an engine.

One option is to shorten the original pushrods by regrinding the ends to bring their original standard length of 8.000in/203.2mm down to whatever is required, followed by re-hardening the ends and polishing them. This is all quite

possible and standard pushrods can be successfully shortened by up to 0.125in/3mm (0.0625in/1.5mm per end), but it does involve precision engineering. Following the precision grinding, each end is re-hardened by localised heating with an oxyacetylene torch set with a medium sized carburising flame so as not to 'burn' the material. The end of the pushrod is slowly taken to 'cherry red' and then quenched in oil. After quenching, the end of the pushrod will be very hard, near to glass hard and can then be repolished. **Caution!** – The critical part of the operation is re-grinding the pushrod ends **exactly** to the original shape so that they fit the lifter plunger's radius, and the rocker arm's contact spherical radius, perfectly. This work is expensive because it requires access to some specialist grinding equipment. If you are an engineer, however, this option is a good one.

An easier option for most people is to use adjustable pushrods. Adjustable pushrods, as made by Crane Cams, for example, are not particularly cheap but they are readily available from most Rover V8 engine specialist companies. They are strong enough for the valve loads that are likely to encountered, and they can be set precisely, although it's time-consuming to get the pushrod lengths right. **Caution!** – The only limitation with adjustable pushrods is

that the 'over the nose' (maximum lift) valve spring load must not exceed 250lb/113kg, because it's then possible that the threaded adjustment section will fail through being overloaded.

Another option when it comes to shorter pushrods is to buy a set of 'modular pushrods' from companies such as J.E. Developments. Its pushrods can be made to any length, however, if you intend using its 'modular pushrods' with a hydraulic camshaft you need to say so because an appropriate set of pushrods requires 32 ball ends (instead of 16 ball ends and 16 cupped ends). 'Modular pushrods' are actually designed to fit J.E. Developments' own adjustable rocker arms, but it will alter the kit to 32 ball ends to make it compatible with standard cast aluminium rocker arms. Alternatively, it will supply assembled ball-ended pushrods to the length you specify.

A further option is to buy US-made shorter pushrods from a major camshaft manufacturer. Most of these companies make a range of pushrods in different lengths, or they'll make pushrods of any length to suit any application. Competition Cams in the USA, for example, is such a company. It will make any length pushrod, or supply you with a kit to make your own. Wildcat Engineering also has a large stock of different length pushrods.

STANDARD ROCKER ARMS

There a few provisos if the standard

Adjustable pushrods can be used to obtain any pushrod length. They're required if a mechanical camshaft is used in conjunction with the standard rockershaft assemblies.

Rocker arm on left has the steel ball cup insert completely worn away; the rocker arm in the centre is brand new; the rocker arm on the right is showing signs of extreme wear.

rocker arms and shaft assemblies are to be reliable. In standard form, with a standard camshaft, the maximum rpm possible is 5800rpm due to hydraulic lifter pump up. Without the pump up limitation, the standard rockershaft assemblies – provided all new componentry is used – are actually very reliable up to 6200rpm.

Caution! – There is a problem with used standard rocker arms, even on standard engines. What happens is that the steel ball cup insert, which has the aluminium of the rocker arm crimped over to lock it in place, wears. The top spherical radius of the pushrod contacts this insert, and so there's considerable pressure on it, even if it isn't really excessive on a standard engine. Not all rocker arms wear out in this manner, but most will.

In many instances it doesn't take long to wear through the insert with 10,000 miles/16,000km not being unknown before one or more

rockers are unserviceable. However, it's more usual for standard rocker arms in standard engines to last for 50,000-100,000 miles/80,000-160,000km. It's usual practise to replace all of the rockers when the first rocker fails.

While the insert is wearing away there will be a squeaking noise coming from the engine, especially when cold. When this noise stops the steel of the insert has worn through and the end of the pushrod is now in direct contact with the aluminium of the rocker arm. If the engine continues to be used the pushrod will quickly wear through the aluminium and exit the other side. The engine will not be running too well by this stage, but it will still be running ...

The complete solution to this problem is to replace the standard aluminium rocker arms with direct replacement Federal Mogul steel ones. These rocker arms are available from most Rover V8

specialist companies. All readers are advised to fit these steel rocker arms to their engines for the sake of reliability.

STANDARD ROCKER ARMS & SHAFT WITH HIGH LIFT CAMSHAFT

A standard engine will rev reliably to the point of lifter pump up (5800rpm).

Caution! – When an aftermarket hydraulic camshaft with higher lift, more duration, and a more aggressive lift rate/closing rate, is fitted the standard rockershaft assembly will suffer breakage: it will fail at between 5500-6000rpm.

The reason for the rpm range for the failure is the variation in loading imposed on the rockershafts, loading due to the increase in the amount of valve lift, and the lift rate of the replacement hydraulic camshaft. The higher the valve lift, and the quicker the lift rate/closing rate, the lower the point of breakage will be within this rpm range. As a general rule, however, take it that 6000rpm will break any standard rockershaft assembly. The rocker arms don't fail at this point, instead the rockershafts break through the end bolt hole.

The solution to the problem of rockershaft breakage is to fit outrigger rockershaft posts (two per rockershaft (it's only the end ones that fail). This a well known fix. Most Rover V8 engine specialist companies sell replacement steel or aluminium outrigger rockershaft pillars.

With outrigger pillars fitted to the otherwise standard rockershafts, an engine equipped with a 0.470in/ 12.0mm lift camshaft, even with the most aggressive lift/closing rate available, and increased tension valve springs (220lb/100kg of 'over the nose' valve spring pressure), will be reliable to 6500rpm. **Caution!** – If such an engine is taken above 6500rpm, then random aluminium rocker arm failure is going to occur.

If higher rpm than this is required from a hydraulic camshaft equipped engine, the use of Federal Mogul replacement steel rockers will ensure reliability up to 7000rpm. Note that he Federal Mogul steel rocker arms are not handed like the standard aluminium ones.

If a mechanical camshaft is going to be used, the rockershaft will be reliable to 7000rpm provided valve lift does not exceed 0.470in/ 12.0mm and valve spring pressure does not exceed 250lb/113kg under any circumstances. Adjustable pushrods will need to be fitted, such as those made by Crane/ Iskenderian, to facilitate valve clearance (lash) adjustments.

Caution! – If 7000rpm is exceeded the valve train becomes a bit fragile, with random failures of pushrods (bent) and lifters coming out of the block. **7000rpm is the definitive proven reliable limit.**

Federal Mogul steel rocker arms: good for 7000rpm.

Chapter 6
Camshafts & valve springs

The standard production camshafts are all designed for use with hydraulic lifters, are all very similar in their timing and duration and all produce identical valve lift. Maximum power is produced typically at 5000rpm with maximum torque between 2500-3000rpm. The torque curve is ideal for the engine's original use in a range of relatively economical road cars.

Aftermarket high performance camshafts improve performance by increasing the duration, altering the timing, increasing the valve lift and increasing the valve opening/closing rates.

Apart from for racing, the vast majority of Rover V8 engines are seldom used above their original design speed of 5500-5800rpm, for reasons that will become apparent. Many readers will be working within fairly tight budgets and, as a consequence, will retain nearly all

of the standard components, such as crankshafts, connecting rods, cast pistons, original equipment standard hydraulic lifters and the sintered valve spring retainers, the latter as fitted to later SD1 engines and all other later engines. Retaining the standard components limits the maximum reliable engine speed to 5800rpm because of hydraulic lifter 'pump up' and likely failure of the later-type sintered valve spring retainers, the latter with potentially disastrous consequences ... In fact, Rover used the hydraulic lifter 'pump up' feature as a crude means of limiting production engine speed to 5800rpm. This also meant it could reduce the valve train design requirements, and hence reduce the production cost, yet still have a powerful and reliable engine.

Throughout this chapter you'll come across references to "hydraulic" and "mechanical"

camshafts. These literally nonsensical terms, simply refer to camshafts designed to work with hydraulic lifters (and no running clearance) and camshafts designed to work with a solid drive train with clearance adjustment built in.

CAMSHAFTS WITH STANDARD VALVE LIFT

The first major point with regard to camshafts used in engines running up to 5800rpm is that the standard arrangement of hydraulic lifters should be retained. It's the most cost-effective solution, and in reality very little difference will be noticed between hydraulic and mechanical camshafts of similar duration, phasing and lift in road use. Mechanical camshafts tend to give the engine a better all round performance and response for the same effective duration and lift, but the resulting improvement in vehicle acceleration will be barely noticed in normal road use.

Continuing to use a hydraulic camshaft reduces the alterations that need to be made to the valve train for most engines to a minimum: a new camshaft with an actual maximum valve lift of not more than 0.430in/10.9mm, new hydraulic lifters, a duplex timing chain and sprockets, and new standard rocker arm and shaft assemblies. It doesn't get much cheaper than that. The amount of money needed to be spent on the valve train for good durability as a whole is minimized, yet the engine performance to 5800rpm is not particularly compromised. Hydraulic camshafts also have the advantage of low noise and low maintenance compared to mechanical camshafts that require frequent valve clearance adjustment.

A key point to note is that the maximum valve lift that the standard single valve springs on the later cylinder heads (1976 onwards) can accommodate is 0.430in/10.9mm. The figure is arrived at by taking the average general valve spring fitted height of 1.575in/40.0mm, and then deducting the approximate coil bind height of the valve springs (1.095in/ 27.8mm) and the required minimum clearance between the coils of 0.050in/1.25mm.

Camshaft choice

Changing the standard camshaft for a longer duration, higher lift, aftermarket one is not necessarily the right thing to do in all circumstances. If 4500rpm is hardly ever going to be exceeded then the standard camshaft is ideal for all road use, especially if maximum fuel economy is a definite requirement. The original camshaft

was designed so that the engine developed good torque coupled with reasonable power and maximum fuel economy. It's a common belief that US automakers never bothered too much about the fuel efficiency of their engines until more recent years, but this has never been the case. They always tried to get the most miles to the gallon out of their standard production engines.

Standard camshafts

There have been various standard factory camshafts over the years, but none of them have been particularly good for engine speeds above 5000rpm. The best of the standard camshafts are the later ones with 32-73-70-35 valve timing. This means the inlet valve opens 32 degrees before top dead centre (BTDC) and closes 73 degrees after bottom dead centre (ABDC), while the exhaust valves opens 70 degrees before bottom dead centre (BBDC) and closes 35 degrees after top dead centre ATDC. The opening and closing points of the factory camshafts are more or less ideal for an engine rarely revving above 5000rpm and give very good fuel economy. Virtually all aftermarket camshafts of similar duration to the standard camshaft give better performance because they have higher lift, and usually have quicker opening and closing rates.

Regrinds

The standard camshaft cannot be reground successfully to its original profile, or to an alternative high performance profile. The lobes are almost always worn too far for a standard regrind and, in addition, the lobes are just too small to be ground to a higher performance profile.

Aftermarket camshafts

All of the aftermarket camshafts that can be used without creating valve spring coil binding have one common feature, they have no more than 0.430in/10.9mm of actual valve lift. This allows for the correct minimum clearance between the valve spring coils at full lift and gives maximum component reliability. The difference between this type of aftermarket camshaft and the standard item is 0.040in/1.0mm increase in valve lift and a faster rate of valve opening and closing. These two features improve the volumetric efficiency of the engine without altering its low rpm characteristics.

The duration of an aftermarket camshaft can often be less than that of the standard camshaft, but don't worry about this aspect as it isn't detrimental to performance. The standard camshafts are slower to open and close the valves, and do so to a lesser height. By comparison, the aftermarket camshafts start to open the valves slightly later but open them to maximum lift quicker, hold the valves open for longer and then close the valves much quicker than the standard camshaft does. The result is that the engine has a bigger 'window' for the induction of air/fuel and the expulsion of exhaust gases than with the standard camshaft.

While all camshafts have advertised valve lifts, few achieve the quoted figures when installed in the engine. Generally, there are two reasons for this. The first is that few camshafts are ground to the precise drawing dimensions; they always seem to be a few thousandths of an in smaller than the correct size (typically 0.003-0.08in/0.075-0.20mm). Secondly, there are other dimensional errors and clearances in the rocker system that stop it achieving the correct cam lift to valve lift ratio. This all adds up to a reduction in the full valve lift that you can measure with a dial test indicator. A camshaft, which is advertised as having 0.430in/10.9mm maximum lift, will often only have an actual maximum valve lift of 0.415-0.420in/10.5-10.7mm. This means that a camshaft with an advertised maximum valve lift of 0.440in/11.1mm might just work without any clearance problems.

Caution! – If you buy a camshaft that achieves an actual valve lift of more than 0.430in/10.9mm, it may fit okay and even allow the engine to run (assuming the spring coils aren't actually binding), but the valve springs will still be compressed too much, resulting in premature valve spring failure.

Overall, it's better to play safe and buy a camshaft with an advertised lift of no more than 0.430in/10.9mm.

VALVE SPRINGS & RETAINERS

The P5, P6, MGB-V8 and early Range Rover engines were all equipped with non-contra-wound dual valve springs (1.300in/33.0mm outer diameter) and steel valve spring retainers that are suitable for the original cylinder heads only. All Rover V8 cylinder heads are 'spot face' machined to provide a seat of the correct size for the valve springs to fit in. Note that SD1 and Range Rover engines changed from dual valve springs to smaller single valve springs (1.225in/31.0mm outer diameter) and these cylinder heads were 'spot faced' to seat the smaller size valve springs. The first

SD1 engines had steel valve spring retainers, which were as strong as those in the early P5/P6 engines: both these retainers are suitable for racing. A change was made to sintered material valve spring retainers early in the SD1 production run: these retainers are not as strong as the earlier ones. These early SD1 type steel valve spring retainers are no longer available from Rover and no Rover V8 specialist makes exact copies of them now. The only components that can be swapped between the P5/P6 engines and all later Rover V8 engines are the valve collets (keepers/split locks), although the early SD1 cylinder heads did use early P5/P6 size valves for a time. All of the standard valve spring pressures are similar regardless of spring type.

HYDRAULIC LIFTERS

On standard Rover V8 engines there's no adjustment on the rocker arms because hydraulic lifters are used. As a consequence, the rocker shaft assemblies simply bolt down on to the cylinder heads pushing the pushrods down into the hydraulic lifter and thus creating some 'preload'. The average amount of preload equates to between 0.020in/0.5mm and 0.050in/1.25mm of lifter plunger travel, with 0.020in/0.5mm being the optimum. Hydraulic lifters can actually operate successfully within a self adjusting working range of between 0.020in/0.5mm and about 0.160in/4.0mm and, as a consequence, are able to compensate for any minor discrepancies, such as cylinder heads or block decks that have been planed.

0.020in/0.5mm is the optimum, preload because, exceeding this

figure can result in lifter 'pump up' at above 5000rpm, although it's worth bearing in mind that lifter pump up can also occur if the oil pressure is above 65psi/44.8kPa. If the hydraulic lifters are set with 0.020in/0.5mm of lifter preload, then they can only pump up 0.020in/0.5mm before the plunger of the lifter comes into contact with its retaining circlip. Setting the hydraulic lifters with 0.020in/0.5mm preload reduces the amount of potential lifter pump up and hence reduces the potential for engine misfire to a minimum.

Hydraulic lifter preload can be altered by shimming the rocker shaft away from the cylinder head. While this works, there is a trade-off in that the rocker geometry is upset.

Whilst optimum preload enables the standard hydraulic lifters to be run at higher engine rpm, the only reliable solution to pump up is to fit Iskenderian 202-HY anti-pump up hydraulic lifters. Iskenderian Racing Cams in America developed and patented these hydraulic lifters over 40 years ago for use in pushrod operated six cylinder and V8 engines. Iskenderian lifters are expensive by comparison with the standard lifters, but are worth the money because of their reliability and the fact that they perform exactly as claimed. They are far more tolerant to higher lifter preload, although Iskenderian recommends adjusting them to between 0.020 and 0.030in/0.5 and 0.75mm preload for high rpm applications.

There are now many other similar anti-pump up hydraulic lifters on the market from other camshaft manufacturers, which are generally reliable, but few if any seem to be able to match the Iskenderian lifter's performance. Iskenderian lifters are unique in that they have two ports (small diameter holes) in the side of the lifter body and can generally be considered 'bullet proof'.

Iskenderian racing camshafts and related components are of excellent quality for which the company enjoys a worldwide reputation. While Iskenderian recommends a maximum engine speed of 6500rpm with these anti-pump up lifters, many people have revved engines to 7000rpm plus and have not experienced any problems whatsoever. These hydraulic lifters are compatible with any standard or aftermarket hydraulic camshaft.

Using old lifters

It's generally stated that it's not possible to use used lifters from one engine in another or with a new camshaft. This is not quite correct, but there are definite criteria for establishing whether used lifters are compatible with a new or used camshaft.

Essentially if the lifter bases are as standard (ie: convex and highly polished) then they can be re-used with any camshaft. New lifter bases are not flat, they're convex, and they wear from convex to flat and then to concave. Lifters can be refaced by regrinding and polishing them, and many engine reconditioning companies will do this. The refaced lifters will then work perfectly, although the lifter bodies and their internals must also be in serviceable condition to make remachining the bases worthwhile. Any pitting of the base of the lifter means it is scrap as even if it is reground it will usually continue to 'break up' after a short period of service. In practice, used low mileage lifters are seldom refaced because of the low cost of

brand new lifters even though they could give excellent service with a new camshaft.

As an aside, unlike most other pushrod V8 engines, the camshaft lobes of the Rover V8 are not parallel ground, but rather taper ground. With the tapers in good shape, the lobes correctly dimensioned and new lifters, or used lifters that have had their bases reground/polished, there will be few compatibility problems which might lead to a failure.

Realistically, any hydraulic lifter that has done 50,000 miles/80,00km or more should not be reinstalled in any engine no matter how good its external condition, at that age the internals will be worn. Low mileage lifters (5000-10,000 miles/8000-16,000km) will seldom show any signs of wear and can usually be re-used just as they are.

Common problems

When the valve train of a well-used Rover V8 engine starts to clatter, it's generally because the hydraulic lifters are no longer able to retain oil pressure and 'leak down'. As the camshaft lobe starts to lift the lifter against the valve spring pressure, the oil just spews out of the lifter body. Then, as the camshaft lobe goes over maximum lift and starts to return to the valve seated position, a considerable valve clearance opens up which is not removed until the hydraulic lifter fills with oil again once the valve is shut. Creaking noises coming from the engine immediately after it has been switched off also indicates that the lifters are worn and, realistically, are due for replacement. Sometimes even new lifters fail, so fitting top quality aftermarket ones, like the

Iskenderian ones, preclude this from happening.

It's possible for a camshaft to have been machined incorrectly and have lobes with base circles that are not of a constant radius, although this is rare. When it happens the engine will have a constant misfire which will prove very difficult to track down. Most engine builders put any camshaft they buy between centres in a lathe and check every lobe for base circle run out, irrespective of which company ground it. It's only a few minutes' work and the integrity of the camshaft in this area is then placed beyond doubt.

Another factor that can cause noisy lifters as the rpm rises is weak valve springs. It's just not possible to run one of these engines successfully if the valve springs are not to factory specification at the very least. Weak valve springs contribute to lifter pump up by stopping the lifters from following the trailing side of the camshaft profile exactly. When it happens the lifter 'thinks' there's a gap and starts to compensate for it by taking in extra oil. As the lifter comes off the camshaft lobe, the valve stays open and eventually the valve spring forces the lifter to 'bleed down' the extra amount of oil it's taken in. This problem can lead to poor engine performance and rough operation. Valve springs are a critical component in any engine, and every valve spring needs to be checked for correct pressure at fitted height and at full lift compression to make sure the specifications are met. This applies to any Rover V8 engine, even a standard one.

Another source of noise in worn valve trains is axial movement of the camshaft at low speed. This affects any engine prior to the fitting of the camshaft 'restraint plate', or the camshaft 'thrust plate' to the 'interim' 3.9 & 4.2 litre engines made from March 1994 onwards. This noise manifests itself as a low speed knock, which is caused by the camshaft having too much axial movement and settling back against the thrust face of the block (knocks each time it does so). This happens once the lobes and the bases of the lifters have worn a bit from original specification (the taper grinding of the lobes versus the convex bases of the lifters creates rearward axial thrust). Rover finally fixed the problem by providing a Teflon thrust button kit from 1996 (part number STC 3620 K), and any 3.5, 3.9 or 4.2 litre Rover V8 which doesn't have a 'thrust plate' should have one of these Rover brand thrust buttons fitted.

Careful adjustment of this thrust button is required to ensure that the end clearance between the front of the camshaft and the underside of the timing chain cover is correct. Ideally it should be 0.005in/0.1mm, but in any case it should be no more than 0.010-0.015in/0.25-0.4mm. Getting it right may take several attempts.

All production camshafts suffer from lobe wear. This is caused by a combination of the camshaft lobes having a fairly small base circle diameter and, to varying degrees, by a low hardness value of the lobe surfaces. The result is that the lobes do not last as long as they should, especially when compared to many other similarly-designed American V8 engine camshafts. Excessive lobe wear, with one or more lobe surfaces often breaking up, can occur on any engine that has covered around

75,000 miles/120,000km, and sometimes less. Once the lobes have worn by 0.004in/0.1mm the camshaft is no longer any good and, in extreme cases, a lobe or two may have worn down by 0.125in/3.2mm or more. The engines are still running but not very well. Replacement is the only option for a worn camshaft and the aftermarket manufacturers seem to have the problem sorted as their products appear to be much more reliable than the standard camshafts.

As a general rule, always fit a new camshaft and lifters if there are any signs of lobe wear. If the camshaft duration and lift are to be altered, buy a new high performance camshaft from an aftermarket manufacturer. All aftermarket manufacturing camshaft companies supply camshafts that are ground using new hardness tested camshaft blanks.

Camshafts for 'Group A' racing
Although standard-type camshafts usually fail to reach their advertised valve lift of 0.390in/9.9mm, there is one exception. This is the camshaft made for use in UK Group A racing in the 1980s. Class rules required the use of standard valve lift and so racing camshafts were made which gave exactly 0.390in/9.9mm of valve lift. Camshafts like this are still available from Piper Cams under its part number V8GPAK. Other suppliers will have similar items.

Rover also made its own high performance hydraulic camshaft in the 1980s and homologated it for racing. About 20 engines were equipped with the WL9 camshaft and quite strong dual valves springs. This camshaft proved to be quite noisy because of its rapid action

valve opening and closing.

A number of other engine improvements were homologated at the same time as the WL9 camshaft and, to satisfy the homologation requirements, about 10 cross-bolted racing blocks ending up being fitted into road cars. In addition about 250 road car engines were fitted with large diameter rockershafts, and forged steel rocker arms which had the adjusters welded up. The owners of these cars wouldn't know that their car had high performance parts in its engine.

Summary
- **Standard valve lift is 0.390in/9.9mm in all cases.**
- **Standard original equipment hydraulic lifters limit revs to 5800rpm.**
- **Standard early steel valve spring retainers (P5, P6 and SD1) have no rpm limit.**
- **Later SD1 sintered valve spring retainers are only suitable for use up to 5800rpm.**
- **The standard valve springs of all engines limit the maximum valve lift to 0.430in/10.9mm.**

INCREASING VALVE LIFT ABOVE STANDARD
There are two important components to remember when increasing valve lift on standard cylinder heads to more than 0.430in/10.9mm: one, valve spring coil bind height; two, the clearance between the underside of the valve spring retainers and the tops of the valve guides (or the valve stem seals, depending on the cylinder heads).

The original 215 cubic in Buick engine's cylinder heads, on which the Rover heads are based, allowed 0.500in/12.7mm of clearance

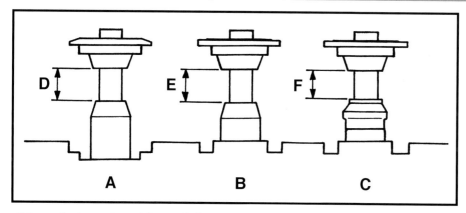

Valve and valve spring retainer variations. 'A' 1967 to 1976, gap 'D' is 0.525in/13.3mm. 'B' 1976 to 1993, gap 'E' 0.525in/13.3mm. 'C' 1994 to 2004, gap 'F' is 0.450in/11.4mm.

between the underside of the valve spring retainers and the top of the valve guide. These heads had single valve springs with a fitted height of 1.625in/41.2mm, and these springs were more or less identical to the later single valve springs of the 1976 on SD1 & range Rover engines, but wound the other way. These standard springs would be coil bound at 1.125in/38.5mm, which allowed for a safe 0.450in/11.5mm of valve lift just as they came from the factory.

Early cylinder heads
While rare these days for road use or racing purposes, the 1967-1976 cylinder heads were made in their thousands and people do still use them. These early P5, P6, MGB-V8 and early Range Rover engine heads had no valve stem seals fitted at all, and this allowed about 0.525in/13.3mm of clearance between the underside of the valve spring retainer and the top of the valve guide when the valves were seated.

The fitted height of the outer valve spring is about 1.600in/40.6mm and it has a coil bind height of 0.975in/24.8mm which, in theory, allows a maximum safe valve lift of about 0.575in/14.5mm (actual

crush height minus 0.050in/1.25mm collective clearance between the coils). The inner valve spring has a fitted height of 1.625in/41.3mm and a coil bound height of about 1.100in/27.9mm which, in theory, allows a maximum safe valve lift of about 5.75in/14.5mm (actual crush height minus 0.050in/1.25mm collective clearance between the coils).

These early cylinder heads can achieve a safe maximum valve lift of 0.475in/12.0mm in standard form, the distance between the underside of the valve spring retainer and the top of the valve guide being the limiting factor.

The standard dual valve springs are quite strong and are suitable for the vast majority of applications, and certainly for all hydraulic camshaft applications. They have approximately 70lb of seated pressure and 165lb of pressure at standard valve lift of 0.390in/9.9mm. These valve springs are suitable for up to 6500rpm with mild action (don't give ultra-rapid valve opening and closing) hydraulic camshafts. **Caution!** – If your requirement is for more than 6500rpm and an aggressive opening and closing action, then stronger dual valve springs **must** to be fitted (use the

valve springs recommended by the camshaft manufacturer).

Today, if you are going to use these early cylinder heads for more than 6500rpm you would convert them to take the dual valve springs of the 1976-2004 cylinder heads. Aftermarket high strength valve spring retainers will have to be used, together with custom-made mild steel spring baseplates. The latter to convert the original dual depth spot-facing registers machined into the cylinder head to match those of the later cylinder heads. You really won't go to all this trouble unless you specifically need to use early cylinder heads because it is much simpler to substitute 1976 on-type heads.

1976-1993 cylinder heads
The single valve springs of all engines fitted with such (1976-2004) will need to be changed to prevent coil binding if more than 0.430in/10.9mm of valve lift is to be used. There are a number of aftermarket single valve springs that allow for valve lift well beyond 0.430in/10.9mm before they become coil bound. This is an easy 'fix' and many Rover specialists and camshaft manufacturing companies offer direct replacement single valve springs with one coil less than standard to safely allow more space between the coils and increased valve lift of up to 0.500in/12.7mm (more than enough for most engines).

The later standard single valve springs (1976 on SD1 & Range Rover) become coil bound at between 1.090 and 1.095in/27.7 and 27.8mm. They are compressed to 1.145in/29.0mm at the maximum possible valve lift of 0.430in/10.9mm, at which point there is only 0.050in/1.25mm of cumulative clearance between all of the coils of the spring.

1976-1993 cylinder heads have a clearance of approximately 0.525/13.4mm between the underside of the valve spring retainer and the top of the valve guide. Unless the valve lift is going to be taken over 0.475in/12.1mm, there is no need to machine down the top of the valve guide for more clearance. The requirement is for 0.050in/1.25mm clearance between the underside of the valve spring retainer and the top of the valve guide at full valve lift. The tops of the valve guides will have to be machined down accordingly to suit any valve lift over 0.475in/12.1mm.

Caution! – It is not advisable to have less than 0.050in/1.25mm of clearance between the coils of a compressed valve spring without risking fatigue and breakage. Doing so also risks rapid and excessive wear of the camshaft lobes and lifter bases if the valve springs become coil bound. Once the 'nose' of a camshaft lobe starts to wear away it doesn't stop, even if the lift is reduced and the excess force removed: premature camshaft failure is inevitable!

1993 on cylinder heads
The cylinder heads fitted with the neoprene valve stem seals (1993-2004) have the problem of the valve spring retainers and collets/keepers/split locks hitting the tops of the valve stem oil seals at anything over 0.450in/11.4mm of valve lift. With the standard camshaft lift of 0.390in/9.9mm there is 0.060in/1.5mm of clearance between the underside of the valve spring retainer and the top

of the valve stem seal.

Once you decide to go above 0.430in/10.8mm of valve lift on 1993 and later cylinder heads (only 0.020in/0.5mm of clearance between the underside of the valve spring retainer and the top of the valve stem seal is acceptable for moderate rpm use), you'll need to cut down the tops of the valve guides to avoid contact between the tops of the standard valve guide seals and the underside of the valve spring retainers. The usual practice is to take the cylinder heads to a Rover V8 specialist and have the tops of the valve guides machined so that they are lower than standard by 0.100in/2.5mm. This is low enough to allow up to 0.500in/12.8mm of valve lift while still retaining the standard valve stem oil seals. Most specialist Rover V8 engine rebuilding concerns do this sort of re-working as a matter of course now. They have a trepanning tool that fits into a drill press chuck/milling machine and the pilot of the trepanning tool locates into the valve guide. The cylinder head is held at the right angle in a jig and each guide then is reduced in height by the required amount. Provided the cylinder heads have been stripped down beforehand, it only takes about 30 minutes to do this work, so it's not expensive.

There aren't many camshafts available for the Rover V8 that have more than 0.500in/13.7mm of valve lift. If you do decide to use more valve lift than 0.500in/13.7mm the tops of the valve guides will need to be further reduced in height, as required, to achieve the 0.050in/1.25mm clearance for the seals. Don't reduce guide height anymore than necessary as shortening

Standard early Rover V8 engine (1967-1976) dual valve spring on the left (both wound the same way) and a 1976-2004 single valve spring on the right. The freestanding height of the early outer dual valve spring is 1.975in/50mm, the inner 1.875in/45.7mm, while the single coil valve spring is 1.935in/49mm.

Standard 1976 and later SD1 & Range Rover single valve spring on the left and a Piper Cams VSSV8 one on the right. The VSSV8 valve spring has one less coil than the standard SD1 & Range Rover valve spring to allow more coil clearance.

reduces the valve stem to valve guide stability).

Removing the seals on later cylinder heads (1993 and later) increases the clearance by about 0.220in/5.6mm to 0.670in/17.0mm in an instant, but is not recommended, despite the earlier engines not having valve stem seals. Without the seals, too much oil will go down between the valve stems and valve guides, especially inlets, and will end up in the combustion chamber

Late model cylinder heads (1993 and later) were fitted with neoprene valve stem seals. The clearance between the underside of the valve spring retainer and the top of the seal (right) limits valve lift unless modified.

The valve guide on the right has had the seal removed to illustrate the difference.

diluting the inlet charge with oil and reducing the power output of the engine. This is why the factory changed the cylinder head design to incorporate seals in 1993.

Another option to avoid the seal contact problem is to have the original valve guides removed from the cylinder heads and have shorter bronze valve guides fitted. This is often done by Rover V8 engine-rebuilding companies, especially if the original guides are going to be removed anyway in order to port the cylinder heads. Caution! – It is important that the original guides are removed from the cylinder heads without damaging the valve guide

holes. It's all too easy to damage the cylinder head when using the common drift punch method where, typically, the cylinder head is heated to 150 degrees C/302F and the old valve guides then driven out using a hammer and a specially-shaped drift punch. Without doubt, the best way of removing the valve guides without damaging the cylinder head is to machine them out. This involves clamping the cylinder head to a milling machine table and machining the original valve guides away, until each one becomes a very thin-walled tube (0.003-0.005in/0.075-0.125mm), it then doesn't take too much effort to remove what's left manually with a special cutter supplied by K-Line.

Caution! – The original cast iron valve guides are almost always correctly fitted into the cylinder heads by the factory and it is not a good idea to disturb them if it can be avoided. This could be necessary if extensive modification of the inlet ports and exhaust ports is contemplated, or if a valve guide is seriously damaged. Once a valve guide bore hole in the cylinder head is damaged, specialised remedial work is required. The original valve guide hole will have to be remachined by boring and reaming oversize to accept specially-made oversize valve guide, followed by recutting the valve seat. In all, it's an expensive process.

Unless you need to remove the original guides for porting work, the best way to restore worn guides is the K-Line valve guide insert replacement system. K-Line phosphor bronze valve guide inserts are quite inexpensive to have fitted, and can subsequently be replaced as many times as you

A phosphor bronze K-Line valve guide insert.

like. Many engine-reconditioning companies use this system now so it is generally not too difficult to find a company that has it. These inserts are extremely hard wearing (five times better than the original cast iron valve guides and twice as good as bronze guides) and are highly recommended. **Caution!** – Note that K-Line inserts are not recommended for fitting into bronze valve guides.

The cylinder head is mounted on the Kwik-Way head shop machine, or similar, the valve guides accurately aligned in turn with the spindle of the machine and the original guide bores machined out to a particular size. The K-Line insert is fitted into the cast iron valve guide and a tungsten carbide ball forced through the bore of the guide with a pneumatic impact tool. The size of the tungsten carbide ball is the valve stem size plus clearance 0.005in/0.127mm for inlet valves and 0.008in/0.203mm for exhaust valves: this is quite tight, but they never seize. The excess insert length is then trimmed off with a special tool. Two types of insert are available, one plain and the other grooved for lubrication: use the grooved ones.

Valve springs for high performance applications

All of the guide measurements given in this section relate to the original standard factory machined sizes. They don't take into account the fact that, for instance, the original valves and valve seats may have been reground, or larger than standard head diameter valves might have been fitted. All of these things can affect the clearance between the top of the valve guide and the underside of the valve spring retainer.

The way to check the actual clearance and find out the true status of the clearance is to partially assemble the cylinder heads and check the measurements individually. This involves fitting the valves, valve retainers and collets (keepers/split locks) to the cylinder head without the valve springs. A vernier calliper can then be used to measure the distance between the top of each valve stem seal and the underside of each valve spring retainer.

Standard single valve springs

The fitted height of the single valve springs in a standard cylinder head (late 1976 on) is 1.575in/40.0mm. Regrinding valves and/or recutting valve seats will possibly increase this to 1.580in/40.1mm, or so. However, in the interests of leaving a margin to avoid coil binding, work with the standard fitted heights in the sure knowledge that you will ultimately end up with enough, or slightly more than enough, clearance.

The standard single valve springs, as fitted to later cylinder heads, exert a (valve seated) force of about 75lb/33kg. At the standard maximum valve lift of 0.390in/9.9mm

Valve spring comparison, left to right: standard P5/P6 and Range Rover to 1976, standard SD1 and Range Rover of 1976 on and all later engines, Piper VSSV8 single, Piper VTSV8 triple.

this becomes 165-170lb/73-75kg and, at a maximum valve lift of 0.430in/10.9mm, becomes 185-190lb/82-84kg. This is enough valve spring force for engine speeds up to 6500rpm, using new standard valve springs.

If more valve lift than 0.430in/10.9mm is going to be used, then these original equipment single valve springs cannot be used and will have to be replaced with ones that allow more spring compression before the onset of coil binding, but without increasing pressure.

Aftermarket valve springs

A reasonably wide range of aftermarket valve springs are available, including singles, duals and triples. Piper Cams valve springs are good examples of what is readily available, but there are many other suppliers of similar parts.

Note that in all of the valve spring information that follows, the standard single valve spring installed height of 1.575in/40.0mm is used as the base figure. Most valve spring suppliers will provide you with their spring length/force details once you have provided them with details of the actual fitted height and

compressed height at full valve lift for your particular engine.

Piper Cams, for example, specifies two valve springs for use with its camshafts. The first is direct replacement single valve spring, part number VSSV8 (for use on 1976 on heads only). This spring is coil bound at 0.975in/24.8mm, which will allow a maximum of 0.550in/14.0mm valve lift on fully clearanced cylinder heads while retaining a cumulative clearance of 0.050in/1.25mm between the coils.

These Piper single valve springs have a fitted valve spring pressure, at the standard fitted height, of about 75lb/33kg and about 180lb/80kg at the standard maximum valve lift height of 0.390in/9.9mm. Pressure increases to 200lb/89kg at 0.450in/10.4mm of valve lift, 210lb/93kg at 0.480in/12.2mm of valve lift and 220lb/102kg at 0.510in/13.0mm of valve lift. These springs are ideal for use with up to 0.510in/13.0mm of valve lift without stressing them unduly. This amount of valve spring pressure is more than enough for an engine revving to 7000rpm.

Caution! – Standard sintered valve spring retainers can be used with these valve springs, but not for engines that are going to rev above 5800rpm. As an alternative to the early standard steel valve spring retainers, Piper Cams SC4T (T for titanium) retainers should be used if engine speeds over 5800rpm are going to be used, or if there is any concern about possible failure of the standard sintered-type retainer.

The other spring specified by Piper (for use on 1976 on heads only) is its VSTV8 triple valve spring which comprises two coils separated by a contra-wound flat damper. These valve springs will allow more than 0.550in/14.0mm of valve lift (there are no generally available hydraulic or mechanical cams with more than this amount of lift). The coil bind height of this valve spring combination is 0.800in/20.5mm. The springs are a direct replacement for the standard production valve spring and fit the spot facings machined into the cylinder head to seat the springs.

These triple springs have a seated pressure of about 75lb/33kg, rising to 180lb/80kg at the standard maximum valve lift of 0.390in/9.9mm. Thereafter, at the following valve lifts: 200lb/89kg at 0.450in/11.4mm, about 210lb/93kg at 0.480in/12.2mm, about 220lb/98kg at 0.510in/13.0mm valve lift, and about 230lb/102kg at the maximum safe valve lift of 0.550in/14.0mm. **Caution!** – Piper Cams' SC4 high tensile steel valve spring retainers must be used in conjunction with these springs.

Caution! – While these Piper valves are direct replacements for the standard items on all 1976 and later cylinder heads, and allow the valve lifts already mentioned, they'll only do so if there is sufficient clearance between the underside of

Piper Cams' VSSV8 single valve spring on the left, and its VSTV8 triple valve spring on the right.

the valve spring retainer and the top of the valve guide/valve stem seals. If the valve lift being used is not greater than 0.430in/10.9mm, there will be no clearance problems on any cylinder head. Above this, the actual clearance must be checked to see that it's adequate. Clearly you must identify which of the three basic cylinder head types you have.

The VSSV8 single valve springs and VTSV8 triple valve springs give virtually the same valve spring pressures at the same heights and are also coil bound at the same height. The justification for using a set of the more expensive triples is their better fatigue resistance, resulting from the coils being less stressed at the same compressed heights. At up to 0.500in/12.7mm of valve lift the VSSV8 singles and SC4T retainers are quite adequate. For maximum reliability, the VTSV8 triples and SC4 retainers should be used for lifts greater than 0.500in/12.7mm and up to 0.550in/14.0mm. Both these valve springs, and associated valve spring pressures, are fine for engines which produce maximum power at 7000rpm, as well as allowing a reasonable safety margin for engine over-speeding.

Kent Cams lists two valve

Piper Cams' VTSV8 valve spring and high tensile steel SC4 valve spring retainer.

springs for use with its range of camshafts. The single VS44 valve springs are used with lower lift camshafts (H180, H200 & H218) because, at 0.440in/11.2mm to 0.465in/11.8mm, the lift is above the maximum permissible for standard Rover V8 single valve springs.

The tops of the valve guides need to be cut down if the H218 camshaft is going to be used as the exhaust valve lift is over the maximum permissible if 1993 and later cylinder heads are going to be used. Otherwise, the VS44 springs are a direct replacement for standard springs.

Kent Cams' VS43 dual valve springs are not direct replacements for the standard units and require the aluminium boss around the valve guide to be machined down to 0.675in/17.1mm from the original diameter of 0.845in/21.4mm. This allows the inner valve spring to sit on the same flat surface as the outer (otherwise it will have edge contact where it sits on the factory machined spot facing). The company states that its ST47 valve spring retainers must be used with the VS43 dual valve springs, but note that they cannot be used with the VS44 single valve springs. This means that, with the VS44 springs, you'll either need to use the standard sintered-type valve spring retainers for engine speeds up to 5800rpm, or change to another company's steel retainers for speeds above this.

It's quite possible, and acceptable, to use a particular camshaft with another company's valve springs provided the seated pressures and the maximum valve lift ('over the nose') pressures are compatible. J.E. Developments, for example, stocks and supplies valve springs that are suitable for use with a wide range of camshaft brands other than the ones it regularly uses.

Caution! – A reminder: don't risk using late model sintered-type valve spring retainers on any engine revving to more than 5800rpm, even if the standard valve springs are retained. Breakage is quite possible and the risk is just not worth taking. If a retainer breaks the resulting damage can be catastrophic. Fit aftermarket high tensile steel, aluminium or titanium retainers which are generally readily available and are a good insurance against a catastrophe.

WHICH AFTERMARKET CAMSHAFT?

All aftermarket camshafts tend to cost about the same, so the natural tendency is to buy a camshaft with the most duration, and probably more than is really needed. When choosing a camshaft other than a 'smooth idle' one (ie: a cam with more than 275 degrees of duration), resist the temptation to use a longer duration camshaft than is absolutely necessary.

The Rover V8 is, for the most part, favoured by drivers who like the 'torqueiness' of these engines, rather than their 'revability' and increasing duration will push power up the rev band. A well-known American saying is 'don't buy more duration than you can use' and this statement is absolutely correct.

If the engine is in a weekend/trackday car, the rough idle caused by overlong duration won't matter too much, but be aware that a camshaft that does not start to 'work' more or less off idle in a road going car is not a very practical option. If the engine is going to be revved to a maximum of 5500rpm, look at 275-280 degree duration camshafts. If the rev range will extend to 6000rpm, look at 280-285 degree duration camshafts.

If you fit a long duration camshaft (300 degrees, for example) to an engine that is used for low rpm work, such as road use, while the engine will have a much rougher idle and sound powerful, it will not start to produce real power until well up in the rpm range, probably around 4000rpm. Not only will the engine perform poorly below 4000rpm, the effective power band will be reduced to just 2000rpm if the redline is at 6000rpm. Such an engine will feel 'flat' under about 4000rpm, and when it does start to go will not perform all that much better than one with a 275-285 degree duration camshaft, for example. You'll also need to keep the engine within its narrow power band via frequent gearchanges. Cars with engine characteristics like this tend to be frustrating to drive. Most enthusiasts are better off with an engine that 'goes' the instant you press the accelerator pedal at idle.

Note that what causes an engine to sound 'the business' with a long duration camshaft is the earlier exhaust opening. But don't be fooled by this, the wild sounding idle is just noise ...

With engines that are being used up to 6000rpm, there is another aspect of the camshaft design that needs to be taken into consideration: the opening point of the exhaust valve. The majority of camshafts for these engines do not need to have the exhaust valve opening too early if good mid-range power is required. Because these engines are rarely required to rev over 6000rpm, the torque curve between 1500-6000rpm is what really matters. This means opening the exhaust valve as late as is practicable. For an engine revving up to 6000rpm, the earliest that the exhaust valve should ever be opened is about 70 degrees before bottom dead centre (BBDC). Any earlier than this (75 degrees, or earlier) and low end and midrange 'punch' is less than what it could be. The appropriate range to consider is 65 to 70 degrees BBDC as this will keep the combustion pressure acting on the top of the piston for as long as possible.

It's worth noting that if a high performance camshaft is fitted to an engine with standard cylinder heads, the benefit is never going to be as good as it could be, although the idle speed roughness will not be very pronounced. This is no reflection on the standard cylinder heads, which were designed for a specific purpose. If the standard cylinder heads are modified correctly the difference with that same camshaft can be quite dramatic, although the engine's idle roughness will also become more apparent. The improvement is caused by better porting in the head allowing more interaction between the inlet and exhaust pulses. Of course, the amount of improvement depends on how well the engine is tuned in the first place.

Correctly modified cylinder heads are expensive but represent good value for money if the amount of time and skill involved in doing them correctly is taken into account.

Armed with this knowledge, a sensible choice of camshaft can be made which will make the engine as usable as possible within the framework of the other modifications built into it.

The critical factors when deciding on a camshaft can be summarised as follows:

1 – What will be the maximum engine rpm? With this factor decided, the valve duration can be narrowed down. As general rule use 265-275 degrees for 'smooth idle' applications, 275-295 degrees for high performance road & occasional race applications, and 295 degrees, and above, for straight racing applications.

2 – If the engine is going to be used for racing only, the camshaft ideally needs to be a mechanical one. With a very few exceptions, all other applications should retain the hydraulic lifters.

3 – The lowest amount of valve lift to consider is 0.430in/10.9mm and the highest amount normally used in racing engines is about 0.500in/12.7mm. Although it's rarely used, up to 0.535in/13.6mm is possible and available.

4 – The maximum amount of 'over the nose' valve spring pressure that ever needs to be used is 230lb/105kg, which is adequate for up to 7000rpm.

The consequences of higher valve lift

Piper Cams makes its shorter duration hydraulic V8BP255 camshaft with 0.430in/10.9mm valve lift to suit the maximum amount of valve lift that the standard valve springs will stand. Piper's V8BP270, V8BP270i and V8BP285 camshafts have 0.445in/11.3mm to 0.450in/11.4mm lift, and hence require a change of valve springs, but once that's been done these camshafts are direct replacements for standard camshafts.

Other aftermarket camshaft manufacturers make higher lift camshafts (over 0.430in/10.9mm and up to 0.450in/11.4mm) that work well in these engines, but a valve spring change will definitely be required.

High performance aftermarket camshafts

There are many companies around the world which make excellent hydraulic and mechanical camshafts and related components for these engines. A few of them are: Sig Erson Cams (USA), Iskenderian Racing Cams (USA), Kent Cams (UK), Piper Cams (UK), Crower (USA), Crane (USA), with Kent Cams and Piper Cams being the most common suppliers in the UK. These two companies make good products and their agents are widely spread throughout the UK and in many countries around the world. All of these camshaft companies list similar products, but there are subtle differences in many instances and these differences can be used to your advantage, with some camshafts being easier overall to install. The range of camshafts is quite wide and there are several

factors that need to be taken into account that will affect your choice.

All camshafts will fit, but some require swapping or reworking of other components, such as valve guide shortening and alternative valve springs, or a valve spring change, while others will require no changes. It's not always as straight forward as you might think and there can be several ways of achieving your objective by different means, this is especially so when it comes to valve springs and valve spring retainers.

Note that all camshaft timing/phasing specifications (eg: 26-66-66-26) given in this section are in the same order: inlet opening point, inlet closing point, exhaust opening point and exhaust closing point.

'Smooth idle' camshafts

Piper Cams is a good example to start with, as it provides a wide range of 'smooth idle' camshafts. The first of these hydraulic camshafts is the V8BP255, which is a direct replacement item with its 0.430in/10.9mm of valve lift, because the standard valve springs can be retained. Expect this camshaft to give a power 'surge' that goes from off idle to approximately 5000rpm on a well-tuned engine. This is an ideal high performance camshaft for anyone who wants a simple modification and yet wants a good result. Use new or refaced lifters and fit a new duplex timing chain and sprocket set. The V8BP255 is not an inferior performance camshaft just because it's been designed around the standard engine components, uses standard valve springs, and doesn't have as much valve lift as others. It has 26-66-66-26 valve timing which means the inlet valves open at 26 degrees before top dead centre (BTDC) and close 66 degrees after bottom dead centre (ABDC). The exhaust valves open 66 degrees before bottom dead centre (BBDC) and close 26 degrees after top dead centre (ATDC). The full lift inlet timing point is 110 degrees ATDC.

Kent Cams offers its H180 camshaft as a direct replacement for the standard item. It has 23-59-59-23 timing, with the full lift inlet timing at 108 degrees ATDC. It's a very mild camshaft and, like the Piper Cams V8BP255, is very good for its intended purpose. However, at 0.441in/11.2mm the lift is past the maximum that the standard single coil spring cylinder heads will take reliably.

The next cams in the performance ranking are Piper Cams' hydraulic V8BP270 and V8BP270i (the 'i' version is designed to have slightly less overlap to create better manifold vacuum for fuel injection engines). These camshafts are 'smooth idle' items and, on correctly tuned engines, are going to give a power 'surge' that goes from off idle to between 5000 and 5500rpm. These cams are not, however, a simple replacement for the standard items because the standard valve springs have to be replaced, using Piper VSSV8 items or similar. In theory these cams can be used with standard valve spring retainers, collets, valve guides and stem seals, but the clearances are tight, and each valve assembly must be checked individually to make sure that there actually is enough clearance. These camshafts have 0.445in/11.3mm of advertised valve lift, and yet late

model cylinder heads (1993 on) can only accommodate 0.450in/11.4mm of valve lift so there is no room for error in this situation. The timing for the V8BP270i is 26-66-66-26. Both V8BP270 and the V8BP270i (injection) require the use of VSSV8 valve springs.

One common feature of all the foregoing high performance 'smooth idle' camshafts is that they open and close the valves quicker which, coupled with the higher lift, provides a bigger 'window' for the air/fuel mixture to get into the engine without causing idle roughness. However, whilst two camshafts can have the same opening and closing points, their rates of opening/closing can be different, and so they can have entirely different efficiency ratings and valve train loadings. So, when you see duration figures from aftermarket camshaft manufacturers that are identical to those of the standard Rover V8 camshafts, be aware that in reality their characteristics may be quite different from the standard unit's.

'Smooth idle' camshafts are not inferior performance camshafts. They are high performance camshafts without the usual rough idle characteristics that long duration camshafts often exhibit. Having a rough idling engine can become very tiresome in a car that is used around town most of the time. The constant shaking and vibration and excessive fuel economy is the downside of having a 'rough idle' camshaft, especially if you are not really using its power range.

Note that cylinder heads do not have to be removed from the engine and stripped to change the valve springs. Garages change valve springs by placing each cylinder in

turn at top dead centre (TDC). Then, with both valves closed and with the engine locked, pressurising that cylinder with compressed air. Now it is possible to compress the valve spring/retainer combination and remove the valve collets (keepers). The valve spring is then removed, the new valve spring fitted. This method of removing and replacing valve springs is really an offshoot of the method used to replace valve stem oil seals quickly and cheaply. On that subject, it's always a good idea to fit new valve stem oil seals if the valve springs are changed.

'Rough idle' camshafts

Rough idle camshafts are generally regarded as those that have a duration of over 270 degrees. The idle speed and low end 'roughness' of camshafts is caused by the large amount of inlet and exhaust valve overlap: the greater the overlap the rougher the idle.

Overlap is that part of the camshaft cycle when, for an individual cylinder, the exhaust valve is closing (very nearly closed) and, simultaneously, the inlet valve is just starting to open. These events occur at preset crankshaft degrees before top dead centre (BTDC) and after top dead centre (ATDC). While both the inlet valve and the exhaust valve of a cylinder are open there is an amount of 'interaction' between the exhaust and inlet parts of the four stroke cycle. The amount of idle roughness is determined by the number of crankshaft degrees that both valves are open together, and by the amount and rate of the valve lift of each valve during this phase. The quicker the inlet valve lift rate and the exhaust valve closing rate, the larger the 'window' for the interaction to take place in. The larger the amount of overlap a camshaft has, the higher up the rpm range before it 'smoothes out' and starts to produce usable engine power.

270-280 degree camshafts

An example of a 280-degree duration hydraulic camshaft is the American-made Sig Erson Cams' E640111 camshaft, which has 27-67-70-30 phasing and 0.448in/11.4mm maximum of valve lift. Sig Frson Cams also supply suitable valve springs for use with this camshaft, otherwise it is a direct replacement for the standard camshaft. This is a very good camshaft which starts producing power from just off idle.

The Iskenderian Oldsmobile/Buick 270 degree duration 270 HL HYD and its 280-degree duration 280 HYD hydraulic camshafts are in the same category. The 270 HL HYD camshaft has 0.470in/11.9mm of valve lift and 23-67-61-29 phasing, while the 280 HYD camshaft has 0.467in/11.85mm of valve lift and 31-71-71-31 phasing.

Kent Cams offers its H200 camshaft in this category, which has 23-67-68-34 phasing, and reasonable lift of 0.429in/10.9mm for the inlet valves and 0.453in/11.5mm for the exhaust valves. This is a low overlap camshaft, with late exhaust valve opening and delivers good low rpm torque from just above idle.

While the idle will be slightly rough with all four of these camshafts, it will 'smooth out' and the engine will start developing good power and torque from just off idle. In all cases modified cylinder heads and the degree of tune of a particular engine will affect the amount of idle roughness, but using standard cylinder heads will reduce it. All four camshafts will allow the engine to rev to 6000rpm plus, provided the sintered-type valve spring retainers have been replaced with stronger items.

280-290 degree camshafts

There's quite a number of different hydraulic camshafts in this category that can be used to really good effect; in fact, this is the start of camshafts that are used for racing/competition purposes. In all cases well-modified cylinder heads are essential if the benefits of the camshaft are to be realised in terms of enhanced performance.

Kent Cams, for example, offers its H218 hydraulic camshaft with 27-71-74-30 phasing, 0.448in/11.4mm of inlet valve lift and 0.464in/11.8mm of exhaust valve lift. The duration of this cam is on the low side for this category.

An alternative here is to get Kent Cams to grind you a 'special order' camshaft which has the H214 hydraulic camshaft inlet profile in the usual phasing (31-73) and the exhaust profile of the H218 camshaft, but instead of phasing it 74-30, have it phased 71-33. The duration of such a camshaft will be 282 degrees for both the inlet and exhaust valves, the inlet lift will be 0.469in/11.9mm, the exhaust valve lift 0.464in/11.8mm and the overall phasing 31-73-71-33. The object of this exercise is to have as late as possible exhaust opening, reasonably high valve lift, and not too much overlap, giving wide torque and power bands which start from just off idle. This 'special order' camshaft works very well with modified cylinder heads, with maximum power being developed at about 6300rpm.

Kent's next hydraulic camshaft in this group is the H214, which has 31-73-78-40 phasing, 0.469in/11.9mm of inlet valve lift and 0.490in/12.45mm of exhaust valve lift. The increased duration also increases the rpm point at which maximum power is developed.

The Holbay 111R camshaft is an example of a true direct replacement high performance hydraulic camshaft with quite long duration, although it does need to be used in conjunction with new standard valve springs. It has 0.429in/10.9mm of valve lift, 292 degrees of duration and 39-73-73-39 timing. For what it is, with the valve lift limited for ease of fitting, it's an excellent camshaft, capable of 5800rpm maximum using sintered valve spring retainers. Its duration also provides good performance up to 6500rpm (**Caution!** – only if the mechanically limited components are replaced with stronger ones). The drawback is that, with this amount of overlap, the low-end response is reduced. Coltech Racing Engines (phone number +44 [0]1473 738738), which now has the Holbay camshaft profiles, still supplies this camshaft.

A mechanical camshaft in this range is the Kent Cams M228. It has 32-68-73-37 phasing, 0.464in/11.8mm of inlet valve lift and 0.470in/11.9mm of exhaust valve lift. That's 280 degrees of inlet duration and 290 degrees of exhaust duration. Next is Kent Cams' mechanical M238 with an inlet and exhaust valve lift of 0.485in/12.3mm. This camshaft is phased 34-70-73-37, with the inlet duration at 284 degrees and the exhaust duration at 290 degrees. These two camshafts can produce power at over 6500rpm, which is nearly at the limit of what well modified standard heads can flow. They are ideal for any application where the engine is revving to between 6500 and 6700rpm on a regular basis.

Long duration (295-305 degrees plus)

This group of camshafts is for racing and, realistically, none of these cams have any place in road cars of any description. Kent Cams' M248 gives 0.506in/12.85mm of inlet and exhaust valve lift and has phasing of 43-77-79-41. This camshaft can take the maximum power point to 7000rpm, and as you would expect there's no really useful torque or power under 4000rpm.

Piper Cams' V8BP300 is in the same category, with its 46-80-80-46 phasing and 0.498in/12.65mm of inlet and exhaust valve lift.

Both these cams are very good for the right application. Avoid using even longer durations than these for racing purposes, it's all been tried before and it doesn't work well unless you have lots of gears in a close ratio gearbox and are keeping the revs up all of the time.

Alternative profiles & phasings

There are a huge number of camshaft grinding/regrinding companies around the world who all seem to have a good range of Chevrolet, Ford and Chrysler camshaft profile masters and, provided they start from a new blank camshaft, can grind virtually any reasonable lift and phasing to suit any application. The Chevrolet camshaft profiles are the ones to use because they use the same diameter lifter as the Rover V8 (this is a vital factor).

There is quite a lot that can be done with different phasings for different applications, such as using 'low overlap phasing'. In cases like this a 275 degree duration profile is phased at 25-70-73-22, for example. Such camshafts tend to 'work' from off idle and go through to about 6000rpm in a very strong surge of power. However, the power surge finishes abruptly.

Summary

- Avoid using cams with over long duration, think more in terms of having the least duration possible so that a broad power band and a good torque curve is realised.
- Road going engines that need to deliver good fuel consumption and a wide band of power and torque from off idle need durations in the range 255 to 270 degrees.
- Engines for high performance road use, such as rally engines, require camshafts with durations of between 275 and 295 degrees. This group is split into two: for applications using up to 6000rpm, use camshafts with a duration of between 275 and 285 degrees; for applications which are going to use more than 6000rpm, use up to 295 degrees of duration.
- Full racing engines turning regularly to 7000rpm will need mechanical camshafts with durations in the 290 to 305 degree range. Mechanical camshafts tend to have a bit more 'snap' to them compared to the engine response of hydraulic cams and, as a consequence, can offer better engine response.
- The best racing engines produce their maximum power at no more than 7000rpm, irrespective of what camshaft is fitted to the engine.
- Low valve lift is 0.390-430in/9.9-10.9mm. Medium valve lift is 0.430-0.480in/10.9-12.2mm. High/maximum valve lift is in the range of 0.480-0.535in/12.2-13.5mm.

For those wishing for more in-depth information about camshafts and camshaft timing, *How to Choose Camshafts & Time Them for Maximum Power* by Des Hammill (published by Veloce) is recommended reading.

Chapter 7
Balance

ORIGINAL FACTORY ENGINE BALANCE

On a mass production basis, Rover didn't need to balance each engine as thoroughly as a specialist does.

Rover ensured basic balance for each engine by making sure that the individual components were pre-balanced to within fairly strict weight limits (measured in grams) prior to engine assembly. The pistons were weighed, and lightened as necessary, to ensure that they all ended up weighing within 4gm of a mean design weight (ie: plus or minus 2gm from the mean). The gudgeon (piston) pins were made to exact dimensions and, as a consequence, all weighed within 2gm of each other (plus or minus 1gm from mean). Rings sets all weighed within 1gm of each other (plus or minus 0.5gm from mean). Similarly, the forged and machined connecting rods were balanced

end for end so that each end of a connecting rod was within 5gm of the mean design weight for each end (plus or minus 2.5gm from the mean), and the overall weight of each connecting rod within 5gm of its mean design weight (plus or minus 2.5gm from the mean). This means that there was a possible weight tolerance (assembled components) of approximately 12gm per cylinder and that the maximum out of balance tolerance over 8 cylinders was 68gm. However, the factory didn't always get the balance within the specified tolerance.

The crankshaft dampers and flywheels were also individually balanced to a strict tolerance by fitting them on to a dynamic balancing machine, and then drilling into the heavy side to bring the flywheel into balance. Note that the crankshaft pulley/damper wasn't pre-balanced in this manner.

The crankshafts were individually dynamically balanced on a balancing machine that spun each at around 500rpm. Before this was done, a mean weight (component design weight) bob-weight was attached to each big end journal. The bob-weight simulated the rotating force component of the connecting rod and piston that is felt at the big end journal (ie: the equal of the mean weight of the connecting rod big end, and 50% of the mean weight of the little end, piston, gudgeon pin and ring set).

During the crankshaft dynamic balancing process, any imbalance of the crankshaft is dealt with by removing metal (drilling holes) in the foremost or rearmost counterweights as and where necessary. The crankshaft was designed to be very slightly over counterweighted after initial production so that an amount of metal is always available for removal when it was dynamically balanced. After this basic balancing procedure, all of the components were deemed ready for assembly into a production engine.

The significant point about the crankshaft's dynamic balancing is that it was balanced with mean **design** weight bob-weights. The actual parts that were subsequently fitted to the engine were all subject to production tolerances, which means that they were almost certainly not going to be the same as the mean design weights. In some cases, each piston, gudgeon pin, and connecting rod assembly could be up to 16gm different from the mean design weight, although it was usual for the all-up discrepancy to be between 4 and 8gm.

Even with the very small allowable weight tolerances of the components fitted into Rover V8 engines, tolerance stacking could occur even when all parts were within the overall factory designated tolerances. To cover this possibility, Rover always carried out a final check balance and adjustment procedure to ensure that every single engine made left the factory correctly balanced to within the maximum allowable factory tolerance.

Using an electric motor to drive it, each engine was dry motored at 500rpm, and strategically placed sensors detected any imbalance at the front and the rear of the engine. If the engine was within acceptable tolerance, it was passed as fit for installation into a car without it being touched. If an engine was out of tolerance, the imbalance was corrected by a combination of strategically mig welding a piece of round bar stock to the back of the rim of the crankshaft pulley to fine

balance the front of the engine, and strategically adding special bolts to the flywheel to fine balance the rear. What the factory did was to add 'external balance' to fully assembled engines to make them meet the acceptable production criteria. The amount of material added was quite small and very acceptable in a mass production situation.

All engines had to be in balance to within 1oz-in/72gm-cm and this is accurate enough for a road going standard production engine.

In the worst case scenarios of factory balanced components expect connecting rod weights different from each other by up to 12gm in a set, and pistons more than 5gm different from each other in a set. Even with the factory final balancing procedures to make sure that all engines were within a specified tolerance, some engines were going to leave the factory technically better balanced than others.

ENGINE BALANCE FOR HIGH PERFORMANCE

The factory procedure just described was fine for original mass production, but is not necessarily quite so good for today's engine builders when components have been swapped from one engine to another. When this happens the engine can immediately lose the factory balance factor. A second-hand engine that's been repaired or modified could have had components fitted to it from two or three different engines and the overall balance could easily have moved well away from the minimum requirement. The only way to be sure that an engine in this category is correctly balanced is to have all

of its components rebalanced from scratch by a specialist balancing company.

The engine rebalancing engineers know what to expect with the Rover V8, and so start by removing any mig-welded bar stock from the back of the crankshaft pulley/damper rim and any extra weights from the flywheel. All components are then individually balanced to very fine limits. That means on average each piston, gudgeon pin and ring set weighing within 0.5gm of each other. The connecting rods are similarly match weighed to within 1.0gm in overall weight and 0.5gm end for end. The bob-weights for the dynamic balancing of the crankshaft are accurately matched to the *actual* weight of the components they represent using the V8 engine balancing formula and a tolerance of 0.5gm. Most engine rebalancing companies dynamically balance the crankshafts to within 50-80gm-mm of residual imbalance. This is viewed as the realistic minimum limit, anything significantly less is Formula One territory and results in minuscule amounts of metal being removed for very little further improvement in overall engine balance.

Next, the flywheel or flexplate is fitted to the crankshaft and balanced, the damper is added and then, finally, the drive pulley is fitted to that and balanced. This procedure results in a perfectly balanced assembly. Needless to say, none of this work entails lumps of metal being mig-welded to the back of the crankshaft pulley rim or extra bolts in the flywheel! This process will be expensive, but consider it worthwhile expenditure.

If you are 100% sure that all of the components in your standard engine are the originals then a rebalance is probably not necessary, unless you're going to use your engine for racing purposes. In the latter case a rebalance is required to reduce the allowable imbalance to the minimum possible.

When an original crankshaft with modified offset ground big end journals (a 'stroked' crank) is being fitted, possibly with various combinations of connecting rods and pistons, significant amounts of metal could have to be added to the crankshaft counterweights to correct the dynamic balance. Adding weight to the counterweights is achieved by several methods, with extreme cases requiring holes to be drilled in the front two or three and rear two or three counterweights to allow 'Mallory metal' or tungsten carbide slugs to be press-fitted into the holes. The specific gravity of Mallory metal is about twice that of nodular iron. It's usual to use ⅝in/16mm diameter slugs and fit them as close as possible to the outer edge of the counterweighting for greatest effect (force times distance applies). Several slugs of Mallory metal are often required to effect correct balance in such instances.

Caution! – All Rover V8 engines revving to more than 6000rpm should be balanced 'internally', **not** 'externally' (weights added to the flywheel/flexplate and pulley/damper). It's a lot cheaper to use external balance (as Rover did) than to add Mallory metal or equivalent to the counterweights of the crankshaft to 'internally balance' the engine, but the finished product is not as good for high rpm applications. 6000rpm is the threshold for using the more expensive balancing method. Internally balanced engines have less of a 'bending moment' in the crankshaft than externally balanced ones.

Note that the standard original equipment crankshaft dampers are fine for all general applications up to about 5500rpm. They are 'elastomer'-type dampers which are tuned to work at maximum torque speed (approximately 3000rpm). They are principally designed to damp the 'first mode' of torsional vibration only. No elastomer-type damper removes torsional vibration, it damps it and reduces its effect (stops the crankshaft breaking). This type of damper is excellent for the standard applications where the revs being used are virtually confined to a 1000-5000rpm band (ie: all round general road going use). Any application that uses more than 5500rpm is effectively operating with the 'second mode' of torsional vibration undamped and big numbers in the forces involved develop rapidly as the rpm increases (can lead to crankshaft breakage).

Fortunately crankshaft breakage is rare on Rover V8 engines.

J.E. Developments offers an elastomer-type 'competition damper' which is capable of damping the torsional vibration of any Rover V8 engine through to a 5.2 litre unit. This damper is effective for engines which produce up to 360 foot pounds of torque, 400bhp, and rev to 7000rpm.

John Eales has had two torsional surveys (measuring crankshaft deflection) done to ensure that his company's competition damper is suitable for the general range of engines. This competition damper is a tighter fit on the crankshaft than a standard one.

Caution! – Many standard dampers are in fact a loose fit on to the crankshafts and, as a result, are not serviceable items and should not be used. They **must** have an 'interference fit' on the snout of the crankshaft (this means that the damper has to be pressed on to the crankshaft and drawn off using a puller). If the fit is not tight enough (the damper bore must be between 0.0007 and 0.001in/0.177 and 0.025mm smaller than the crankshaft snout) the result could be a ruined crankshaft and damper.

Caution! – Note that both the flywheel/flexplate and the crankshaft must be tightly and accurately located on the crankshaft: if they are not, the balance job will be flawed.

Chapter 8
Lubrication

LOW OIL PRESSURE

Low oil pressure on 1967 to 1993 engines (as well as the later 1995 and 1997/98 3.5 litre 'Service' engines) is a well known problem, and revolves around the early type of pump and the oiling system circuitry. The system is generally good enough for normal road use, even with a well-worn engine, but is a serious limitation if the engine is tuned for fast road work or competition. The Achilles Heel is the pump drive, which comes off the front of the camshaft. Any attempt to significantly increase the oil pressure overloads the skew gears and they fail (teeth rapidly wear away).

The problem was completely solved by a crankshaft-driven oil pump, part of the 'interim' engine improvement package introduced in January 1994 on Classic Range Rover and Land Rover Discovery models with 3.9 and 4.2 litre engines.

The capacity of the oil pump was increased by a significant 40% over the original pump and, being driven directly off the crankshaft, also meant that the oil pressure could be increased for competition without the associated distributor drive gear wear problems of the earlier design.

The vast majority of road going pre-1994 (and 'Service' 1995 and 1997/98) 3.5s in use usually retain the standard distributor driven oil pump, although some engines are being modified by enthusiasts. **Caution!** – Engines that are being used for racing really should have the oil pump changed for the 'interim' pump, a modification that's already a well-accepted practice for wet sump racing engines.

Fitting the interim oil pump to a pre-'94 (or 'Service') block also involves using an interim engine's crankshaft damper and front cover complete with integral oil pump, but

it's not quite a bolt-on exercise. The problem is that the original Woodruff keyway and key in the crankshaft aren't long enough to engage the crankshaft damper as well as the oil pump. In addition, the distributor, which has a 'wobbly drive' on '76-'93 engines, needs to have the oil pump drive removed.

The crankshaft's original keyway has to be machined to take the longer interim Woodruff key. This involves mounting the crankshaft in a milling machine and lengthening and deepening the original keyway slot to suit the later type key. It's not involved work and any competent engineering company will be able to do it for you. With this machining work done, your 3.5 litre or 'pre-interim' 3.9/4.2 litre engine's crankshaft nose will be up to the later standard.

The only other work to be done is to maintain the correct oil flow to the rockershafts. This is to prevent oil flooding the rocker covers and getting pumped out of the engine ventilation system. No other internal modifications to the engine are required. These crankshaft driven oil pumps can be set to a maximum of 75psi/51kPa (or 10psi/6.9kPa per thousand rpm of engine speed being used), hot, for racing purposes.

IMPROVING OIL SYSTEMS OF NON-CRANK-DRIVEN OIL PUMP ENGINES

Before increasing the oil pressure, or fitting a later pump, there are a number of modifications that can be made to limit unnecessary losses in the oil system by restricting the flow of oil to certain areas of the engine.

The oil starts its path through the engine by being sucked up from the bottom of the sump via a gauze strainer. The oil is then drawn vertically upward about 8¼in/210mm into the block, where it makes a right angle turn and flows 18in/610mm towards the front of the block and directly to the primary side of the oil pump. The oil gallery that goes forward to the oil pump is higher than the centreline of the crankshaft's main bearings. This is quite high, and it is not a particularly good design feature, although necessary because of the position of the oil pump on the front of the block. It's this design feature that causes the oil priming problems. To put it in perspective, the oil system of the Rover V8 is quite different to, say, that of the Small Block Ford V8 engine which has the oil pump right down at the bottom of the sump, nearly level with the pickup. A small block Ford V8 engine will always self-prime.

The solution for the first time start up of a rebuilt Rover V8 engine is to fill the oil pump with petroleum jelly (Vaseline), Wynns Additive or Wynns Gear Oil. Once the pump is pre-primed with oil, priming of the Rover V8 engine's oil system is not normally a major cause for concern, because the design of the oil pump does not allow oil to drain back out of the pump gear chamber. However, if an engine has not been turned over for a long time, it is possible that the oil will not pick up. If this happens then it's simple to remove the external baseplate from the oil pump and pack it with Wynns or petroleum jelly.

Once it enters the pump (primary side), the oil goes around the outside of the two pump gears in their housing and is then under pressure (secondary side). After this the oil goes through the filter and into the engine block's main oil gallery. The oil gallery makes a 90 degree turn and goes up to just above the camshaft where a single main gallery feeds oil into two longitudinal lifter galleries that go back along the block. These two lifter galleries supply oil to the hydraulic valve lifters, with each gallery supplying the oil for the 8 lifters on that side of the engine. The left hand lifter gallery (that's the one on your left if you are standing directly in front of the engine block) supplies oil to the lifters on this side of the engine, the camshaft bearings and **all** of the main and big end bearings of the engine. There's a lot of items taking oil from this left hand oil gallery, and herein lies part of the problem. Tests have proved that with all of the lifters and bearings taking oil from this one gallery, the oil pressure can be as low as 15-

25psi/10-17kPa at the far end of end of the oil gallery while it is 60psi/54kPa at the front of the block. There are several worthwhile modifications that can be incorporated to improve things here, some obvious and some not quite so obvious.

Increasing oil pressure

If you're not going to fit the later crank-driven oil pump, then there are a number of modifications that can be carried out to improve the oil system on the pre-1994 and later 'Service' engines. As a starting point, a typical rebuilt Rover V8 engine, which has normal factory clearances, should have a range of oil pressures like this –

10psi/7kPa at 1000rpm
28psi/21kPa at 2000rpm
32psi/22kPa at 3000rpm
38psi/26kPa at 4000rpm
40psi/28kPa at 5000rpm

These are reasonable oil pressures for a standard road going Rover V8 engine, and are quite acceptable. However, in some instances the oil pressure readings are much lower: 3-5psi/2-4kPa at 1000rpm and 25-30psi/14-20kPa at 5000rpm plus, for example, being not uncommon. There are reasons for this very low oil pressure; the engine may not have been rebuilt to factory standards, it may be a well used with high mileage, or it may just be worn out but still running. Rebuilt engines with this amount of oil pressure don't necessarily fail, but something is not right, and incorrect running clearances are the most likely reason. Possible causes are a worn oil pump gear chamber, worn oil pump end cover, worn camshaft bearings, maximum tolerance, or over, main and big end bearing clearances, worn lifter bores, etc.

As a general rule, competition V8s of all types with pushrod valve operation are universally set with 8-10psi/5.5-6.9kPa of oil pressure for every 1000rpm of engine speed that is going to be used, with 10psi/6.9kPa being a much liked figure. Using 10psi/6.9kPa of oil pressure per 1000rpm on an engine that is revving at 6000rpm means having 60psi/42kPa of hot oil pressure, for example, and this is the **absolute maximum** reliable limit for the standard pre-1994 and 'Service' oil pump drive system. Any more than this and excessive, fast camshaft/distributor drive gear wear is inevitable, irrespective of how much oil is sprayed on to the two gears.

What the standard drive gears will stand is having the oil pressure relief valve modified so that the pump gives a maximum of 60psi/42kPa of oil pressure when the engine is hot and revving at 5000rpm plus. This can be achieved in two ways.

The first method is to fit the stronger pressure relief valve spring as used on the factory-built MGB V8s. They're no longer available from Rover, but specialist Rover V8 engine builders get them made to the original factory specification, so they are still available. Fitting one of these MGB-V8 type relief valve springs increases the oil pressure to 55psi/38kPa (up from 45psi/31kPa) and 25-30psi/17-21kPa at idle, provided that everything else in the oil system and engine is within specified standard tolerance. Fitting one of these MGB V8 springs involves removing the original spring and directly replacing it with a new spring, and takes about 5 minutes. **Caution!** – Don't forget to check that the valve seat and relief valve bore

is in good condition: not scored or damaged. The standard relief valve will likely stick or jam if the bore is scored and damaged, and the oil pressure won't be stable.

The second method involves taking the relief valve spring cap off the oil pump, drilling a hole in it and then tapping the drilling to take a 10mm x 1.25mm pitch bolt fitted with a locknut. This allows the oil pressure to be raised by reducing the spring's fitted height, and a standard, or an MGB V8 spring, can be used. With the engine hot, the bolt is screwed in until the required amount of oil pressure is being read at the gauge. With the bolt adjusted to the correct position, tighten the locknut. An alternative is to buy a Kenne Bell 'adjustable oil pressure regulator unit' which simply bolts on in place of the standard relief valve cap and does exactly the same thing. These are available from most Rover V8 engine specialists.

Caution! – Do not be tempted to increase the hot oil pressure beyond a maximum of 60psi/41kPa, otherwise increased distributor gear wear and camshaft drive gear wear will be the direct result. In any case, 60-70psi/42-48kPa is the limit for hydraulic lifters because of 'lifter pump-up'. You should also check the accuracy of the oil

Early gear pump endplate with a modified cap drilled and tapped to 10mm x 1.25mm, for the bolt and locking nut.

pressure gauge, either by comparing the readings with a known to be accurate gauge, or by getting the gauge calibrated at an instrument repairer.

Caution! – With the hot oil pressure set to 60psi/41kPa, the engine will have a very high cold oil pressure of about 100-120psi/69-83kPa. The use of high rpm with the oil cold will cause excessive wear of the camshaft/distributor drive gears, so when the engine is first started it must be allowed to idle at as low a speed as possible (1200-1800rpm) until the oil temperature starts to increase and the oil pressure starts to reduce. The racing fraternity get over this problem by pre-heating the oil in the sump, using a heat gun, before the engine is started. Heat guns need a mains electrical power supply but most race teams have a generator to run their pit equipment.

Oil pump

Early 1967-1976 oil pumps fitted to the P5, P6 and early Range Rover engines (1970-1976) are good enough for any road use, provided the engine has good standard bearing clearances. What can happen with the P5/P6/early Range Rover pumps is that the oil pressure falls because wear in the bearings, etc, increases the clearances, the pump cannot keep up with the demand for oil and maintain the pressure, and the pressure relief valve just remains shut. The later SD1/later Range Rover type oil pumps (1976-1993) have longer gears than the P5/P6/early Range Rover pumps (0.875in/22.2mm versus 1.045in/26.5mm) and, as a consequence, flow a higher volume, although the pressure relief valve is still set for the same overall pressure.

The tops of these gears are worn. They've worn because dirt particles/metal fragments have become embedded in the gear chamber housing, rubbing away at the tops of the gears.

The tooth flanks of the driving and driven gears wear against each other, as well as picking up dirt particles/metal fragments which adhere to the flanks of the teeth and wear away at the mating gear tooth flanks.

Any early P5/P6/early Range Rover engine can be fitted with the later SD1/Range Rover-type oil pump, provided the whole front cover assembly is changed over. An early engine being used for racing should either have the later, taller, SD1/Range Rover gear pump fitted, or have one of the 'tall gear' conversions fitted which are available for the pre-1976 engines. Better still, fit an 'interim' engine timing chain cover and crank-driven oil pump.

Just because it's pumping oil doesn't mean that an oil pump won't wear out. The oil filter is on

Gear chamber with score marks and particles embedded in the sides and base.

the delivery side of the pump, so un-filtered oil goes through an oil pump, taking with it all manner of small bits and pieces, fragments of steel and so on. Much of this debris doesn't leave the pump, but gets embedded in the aluminium of the oil pump housing or adheres to the teeth of the gears. It's this debris that causes the majority of wear in the oil pump components. The size and shape of the gears is critical to the pump's efficient operation, which is why used gears almost always have to be replaced. Excessive wear and scoring of the gear housing, and particularly the bottom end cover, also affects the pump's performance and hence the oil pressure. Making sure that the oil pump is to standard specification and in as new condition is a definite requirement: nothing less will really do. **Caution!** – Any engine used for racing needs to have the oil pump checked quite frequently for wear and tear; any unit that shows signs of wear being replaced immediately. Without the oil pump being in excellent condition, no Rover V8 engine will be reliable in the long term.

The standard gear-type oil pump housing is a maze of drilled oil holes and cast-in rectangular slots, all of which the oil has to pass through before it flows to the main oil gallery: hardly conducive to all-round oil pump efficiency. To maintain the maximum available oil pressure, every facet of the oil pump's condition should be kept as near to standard as possible. Brand new front covers and gears are the ideal, but new front covers are now hard to come by, so it means picking the best of the used ones. The gear chamber of the front cover is a key area to look at, and its condition largely depends on how clean the oil has been that has passed through it throughout the life of the engine. A visual inspection of the gear chamber will reveal its overall condition (diameter and depth of scoring, for example), and whether it is re-usable. If the front cover has a scored oil pump gear chamber, look for another one in a good serviceable condition. The clearance between the tops of the gears and the housing of an old well-used oil pump can be anything from 0.006-0.010in/0.15-0.25mm, depending on how many miles/km the engine has covered and the number of oil and filter changes the engine has had.

New, replacement oil pump gear sets are readily available, so if the gear chamber is within tolerance and free of scores, fit new gears into it and check the clearance between the tips of the gears and the sides of the housing. A new oil pump will have a clearance of 0.002in/0.05mm between the tips of the gears and the housing, which is ideal. Wear of a used gear housing has to be expected, and obtaining 'as new' clearances after fitting new gears to one is not realistic. A used timing cover with a slightly worn, but otherwise unmarked gear chamber, with new gears fitted to it, could have as little as 0.004-0.005in/0.1-0.125mm side clearance between the tips of the gear teeth and the gear chamber walls: at the very least twice the standard minimum clearance. This will cause the pressure to be down by about 2-3psi/1.8-2.1kPa on what it would be in with an all new pump.

With new oil pump gears in the timing cover, check the height of the gears above the aluminium surface of the gear chamber. The optimum distance is 0.0058in/0.15mm which, when subtracted from the 0.008in/0.20mm thickness of the oil pump gasket, means that the minimum endfloat (lash) will be 0.0022in/0.056mm. Clearly, the whole system relies on the correct thickness of gasket being used. End float of 0.005-0.010in/0.125-0.25mm, will cause a pressure loss of 2-3psi/1.8-2.1kPa. **Caution!** – No engine should ever be reassembled with old, worn, oil pump gears in it, and the pump should have the minimum endfloat.

The oil pump bottom cover is made of aluminium with an anodised facing to increase the wear resistance of the surface that's in contact with the oil pump gears. **Caution!** – A worn or scored oil pump cover surface can be remachined, but the surface **must** be

This oil pump's endplate has most of the anodised surface worn away where the two oil pump gears rotate against it, and is **not** reusable in this condition.

re-anodised afterwards to restore its wear resistance. The best solutions are to buy a new oil pump cover, or fit a nearly new unmarked one.

Another alternative is to buy a Kenne Bell 'oil pressure booster plate kit'. It's claimed that this plate increases the oil pressure by 4-7psi/2.7-4.8 kPa, but what it also does is to effectively restore the baseplate surface because the booster plate is sandwiched between the original baseplate and the original oil pump housing.

When an engine has been rebuilt and run-in, the oil pressures need to be recorded at 1000rpm when cold and hot, at 2000rpm when hot, at 3000rpm when hot and finally at 4000rpm when hot. **Caution!** – If these pressures start to drop over time, then inspect the oil pump immediately.

Pressure relief valve

Caution! – The pressure relief valve must be free to move in its bore or the oil pressure will not be regulated properly. If the relief valve jams in the open position the engine will have

low oil pressure or, worse still, none. What happens is that particles and fragments get lodged between the steel relief valve and the bore of the pump housing cover. It's a fairly easy task to remove the oil pump cover, and to inspect and clean the valve.

An alternative to using the standard relief valve is to use a 'tadpole'-type relief valve (available from J.E. Developments). This is a 'drop in' item and it allows a much larger flow across the relief valve, reduces the excessive cold oil pressure and gives steadier control of oil pressure. A drawback is that,

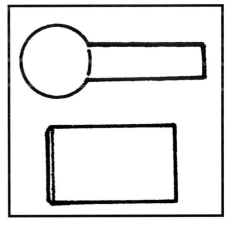

'Tadpole'-type relief valve (top) and the standard relief valve (bottom). The tail of the 'tadpole' fits in the relief valve spring.

unless great care is taken to seat it in the oil pump housing, there's a tendency for the oil to drain back into the sump. This means that the oil pump will require repacking with petroleum jelly or Wynns to prime the system. The problem is caused by contact between the radius of the 'tadpole' and the edge of the hole in the pump housing. To avoid the problem the 'tadpole' needs to be lapped into the housing using fine lapping paste (400 grit). An odd characteristic with a 'tadpole' is that the oil pressure will drop on initial opening of the valve and will need another 500-1000rpm to see it build back up.

Extra oiling of the distributor & camshaft skew gears

The alignment of the distributor spindle to the camshaft drive gear is preset by design and, provided it's properly assembled, this is never a problem. These drive gears, however, rely on splash lubrication, largely from the timing chain. The chain certainly moves a lot of oil up into the front of the engine, but not necessarily directly onto these gears. This is the one aspect of the design that can be improved by drilling a strategically placed 0.020-0.025in/0.50-0.60mm hole into the main oil gallery in the front cover. This small hole ensures that there is a jet of oil directed straight onto the two gears. However, it does **not** mean that these gears will not wear quickly if the oil pressure is increased: it just ensures that there is a good steady supply of oil to improve gear lubrication. **Caution!** – If the drive gears are not properly aligned, or if the oil pump has been adjusted to give over 60psi/42kPa, then no amount of oil being directed onto the gears can ever prevent them from wearing out quickly.

Although increasing the flow of oil to a certain area (in this case the oil pump/distributor drive skew gears) results in a slight loss of oil pressure (because it is effectively a leak in the system), it's still a good trade off as it improves the engine's overall reliability.

For road use, any further work should focus on reducing the losses possible in the original system by restricting the flow of oil to certain areas of the engine such as the rockershafts and, perhaps, the camshaft bearings; also not tweaking the pressure relief valve to give beyond 60psi/42kPa when hot.

Camshaft bearing modification

Each camshaft bearing receives its oil from the same oil hole that also feeds a main bearing and two connecting rod bearings on the crankshaft. The oil gallery design is such that the oil reaches the camshaft bearings before it gets to the main bearings and the connecting rod bearings.

There is a significant modification that can be made to replacement camshaft bearings, which reduces the amount of oil they receive. Camshaft bearings come with one oil feed hole in them which is about $3/16$in in diameter (4.76mm) diameter. New holes which are 0.060in/1.5mm in diameter can be drilled in the bearings **opposite** the existing holes (180 degrees away). The new camshaft bearings are installed in the block so that the new, smaller diameter holes line up with the oil gallery holes in the block and not the original larger feed holes. **Caution!** – the new, smaller oil feed holes **must** line up with the oil gallery holes which are feeding oil down to the main bearings.

The amount of oil that the reduced feed hole allows into each camshaft bearing is still sufficient, despite being reduced by about 60%. With the camshaft bearings now receiving a lesser amount of oil, more oil is directed to the main and connecting rod bearings, which is where it is needed most.

When the camshaft bearing surfaces get a bit worn through high valve spring pressure, the oil feed to the bearings is still controlled by the new smaller sized hole, whereas previously the greater the wear of the camshaft bearings the greater the flow of oil through them until the flow rate of the original hole size was reached.

Dual oil feed to the centre three main bearings

This is a modification for racing engines only which can be carried out when the engine is being built up, although generally it's done just after the block has been first cleaned and inspected to make sure that the block is sound and suitable to be rebuilt.

If you were to take an oil pressure reading from the end of the lifter gallery that feeds oil to the main bearings (left hand gallery when standing in front of the block) and a simultaneous reading from the oil pump, the two oil pressure readings would differ when the engine is run at high rpm. This is because of the pressure losses along the way to the back of the block where the second oil pressure reading was taken. The difference in the pressure readings will be normally be in the vicinity 8-15psi/5.5-10kPa, and the following enables it to be reduced to only 2-3psi/1.7-2kPa at all times.

It is a well-known fact that, on all V8 engines, the centre three main bearings are stressed more than the front and rear main bearings. On an engine that is going to be running constantly at high rpm, there is a distinct advantage in drilling the block so that the three centre main bearings are fed oil from **both** lifter galleries. When facing the front of the block, the lifter gallery on the left hand side feeds the camshaft bearings and the main bearings, as well as the connecting rod bearings. The lifter gallery on the right hand side normally only feeds the lifters on the right hand side of the block. **Caution!** – Only the centre three bearings can be drilled in this way because there is insufficient material in the block to drill similar holes for the front and rear main bearings.

Caution! – This work requires precision and is best done by an engineering company with a radial arm drill. The block can be clamped down on to the table of the machine and a skilled operator will virtually guarantee that the holes will be drilled in the right place.

After the three holes have been drilled, the block is then placed on a milling machine and a slot milled between the two holes of each of the three centre main caps. These should be $5/16$in/8mm wide by $1/2$in/13mm long and about $1/4$in/6.5mm deep at the shallowest point. It's possible to do this using a small hand-held die grinder; a dexterous engineer can do the work quite easily. Machining these troughs positively links each pair of two cross-drilled oil feed holes into a common chamber, which then feeds oil through the hole in the top of each bearing shell. The volume of oil available at the three centre bearings is greatly increased as the opposite side lifter gallery is now also feeding oil. The work is not particularly expensive to have done, but it has to be done accurately. Certainly any engine being used for racing purposes and which retains the original pre-1994-type oil pump should have this work done. Engines with crank-driven oil pumps, or a dry sump system, don't need this work as these designs can maintain uniform oil pressure throughout the oil system.

360 degree main bearing oiling

In standard form the big end bearings receive the vast majority of their oil during only 180 degrees of crankshaft rotation. This is because there is only a single oil feed groove in the upper main bearing shell, the bottom half bearing shell is plain. This oil feed design is an industry-wide practice, and provides quite sufficient lubrication for any engine running up to 6000rpm, but it is not always enough for a racing engine running to 7000-7500rpm.

The reason for using a plain bottom main bearing shell is that the load carrying capacity of the bearing is greater than that of a grooved bottom bearing shell. Having the groove in the bottom bearing shell reduces the load carrying capacity of the bearing by approximately 18%.

There are two ways that a standard crankshaft can be modified for 360 degree main bearing oiling, which also results in 360 degree connecting rod big end bearing lubrication. The first is to machine an identical groove into the plain bottom bearing shells. This is a complex task which requires a jig to hold the plain bearing shell: in fact, it's never done these days because of the complexity of the work and the fact that the load carrying capacity of the main bearings is reduced. 'Fully grooved' main bearing shells were available for some USA V8s, but you don't see these bearing sets much these days and, if you do, they're always old stock. The reason why you don't see this kind of bearing shell in regular use on racing engines these days is because there is now a better way of achieving improved oiling without any loss of load carrying capacity.

The second method of achieving 360 degree connecting rod bearing oiling is to groove the five main bearing journals of the crankshaft. This work is done in a lathe using a radius-edged form tool. The end result is a groove in the main bearing journals that is 0.175in/4.5mm wide and a maximum of 0.060in/1.5mm deep. The finished groove is a mirror image of the groove in the top main bearing shell. The groove must be highly finished to the same standard as the main bearing journal surface to prevent crack initiation in the surface. The radius in each of the two corners of each groove is 0.060in/1.5mm. The corner so formed on the journal surface is also radiused with a small 0.010in/0.25mm radius. It takes careful work to do all of this, but once done it only requires a standard set of main bearing shells at each rebuild. Although the crankshaft is not significantly weakened through being grooved, it does reduce the load carrying capacity of the main bearing journals because the effective bearing width is reduced. As with grooving of the bearing shells, grooving the main bearing journals is seldom seen these days because there is now a better way of improving the supply of oil to the big ends (see the following section).

CRANKSHAFT BEARING CLEARANCES

Crankshaft bearings need the correct clearance to perform properly, but the clearance shouldn't be excessive. **Caution!** – Don't run one of these engines with more than 0.0025in/0.065mm main bearing clearance, or more than 0.0022in/0.055mm big end bearing clearance. Less than this is preferred, such as 0.0022in/0.056mm for the main bearings and 0.0018in/0.044mm for the big end bearings. Keep the endfloat of the crankshaft at the minimum specified factory size of 0.003-0.004in/0.075-0.10mm. Grinding more side clearance between the connecting rods over the maximum standard recommended amount is not necessary, or desirable. You should be able to get a 0.010in/0.25mm feeler gauge between the connecting rods when fitted to the big end journals, and certainly not more than a 0.012in/0.30mm thick feeler gauge.

LIFTER TO LIFTER BORE FIT

The lifter bores wear out in the block and can be a considerable source of oil leakage when the clearance between the lifters and their bores is excessive. When new, the clearance is approximately 0.0008in/0.02mm to 0.001in/0.025mm (maximum 0.0015in/0.038mm). The lifter bores can wear quite markedly so that, when the engine block is at ambient temperature, the clearance can be as much as 0.0015in/0.038mm, or even slightly more. This is quite a lot of clearance because, when the engine's up to normal operating temperature, the aluminium of the block will have expanded more than the steel lifter, and it's possible to end up with a working clearance of 0.002in/0.05mm or more. Aluminium has a coefficient of expansion nearly twice that of steel.

If you can fit a 0.003in/0.075mm feeler gauge between the lifter and the lifter bore, then the block is really too worn for further use, and there is no cheap fix. The good news is that most blocks won't be found in this condition. If you're faced with excessive bore wear, then finding another block with minimum specification lifter to lifter bore clearance is the cheaper solution. A not too expensive option is to have the lifter bores bored and sleeved back to minimum specification. Wildcat Engineering does this to its own racing blocks and has all of the facilities to do it for customers.

ADJUSTABLE OIL PRESSURE RELIEF VALVE: CRANK-DRIVEN OIL PUMPS

The standard oil pressure relief valves (as fitted into 'interim' engine front covers from January 1994 on and '38A' 4.0 & 4.6 litre engines from late 1994 until 2004) deliver approximately 45psi/31 kPa of oil pressure.

Wildcat has offered adjustable relief valves since the 'interim' 3.9 & 4.2 litre engines were introduced. The kit comprises a set of duplex springs and a new end cap that fits into the front cover. Integral with this new end cap is a screwdriver slotted spindle and locking nut system which is used to increase or decrease the compression of the two relief springs.

Caution! – Modified engines fitted with crank-driven oil pumps should have 8 to 10psi/5.5 to 6.9kPa of oil pressure per 1000rpm of max engine speed –
5000rpm: 40-50psi/27-34kPa
6000rpm: 48-60psi/33-41kPa
7000rpm: 56-70psi/38-48kPa

To adjust the oil pressure the locknut is undone, a screwdriver used to either wind the spindle in or out and the locknut done up again once the desired oil pressure requirement is met. The oil pressure is adjustable from 45 to 70psi/31-48kPa which is enough for any application. **Caution!** – always use an accurate oil pressure gauge of known integrity. It's a common misconception that these gauges always remain accurate irrespective of what treatment they receive: this just isn't so and disastrous errors can be made!

IMPROVED MAIN & BIG END BEARING OILING (ALL ENGINES WITH STANDARD CRANKSHAFT OILWAYS)

260-270 degree main bearing oiling

This is a very good compromise that doesn't require too much reworking of a standard set of main bearing shells. It yields 260-270 degree oiling, as opposed to the standard 180 but without the reduction in load carrying capacity of a 360 degree-type oiling modification. Engine builders have been modifying standard bearing shells for years to create this feature and many bearing replacement companies now make this sort of bearing shell for racing use.

The current method of 260-270 degree oiling is widely accepted as being the way to go with any standard oilway crankshaft. In recent years various well known bearing companies have developed main bearing shells for competition purposes which have a couple of interesting features.

Firstly, the bearings look old at first glance, even when they're brand new, and this is because of their

ACL HP competition bearings offering 260-270 degree oiling. In spite of the 'discolouration' you see because of the lack of tin-plating, the bearings shown are new.

The length of the slots in each of the shells is easy to see. The centre portion of the bearing is plain (80-90 degrees worth) so still has good load bearing characteristics.

surface colouring. This is misleading because the only difference is that they have not been tin-plated (bearing shells have been tin-plated for the past 50 odd years). The heat transfer of the bearing shells is improved by leaving out the tin plating process because it's one less barrier to heat dissipation.

Secondly, the bottom half shells have partial grooves running down each side from the parting line, a feature which effectively extends the groove in the top bearing shell by 0.75in/20mm on each side. The increase in oiling period to the big ends is significant, so these bearing shells are well worth having.

Wildcat Engineering, for example, supplies this type of racing bearing, based upon Australian-made ACL HP triple metal bearings which are, in fact, Holden V6 main bearing shells (Buick 300 size). It buys in several sets of V6 main bearings and makes up full sets to suit the Rover V8. The blocks have to be line bored to suit these main bearings as they require an approximately 0.007in/0.175mm larger main bearing tunnel size, compared to the standard '38A' main bearing tunnel bore size. This may sound like a major rigmarole to get a good competition bearing, but

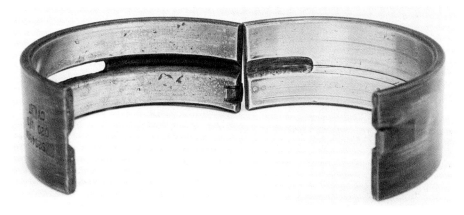

Main bearing shell on the left is the standard upper shell, which fits into the block. The one on the right is a standard plain bottom shell which has had two short grooves cut into it by hand, extending the oil grooving by 0.75in/19mm each side.

it's a one off machining operation, the ACL Holden HP bearings are readily available and are likely to be so for a very long time, and at reasonable cost. Suitably modified engines have 260-270 degree oiling **and** premium quality racing shells. This system has been in very common use since about 1990. Wildcat Engineering crankshafts are not cross-drilled, they retain the standard configuration.

Altering standard bottom main bearing shells

Standard Rover V8 bearing shells can be altered to 260-270 degree specification using a small die

grinder fitted with a 1/8in/3mm ball-nosed rotary file. There's no need to make the slots longer than 0.75in/19mm and, if you do, the load carrying capacity of the bearing starts to be compromised. A neat enough job can be made of modifying the plain bottom bearing shells by someone who is reasonably dexterous, the material being removed is, of course, quite soft.

This method of improving the oiling to the big ends is for **all** crankshafts with standard oilways, as opposed to cross-drilled cranks. It isn't necessary to use these extended groove types of bearing shell with a cross-drilled crankshaft.

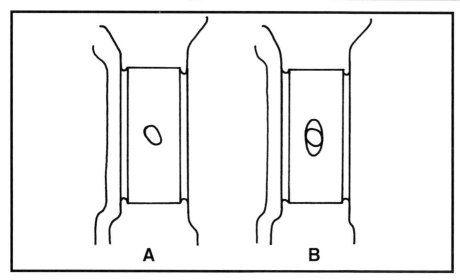

Oil holes in the main bearings of the crankshaft come standard as shown at 'A'. Altered shape 'B' is for improved oiling to the connecting rods.

Big end bearing oiling improvement summary

Any road going application can retain the standard main bearing arrangement in conjunction with a crankshaft with standard oilways. However, for racing purposes there are a few choices.

John Eales of J.E. Developments cross-drills the crankshafts (starting from a raw crankshaft casting. 360 degree big end bearing oiling is achieved. The standard type bearings (Vandervell VP material) are then very acceptable for racing purposes.

Ian Richardson of Wildcat Engineering uses forged and cast crankshafts with conventional Rover V8 oilway drillings, but with Australian-made ACL bearings. These bearings have extend slots in the lower shell which increases the big end bearing oiling period to 270-280 degrees which has proven to be sufficient.

Any standard set of replacement Rover V8 bottom bearing shells can be modified to extend the oiling period by anyone with the dexterity to do it, or an engineering workshop could be contracted. The oil outlets in the shell are extend by cutting a small groove using a small hand held die-grinder with a small diameter rotary file fitted. This modification will give any engine a 270-280 degree big end bearing oiling period.

Radiusing crankshaft oilways

The oil holes in the crankshaft main bearing journals and big end journals can be radiused so that sharp edges are made smooth, or they can be reshaped to be oval using a die grinder (as shown in the diagram at 'B'). **Caution!** – Dexterity and confidence is required to do this as it is easy to make a mistake and grind into the journal surface. The radiusing of these holes is usually done before the crankshaft is reground but if it isn't being reground great care is needed to ensure that the journal surfaces aren't marked

through the grinding wheel slipping.

Within reason each oilway exit slot should be as long as possible, but don't over do it. About $^7/_{16}$in/ 11mm long is about right, and the width of the original drilling should not be increased anymore than is necessary to put a small radius on it. **Caution!** – If you go too far, the load carrying capacity of the bearing starts to get reduced.

Lengthening the oilway exit aperture has the effect of increasing the duration of oil supply to the big ends. (The effective interruption of the oil flow to the big ends is from just before where the trailing edge of the hole in the crankshaft main bearing passes the end of the oil groove on one side of the bearing shell, until the leading edge of the hole in the crankshaft lines up with the end of the oil groove on the other side of the bottom main bearing shell.)

The oil holes of the big end journals only need to be radiused so that there isn't a sharp edge where the hole meets the journal's surface. These holes can have the same basic treatment as the main bearing journals if you want to go to the trouble of doing it (many do) but, normally, placing an approximate 0.020in/0.5mm radius all the way around the edge of the hole is all that is needed.

RESTRICTING ROCKERSHAFT OIL FEED (ALL ENGINES)

There is a $^3/_{16}$ in diameter (0.1875in/ 4.76mm) hole feeding oil to each of the two rockershafts, with the result that they can be swamped with more oil than they need, especially in a high revving engine. Restricting the amount of oil that goes to the

Standard oilflow path to the big ends is represented by the dotted area. The oiling is uninterrupted for approximately 180-190 degrees, as indicated by the length of the arc.

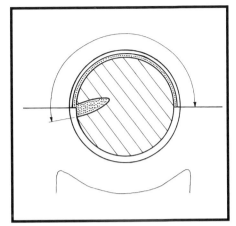

Non-standard oilflow path to the big ends is represented by the dotted area. The oiling is uninterrupted for approximately 250-260 degrees, as indicated by the length of the arc.

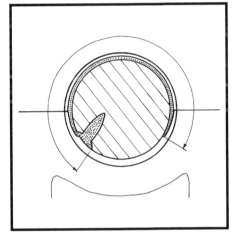

engineering works will drill holes through two high tensile steel grub screws in about five minutes, or you can do it yourself with a pistol drill/pedestal drill if you take care not to turn the drill too fast or put too much pressure on the drill and break it. **Caution!** – The grub screws **must** be screwed into the holes so that they are **below the block's deck,** to avoid touching the cylinder head when it's tightened down on to the block, 1/16in (0.0625in/1.5mm) below the block's deck surface is about right. Just screw them in tightly with an Allen key to a reasonable tension. They can't go anywhere as they are trapped but screw them in reasonably tightly anyway. This operation should only be done when the engine is being rebuilt so that any swarf from the tapping process can be removed from the oilways in the block.

The second method, which achieves the same result, is to tap the oil feed hole that's actually used in each cylinder head, and then install a grub screw with a 0.035-0.040in/0.75-1.0mm diameter hole drilled through the centre. This does mean that the cylinder heads will be left or right hand fitting (unless both of the holes in each cylinder head are tapped). **Caution!** – If you do use this method, clearly mark the cylinder heads as being left or right hand fitting.

While restricting the oil flow to the cylinder heads in this manner is certainly enough to give an overall increase in oil pressure, it's not usually enough on its own for a racing engine.

WET SUMP (OIL PAN)

All standard Rover V8 engines have a wet sump (oil pan) and for the

rockershafts still provides enough for their lubrication, but generally results in a uniform increase in hot oil pressure of about 5psi/3.5kPa (if the oil temperature is kept to a reasonable level, 75-85 degrees C/165-185F maximum).

There are two oil feed drillings for the rockershaft in each cylinder head, but only one of them is used. This is because the cylinder heads are not handed and are, therefore, drilled for left hand or right hand fitting. The single oil feed hole going to each cylinder head exits from the cylinder head underneath the front rockershaft pedestal, and then feeds up through the centre of each

pedestal which has the 3/8in securing bolt going through the middle of it and into the rockershaft (the oil feeds up to the rockershaft between the outside diameter of the bolt and the hole drilled in the rocker pedestal).

Restricting the oil flow to the rocker shafts can be done in two ways.

The first method is to tap the two 3/16in diameter (0.1875in/4.76mm) oil gallery holes in the block which feed oil to the rocker shafts with a 1/4in UNC or 6mm course thread. Then fit a grub screw – which has had a 0.035-0.040in/0.75-1.0mm diameter hole drilled through the centre – into each tapped hole. An original road going application this design is perfectly adequate. There have been four basic sump types –

P5 & P6-type
Range Rover-type
SD1-type
HSE-type

As soon as Rover V8 engines started to be modified and used in racing applications problems with oil starvation in turns and sweeping bends became apparent; problems were cured or reduced by enlarging sump reservoirs and fitting internal baffling. All sorts of ideas have been tried to cure the problem of oil starvation which occurs when the oil pickup is no longer submerged and air is drawn into the oil system. However, over the years, as speeds have increased and tyre adhesion has improved, the 'G' forces encountered during racing have meant that ensuring adequate oil is available at the oil pickup at all times has become more and more difficult. The dry sump is the cure for this problem, but the comparative cost is high and, in many cases, a dry sump is not really needed.

Today the procedure for creating an effective wet sump has been narrowed down to one basic configuration. The best way to obtain one of these modified sumps is from a Rover V8 specialist company. The vast majority of Rover V8 specialists alter a standard Range Rover sump because it has the largest capacity and is made of thicker material which makes it more resistant to impact damage and subsequent leakage.

The design configuration used has baffles fitted into the reservoir of the sump and a pre-formed steel plate mig welded across the top of the reservoir part of the sump at approximately full oil level height. With this steel plate in place, the sump of the reservoir is effectively sealed around the edges and returning oil gets back down to the pickup by going in through the hole in the centre of the plate and via the longitudinal drains. What this plate does is prevent the rapid movement of oil away from the pickup during quick hard cornering or when negotiating a long sweeping bend at high speed.

One problem which has cropped up with the Range Rover sumps is the fact that the right hand threaded sump plug is on the left hand side of the sump reservoir. If the base of the sump is grounded, the forces involved are in the right direction to undo the sump plug! This has happened on numerous occasions and engines have failed because of it. Extra strong locking wiring is required (1/8in diameter) or a pin location method.

There is a limit to the effectiveness of this type of modification because of its design of central hole and central channel drain for returning oil, but for the vast majority of applications it works very well. However, there comes a time in certain wet sump applications where an amount of drain back is required at the sides of the sump to avoid oil starvation problems. **Caution!** – Anyone using a Rover V8 engine in a form of motorsport featuring long sweeping curves, needs to be aware of the fact that it isn't impossible for the pick-up to suck on air with some sump and pick-up designs. In a long sweeping bend a huge amount of oil can be held out of circulation by centrifugal force, yet the engine's oil pump will continue to draw oil from the reservoir until it is no longer immersed. In effect, the reservoir will run dry and, when it does, the bearings will not receive oil at full pressure as air enters the oiling system. Serious engine damage is always the result.

With the advent of the fitting of Rover V8s into low-slung sports cars/kit cars, such as Westfields, which require the engine to be as low in overall height as possible, the depth of wet sumps has been taken to its logical minimum at 1in/25mm shallower than the standard Range Rover item. As a result of this requirement, Rover V8 specialists make the reservoir section of the sump full engine length (to hold a similar total amount of oil as a standard Range Rover sump): the base of the sump reservoir is exactly level with the bottom of the bellhousing. There is no point whatsoever in making the base of the sump shallower than this because the bellhousing then sticks out below it.

It isn't impossible in some engine installations to be able to increase the depth of the sump and pickup by 3in/75mm (a boat installation for example or, perhaps, some types of off road vehicles). The oil level can then be lowered by 1-1½in/25-37mm (re-mark the dipstick).

While the oil will be able to climb the side of the sump and to a certain extent the block, the fact that the general oil level is lower will tend to keep it well away from the rotating crankshaft (so it won't get flung around the crankcase). In such cases a baffle/windage tray is still used (mig welded or bolted into place) but 1-1½in/25-37mm lower than it otherwise would be.

Caution! – Note that if major

alterations are going to be made to a standard type sump, always bolt the sump on to a block before mig welding to prevent distortion. If you don't do this the result will almost certainly be a sump that does not bolt to the block correctly.

CRANKCASE VENTILATION

In the majority of instances all that is required to vent a Rover V8 engine is to run a ⅝in (15.87mm) inside diameter pipe from a stub on each rocker cover to a catch tank which has good ventilation to atmosphere. **Caution!** – The take off point on the valve cover should be between rocker arms, not in line with one (if it is, a baffle plate may have to be fitted in the rocker cover) to avoid oil being 'pumped' into the piping.

Chapter 9
J.E. Developments
& other specialists

J.E. DEVELOPMENTS

Telephone (UK) [0]1455-202-909
E-mail <john@ealesxx.fsnet.co.uk>
www.rover-V8.com
J.E. Developments, Claybrooke
Mill, Frolesworth Lane, Claybrooke
Magna. Nr. Lutterworth, LE17 5DB,
England.

J.E. Developments is run by John
Eales who's had an interest in
the Rover V8 engine since the
late 1960s, and who has huge
experience of working on this unit.

The company modifies original
Rover parts and commissions
production of components like
connecting rods and rocker arms.

This chapter describes the
specifications of the replacement
and modified components/
assemblies available from J.E.
Developments to guide you in your
choice of engine specification for
your particular application.

CYLINDER BLOCKS

J.E. Developments uses the
standard and standard oversize bore
diameters in conjunction with the
standard liners in virtually all of the
engines it builds. John Eales prefers
to use the later cross-bolted blocks
for all applications. The bores used
are standard, plus 0.020in/0.5mm or
plus 0.040in/1.0mm, that is –
Small bore blocks: 3.500in/
88.90mm to 3.540in/90.00mm
Large bore blocks: 3.702in/
94.00mm to 3.722in/94.50mm

For racing purposes, where a
3.5 litre engine block is to be used
and 3.500-3.540in/88.9-89.9mm
bore size retained, readers need
to be aware of the fact that the 3.5
litre 90, 110, 130 Land Rover and
3.5 litre engine 'Service' units made
in 1995 and 1997/1998 used the
later cross-bolted (X-bolted) blocks
without the cross-bolt drilling work
being completed by the factory.

Westfield sportscar with J. E.
Developments engine.

These blocks have the original
small diameter main bearing sizes
of 2.300in/58.40mm and not the

later main bearing size of 2.500in/ 63.45mm as found in 4.0 and 4.6 litre 1994 and later '38A' units. All that has to be done to make these blocks true cross-bolted four bolt main cap units is to drill and tap the holes and fit the extra bolts. Brand new blocks that have been reworked like this are available from the likes of J.E. Developments.

This block is the strongest of the standard built 3.5 litre units. It has the thicker liners of the original 3.5 engine and the original thickness aluminium walls behind the liner and, once drilled and tapped, is a cross-bolted block in terms of maximum bottom end strength and stability. An 'interim' 3.9 and 4.2 litre engine's front timing chain cover with its crank-driven oil pump can also be fitted. The 3.5 litre 'Service' engines were not equipped with the 'interim'-type front cover assembly because they were mainly made for military replacement use (all previous Rover V8 engines had the early type front cover so they continued with them to maintain uniformity).

Note that these 3.5 litre 'Service' engines have a 'liner dropping down' problem, which results in a near 100% failure rate, even in normal road going service. This situation means that the fitting of flanged liners is recommended for all applications so that the potential problems are removed before the engine has even fired. Please refer to Chapter One for details of these particular blocks and flanged liners.

Caution! – The use of the cross-bolted block is really essential for reliability for any 3.5 litre race engine revving to 7500rpm on a continuous and frequent basis. This block type removes the bottom end block problems (main cap to block fretting)

associated with two-bolt mains.

Note that, nowadays, all older blocks rebuilt by J.E. Developments are converted to thrust plate camshaft retention using genuine Rover componentry: in the past the company used a Teflon thrust bolt/Teflon button system, which it machined itself. Today, and since 1996, Rover has also offered a Teflon thrust bolt and spacer kit (part number STC 3620K) to prevent the camshaft moving forwards in the block.

CRANKSHAFTS

All J.E. Developments competition engines use standard Rover cast iron crankshafts or, to give the material its correct name 'nodular iron' or 'spheroidal graphite iron' ('SG iron'). Nodular iron is a modified form of grey cast iron. Grey cast iron has a tensile strength of 20,000psi/138N/mm, but with the impregnation, while in its molten state, of nickel, magnesium or cerium bearing alloys, the structure is altered and the tensile strength factor increases to approximately 60,000psi/413N/mm. This increase in tensile strength is achieved without making the material any more difficult to machine which is a real advantage as far as engine manufacturers are concerned. Another advantage of cast iron/ nodular iron is its natural damping characteristic.

Cast crankshafts are used by J.E. Developments because they are cheaper and easier to make than forgings and, for all of the relevant applications, they're quite strong enough. Cast cranks don't break in racing engines revving to 7000rpm, the general maximum J.E. Developments recommends for its

engines. This rev limit is not imposed because the crankshaft's a limiting factor either, the valve train is the real limitation.

The cast crankshafts used by J.E. Developments are purchased from Rover as rough crankshaft castings which are then machined by an outside contractor. Starting with a raw casting means that the crank throw (and therefore the stroke) can be ground to any specific size within the original crankshaft casting's limitations and, vitally, the oiling drillings can also be made as required without having to take the original factory drillings into consideration. This means that strokes from 2.482in/63.0mm to 3.603in/91.5mm are possible, with all custom machined cross-drilled crankshafts having a 2.000in/ 50.8mm big end journal size.

John Eales built one experimental engine fitted with a 3.780inch/96.0mm stroke crankshaft engine many years ago, but found the engine harsh and so discontinued the research into engines with strokes longer than 3.603in/91.5mm.

J.E. Developments supplies cast crankshafts (all with 2.000in/50.8mm crankpins/big end journals) with the following strokes, the choice of main bearing journal diameter depending on the block being used –

Crankshaft strokes:
2.482in/63.00mm
2.800in/71.12mm
3.030in/77.00mm
3.125in/79.40mm
3.150in/80.00mm
3.230in/82.00mm
3.400in/86.30mm
3.540in/89.90mm
3.605in/91.50mm

J.E. Developments can also offset grind a standard factory-ground 82mm stroke 4.6 litre engine's crankshaft so that the stroke is increased to 3.400in/86.3mm (the original oiling system drillings remaining as per standard). During this process the crankpin diameter is reduced from the standard size of 2.185in/55.5mm to 2.000in/50.8mm. John Eales does not consider this variation of the standard crankshaft to be as good as his cross-drilled versions and the conversion requires the fitting of alternative connecting rods to suit the smaller big end journal size. However, engine capacity is increased from the 4.6 litres (4552cc) to 4.8 litres (4795cc) by this process.

All J.E. Developments cast crankshafts destined for competition engines are cross-drilled in the big ends and mains (a drilling straight through each journal). All of these through drillings are interlinked by strategically drilled axial, angled drillings. (This is the way that the highly successful Coventry Climax FWMV 1.5 litre V8 Formula One Grand Prix racing engine's dual plane crankshafts were made between 1961 and 1963.) Many V8 engines have been drilled this way in past years, especially racing versions of stock block engines such as the 'heavy duty' High Performance Ford 289s of the mid-1960s and the Boss 302 small block Ford V8 engine of the late 1960s, for example. Even the road going version of these Boss 302 engine had a forged cross-drilled crankshaft in 1969. Today, in the UK, this cross-drilling is commonly referred to as being machined 'BDA-style' after the way the 1600cc in-line four cylinder Ford BDA engine's racing crankshafts were machined in the mid-1960s. This is all well tried and tested technology, although you seldom see it on cast crankshafts.

On J.E. Developments' cross-drilled competition engine crankshafts, oil enters the crankshaft via two, or three, drillings in each of the five main bearing journals in the usual manner, which is through the feed hole in the upper bearing shell inserts. The three centre main bearing journals have an extra drilling at 90 degrees to the through drilling to allow maximum continuous oil flow to the centre of the crankshaft.

With the crankshaft drilled in this manner, oil that is fed into the front main bearing journal holes can, theoretically, reach the rear main bearing journal. The lower main cap shells are plain. This crankshaft oiling configuration is extremely good.

J.E. Developments uses Vandervell VP2 (or Clevite 77) lead indium main and big end bearings in all of its competition engines. It doesn't use, or recommend the use of, the harder 'rectilinear tin bearings' that are available. These Vandervell bearing shells are essentially standard replacements and they are also available from J.E. Developments in 0.010inch undersizes for large main bearing 1994 late model blocks.

Connecting rods

J.E. Developments competition engines are fitted with one of two sizes of connecting rod that it has forged and machined. Both have the same big end bearing diameter at 2.000in/50.8mm and the standard gudgeon pin diameter too. The centre to centre lengths of the two different rods are 5.700in/144.8mm (0.040in/1.0mm longer

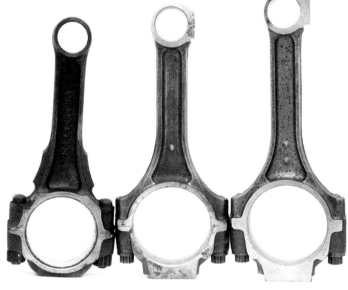

Conrod comparison: 3.5, 3.9 and 4.2 litre left, 4.6 litre centre, 4.0 litre right.

than the stock early length) for the shorter ones and 6.000in/152.45mm for the longer ones. The reason for making the shorter connecting rods 0.040in/1.0mm longer than standard is to bring the piston crowns up flush with the top of the block deck. This increases the compression ratio

Left: J.E. Developments' custom-made connecting rod. These connecting rods use standard late model 4.0 and 4.6 litre connecting rod bolts.

without having to plane the block, it also increases the connecting rod to stroke ratio slightly. The standard engine's piston crowns are on average 0.040in down the bore from the deck at TDC.

SPECIAL CAPACITIES FOR RACING APPLICATIONS

There are racing classes in which these engines are limited to 3.5 litres capacity. It might seem logical to use the 3.500in/88.9mm bore block in these circumstances, but that isn't necessarily so. To take advantage of the larger valve sizes afforded by using a 3.702in/94mm bore block, what can be done is to use a 'red'-graded cross-bolted '38A' engine block and fit a specially machined 2.482in/63mm stroke, cross-drilled cast iron crankshaft. The cylinder liners are rebored to 0.020in/0.5mm oversize giving a bore of 3.722in/94.54mm which, in combination with a crankshaft with a 2.482inch/63mm stroke, results in an engine capacity of 3498cc. That's a reduction in stroke over the 3.5 litre engine of 0.320in/8.1mm (2.800in/71.1mm down to 2.480in/62.95mm).

The (standard material) connecting rods used are 5.700inch/144.8mm centre to centre distance

Standard-type high strength piston made for J.E. Developments by Omega.

3.702-3.722in/94.0-94.5mm diameter Omega forged piston made to J.E. Developments' specifications.

Omega 'full skirted' forged piston.

ones which suit the stock-type cast replacement pistons made by Omega for J.E. Developments for this application. The connecting rod to stroke ratio is, in this instance, 2.3.

All other engine applications use the standard Rover-manufactured connecting rods, with which John Eales reports no problems (all three types).

Using this method, the crowns of the pistons are flush with the top of the block's deck without the top of the block having to be machined down. The chosen pistons having the gudgeon pin to top of piston dimension making up the difference needed to get the piston crown flush with the top of the block.

As cast aluminium pistons are also a requirement of the class rules, the pistons used in these engines are much the same as the full skirted standard cast pistons. A difference is that the skirt is tied into the crown of the piston better because there is no oil grove slot, rather drillings for the oil to drain through to the underside of the piston (just like a forged piston). This is Omega's high strength version of a replacement standard cast piston which is made exclusively for J.E. Developments to its specifications. These pistons in this combination have proven to be reliable to 7500rpm.

For these 3.5 litre specials, the cast nodular iron crankshaft starts out as a standard raw casting which is custom machined to suit and is suitable for use up to 7500rpm with near guaranteed reliability. The big end journals are made 2.000in/50.80mm in diameter (standard pre-1994 size) which keeps the 'bearing speed' down, as well as still being strong enough. Main bearing journal diameter is 2.500in/63.5mm which is what all '38A' cross-bolted blocks require. The chosen bore size allows the use of the largest valves J.E. Developments uses in its racing cylinder heads. That's the valves in one basic 'top of the range,' fully modified from standard cylinder head fitted to all of J.E. Developments' 3.702 to 3.722in/94.0 to 94.5mm bore competition engines, irrespective of crankshaft stroke. A WL3 mechanical (non-hydraulic lifter) racing camshaft is used, as are J.E. Developments-made forged steel rocker arms with a special rockershaft arrangement.

Class rules require the use of the original twin SU carburettors and inlet manifold which does tend to limit power but, nevertheless, these engines perform extremely well.

Other racing engine capacities

All other cross-bolted large journal crankshaft racing engines made by J.E. Developments use one of the two connecting rods J.E. Developments has made for them. The rods are used in combination with a range of stroked crankshafts, all machined from raw crankshaft castings bought from Rover. A range of custom piston compression height sizes are used in conjunction with the various strokes and the two connecting rod lengths. The following are the bore/stroke combinations available from J.E. Developments –

Standard bore size 1994 and later cross-bolted blocks –
3.702in/94.0mm bore x 2.800in/ 71.12mm stroke = 3948cc
3.702in/94.0mm bore x 3.033in/ 77.0mm stroke = 4275cc
3.702in/94.0mm bore x 3.150in/ 80.0mm stroke = 4441cc
3.702in/94.0mm bore x 3.230in/ 82.0mm stroke = 4552cc
3.702in/94.0mm bore x 3.400in/ 86.3mm stroke = 4795cc
3.702in/94.0mm bore x 3.540in/ 90.0mm stroke = 4997cc
3.702in/94.0mm bore x 3.605in/ 91.5mm stroke = 5080cc

0.020in/0.5mm oversize 1994 and later cross-bolted blocks –
3.722in/94.5mm bore x 2.800in/ 71.12mm stroke =3991cc
3.722in/94.5mm bore x 3.033in/ 77.0mm stroke = 4320cc
3.722in/94.5mm bore x 3.150in/ 80.0mm stroke = 4488cc
3.722in/94.5mm bore x 3.230in/ 82.0mm stroke = 4601cc
3.722in/94.5mm bore x 3.400in/ 86.3mm stroke = 4845cc
3.722in/94.5mm bore x 3.540in/ 90.0mm stroke = 5049cc
3.722in/94.5mm bore x 3.605in/ 91.5mm stroke = 5134cc

CYLINDER HEADS

J.E. Developments uses modified standard Rover V8 cylinder heads for the engines that it builds for customers and these follow fairly straightforward criteria.

The heads use four types of inlet valve and four types of exhaust valve. There are two valve stem diameters and two types of collet grooving for two types of collet (the standard Rover made collets and Ford Pinto ones). All valves are the standard length.

Valve set 1

The first pair of inlet and exhaust valves for fast road use or competition purposes J.E. Developments has manufactured are for the earlier P5/P6-type cylinder heads. Valve head sizes for the inlets are 1.500in/38mm in diameter, while exhausts are 1.350in/33mm. The standard valve seat insert outside diameter sizes limit the valve head sizes to standard.These valves are standard overall dimensionally, but much smoother shaped around the head of the valve and a similar shape to J.E. Developments' other racing valves. Valve seat widths are 0.040 to 0.050in/1.0 to 1.25mm (both valves). The inlet valves have waisted stems and weigh 78gm. The exhaust valves do not have waisted valve stems and weigh 71gm. Both valves have 0.343in/8.72mm diameter valve stems, are made from 214NN and use the standard collets.

Valve set 2

There are two inlet and two exhaust valves used by J.E. Developments in SD1 and later modified road going engine cylinder heads. All 3.500in/88.9mm bore road going engines use the standard SD1 inlet and exhaust valve head size, while 3.702in/94.0mm bore road going engines can larger valves. The larger inlet and exhaust valves J.E. Developments uses are bought in and are what John Eales terms 'medium valves'. The head diameter of the inlet valves is 1.625in/41.25mm, exhausts 1.400in/35.5mm. Both have waisted valve stems, 0.343in/84.72mm valve stem diameters and use standard collets. The inlet valves weigh 89gm, exhausts 79gm. These are the largest head diameter valves that the standard valve seat inserts can accommodate.

Valve set 3

Another set of valves that J.E. Developments uses for SD1 and

Medium-sized inlet valve (left) and medium-sized exhaust valve, as available from Real Steel.

The racing valves use different collets (keepers) because of the fact that the original Rover V8 engine valves and collets have square edged grooves in the valve stems, but John Eales decided that round grooves were more desirable (less prone to fracture). Therefore, Ford Pinto triple groove keepers (inexpensive and strong) are used in conjunction with valve spring retainers made in steel and aluminium to suit the Ford collets' taper locking angle. The undersides of the special valve spring retainers are designed to fit standard-sized single valve springs and dual valve springs that J.E. Developments has made. These retainers are identical in size and are interchangeable.

The grooves machined in the valves are not to original Ford dimensions, but are machined for a tight collet to valve stem groove fit. This means that instead of the valve stems being able to spin freely when the collets and valve spring retainer is fitted via the normal 0.002-0.003in/0.05-0.075mm clearance fit, in this application there is no clearance whatsoever (instead a locking fit prevents 'flogging out' of the grooves of the valve stem). These valves, being standard head sized, are used in conjunction with the original valve seat inserts which are re-cut/reshaped.

Valve set 4

The largest racing valves that J.E. Developments has made are similar to the previously mentioned racing valves, but have larger head sizes: inlets 1.700in/43.2mm diameter, exhausts 1.500in/37.0mm. Inlet valves weigh 90gm and exhausts 80gm. The inlet valves have waisted valve stems, the exhausts do not.

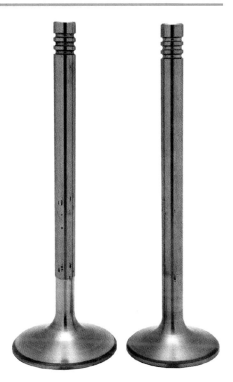

J.E. Developments' standard SD1-sized racing valves with 0.312in/7.92mm diameter valve stems and Ford Pinto type collet grooves. 1.575in/40mm diameter inlet valve on the left, 1.375in/34.9mm exhaust on the right.

These valves use the same Ford Pinto collet (keeper) arrangement as previously described.

These largest valves are used for top of the range cylinder heads and entail the removal of the standard valve seat inserts (milled away). The valve seat insert recesses are then remachined to take larger valve seat inserts.

The valve guides are also removed by milling them away (so as not to mark the as-factory bore holes).

The inlet and exhaust ports are then enlarged to J.E. Developments' specified sizes by an outside contractor. The ports are made as large as the standard cylinder heads will sensibly allow. The enlarged

later standard valve seat insert cylinder heads are standard-sized racing valves (1.575in/40.0mm inlet, 1.375in/34.9mm exhaust) which it has made to its own specifications. The inlet valves weigh 71gm and the exhaust valves weigh 80gm and are used in all of J.E. Developments' 3.500in/88.9mm bore racing engines. These racing valves have 0.312in/7.92mm diameter valve stems (used in conjunction with special bronze valve guides) and the inlet valves have waisted valve stems, while exhausts do not.

The original guides are removed from the cylinder heads (milled out, not pressed), the inlet and exhaust ports are then ported to J.E. Developments' racing use specifications by an outside contractor and, after that, the new guides are fitted.

J.E. Developments' top of the range cylinder head's combustion chamber fitted with larger valve seat inserts, 1.700in/43.1mm diameter inlet valves and 1.500in/38.0mm exhaust valves. This cylinder head has been O-ringed for better sealing with high compression.

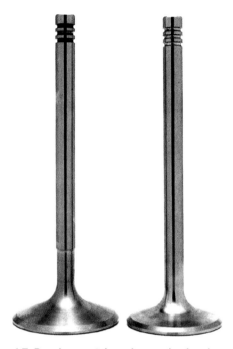

J.E. Developments' maximum-sized racing valves with 0.3125in/7.92mm diameter valve stems and Ford Pinto collet grooves. 1.700in/43.15 diameter inlet valve on the left and the 1.500in/38.0 diameter exhaust valve on the right.

inlet port openings measure 1.850in/ 47mm high by 1.100in/28mm wide but, at the point inside the inlet port adjacent to the pushrods, reduce to 0.850in/21.5mm wide by 1.850in/ 47mm high. The enlarged exhaust ports measure 1.550in/39mm high by 1.100/28mm wide at the exit of the cylinder head. The inlet and exhaust port tracts are more or less uniformly enlarged, although very little material is removed from the 'floor' of the inlet or exhaust ports as they turn into the valve throat and seat area. The porting is carried out

up to within 0.250in/6.3mm of the valve seat inserts.

Next, new Brico-made inlet valve inserts (of exactly the same material as the standard originals) are fitted into the cylinder heads. The larger inlet valve seat inserts are 1.725in/43.80mm in diameter, exhausts 1.525in/38.75mm. The inserts are 0.004in/0.10mm larger than the counter bored recess that they fit into (giving interference fit). To fit the new valve seat inserts they are frozen using dry ice, while the cylinder heads are uniformly heated to 150 degrees C/300F so that there is a clearance of about 0.001-0.002in/0.050-0.076mm for fitting purposes (the valve seat insert now smaller than the aperture it fits into). The inserts are installed using alignment jigging to avoid any possible damage to the aluminium of the cylinder head (any removal of material from the counter bored recess could affect the interference fit of the insert, causing them to fall out in service!). The inside shape of each insert is fully machined when

they're made. The larger inlet valve seats have 1.425in/ 36.1mm diameter throats (minimum diameter sizes), while the exhausts have 1.325in/ 33.6mm.

New bronze valve guides are now fitted. After this the porting of the cylinder heads around the valve seat inserts is completed to match the inserts and the valve seats 'trued' by grinding. Next, the valves and seats are lapped together using very fine (400 grit) lapping paste. The cylinder head gasket faces are planed 0.004-0.005in/0.10-0.127mm to clean them up and remove any distortion which completes the head work.

VALVE SPRINGS

J.E. Developments uses two valve spring combinations on the engines it builds. All engines using up to, but not exceeding, 0.450in/11.5mm of valve lift, and which are not going to rev at more than 6000rpm, use standard single Rover V8 valve springs giving a seated pressure of 80lb/35.5kg and an 'over the nose' (full valve lift) pressure of 180lb/80kg at 0.450in/11.5mm of lift. This specification applies to engines with hydraulic lifters such as those using the J.E. Developments 2665-(101) or the Crane H-218 hydraulic-type camshafts.

The dual valve springs are used for revs higher than 6000rpm (up to 7500rpm) and for higher lift camshafts. These dual valve springs have a seated pressure of 85lb/38kg and an 'over the nose' pressure of 225lb/100kg at 0.500in/12.6mm of valve lift. This amount of valve spring pressure is enough for 7500rpm operation with the low weight of racing engine valve train componentry. That's lightweight Crane flat tappet mechanical lifters, J.E. Developments' modular pushrods and its forged steel rocker arms (or Yella Terra roller rocker arms), J.E. Developments' lightweight large diameter racing valves, J.E. Developments' aluminium or steel valve spring retainers and Ford Pinto valve keepers. The emphasis is on using sufficient valve spring pressure with a reasonable safety margin against valve float and – most definitely – without excessive valve spring pressure. John Eales has not gone down the route of roller camshafts.

Caution! – J.E. Developments does not recommend that any of its racing engines be revved higher than the point of maximum power. This means keeping the revs limited to about 7000rpm in most cases, perhaps 7500rpm for some of the shorter stroke engines (2.800inch/ 71.12mm stock type ones, for example). Short stroke 3.5 litre engines which develop maximum power at 7300-7400rpm can be revved to this rpm level reliably. J.E. Developments gives engine rpm limits on all of the engines it sells and strongly recommends that **all** engines be electronically rev-limited to prevent over speeding.

Caution! – Early SD1-type steel valve spring retainers are quite acceptable for use in a high performance or racing engine,

J.E. Developments' single coil spring on the left and its dual valve spring on the right: these springs are made in the UK to J.E. Developments specifications.

but the later sintered valve spring retainers most definitely **are not,** and 5800rpm cannot be exceeded without a **high risk** of failure. The sintered retainers **must** be replaced with early standard steel ones, or aftermarket steel or aluminium ones, if more than 5800rpm is going to be used. Steel valve spring retainers were used on all SD1 engines built between 1976 and 1980.

There is one size of steel valve spring retainer for P5 and P6 engines fitted with dual valve springs, and one size steel valve spring retainer used on early SD1 engines with single valve springs. Stocks of these original retainers are universally low, but J.E. Developments-made steel and aluminium retainers are readily available.

J.E. Developments' aluminium (anodised) valve spring retainer on the left, high tensile steel item on the right.

CAMSHAFTS

Caution! – Competition engines, consistently and frequently revving to 7000rpm plus, need mechanical camshafts and lifters, as opposed to hydraulic lifters and 'hydraulic' camshafts. The action of the mechanical camshaft is better for high performance use (more 'snappy' engine response) and the system is generally more reliable (no possibility of lifter problems).

J.E. Developments uses either Crane mechanical camshafts or the original British Leyland WL3 mechanical camshaft: the latter cam's profile is ground on to a new blank by an outside contractor. John Eales favours the BL camshaft over all others, in spite of its technological age. The specifications for this camshaft are: inlet valve opens 49 degrees before top dead centre (BTDC), closes 77 degrees after bottom dead centre (ABDC); the exhaust valve opens 81 degrees before bottom dead centre (BBDC), closes 45 degrees after top dead centre (ATDC). This equates to 306 degrees of duration using absolute figures (actual opening and closing points).

Both inlet and exhaust valves have 0.500in/12.6mm lift and the valve clearance for both is 0.017in/ 0.42mm (hot). On smaller capacity engines like this, the inlet full lift timing point is 104 degrees after top dead centre (ATDC). If used in a large capacity engine (more than 4.6 litres), the full lift timing point is moved to 108 degrees after top dead centre (ATDC). No other camshaft tested in recent years has bettered the general high rpm race style performance obtainable from the WL3 camshaft. Other very similar profile camshafts are Piper Cams' V8BP300 and Kent Cams' M248.

VALVE TRAIN

The valve train componentry J.E. Developments uses on all of its competition engines is largely made to its own specification by outside contractors, and all parts are stocked in reasonable quantities.

The valve train used on all high power, high revving J.E. Developments racing engines isn't all that far removed from what was used in the days of Group A racing (1980s). While all manner of complicated roller rocker assemblies and roller camshafts have been tried, few have proven as reliable as the system that's used today.

When the Rover V8 engine was originally being prepared for serious racing use (Group A) the standard componentry was tested to destruction. This was done to see what broke, and to give the engineers some idea of what was going to have to be altered to make the engine reliable.

The standard sintered valve spring retainers broke at about 5800rpm and the stock rocker arrangement broke at about 6000rpm. However, it wasn't the cast aluminium rocker arms that broke, as you might expect after looking at them. In fact, it was the steel rockershafts which consistently broke at the ends on a random basis after a very short time (as little as half an hour to one hour's running). Brand new rockershafts cracked through the last drilled hole in each shaft, where the end securing bolts passed through. The loading imposed on this area by the end

Steel rockershaft end pillar for fitting to each end of each rockershaft ...

... also available in red anodised finish.

(unsupported) rocker arm being the problem. To counteract this, steel pillars were fitted to each rockershaft end (four per engine). This solved the problem of standard rockershaft breakages.

Today J.E. Developments makes rockershaft end pillars out of steel and aluminium. The aluminium units are red anodised and of identical dimensions to the steel ones. The company also makes replacement aluminium central pillars, which are blue anodised, for competition engines.

With the standard rockershaft assembly fitted with end support pillars, the standard aluminium rocker arms only started to cause problems when the revs went above 6500rpm. At this point there were random rocker arm breakages and the bore of the rocker arms started to pick-up (gall) on the rockershaft. Engineers started looking around for a production engine's rocker arm that would fit and discovered that Volvo rocker arms fitted these engines and were then universally adopted for Group A racing use.

While J.E. Developments has tried various roller rocker arm systems, few have proved to be as reliable as the company's current forged steel rocker arms. These are very similar to the Volvo ones that were used in the 1980s for Group A racing engines. All that's left of the standard components on a J.E. Developments rockershaft assembly is the actual rockershaft and the three coil springs which keep the rocker arms apart. Spacer sleeves can be used in place of these springs, but J.E. Developments reports no problems with the standard spring arrangement.

An alternative that can be used here are the Federal Mogul USA-made replacement steel rocker arms

J.E. Developments' forged steel rocker arms which are based on the Volvo rocker arms used for racing purposes in the 1980s. They are handed left and right.

J.E. Developments' forged steel rocker arm, ball and screw and adjusting nut assembly. The assembled rocker arm is very conventional, simple, efficient and strong.

intended for the Buick engines. They used to be distributed in the UK by Zephyr Cams which is no longer in business, but most Rover V8 engine specialists can access them, though they can be hard to source if, as is the case at the time of writing, there hasn't been a recent production run. This sort of obsolete part only gets produced when there is a sufficient number of backorders from retailers.

The Federal Mogul rockers are not handed, like the original aluminium Buick or Rover ones, but are more than twice as strong as the standard aluminium ones and don't wear or break. They're very good heavy-duty replacements for the standard cast aluminium rocker arms for all road going and high performance applications (standard aluminium rockers fail when the pushrod wears through the rocker arm, and this point needs to be kept in mind).

The only factor with the Federal Mogul made rocker arms that needs attention before they're used, is that they have a small hole aimed directly at the valve stem (there for manufacturing purposes). This hole causes high revving engines (not so

much standard road going engines) to use excessive oil, but there's a simple solution: 'tig' weld the hole closed. This is achieved by placing all of the rocker arms on a close fitting aluminium bar and welding closed each hole in turn.

With these Federal Mogul rockers on a rockershaft fitted with support pillars, the assembly will stand 7000rpm reliably. Rockershafts prepared in this manner can be used with either hydraulic or mechanical camshafts, through the use of adjustable pushrods (Crane). Adjusting the valves for tappet clearance is fiddly and time consuming. These Crane adjustable pushrods can also be used to good effect on hydraulic camshaft-equipped engines for setting lifter preloading. These adjustable pushrods are reliable with this amount of valve spring pressure. **Caution!** – However, if too much valve spring pressure is used with these adjustable pushrods, they can fail in the thread. The sort of pressure that will cause failure is 250lb/114kg plus, at 6500-7500rpm.

J.E. Developments also imports the Australian made 'Yella Terra' roller rocker arms and fits them on request. Its own forged steel rocker arms are, in fact, lighter than the aluminium roller rockers, but many customers today insist on having roller rockers and these are the ones J.E. Developments has chosen to stock.

PUSHRODS

J.E. Developments makes its own tubular modular pushrods. The company has high tensile steel case hardened ball ends and cup ends, manufactured by an outside contractor, which are pressed into

J.E. Developments' assembled modular pushrod on the left, cup end (top middle), ball end (bottom middle) and a length of tube on the right.

the ends of the tubing. With the tube cut to the required length and the ends squared off neatly, the ends are pressed into the tubing. Any length of pushrod is possible by this means. The cup type ends are required for use with the forged rocker arms, but the pushrods can alternatively have two ball ends fitted to them to make them like a standard pushrod.

A J.E. Developments competition engine with the rocker cover removed is shown in an accompanying photo. Fitted to this engine are dual valve springs, aluminium valve spring retainers, Ford Pinto triple groove collets, racing valves with triple grooves and 0.312in/7.92mm diameter valve stemmed valves, forged steel rocker

Standard Rover V8 pushrod on the left, J.E. Developments' modular pushrod in the centre and an adjustable Crane brand one on the right.

J.E. Developments' rockershaft assembly in-situ.

arms, standard Rover rockershafts and springs, aluminium red anodised end support pillars, aluminium blue anodised pillars (the centre two) and three piece modular pushrods. Specification is reliable to 7000rpm.

ENGINE BALANCE

J.E. Developments has its own dynamic balancing machine and does everything in-house.

Each individual piston, with its rings and gudgeon (piston) pin is balanced as a single component to within 0.1 to 0.2gm of each similar set within the same engine.

Connecting rods are balanced end for end to within 0.1 to 0.2gm over the set of eight. This is quite exacting, and is quite time consuming but it is required if the engine's final balance status of 80-100gm/mm is to be realised.

These values are input to the general V8 engine balance formula: half of the reciprocating weight of the engine multiplied by all of the rotating weight of the engine componentry acting as 'bob-weights'. That's half of the piston, rings, gudgeon pin and little end portion of the connecting rod (as found by end for end weighing) and all of the big end portion of the connecting rod (as found by end for end weighing of big end journals). Four 'bob-weights' of the exact calculated weight (to within 0.1 to 0.2gm) are bolted onto the crankshaft's big end journals and the crankshaft rotated (500rpm) on a dynamic balancing machine. Material is then removed from appropriate areas of the crankshaft (as indicated by the balancing machine) to effect as near perfect balance as possible.

Note. The term gm/mm may well be new to many. The simple analogy is that gm/mm relates to the amount of residual imbalance present in the rotating assembly. If the amount of imbalance is registered as 100gm/mm, this can be taken to mean that the imbalance is equivalent to 1gm of weight at a radius distance of 100mm from the crankshaft axis or 100gm of weight at a radius distance of 1mm from the crankshaft axis. In practical terms, convenient equivalents are easily worked out. For example, if the amount of residual imbalance at the front of the crankshaft is registered as being 1200gm/mm (that's equivalent to 1gm at a distance of 1200mm from the crankshaft axis, or 2gm at 600mm, or 4gm at 300mm, or 8gm at 150mm, or 16gm at 75mm distance, and so on). In our example, a realistic amount of material that could be removed from the front of the crankshaft, to effect correct balance of the front of the crankshaft assembly, would be 16gm at a distance of 75mm (by grinding or removing metal with a drill point).

J.E. Developments' balanced engines (racing or otherwise) are internally balanced, including all of the long stroke engines. The common practice is to use external balance weight added to the crankshaft damper and flywheel/flexplate to bring the engine into balance. However, John Eales doesn't do this, instead he adds 'Mallory metal' or tungsten carbide to the crankshaft counterweights. This process involves drilling/reaming 5/8in/15.875mm holes into the first and last three counterweights of the crankshaft.

The Mallory metal or tungsten carbide slugs are then pressed into place in the holes. It's an expensive operation because, quite frequently, a lot of Mallory metal has to be added. In many instances 8-9 slugs, sometimes more, have to be installed into each end of the crankshaft.

The reason for internally balancing the engine, rather than externally, is to reduce the 'bending moment' of the crankshaft to a minimum. On a high revving engine (over 6000rpm) maintaining internal balance is essential.

IGNITION SYSTEMS

John Eales favours the Lucas distributor, sparkplug (HT) leads (wires) and coil/coil packs over all other possibilities because they have proven to be very reliable. All Rover V8 engines can be fitted with the 1994-1996 'interim' timing cover, which means that engines can use the crank driven oil pump (replacing the troublesome original style oil pump system) and maintain the use of a conventional Lucas 'electronic' (breakerless) distributor.

There has been quite a range of internal specifications for these Lucas distributors (amounts of advance and rates of advance) depending on engine requirements. Amounts of total ignition advance as used by J.E. Developments are –
3.5 litre engines: 35-36 degrees.
3.9 and 4.2 litre engines: 32-34 degrees.
4.6 litre engines: 28-30 degrees.

Note that these amounts of total advance apply to **all** Rover V8 engines, not just racing ones.

Each competition engine is tested and set with the optimum amount of advance for maximum torque. Distributors are calibrated by J.E. Developments to suit each individual engine's specification. Other distributors are available to suit the Rover V8, such as the Mallory dual point, or the same company's electronic versions.

Distributorless electronic ignition system-equipped engines can have different amounts of advance programmed into them in any part of the rpm range, unlike conventional distributors which tend to be linear in their action. The flexibility of distributorless systems means that the amount of advance can sometimes be beneficially increased for high rpm work over what is required to develop maximum torque or, if the compression ratio of the engine proves to be a little bit too high, a slight dip can be incorporated into the advance curve. This sort of advance regime was not possible until the advent of electronics.

The vacuum advance mechanism is disabled in all instances and firmly fixed so that no movement is possible, making the ignition advance centrifugal only.

Engines are tested for the ideal amount of initial advance (for starting purposes), idle speed/low rpm speed and total advance. With these tests concluded the amount of advance that a particular engine will require is a known factor, and replacement internals that give this amount of advance are fitted into the distributor or the original components are altered to suit. The rate of advance is controlled by the two springs in the mechanical advance mechanism. Changing springs for lighter or stronger ones alters the rate. Stronger springs in combination retard the rate of advance while lighter ones do the opposite. On average the total advance is all-in between 3000 and 3500rpm.

There is another title in the Veloce SpeedPro range of books that deals specifically with optimising distributor type ignition systems called *How To Build & Power Tune Distributor-type Ignition Systems*. This book covers all aspects of modifying ignition systems for high performance and has numerous photos in it to assist you to gain a full understanding of the requirements.

INDUCTION SYSTEMS

J.E. Developments will fit, and tune, any induction system required. On request, engines are 'run-in' and dyno-tuned in-house before being shipped to customers; this is to ensure that the maximum power has been realised.

There aren't many carburettor and fuel injection systems that John Eales hasn't fitted over the years. His experience includes the following set ups:
● 4 x downdraught Weber or Dellorto twin barrel carburettors.
● 4 x sidedraught Weber or Dellorto twin barrel carburettors on custom made 'crossover' inlet manifolds.
● Holley carburettors on a range of 180 degree/dual plane and 360 degree/single plane aluminium inlet manifolds.
● Standard twin SU and Zenith carburettor induction systems.
● All of the Lucas fuel injection systems.
● Many aftermarket individual inlet tract fuel injection systems.

In fact, you can have exactly what you want from J.E. Developments!

OPTIMUM FUEL MIXTURE SETTINGS

John Eales sets all of the engines his company builds to the following criteria. Note that, while the engines he builds are predominantly racing engines, the following criteria apply to **all** Rover V8 engines.

Induction systems are set to give the following:

- **Low/idle rpm: 0.92 Lambda.**
- **Full throttle: 0.88 Lambda.**
- **Acceleration phase: rising to 0.85 Lambda.**
- **Cruise (road engines): 1.05 Lambda for maximum economy.**

Note that peak power is **always** developed at 0.87-0.90 Lambda, but **Caution!** – **all** engines are set to 0.87-0.88 Lambda to avoid any possibility of leaness and the overheating of internal componentry, such as pistons.

FUEL

The fuel recommended for use in all J.E. Developments' competition engines in the UK is the 98.3 RON Shell Optimax which is an unleaded fuel. This fuel will generally support up to 12.5:1 compression ratio (CR). John Eales has tended to keep CRs down to stay away from using additives, not because the additives don't work but because there always seems to come a time when owners don't have a bottle of additive and then run the engine on standard fuel. He has found from experience that it is safer to build engines to suit readily available fuels, then you don't have to worry about the availability of additives. He recommends that the fuel being used in racing engines be guaranteed fresh, like the fuel that can be bought at the major racing circuits which is mixed a day or two before race day and then dispensed

Conversion chart

Lambda	Air/fuel	%CO
0.80	11.8	8.0
0.81	11.9	7.3
0.82	12.0	6.5
0.83	12.2	5.9
0.84	12.4	5.4
0.85	12.5	5.0
0.86	12.6	4.85
0.87	12.8	4.35
0.88	13.0	3.8
0.90	13.2	3.3
0.91	13.4	2.85
0.92	13.5	2.6
0.93	13.7	2.15
0.94	13.8	1.9
0.95	14.0	1.6
0.96	14.1	1.4
0.97	14.3	1.0
0.98	14.4	0.8
0.99	14.6	0.6
1.00	14.7	0.5
1.01	14.8	0.6
1.02	15.0	0.3
1.03	15.1	0.15
1.04	15.2	0.2
1.05	15.4	0.15

from a Shell tanker at the circuit. John further recommends adding 10cc of two-stroke oil to every 5 (imperial) gallons of unleaded fuel for fuel injection engines (to lubricate pumps and injectors which are susceptible to sticking).

There is some variation in the way fuel octane ratings are listed around the world. In the UK, for example, all fuels are advertised as being rated using the Research Octane Number (RON) and this is the system seen written on the pumps in petrol stations. The fuel companies in the UK actually use another method of grading fuel as well: the Motor Octane Number (MON). MON figures are seldom ever publicised, but it is, in fact, a vital indicator of

how good the particular fuel is. For example, Shell Optimax is 98.3 RON and 91 MON.

The USA uses a slightly different rating system for its fuels which is a combination of RON and MON added together and then divided by two. The result of this is an Anti Knock Index (AKI) or a Pump Octane Number (PON). This system results in a number that appears on the dispensing pump in a service station that is lower than the RON number for the same fuel.

The USA is somewhat better off for racing purposes than most other countries around the world because high RON octane tetraethyl leaded fuels are still there for racing purposes. Fuels with a 118 RON are available in the USA and unleaded fuels which have a 104 RON are available for road going cars. However, a premium price does have to be paid for these fuels.

Some countries still have aviation fuel (leaded) available for car racing purposes. This 'racing fuel'/'Avgas' typically has a 107 RON octane rating/100 MON octane rating and 0.80-0.85gm of tetraeythl-lead per litre. This fuel used to be called '100/130'. The '100' is the MON rating, while the '130' is a rating obtained by a supercharge method.

Note that modified Rover V8 engines which are based largely on standard components, such as the type John Eales builds, all seem to respond best to air/fuel mixture ratios of Lambda 0.88 which is equivalent to 13.0:1 air/fuel or 3.8% CO. Whenever an engine is being set up on a dyno it will be found that this sort of mixture ratio is required to achieve maximum torque and bhp. It's quite a lean mix really, but it's what this engine 'likes'.

EXHAUST SYSTEMS
The exhaust systems recommended follow usual practice. For example, if one these engines is fitted into a Westfield sports car, a four into one or a four into two into one-style exhaust extractor is used because it's the easiest to fit. The primary pipe diameter sizes are universally 1⁵/₈ or 1³/₄in/41 or 44mm outside diameter, 26 or 36in/710 or 915mm long going into a 2¹/₂ or 2³/₄in/63.5 or 70mm outside diameter main pipe, and an appropriate silencer on each side of the car. This is a good all-round system with 7000rpm capability. Such set ups provide two independent exhaust systems.

Other systems are available which are an improvement on the foregoing arrangement. These alternative systems involve the use of either –

A four into one primary pipe system, using 1⁵/₈ or 1³/₄in/41 or 44mm) outside diameter primary pipes leading into a 2¹/₂ or 3in/63 or 76mm outside diameter main pipe extractor system, or –

A four into two into one primary pipe system, using 15/8in or 13/4in/41 or 44mm outside diameter primary pipes, 2in/50mm outside diameter secondary pipes which then merge into a 2½ or 3in/63 or 76mm outside diameter main pipe extractor system.

The two extractor manifold main pipes (either system) are then joined. This joining of the two primary main pipes into a single main pipe makes quite a difference to torque and power output as it achieves optimum scavenging. This is a

practice followed worldwide when such configurations are possible for a particular application.

Two exhaust systems are used on the J.E. Developments engine dyno. The first one is a very expensive four into one system (times two of course), which ultimately has the two main pipes of each bank joining into one large main pipe. The system is, as you'd expect, all sweeping curves, very elaborate and delivers excellent all round power.

The second system uses two Dakar Rally cast iron exhaust manifolds from a Range Rover which has the four exhaust tracts joining into two downpipe outlets within the inlet manifold configuration. The internal passageway configuration of these exhaust manifolds joins each pair of non-consecutive exhaust pulses of each side of the engine which is quite different to what happens with a four into one system. This firing pulse phasing is what is frequently termed 'Tri-wy' in the USA, has been around since the early 1960s and was always known to be very efficient in the mid-rpm range. The castings look quite rough and ready on the outside, but they're not what they might seem. The internal passageways have been smoothly cast so that a 13/4in/44.5mm diameter ball can be rolled from each of the two outlets right up to the exhaust port outlet of the cylinder head! Two 21/2in/63.5mm outside diameter tubular steel downpipes attach to the underside of these cast iron exhaust manifolds and, at a distance of about 24in/610mm, they bifurcate into a single main pipe. These two

main pipes are in turn bifurcated into one large diameter (4in/101mm) main pipe. This system looks quite rough and ready compared to the expensive custom made system, but, ultimately, the only difference in power between the two systems measured on any one engine was a maximum loss of top end power of no more than 8bhp, with no difference in torque values (although the maximum torque is maintained for a further 500rpm with the very elaborate custom made exhaust system).

OTHER SPECIALISTS
Other companies in the UK which build high performance and competition engines largely from stock componentry are –

J.E. Engineering:
Telephone (UK) [0]247-630-5018
E-mail <sales@jeengineering.co.uk>
www.jeengineering.co.uk
Progress Engineering:
Telephone Nick Law on (UK) [0]162-687-070
Fax (UK) [0]1622-692-2753
E-mail <nlaw0000@aol.com>
D.J.E. (D.J. Ellis Ltd):
Telephone Dave Ellis (UK) [0]24-7635-2888
E-mail <djev8@aol.com>
www.djev8.com
Graham Nash Motorsport
Telephone UK [0]1455-840-140
E-mail
<info@grahamnashmotorsport.com>
www.mimsport.co.uk
34 Main Street
Kirkby Mallory
Leicester
England
LE9 3PS

Chapter 10
Wildcat Engineering

WILDCAT ENGINEERING
Telephone (UK) [0]1341-450-200, fax 01341-450-695
E-mail <roverv8engine@tiscali. co.uk>
www.roverv8engine.co.uk
The Old Creamery, Rhydymain Dolgellau, Gwynedd, North Wales LL40 2AY, UK.

Wildcat Engineering (hereinafter referred to simply as 'Wildcat') is a company run by the hugely experienced Ian Richardson.

This chapter describes the specifications of the replacement and modified components/ assemblies available from Wildcat to guide you in your choice of engine specification for your application.

Wildcat makes and supplies a very large range of componentry for the Rover V8 engine including cylinder heads in three versions,

Wildcat development engine.

custom machined forged and cast crankshafts, I-beam and H-beam connecting rods, all manner of cast pistons, eutectic and hypereutectic cast pistons, forged pistons, two special large bore, high strength Rover derivative blocks, plus all manner of camshaft and valve train components. It has large machining capacity and is geared up to machine every single aspect of blocks, cylinder heads and crankshafts. Engine capacities of up to 6.0 litres are possible using its componentry.

The longest stroke crankshaft Wildcat makes out of an existing factory standard (82mm/3.150in stroke, 4.6 litre, non-reground crankshaft) has a 86.35mm/3.400in stroke. To get this stroke, the big end journals are offset ground and go down to 2.000in/50.8mm diameter from the original factory size of 2.185in/55.5mm.

Alternative Wildcat connecting rods are used with this long stroke crank as are ACL-Wildcat eutectic pistons in the standard bore size of 94.0mm, or 94.5mm (the first oversize). Wildcat buys in semi-finished pistons from ACL (an Australian replacement part company, the origins of which go back to Repco Engineering) and machines these pistons to suit a range of combinations. There's a wide choice of piston top dish cc sizes and shapes (15cc to 30cc) and gudgeon pin positions.

With this longest stroke, engine capacity is increased from 4525cc to 4795cc. A larger bore of 3.780in/96.0mm is available which involves the removal of the original liners, fitting new ones and fitting KB hypereutectic pistons (pistons that usually fit a small block Chevrolet V8 engine). The gudgeon pin size of these two piston types is 0.927in/28.56mm diameter. With this combination of crank, rod, piston and bore the engine capacity is increased from 4525cc to 4997cc.

CONNECTING RODS

Wildcat buys in (from the USA) semi-finished forged H-beam section connecting rods and machines them to a range of sizes to suit various applications. Conrods are available in the following centre to centre measurements –

5.660in, weighing 600gm
5.700in, weighing 610gm
5.850in, weighing 620gm
6.000in, weighing 630gm
6.125in, weighing 640gm
(The weights of the bearing shells are not included in the foregoing weights.)

All connecting rods are supplied in matched sets weightwise, and are machined to suit either 2.000in/50.8mm or 2.100in/53.3mm crankshaft big end journals.

Wildcat has also recently introduced a super lightweight I-beam connecting rod which comes in two centre to centre lengths: 5.700in/144.8mm and 6.000in/152.5mm. These two connecting rods are available to suit 2.000in/50.8mm diameter crank pin crankshafts or the company's new 1.770in/45mm diameter

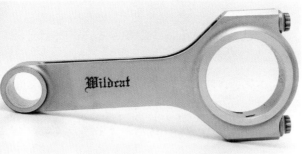

Wildcat H-section connecting rod.

crankpin forged steel crankshafts. The lightweight rods weigh in at approximately 510gm, minus bearing shells.

A range of connecting rod lengths is required to keep the crankshaft stroke to connecting rod ratios within the criteria known to work well. The standard 3.5 litre engine, for example, has a stroke of 2.800in/71.1mm and a connecting rod which has a centre to centre measurement of 5.660in/43.7mm. To obtain the stroke to connecting rod centre to centre distance ratio, the length of the connecting rod is divided by the stroke.

In the case of the 3.5 litre engine, that's 5.660 divided by 2.800 which results in a 2.02 connecting rod ratio.

The 4.0 litre engine has a 2.800in/71.1mm stroke and a 6.105in/155.0mm centre to centre length connecting rod: that's 6.105 divided by 2.800 which results in a 2.18 connecting rod ratio.

The 4.6 litre engine has a 3.232in/82mm stroke and 5.883in/149.5 centre to centre length connecting rods. That's 5.893 divided by 3.232 which results in a 1.82 connecting rod ratio.

Wildcat endeavours to keep its engines with connecting rod ratios of 1.7 and above. Its latest 3.625in/92mm stroke forged steel crankshaft

fitted with the 1.770in/45.0mm crank pins uses the new 6.000in/152.4mm centre to centre length super lightweight I-beam connecting rods. That's 5.850 divided by 3.625 which results in a 1.61 connecting rod ratio, which doesn't meet the company's regular criteria.

By comparison, the mass production V8 engine with the shortest centre to centre length connecting rods in the business is the 302 cubicin small block Ford with its 5.090in/129.3mm rods and its 3.000in/76.2mm stroke. That's 5.090 divided by 3.000 which results in a 1.7 connecting rod ratio. The earlier 289 cubicin small block Ford had 5.155in centre to centre length connecting rods and a 2.870in stroke. That's 5.155 divided by 2.870 which results in a 1.8 connecting rod ratio. Ford engineers took this factor to the lowest possible figure they thought acceptable with the 302 and, realistically, 1.7 can be considered the figure not to go under.

Nevertheless, a few production engines have been under this and have gone very well and been reliable, such as the 350 cu in small block Chevrolet engine. This engine has a 3.480in/88.5mm stroke and 5.700in/144.8mm centre to centre length connecting rods. That's 5.700 divided by 3.480 which results in a 1.64 connecting rod ratio. Take it that this is the low side of acceptable: the problem being connecting rod angulation. A very common modification for the last 30 years has been to fit 6.000in/152.5mm centre to centre length connecting rods to these engines for racing purposes. That's 6.000

ACL-Wildcat piston.

KB hypereutectic piston (is actually a small block Chevrolet item).

divided by 3.480 = 1.72 connecting rod ratio. The 265/283/302 cubicin versions of this very same family of engines also used 5.700in/144.8mm centre to centre length connecting rods, but they had a shorter stroke at 3.000in/76.2mm. That's 5.700 divided by 3.000 which results in a 1.9 connecting rod ratio. The 307/327 cu in versions with their 3.250in stroke had a 1.75 connecting rod ratio.

CRANKSHAFTS

Alternative longer than stock stroke crankshafts are available from Wildcat with strokes up to 3.540in/

90.00mm. These are machined from raw castings bought in from Rover. The maximum stroke possible out of any raw casting is 3.540in/90.0mm and, as a consequence, the maximum Wildcat can go to.

There are two big end journal diameter sizes to choose from. One is 2.000in/50.8mm, the other 2.100in/53.3mm. The reason for offering the 2.100in/53.3mm size is to provide more main to big end journal overlap (stronger crankshaft). The largest stroke possible with the 2.100in/53.3mm big end journal size is 3.450in/87.5mm. The engine capacities possible using cast crankshafts and derived from the standard 4.6 litre engine are as follows –

3.702in/94.0mm bore
x 3.385in/86.3mm stroke
  = 293 cubicines/4.8 litres
3.722in/94.5mm bore
x 3.385in/86.3mm stroke
  = 296 cubicines/4.85 litres
3.702in/94.0mm bore
x 3.450in/87.5mm stroke
  = 297 cubicines/4.85 litres
3.702in/94.0mm bore
x 3.540in/90.0mm stroke
  = 305 cubicines/5.0 litres
3.780in/96.0mm bore
x 3.385in/86.3mm stroke
  = 305 cubicines/5.0 litres
3.780in/96.0mm bore
x 3.450in/87.5mm stroke
  = 309 cubicines/5.1 litres
3.780in/96.0mm bore
x 3.540in/90.0mm stroke
  = 318 cubicines/5.25 litres

Connecting rod centre to centre distance lengths for each of the above combinations are 5.700in/144.8mm and the big end diameter size is to suit a 2.000in/50.8mm or a 2.100in/53.3mm crankshaft journal.

MAXIMUM BORE (UP TO 6000CC) ROVER V8 COMPETITION ENGINES

Wildcat has a genuine late model factory '38A' block mould which it has further modified to make special large bore blocks for competition use. The main modification is that the bores of the largest block are all Siamesed with there being no water passage between the cylinders (much the same as the 400 cubicin small block Chevrolet block). A considerable number of other small modifications were made to the block. This results in there being room for a maximum 4.000in/101.6mm bore with 0.070in/1.80mm wall thickness liners and a more or less uniform 0.110 to 0.120in/2.80 to 3.00mm of aluminium around each liner.

These blocks have more head studs than the other Rover blocks and, in this respect, are exactly the same as the original Oldsmobile block of the early 1960s (effectively six head studs around each cylinder). The mould was altered so that the bosses that the head bolts/studs screw into are not just connected to the block wall but to the bore wall as well. The block deck thickness was not increased over standard in an effort to keep as much water as possible close to the top of the block and the top of the liner. The cylinder head bolt/stud threaded holes remain block deck mounted as per standard. This block uses Wills rings only.

The top of the range steel crankshaft they supplied until 2003 for these special blocks were rough forged in the USA and finish machined in the UK. They are in fact SVO small block Ford V8 rough forgings and were chosen by Wildcat

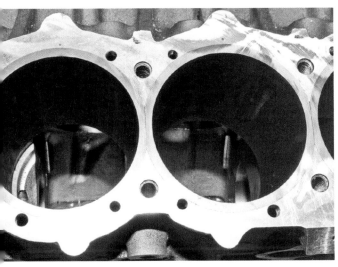

4.000in/101.6mm bore Wildcat block.

Small block Ford based forged steel crankshaft machined to suit the Rover V8.

because they are very close to the Rover rough casting and the thrust is taken on the centre main just like the Rover V8. The design of the Ford crankshaft is overall very similar to the Rover V8 one in terms of counterweighting. The connecting rods and the pistons of the Ford engines are of similar weights to those used in the Rover V8 engines, so there are no balancing problems in so far as there not being enough counterweighting to compensate for a large weight change. From 2003 on, Wildcat has sourced small block Ford-style rough forgings to its exact specifications from a crankshaft forging specialist company in Detroit, USA. These raw crankshaft forgings are made slightly over-counterweighted to ensure that, even with the longest stroke option possible, used in conjunction with lightweight connecting rods and pistons, there will not be any need to add 'Mallory metal' to the front and rear counterweights to effect full internal balance. An amount of metal will always have to be removed to effect correct dynamic balance.

Forged crankshafts are available in many strokes using a 2.000in/50.80mm or a 2.100in/53.3mm diameter big end journals (for maximum journal overlap) for strokes up to 3.540in/89.5mm. After this there may be clearance problems, with things like the camshaft lobes, inside the block so it can become quite awkward.

Caution! – If a mild duration, low lift, small base circle camshaft is used, there won't be any interference between the connecting rods and the camshaft lobes, but if a long duration, high lift roller type of camshaft is used the lobes **will** contact the connecting rod big ends. Reducing the big end journal diameter and the outer dimensions of the big end of the connecting rod is the solution to this problem and the reason why Wildcat has introduced a new connecting rod and big end journal size (NASCAR size) to its range.

The popular strokes Wildcat makes which don't have any crankcase clearance problems are: 3.4000in/85.40mm, 3.440in/87.30mm, 3.500in/88.9mm and 3.540in/90.0mm. The longest stroke crankshaft that is a straightforward fit, provided the camshaft situation is taken into consideration, is the 3.625in/92.0mm one, which usually comes with a 2.000in/50.80mm diameter big end journal size.

Big bore engine capacities –
4.000in/101.6mm bore
x 3.400in/86.35mm stroke
= 342cu in/5.6 litres
4.000in/101.6mm bore
x 3.440in/87.35mm stroke
= 346cu in/5.67 litres
4.000in/101.6mm bore
x 3.500in/88.9mm stroke
= 352cu in/5.77 litres
4.000in/101.6mm bore
x 3.540in/89.90mm stroke
= 356cu in/5.83 litres
4.000in/101.6mm bore
x 3.625in/92.0mm stroke
= 365cu in/5.98 litres

The connecting rods they used for these applications are H-section USA forgings which are bought in as rough forgings and finish machined by Wildcat to suit either 2.100in diameter big end journals or 2.000in diameter ones. The connecting rods feature fully floating piston pins/ gudgeon pins and the pistons use single round wire circlips for gudgeon pin retention or dual Spirolox retainers (two each side of the gudgeon pin).

A new edition to the line up is the use of a 4.000in/101.6mm bore block in conjunction with the the new lightweight I-beam connecting rods (510gm/18oz) with 6.000in/152.5mm centre to centre lengths which have 1.7700in/45.0mm diameter big end journal sizes. This a development which follows current NASCAR practice and uses Honda engine bearings. The crankshaft is, of course, a steel forging. It's not necessary to move the camshaft position in the block to provide enough rotational clearance for the componentry. With a 4.000in/ 101.6mm bore and 3.625in/92mm stroke, here's another version of the six litre engine (but with the lightest weight internal componentry used to date). The pistons for this combination are Diamond forgings (machined all over) which weigh approximately 380gm/13.4oz. The piston is of slipper skirt design and very squat.

The pistons used on the larger capacity engines are either USA- made Ross or Diamond forgings made to Wildcat Engineering's specifications or USA-made KB 'off the shelf' hypereutectic castings which are in fact small block Chevrolet engine pistons. The KB

This block has a 3.800in/96.5mm bore with deck mounted studs.

(Keith Black) hypereutectic pistons, as marketed by Silvolite, can be used in conjunction with the Wildcat cylinder heads as the raised top section of these pistons is virtually identical to the tops of the forged pistons Wildcat has custom made. **Caution!** – Re-machining of the piston crowns of the finished KB pistons is not recommended as it tends to upset the expansion characteristics of the piston. The Ross forgings, on the other hand, can be ordered with a raised top that suits either the original Rover V8 cylinder head combustion chamber shape or the Wildcat cylinder head combustion chamber shape. Essentially, Ross pistons will make whatever is required. The KB pistons are off the shelf items, and the least expensive option, while being extremely strong cast pistons suitable for competition applications.

CRANKSHAFT DAMPERS

The crankshaft dampers supplied by Wildcat are of the 'viscous' type. This type of damper is noted for its general ability to damp torsional vibration over quite a wide rpm band and its increased cost over elastomer-type dampers.

Two types of viscous damper are available, both using the same damping unit but one has a steel hub, the other an aluminium (lighter) hub. Both these hubs allow the fitting of a Wildcat-made 36 degree minus 1 degree ignition timing trigger plate between the back of the damper rim and the front cover of the engine. A Ford-made pick-up is used which is mounted on the engine using a Wildcat-made aluminium bracket.

This overall design makes for a very compact, out of the way, crankshaft trigger-type ignition system.

TURBO BLOCK

Wildcat also makes what it calls the 'turbo-block.' The same modified '38A' block mould is used, but with a different core. This block is different from the six litre block in that the bore size is 3.800in/96.5mm. The bores are not siamesed as the circulation of water around the full 360 degrees of the bores is deemed to be necessary for best possible cooling efficiency. The wall thickness of aluminium around each cylinder liner is 0.120 to 0.140in/3.0 to 3.5mm, except between the cylinders where the aluminium wall thickness of the block casting reduces to a approximately 0.110in/ 2.8mm and there is a 0.080in/2.0mm waterway gap between the bores. The steel liners of this block are of 0.070in/1.80mm wall thickness. The liners are flanged at the top. The tops of each bore cylinder liner bore in the block are machined to provide a recess which is 0.125in/3.20mm vide by 0.200in/5.0mm deep. The ners are shrunk into the block, ust the same as standard blocks, out there is 0.003in/0.075mm of interference fit between liner standard blocks 0.007in/0.175mm).

The head studs of the Turbo-block are not normally fixed the same as the six litre block's. The Turbo blocks have long head studs that are screwed into the block down at the bottom of the water jacket. These blocks are also similar to the original Oldsmobile block in that there are effectively six cylinder head securing studs per cylinder (18 studs per cylinder head).

Note there have been variations in the drilling of the cylinder head stud holes on both types of blocks. Essentially, customers can have what they want: four, five or six bolt per cylinder head retention to suit their application and existing cylinder heads.

Specially made conventional type cylinder head gaskets are available for use on these blocks and are termed '97mm gaskets' by Wildcat. The other option is Wills rings.

The forged steel crankshafts used in the Turbo block are the same as for large bore versions of the block and the range of strokes is the same.

Ross forged, custom machined pistons only available for these blocks with a range of compression ratios and piston crown shapes to suit turbo-charging or natural aspiration. The connecting rods are the same forged and machined ones used in the large bore version of the block.

Turbo block engine capacities –

3.800in bore x 3.400in stroke
  = 308.5cu in/5.06 litres

Ross forged piston.

3.800in bore x 3.440in stroke
  = 312cu in/5.11 litres
3.800in bore x 3.500in stroke
  = 317.5cu in/5.2 litres
3.800in bore x 3.540in stroke
  = 321cu in/5.26litres
3.800in bore x 3.625in stroke
  = 329cu in/5.39 litres

What does vary from the standard cross-bolted large main bearing crankshaft journal Rover V8 engine in both Wildcat-made blocks is the main bearings used. Ian Richardson of Wildcat noted the fact that Rover dispensed with the 360 degree thrust bearing arrangement of all previous Rover V8s when they introduced these blocks in the 1990s and, instead used a 180 degree thrust. Wildcat as a consequence machine these special blocks to use the Buick 300 main bearings which are a full 360 degree thrust type bearing. The main bearing tunnel bore diameter size is 2.687in/68.2498mm for 'bottom size' and 2.688in/68.2752mm for 'top size'. The finished align-honed size aimed for is 2.6875in/68.2625mm diameter.

Gear drives are available from Wildcat and are recommended for use on all out racing engines.

CYLINDER HEADS

Wildcat makes three specifications of cylinder head to suit its own blocks, or standard Rover blocks. The criteria these new cylinder heads had to meet was worked out in 1992 and development was done during 1993. From one basic casting Wildcat initially made two different cylinder heads. The first was the 'Stage I' high performance cylinder head and the second was the 'Stage II.' The Stage I specification cylinder heads also preceded the Stage II cylinder heads in production by about six months, but both were in production in 1994.

In 1998 Wildcat introduced a third version of the cylinder head for road going use which was simply termed the 'High Performance' cylinder head. This later specification cylinder head shared the same sized inlet and exhaust valves at the Stage I heads, but the valves were stock production Chevrolet ones, as opposed to the racing type of valves used in the Stage I heads (less expensive). The inlet port was not as large as the Stage I cylinder heads were while both the High Performance and the Stage I head used the same exhaust port contour and sizing. The inlet port

Wildcat cylinder head.

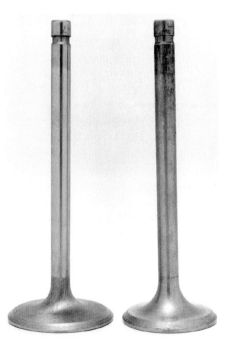

Standard Chevrolet inlet valve on the left and exhaust on the right.

length of these valves is 4.880in/124mm and they are, in fact, standard small block Chevrolet valves. These valves have a tip length of 0.25in/6.3mm. That's the distance from the top of the valve stem to the top edge of the collet (keeper/split lock) groove.

The rockers are

Posi-lock on left, screw in rocker stud in centre, roller rocker on right and ...

... the three components assembled.

Wildcat cylinder head's combustion chamber.

contour of the High Performance cylinder heads was revised in 2002 to improve low rpm engine response.

All three types of Wildcat cylinder head use Buick 300 rocker cover and inlet manifold gaskets, and the very distinctive Wildcat rocker covers. The valley cover gasket from a standard Rover V8 is used with Wildcat cylinder heads, but not the two parts on either side of the gasket that seal between the inlet manifold and cylinder heads which have to be cut away. There's a steel rail along the bottom edge of each Wildcat cylinder head which the cut down valley cover gasket is clamped by. This effectively seals the valley of the block in the normal manner, the cylinder head inlet ports now being sealed with separate

Buick 300 inlet manifold gaskets. The system is not complicated, although it's a bit different from the original Rover V8 setup.

High Performance cylinder heads

The basic 'High Performance' cylinder head comes with 1.850in/47.0mm head diameter inlet valves, 1.550in/39.3mm exhausts and both valves have 0.343in/8.72mm diameter valve stems. The overall

stud-mounted, just like a small-block Chevrolet or small-block Ford V8 engine, and only stud mounted roller rockers are available for standard High Performance and Stage I cylinder heads. Each individual 1.6:1

Stud mounted roller rocker arm as used on 'High Performance' cylinder heads and 'Stage 1' cylinder heads. The guide plate is clamped in position by the screw in rocker stud.

Aftermarket chrome-moly steel valve spring retainers on the left and standard 7 degree taper section collets (keepers/split locks) on the right.

Range of three collets (keepers/split locks) showing the different positions of the locks. The red standard keeper is on the left, the green keeper is in the middle and the blue one is on the right.

The two types of pushrod available from Wildcat. One piece on the left, three piece on the right.

roller rocker on its individual stud is adjusted, and kept in place, by 'Posi-locks.'

The pushrods are located by and run in hardened guide-plates which Wildcat has laser cut to exacting dimensions. These guide-plates, which each control two pushrods, are bolted to the cylinder head sandwiched between the underside of the rocker studs and the cylinder in the manner as used on many USA-made V8 engines. There are four individual guide-plates per cylinder head and, while the valve train system is quite different from a standard Rover V8, it is nevertheless a very common system on a USA-made engine.

The High Performance cylinder heads have a single valve springs, with contra-wound flat dampers fitted on the inside. The valve spring fitted height is 1.700in/42.2mm and they have approximately 95lb/43kg of seat pressure and 280lb/127kg of 'over the nose' valve spring pressure at 0.500in/12.7mm (maximum valve lift). These valve springs suit road or competition use and are, in fact, aftermarket manufacturer Chevrolet

Camaro Z28 replacement valve springs. The valve spring retainers used are USA made aftermarket chrome-moly ones which have the standard 7 degree degree collet (keeper/split lock) taper angles. The High Performance cylinder heads are designed for valve lifts of between 0.400in/10.1mm and 0.500in/12.7mm, but are clearanced for up to 0.600in/15.2 of valve lift.

Valve spring pressure is able to be reduced, or increased slightly, by changing the valve keepers (collets/split locks) for alternative ones that Wildcat supply which have the actual locks in different positions. There are three colour coded valve collets: standard is red, the one that increases valve spring pressure is green and the one that reduces the valve spring pressure is blue. These 7 degree collets work across the range of Wildcat cylinder heads.

The pushrods for High Performance cylinder heads are bought in by Wildcat from several USA-based companies, and they

range in length from 8.400in/212.3mm to 8.550in/217.2mm in incremental sizes of 0.025in/6.3mm. This means that there are seven sets of pushrods. When a set of cylinder heads are ordered, customers are asked what camshaft is going to be used and what base circle diameter it has so that the maximum valve lift is known, also whether the cylinder heads are going to be planed. Wildcat will then include in the cylinder head kit the appropriate length of pushrods from their selection to suit the individual application.

The inlet port opening dimensions are 1.800in/45.7mm in height and 1.060in/26.9mm in width. The inlet port shape was altered as a result of further development in 2002. The exhaust ports on High Performance and Stage I cylinder heads are cast using the same coring, but there's sufficient material wall thickness available around the one basic exhaust port to make the exhaust port just about any size you like within reason. Wildcat supplies a product that is capable of being ported to virtually any specification.

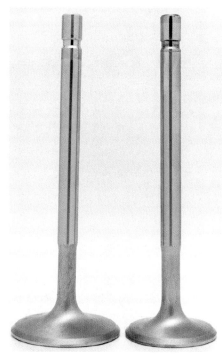

These are one piece stainless steel racing valves with waisted valve stems.

are equipped with fully waisted valve stems (down to 0.295in/7.5mm diameter) and the overall length of these valves is longer at 5.090in/ 129.3mm.

The variation in the length of valves for Wildcat cylinder heads is to cater for various rocker geometry in order to accommodate correctly the amounts of valve lift likely to be used. The rocker arm system is exactly the same as on the High Performance cylinder heads.

Inlet ports are 2.000in/50.8mm in height by 1.060in/26.9mm in width which represents an increas in port height only. These Stage 1 cylinder heads have a valve spring fitted height of 1.800in/45.5mm and use a strong single coil spring which has a contra-wound flat damper inside it. These valve springs give 110lb/50kg of seat pressure and 320lb/145kg of

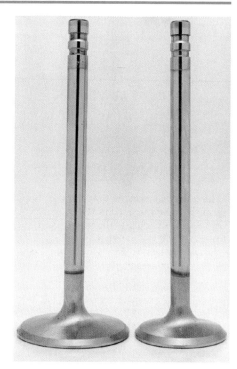

Stage II 1.940in/49.3mm diameter inlet valve on the left and 1.600in/40.6mm diameter exhaust valve on the right.

Stage 2 cylinder heads

These have the largest valve sizes and largest inlet ports available from Wildcat. The inlet ports are 2.100in/ 53.3mm high and 1.025in/26.0mm wide. The exhaust ports are larger than the those of the other two Wildcat heads.

The inlet valve heads are 1.940in/49.2mm in diameter, exhausts 1.600in/40.6mm and both valves have 0.343in/8.72mm stem diameters. Overall valve length is 5.180in/131.6mm. Both inlet and exhaust valves are one piece stainless steel racing items with minimally waisted stems.

These cylinder heads have been designed to be used in conjunction with rapid action roller camshafts which have a lot of camshaft lift. They are clearanced for 0.700in of valve lift and the dual valve springs

Stage II cylinder head inlet ports.

Note that the use of certain parts overlaps from one cylinder head type to another.

Stage 1 cylinder heads

These are Wildcat's intermediate configuration cylinder heads. The valve head diameters are the same as the standard High Performance cylinder head's, but they're not the same valves. These cylinder heads

'over the nose' valve spring pressure at 0.600in/15.2mm (maximum) valve lift. The valve spring pressure can be reduced slightly by using the 'blue' valve collets (keepers/split locks) that Wildcat can supply. These High Performance Stage 1 cylinder heads are clearanced for 0.600in/15.2mm of valve lift.

The four valve springs that Wildcat supplies. Left: the single coil spring and damper for the High Performance head. Centre left: the single coil spring and damper for the Stage I head. Centre right: the dual contra-wound valve springs for flat tappet camshafts and Stage II heads. Right: the contra-wound dual valve springs for rapid action roller camshafts and Stage II heads.

Stage II rockershaft assembly.

Shims are used under the valve springs. The number and thickness of these shims can be used to reduce the springs fitted height in order to equalise valve spring pressures.

Detachable 'saddle' to which the roller rockers are fixed.

supplied will cope with this.

The heads can be used in conjunction with conventional mechanical camshafts or hydraulic camshafts if you wish and these will require less valve spring pressure.

Two sizes of dual contra-wound valve springs with two different pressure regimes are available for these cylinder heads –

1) Lower pressure type dual valve springs (used in conjunction with flat tappet camshafts) have a fitted height of 1.800in/45.7mm on these particular cylinder heads, 130lb/59kg seated pressure and 340lb/154kg at maximum valve lift pressure (0.600in/15.2mm).

2) Higher pressure dual valve springs (designed to be used with rapid action roller cams and valve lifts of up to 0.700in/17.8mm) have a fitted height of 1.900in/48.2mm and seated pressure of 160lb/73kg and 420lb/191kg at maximum lift (0.700in/17.8mm). With these stronger springs the retainers can be chrome-moly steel or titanium. The titanium retainers use 10 degree collets (keepers/split locks) to prevent the collets pulling through the retainer. 'Blue' stepped collets can be used to reduce the valve spring pressure slightly. All Stage I and II valve springs are made out of 'superclean silicone' steel.

These cylinder heads come equipped with roller rockers as standard and tappet adjustment is made by the usual screw adjustment system. The roller rockers are paired on short shafts (four individual shafts per cylinder head), with each pair of rockers being secured to an aluminium 'saddle,' which runs the length of the cylinder head, by three bolts. The saddle is fixed to the cylinder head by 8 cap-screws and

Roller rockers are handed.

is bolted to the cylinder head before the rockers are bolted to it. Once assembled, it's all very rigid.

The reason for the detachability of the saddle and roller rockers is to make rocker geometry adjustments easier. When these cylinder heads are ordered the camshaft

Rocker arm can be positioned (adjusted up or down) for optimum geometry.

specifications must be given to Wildcat, the company will then machine the base of the saddle to suit the particular camshaft lift to be used. The geometry only needs to be reset if a camshaft with a different amount of lift is fitted.

There is quite a range of roller camshafts available for Rover V8 engines and quite a range of valve lifts, but few camshafts will exceed 0.700in/ 17.8mm of valve lift. Wildcat has a special jig for measuring and checking the position of the shaft-mounted roller rockers during a dummy assembly. This allows the roller rockers to be positioned to give the ideal arc of travel before the cylinder heads are shipped from the factory.

The next aspect of the setting up of the valve train is the pushrod length. Wildcat buys in pushrods which vary in length by increments of 0.25in/0.63mm. The pushrods suitable for these Stage II heads start at a length of 8.750in/422.3 and go up to 8.900in/225.0. Within this range the perfect length of pushrod is available. Pushrod lengths need to be able to be varied to take into account things like camshaft lobe base circle diameters which vary from camshaft manufacturer to

manufacturer, also whether or not the cylinder heads are planed from the standard size and possibly the block decks too.

Wildcat buys pushrods from various sources, but all of them are made from chrome-moly in the USA: they're very light and very strong. On the Stage II cylinder heads the rockers are shaft mounted and there

Wildcat makes three sizes of exhaust manifold flanges to suit its cylinder heads. The customer has the exhaust system made to suit the application.

is no need for guide plates.

Note that Wildcat does not normally assemble engines. It supplies high performance/ competition engine components for Rover, Buick and Oldsmobile engines.

Caution! – all parts have to be carefully cleaned and prepared before they are fitted to an engine.

Inlet manifolds

The fact that the Wildcat cylinder heads are spaced further apart than standard would normally mean that induction manifolding would be limited for engines equipped with Wildcat High Performance cylinder heads. This isn't the case as Wildcat makes pairs of pre-drilled adapter plates which bolt onto each cylinder head before the inlet manifol, a method which neatly solves any inlet manifold compatability problems.

All the standard-type fuel

injection units made by Rover, and the range of four barrel carburettor inlet manifolds made by aftermarket companies, will fit an engine equipped with Wildcat cylinder heads (Wildcat adapter plates required). This means, for example, that the simply excellent Edelbrock Performer, with its very good distribution characteristics, can be used. The Edelbrock Performer is the best of the 180 degree-type inlet manifolds available for the Rover V8 engine.

Wildcat makes a 360 degree medium rise inlet manifold (spider inlet manifold) which bolts directly to the company's cylinder heads. This inlet manifold has an aperture and bolt pattern to take a 4 barrel Holley carburettor. A 350 or 500CFM two barrel Holley carburettor can be fitted onto this inlet manifold if a Holley adapter plate, or similar, is used.

Wildcat also makes an identical looking 360 degree inlet manifold, but it's a narrower one that fits engines equipped with standard Rover V8 cylinder heads. Huffaker and Dart, which has made 360 degree inlet manifolds, no longer does so but the Wildcat 360 degree inlet manifold is currently available from Wildcat and other sources. At the time of writing, the Wildcat manifold is the only medium rise 360 degree inlet manifold available new.

Wildcat can supply inlet manifolds to mount four 48mm twin barrel downdraught Weber or Dellorto carburettors to any of its cylinder heads. These manifolds are neatly cast and can be ported to very large sizes, if required, as there is plenty of material in them. These inlet manifolds can also be fitted to standard type Rover V8 engine cylinder heads. Wildcat doesn't supply carburettors or linkages for carburettors.

FUEL INJECTION THROTTLE BODIES

Wildcat also makes individual runner fuel injection throttle bodies in pairs, together with a substantial throttle linkage. Each throttle body assembly bolts directly to each cylinder head. They're available with butterfly diameters of 50mm, 52mm, 55mm and 58mm: the 50mm and 52mm diameters being the most popular. These throttle bodies have vertical tracts, which means they turn 45 degrees as they come from the cylinder heads and the inlet trumpets are vertical. A recent development by Wildcat is throttle bodies which are angled 20 degrees from vertical, which means that the inlet tracts turn 25 degrees as they come from the cylinder heads, as opposed to 45 degrees. Both types will be available from now on. The object of the exercise is an inlet tract with the least curvature possible (straighter is better). The steel throttle shafts are 8mm in diameter and each butterfly is held in place by two small screws. The manifolds are drilled to take standard Rover V8 electronic fuel injection nozzles.

Wildcat does not supply fuel injection software, but can advise good sources for the sort of equipment that suits its hardware. These throttle bodies do not fit standard Rover V8 engine cylinder heads.

DRY SUMP SYSTEM

In 2003 Ian Richardson decided that

Carl Hansen's Wildcat-based engine. Note dry sump pump, fittings and belt-drive system at base of picture.

it was time to work out a complete dry sump package for the Rover V8 engine, one which would suit all known applications.

The requirement was really driven by the need for a fully integrated dry sump system that could be easily fitted to TVR cars. This has been achieved with only the TVR Griffith & Chimaera requiring a reasonably straightforward exhaust pipe modification for the Wildcat dry sump system to be accommodated.

A further consideration was that many of these engines were having long stroke crankshafts fitted, and there was no extra clearance in the existing dry sump pans to accommodate the extra throw. What people had to do was make a spacer rail to sandwich between the block rails and the dry sump pan. The Wildcat dry sump pan is made with a deeper railing which can be left in place on all engines or be machined down if required.

Working with TVR and TVR

specialists, Ian sorted out their exact requirements and the dry sump package/kit he now offers is the result. The dry sump pan has two scavenge take off points and the pipework can be taken off from either side of the reservoir. There are two replaceable filters in the pan in front of each scavenge pipe fitting.

The front cover is cast to accommodate a distributor but, when you order a dry sump kit, you'll have to specify whether you want it machined to take a distributor or not.

The front cover and sump, while normally cast in LM 25 aluminium alloy, is also available in elektron magnesium (which costs three times as much).

Before the advent of the Wildcat front cover, designed to take a three stage dry sump pump pack, dry sump pumps tended to be mounted less firmly than they really should have been. However, the Wildcat front cover and dry sump pan has effectively solved all known problems.

The three stage type dry sump pump pack (Weaver, Pace & Aviad have been used to date, but virtually any type can be fitted), is mounted directly on the Wildcat front cover's substantial mounting using a double blade system. There's one mains pressure pump and two scavenge pumps in the pack. Also supplied in the kit is a Gilmer-type belt drive and drive cogs.

Wildcat stocks all fittings and piping for the dry sump system, but there isn't a single kit as such because of the diverse range of fitting applications. If you give Ian Richardson the exact pipe length dimensions, he will then supply you with an individualised kit. He doesn't stock pump remote oil filters because they are readily available, as are dry sump supply tanks from specialist suppliers.

An aluminium, high flow rate, low cavitation (via the curved blades on the cast impellor) Buick water pump is used. This water pump turns clockwise and can, if required, be under driven down to a ratio of 0.8:1, although most people stay with a 1:1 ratio. Water pumps can be driven by a vee-belt, a poly-vee or a Gilmer belt. Wildcat can supply suitable pulleys for each type to suit individual requirements, and can also supply alternator pulleys to suit the three types of belt.

STEEL FLYWHEELS

Wildcat supplies two types of steel flywheel.

The first type is a lightweight direct replacement of the standard original type (stronger and lighter). These flywheels can be supplied drilled and dowelled for any clutch cover assembly which suits the AP or Quartermaster 7¼in triple plate clutches frequently used for racing. Wildcat does not stock clutches.

The second flywheel type is about 2ines/50.8mm smaller in diameter than the standard-sized ones and is used in conjunction with an Ark Racing offset geared starter. Wildcat aluminium starter

housings are used by Ark Racing which uses Nippon Denso electrical components to make up either a 1.4 or 1.8kW starter: both are extremely powerful. The flywheels are normally drilled and dowelled to suit AP or Quartermaster 7¼in triple plate clutches, but can be drilled and dowelled to suit any alternative fitment.

The Wildcat dry sump system was designed to be compatible with the second type of steel flywheel described, meaning the bottom of the dry sump pan is level with the ring gear on the flywheel. Tying these two factors into each other means that an engine can be installed in a chassis as low as possible given other constraints in particular applications.

WILDCAT ENGINE EXAMPLE

An example of an engine featuring Wildcat components is that of Carl Hansen's racing TVR Tuscan in New Zealand.

Having spent years working with the standard Rover V8 componentry (even going to the extent of downdraughting the original cylinder head castings), Carl decided that he would keep on developing the engine, but would switch to Wildcat componentry to gain capacity and to use the then all new aftermarket cylinder heads.

In 1999 Carl built a 4.8 litre engine using Wildcat cylinder heads, block, forged crankshaft, lightweight connecting rods and

Carl Hansen's Wildcat based engine in his TVR Tuscan.

forged pistons as well as most of the other components Wildcat offered. This 540bhp engine was in use from 2000 until the end of 2004. In 2003 Carl decided to build a new 5.8 litre engine, again using all of the latest Wildcat componentry. He went to England and bought every bit of gear Ian Richardson makes and took it all back to New Zealand and got to work on the new unit. The engine dyno sheets for this latest engine is the one that follows:

As you can imagine, with 525lb. ft of torque and 747bhp, not too many cars pull out and pass Carl. Interesting aspects are that the engine produced more power on USA imported high octane unleaded fuel than on the leaded Avgas readily available in New Zealand for auto racing purposes (107 RON – 100 MON). In short, the unleaded fuel is faster-burning which translates into more pressure being available to push the piston down the bore. A pushrod problem caused an initial 100bhp loss. This has since been rectified. An alternative camshaft has since been ground to see if the power output can be further

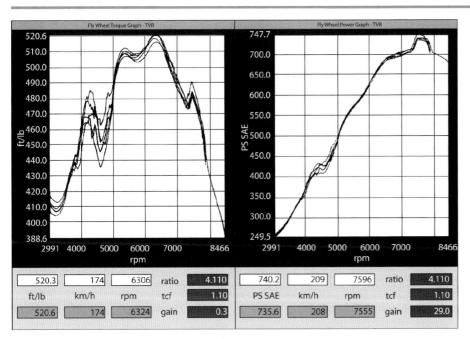

Dynapack dyno printout for Carl Hansen's 747bhp Wildcat Rover V8.

increased even though the existing power is not proving easy to get down to the ground. The careful application of the accelerator pedal is now required at all times especially out of corners to avoid wheelspin. When the wheels spin the car loses forward momentum instantly.

Chapter 11
Cylinder head modifications

Many companies modify Rover V8 cylinder heads: the available range of modifications runs from mild to radical. This is an area of modification about which it can be said, with certainty, that you get what you pay for. Head modification is a time consuming business and, done properly, will be expensive.

The Rover V8 specialists have taken the modification of the standard cylinder head to its logical conclusion, having narrowed down the options to those that really work over the last 30 years. J.E. Developments, for example, removes the valve seat inserts and replaces them with larger ones of the same material, then fits its specially-made large inlet and exhaust valves together with new valve guides. The inlet and exhaust ports are opened out/reshaped to the reliable limit (in relation to casting wall thickness).

However, it has to be said

that the vast majority of high performance engines are not fitted with cylinder heads modified to anything like this level. J.E. Developments prepares its cylinder heads for racing purposes, with the porting designed to match the valve sizes/flow rates of engines revving to 7000rpm at each gear change. These cylinder heads are precisely done because the original castings limit how much material can come out of the cylinder heads. The modified port wall, floor and roof contours are intersecting curves done as smoothly as possible within the limitations of wall thickness. Virtually every part of the standard porting is altered (enlarged) with the exception of the inlet port floor (where the port turns into the valve throat area) which is kept as high as practically possible to avoid having a too tight radius on the 'short turn' (very important).

WHICH HEADS?
Early cylinder heads 1967-1976 (pre-SD1) have the small diameter inlet and exhaust valves and cast iron-type valve seats. The inlet and exhaust ports of all Rover V8 engines (1967-2004) are all pretty much the same shape and size, but there are slight differences in size: the later the cylinder head, the larger the ports are likely to be. The actual size difference will be within $1/16$in/1.5mm overall, which isn't much. The later fuel injection engine cylinder heads (1988 on) have slightly different port turn areas than the earlier cylinder heads, but even then the difference in the height measurement early to late is only $3/32$in/2mm.

Of all the standard cylinder heads available, the later large valve cylinder heads are better. Heads made from 1982 onward are designed for use with lead free fuel which is an advantage

CYLINDER HEAD MODIFICATIONS

as all previous heads require a fuel additive, or to have hardened exhaust valve seats fitted, to prevent valve seat recession (VSR). It isn't all that difficult to find a good pair of later cylinder heads and they do offer the best basis for obtaining the best possible gasflow for the least amount of rework/cost.

The latest cylinder heads (injection engine cylinder heads, which are easy to recognise by the cutout for the injector nozzle spray pattern) have better inlet ports, with more uniform sizes and a slightly larger cross-sectional area offering better airflow compared to the early small valve heads. Small valve heads can be uprated to equal the performance of the later larger valve heads, but it's not worth doing on economic grounds given the ready availability of later heads. Essentially, later is best, with 1988 to 2004 heads being the ones to go for. However, in reality, there are no bad Rover V8 cylinder heads, its just that some are slightly better than others within the full range.

MODIFICATIONS
Preparation
Rover V8 cylinder heads don't have a fault history (cracking, etc), but it is still advisable to have them pressure checked, especially if you are going to spend quite a lot of money refurbishing them. Many engine reconditioners have proper pressure testing equipment and it doesn't take very long to test a pair of cylinder heads and to confirm that they are sound. If one or both heads happen to be faulty, at least you have found out before any serious work has been done.

At the very least all of the ports of a used head should be thoroughly cleaned to remove all carbon build-up and other accumulations. This cleaning is normally done with rotary wire brushes which make short work of it. Use a high speed (1800-4500rpm) pistol drill with the wire brushes and clean the walls back to bare metal.

Warning! – Avoid inhaling (use a mask) the material that comes out of the ports, especially the exhaust ports. Use a vacuum cleaner to suck up all of the debris.

Next, the cylinder heads should be chemically cleaned so that all of the coolant passageways are as clean as when the head was new. This is done to ensure that there is no material deposited on the coolant passageway walls which will reduce the heat conducting efficiency of the cylinder heads. Aluminium heads, like these, are placed in a tank which contains an undiluted cold solution of cresylic acid and methylene chloride. The parts must be left in the tank for a minimum of 1 hour, with overnight being quite acceptable (no damage to the aluminium if the heads are left in for a long period of time). Parts so treated come out with a matt surface finish appearance.

Caution! – **Do not** bead blast cylinder heads. While there is no doubt that bead blasting can clean any surface that the glass beads come into contact with, there's a problem with the beads lodging in inaccessible places. Oilways and the water jacket come to mind here and, even though you may think you've got all the beads cleaned out, in far too many instances this will prove not to be the case and engine failure can be the direct result ...

Valve guides
Whether or not the valve guides are worn, they should all be 'K-Lined' back to minimum clearance. A secondary benefit of this process is to prevent the problem of valves sticking (a fairly recent problem to do with the removal of tetraethyl lead from the fuel). Note that K-Line inserts can be replaced as many times as you like. These inserts are used around the world nowadays to restore worn valve guides and they are simply excellent. **Caution!** – K-Line inserts are designed to be fitted into cast iron valve guides only: **not** bronze ones.

Note that 'Tufftriding' of the valves is now another recognised way of preventing the valves from sticking when unleaded fuel is being used.

Minor porting
An option at this point is to blend the aluminium at the juncture of the valve seats and the cylinder head back into the ports for about 0.375in/10mm. The standard finish here is not all that smooth in contour and an improvement in gasflow will result if this single area of the ports is cleaned up. Removal of material from the actual valve seat insert (to make it larger in diameter to gain flow) is not required, but some smoothing of the insert is quite acceptable (even unavoidable) when the junction between seat and port is being smoothed: this won't have a detrimental effect. This work can be done by anyone who is reasonably handy with a die grinder or a pistol drill fitted with a ball-nosed rotary file. Not a lot of material has to come out of the ports and it doesn't take too long to do this work, but you do have to be careful. **Caution!** – If the

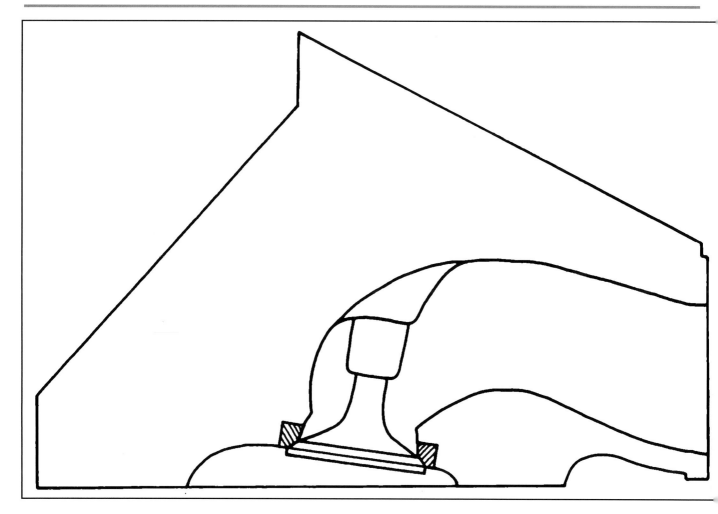

1: Actual size diagram of standard P5, P6 and early Range Rover inlet port/valve/valve seat.

rotary file slips and runs over the valve seat you'll damage it. If the file does slip in this manner, the valve seat cutting will have to be deeper to remove the damage.

Beyond the valve seat/port junction the standard ports are well shaped and sized as standard and really don't need attention except for extreme applications. 'Porting' of cylinder heads to improve the gasflow seems to mean different things to different people. Some reworked cylinder heads look to have very large inlet and exhaust ports but, frequently, all that's been

done is to enlarge the inlet port for the first 0.625-0.75in/16-19mm into the port from the inlet manifold gasket face. These port openings can measure 1.065in/27mm wide by 1.730in/44mm in height (up from 0.970in/24.5mm wide by 1.575in/40mm high). After being altered exhaust port openings at the manifold face can measure around 0.950in/24mm wide by 1.420in/36mm high (standard 0.800in/20mm wide by 1.200in/31mm high), but this enlargement may taper back to the standard port size within 0.75in/19mm. If you do this work, or have

it done for you, consider it to be a cleaning up process of those areas of the cylinder heads which are easy to get at. An improvement in gasflow will be achieved, but it will be very small because the overall porting remains as originally cast.

Valve seats

The valve seats are machined next, and there are several ways this can be done. One of the most popular ways is to get the seats cut using a machine that cuts a three angle valve seat in one hit (eg: Cerdi). These machines cut the seats precisely to

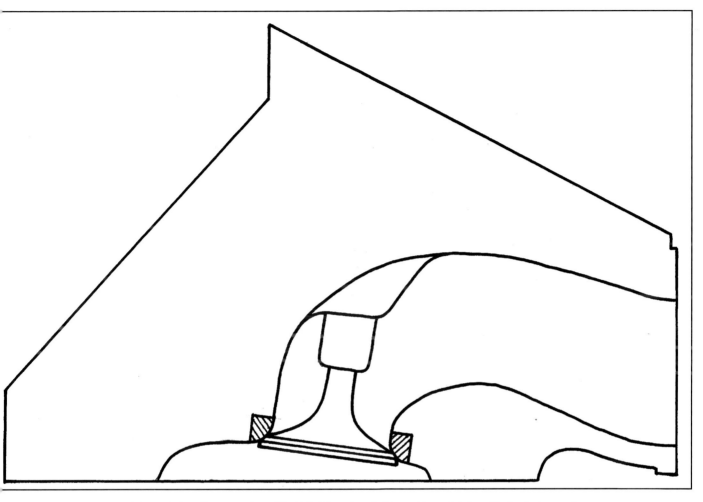

2: Actual size diagram of modified P5, P6 and early Range Rover inlet port/valve/valve seat.

a width of 0.050in and 0.060in/1.25 and 1.5mm respectively for the inlet and exhaust seats. Valve seat widths can be reduced for racing purposes to 0.040in/1.0mm for inlets and 0.050in/1.25mm for exhausts.

A good job can also be made of the valve seats using any of the usual reconditioning methods.

The standard valve seating regime has a 20 degree 'top cut' (combustion chamber to valve seat), a 45 degree valve seat and a radiused inner machined section on both inlet and exhaust valve seat inserts.

The standard valve seats of 1982 on cylinder heads have proved to be absolutely reliable, with deterioration, including after heavy use, being quite minimal even when unleaded fuel is being used exclusively. Since unleaded fuel's widespread use, you're more likely to find the standard exhaust valve's contact area (seat contact area) quite badly deteriorated, with refacing or replacement being required. The valve seat, however, cleans up as good as new with a wire brushing.

One oddity about the standard cylinder heads is the fact that the valve head diameters are larger than the outer diameter of the valve seats. To maximise the gasflow the valve seat of the valve seat insert needs to be re-cut so that it is the same diameter as the valve head. The standard factory valve seating criteria with regard to valve seat widths are perfectly acceptable, but most cylinder head modifiers will narrow the valve seating from standard if they are to be used in high performance applications.

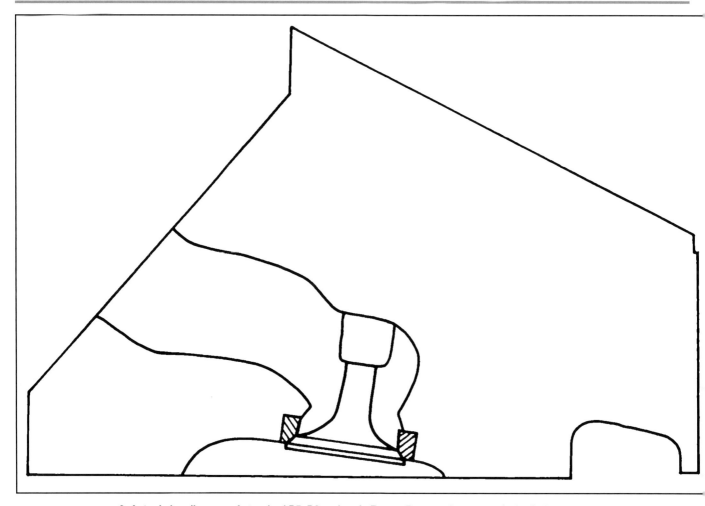

3: Actual size diagram of standard P5, P6 and early Range Rover exhaust port/valve/valve seat.

Refacing

At this point all cylinder heads should be skimmed by a minimum of 0.003in/0.075mm to clean them up and remove any surface warping that might be present. **Caution!** – It would be unrealistic to expect a pair of cylinder heads still to be as the factory machined them after many years of use, and the same holds true for the block decks. The removal of this small amount of material from head and block deck surfaces can be regarded as a preventive measure against blowing cylinder head gaskets.

FULLY MODIFIED CYLINDER HEADS

The requirement for all out racing engines is that everything possible should be done to the cylinder heads to ensure maximum volumetric efficiency in order to allow the production of maximum torque and maximum bhp.

J.E. Developments, for example, has one maximum specification cylinder head which the company uses for all its large bore engines. There is nothing more that can be done in terms of cylinder head modification (within the confines of using a standard cylinder head casting – no welding or building up with plastic steel, etc) as far as John Eales is concerned.

If you buy your cylinder heads from J.E. Developments, for example, expect to pay good money for them because a lot of work has gone into them. Bigger valves, bigger ports, de-shrouding of the valves (which alters the combustion chamber shape slightly) will all allow higher revs and increased engine performance. There is a bit more to it than this, however, because with these modifications fuel economy

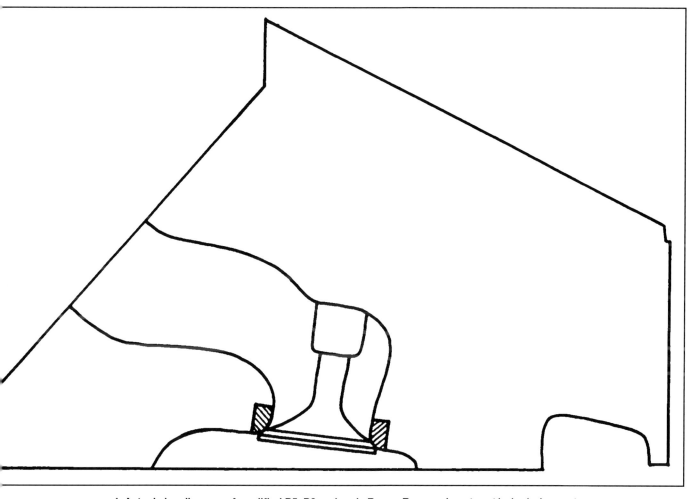

4: Actual size diagram of modified P5, P6 and early Range Rover exhaust port/valve/valve seat.

reduces, even if you're not using the extra power. The GM engineers didn't arrive at the port and valve sizes they chose for nothing. They'd been designing engines for years and had a lot of experience in what they were doing and chose a well-balanced compromise offering good performance with good fuel economy.

In some applications, minor reworking of the cylinder heads, such as tidying up the valve throat areas and, maybe, the inlet port openings at the manifold end, is all you should be doing. A road car

engine that has to deliver reasonable fuel economy doesn't want to be altered too much from standard. Readers should note that a Rover V8 engine that has been modified for racing purposes is going to get between 2 and 5 miles to the gallon when it is being raced!

Cylinder head work has to reflect intended end use! The vast majority of Rover V8 engines being modified for higher performance do not need to have fully modified cylinder heads.

For those that need them, the associated diagrams show the inlet

and exhaust porting, in profile, of all the standard Rover V8 cylinder heads. The shaping and the sizing of the valve throats is uniformly circular making one example all that is really necessary to gain an overview. Diagrams 1 to 4 show the valve throats of the P5, P6 and early Range Rover small valve cylinder heads 1967-1976; diagrams 5-8 show the later, larger valve cylinder head inlet and exhaust porting of 1976-2004. The change to the cylinder heads of 1994 on, when the combustion chamber was made shallower, has no effect on porting

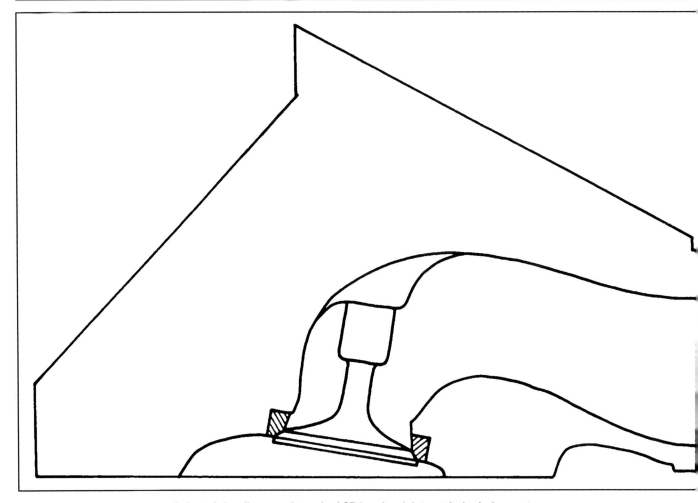

5: Actual size diagram of standard SD1 and on inlet port/valve/valve seat.

criteria. Diagrams 9 and 10 are of modified J.E. Developments racing engine cylinder heads. The widths of the inlet and exhaust ports are maximised on these cylinder heads. All of these diagrams are to scale and actual size.

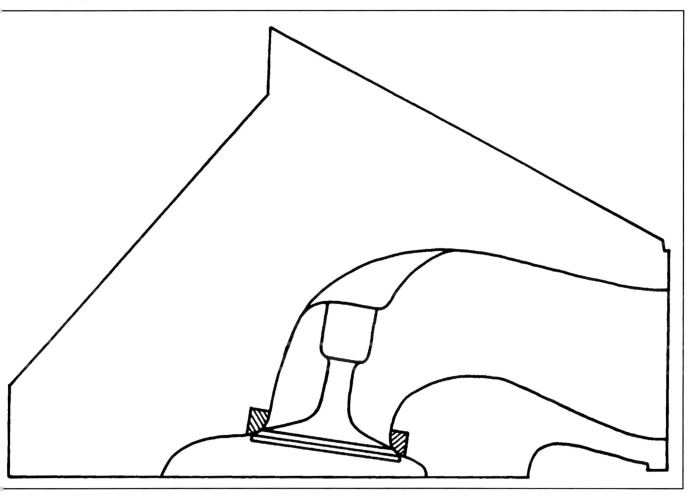

6: Actual size diagram of modified SD1 and on inlet port/valve/valve seat.

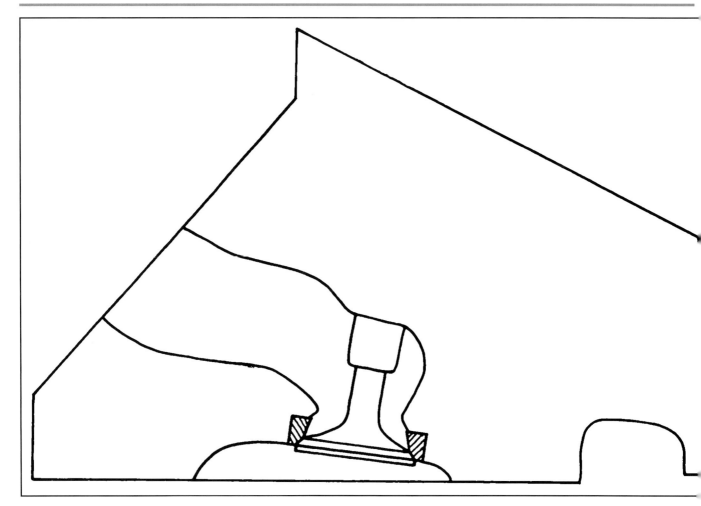

7: Actual size diagram of standard SD1 and on exhaust port/valve/valve seating.

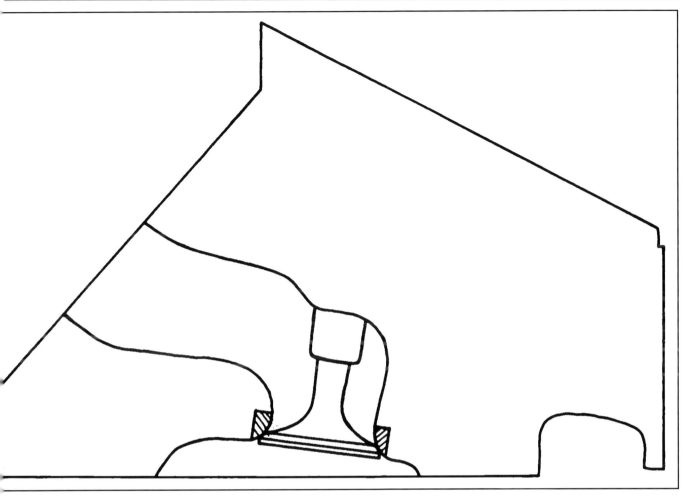

8: Actual size diagram of modified SD1 and on exhaust port/valve/valve seating.

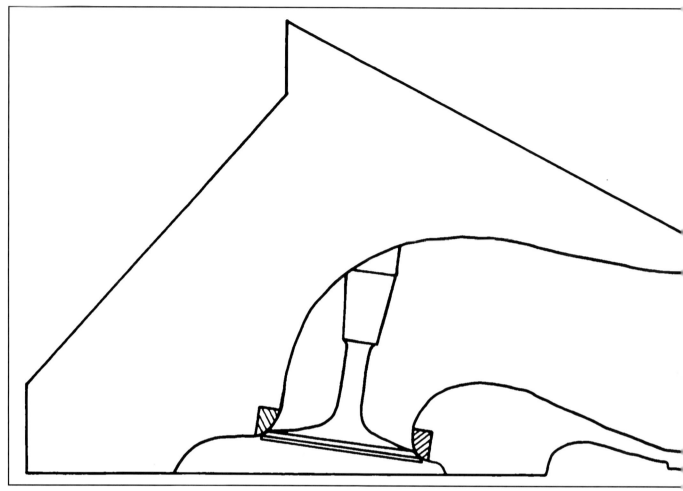

9: Actual size diagram of maximum performance cylinder heads: J.E. Developments' inlet port/valve/valve seating.

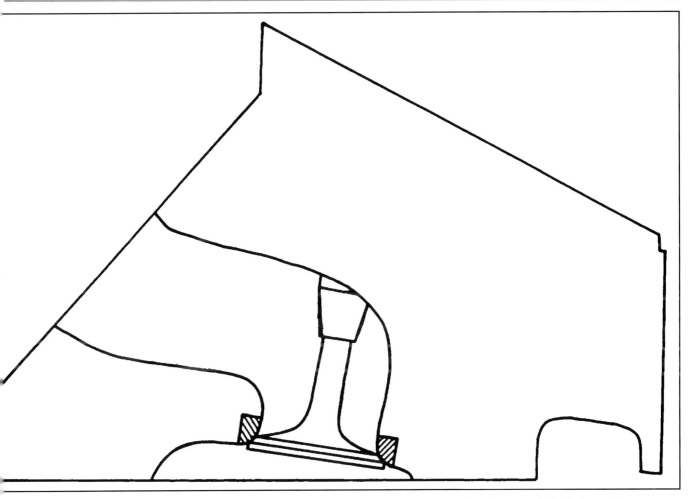

10: Actual size diagram of maximum performance cylinder heads: J.E. Developments' exhaust port/valve/valve seating.

Chapter 12
SU carburettors

The first thing that many tuners do is look for an alternative carburettor, regarding the standard twin SUs as inferior. The alternative choice tends to be the 390 or 465 CFM Holley and, latterly, the 500 CFM Edelbrock/Carter Thermoquad carburettor, this in conjunction with a four-barrel inlet manifold (eg: Edelbrock Performer 3.5), and it's a very efficient system.

In fact, up to a certain level of performance, the standard twin SU set up with its dual plane inlet manifold is very good. If you concentrate on getting the best out of what you have, the results can be very acceptable. The standard 1¾in/44mm twin SUs are quite capable of supplying sufficient gasflow for over 6000rpm: it's the inlet manifold that impedes gasflow, causing poor throttle response.

An important thing to recognise with SU carburettors is that maximum engine power is limited by the maximum airflow through the carburettors. This occurs with the throttle fully open and the piston at its maximum height. The bridge in the throttle bore is there to create a depression and so draw up the fuel from the jet, so it's not something that can be changed. As a result, an SU-equipped engine will never produce quite as much top end power as one equipped with other similar sized, but more sophisticated carburettors, such as a single twin barrel downdraught Weber or Dellorto.

The reason for the SUs not being able to match these carburettors is to do with the difference between a fixed venturi, fixed jet design (as used by both Weber & Dellorto) versus the variable choke (venturi) and moving jet/needle design (used by SUs). Unfortunately, with the latter there is an unrecoverable loss of potential performance. Having said that, SUs are extremely good carburettors and give within 5% to 7% of the performance of a Weber or Dellorto at a lower cost.

SETTING UP

Countless engines are seen running with carburettors that are poorly set up, yet setting them up correctly is relatively straightforward.

There are several settings on an SU carburettor that simply have to be right before the engine will give top performance, but before this can happen the engine needs to be in perfect mechanical condition and the ignition system must be correctly set up as well.

1) Float levels
The float levels must be set to the factory specifications, and for the HIF type SU this means at the top end of the 0.040in/1.0mm to 0.060in/

.5mm tolerance band. Setting the floats at 0.060in/1.5mm makes sure there is slightly more fuel in the fuel bowl, which is an advantage. Fill up the fuel bowls and then carefully drain them, measuring the volume of liquid drained from each one to ensure that it's equal. Adjust the float levels within the standard float height tolerance until you arrive at equal volumes of fuel in both bowls. This balance is essential to ensuring that both carburettors give the correct fuel/air mixture throughout the running range. On the earlier HS6 carburettors with side hung fuel bowls, the fuel volume is checked by removing the top of the fuel bowl and measuring the level of the fuel from the top of the bowl with the tail of a vernier caliper or a narrow 6in/150mm rule. The level is near enough to the top for any difference to be visible. The levels need to be within 0.010in/0.25m of each other (if you're doing this with the carbs installed, the car needs to be level).

2) Needle heights

Next, the two needles must be positioned in their pistons. That is, the shoulder of the needle must be **exactly** level with the base of the piston. This is not always easy to achieve on carburettors with spring loaded needles because the securing screw may have been tightened onto the needle guide so hard that it has become distorted and the needle will only settle in one place. In this case, buy two new needle guides and don't overtighten the securing screws.

3) Main jet heights

Before the piston and dashpot assembly is fitted to the body of the carburettor, screw both main

jets down so that the tops of the jets are 0.040in/1.0mm below the surface of the bridge. You will need to use the tail of a vernier calliper to measure this. This is the easiest way to measure and adjust the height of the jets, which need to be set within 0.003in/0.075mm of each other. This setting will ensure a reasonable fuel/air ratio at idle speed and for starting the engine, although they both may need to be changed equally to effect an ideal idle mixture. It's important to maintain the distance between the top of the main jet and the top of the bridge in both carburettors, whatever the distance is. If an engine will only run correctly with the main jets set at vastly different heights there's a problem somewhere (worn main jet, worn needles, etc), which needs to be rectified.

The needles' first three measuring point sizes in relation to the main jet and its distance below the bridge determine the idle mixture. Once the distance between the top of the main jet and the top of the bridge is set, it should **not** be subsequently altered to effect any slight mixture alteration off idle! To alter the mixture you change the needles' measuring point sizes by increasing, or decreasing, the diameters at the offending measuring points (if you change needles, make sure that the alternative needles used have the same diameters at the 1st, 2nd & 3rd measuring points).

4) Idle adjustment screws

The idle adjustment screws are then adjusted so that the butterflies are half a screw turn from their fully closed position. This will ensure that both carburettors will have a

near equal amount of throttle for initial starting and idling. With these adjustments completed the engine can be started.

5) Balance

The next step is to make sure that the two carburettors are flowing equal amounts of air at idle. Each carburettor has an idle speed screw, which is adjusted whilst using a handheld airflow meter, such as a Gunson or Motometer. With the two carburettors flowing equal amounts of air, the idle adjustment screws are then altered **equally** to either raise or lower the idle speed as required.

6) Idle mixture

The idle mixture is now adjusted, altering both carburettors by **exactly** the same amount. The main jets are either raised or lowered equally to effect optimum idle smoothness. Expect this to usually occur with a 0.92 Lambda/13.5:1 air-fuel ratio/2.5% CO reading. Some engines might require a richer idle mixture, such as a 0.90 Lambda/13.2:1 air-fuel ratio/3.0% CO reading. Trial and error is required to get the mixture strength just right, but this is the range to work within. It's most important that both main jets are altered by **equal** amounts, and you should cross check this by taking both dashpots off again and measuring the position of the main jets relative to the top of the bridges with the tail of a vernier calliper and, if necessary, adjusting them to be within 0.002-0.003in/0.05-0.075mm of each other. Then check the Lambda/%CO reading again.

7) Synchronising butterflies

Next thing on the list is to ensure that both of the throttle butterflies open together when the accelerator pedal is pressed from idle. It needs two people to carry out this check, one presses the accelerator pedal while the other checks the airflow readings of each carburettor. The standard throttle linkage looks a nightmare, but with care it can be set very accurately and remain set correctly for some time, although it is a fiddly task to get it just right.

With the engine running, the accelerator pedal is depressed slowly until the engine reaches about 2000rpm and is then held at that speed. Measure the airflow of each carburettor and compare the readings, if they're not the same, adjust the linkage of one carburettor to suit the other. Let the engine settle back to idle and check the airflow at idle again to make sure that the original settings have not been interfered with by the throttle arm adjustment. Depress the accelerator pedal again until 2000rm is reached, hold it there and check the air flow readings for a third time. With the readings identical, increase to 2500rpm and check them again and, finally, at 3000rpm. If the readings for both carburettors are identical from idle through to 3000rpm, they're balanced for airflow. There's really no need to do this at higher rpm, although many people check the engine through to 3500 and then 4000rpm.

With the engine switched off, the accelerator pedal should be pressed fully to the floor and then both butterflies checked to make sure they're wide open. At full throttle the butterflies should be at precisely 90 degrees to the throttle bore. If they're not, then four cylinders will be getting less air fuel mixture than the other four, and you'll need to check for wear in the linkage and, if this is the case, replace parts as necessary. This full throttle check needs to be carried out frequently and, if it's a racing engine, before each race day.

People often swap to an American two or four barrel carburettor just to avoid the problems of synchronising twin carburettors.

FUEL PRESSURE

After setting up the carburettors, the fuel pumps need to be checked. They must be able to supply 3.5 to 4.5psi/2.4 to 3.1kPa of fuel pressure **throughout** the rpm range and maintain it at maximum rpm. If the fuel pressure is low, the fuel level in the carburettors will drop and the air/fuel mixture will go lean.

To check fuel pressure, connect a fuel pressure gauge to a take-off union placed in the fuel line between the two carburettors. Any reduction in fuel pressure that occurs, especially on a long straight at full throttle, is a cause for concern. Change the pump, or add a supplementary one at the fuel tank if the existing one cannot keep up with demand.

There should be a fuel filter in the line between the fuel pump and the two carburettors, check it and change it if you think it may be partially blocked and restricting flow.

Finally, make sure that the fuel lines aren't crimped, kinked or have sharp bends in them that might restrict the fuel flow.

EMISSION CONTROL POPPET VALVES

The emission control poppet valves when fitted, restrict airflow. They can be removed from the butterflies and the holes soldered over, or new butterflies can be fitted which don't have provision for the poppet valve.

CRANKCASE BREATHER

Another small improvement that can be made to the carburation is to remove the crankcase ventilation pipes from the carburettors. The connection on the carburettors can be blocked off with a rubber cap or even brazed over. The crankcase st needs to be ventilated, and you can do this using a system of breathers in the rocker covers or a vent off the lifter valley.

AIR CLEANERS & RAM PIPES

For most applications the standard air cleaner system is removed and replaced by individual bolt-on air filters fitted to the existing adapter, or by flared ram pipes fitted directly to the carburettor intakes. In some instances, racing engines have no air cleaners and have the adapter removed as well so that the air goes directly into the body of the carburettor. However, all of these options have been proven, beyond doubt, not to be optimum, although the engines still produce good general power.

The following back-to-back tests give a real insight into the effects of these options. The test engine was a 3.9 litre prepared by John Eales of J.E. Developments and fitted with twin SUs on a standard but modified manifold. With the air going directly into the SUs (ie: no air filter or adapter) the engine

FRONT OF ENGINE

P

The standard moulded hoses are retained in their original positions. A K&N air filter is fitted to the end of each hose. The air separation plate "P" fits between the ends of the two air filters.

eveloped 240bhp. When full radius aluminium ram pipes, with or without ram-pipe socks' were added, the power increased to approximately 247bhp. With rubber-necked universal cone air filters fitted to the standard aluminium adapters, power showed 242bhp. With the cone filters removed and the adapters left in place, the power was about the same.

The system that gave the best result was not far removed from the standard air filter set-up. The standard cast aluminium adapters were retained with both of the air intake elbows and a large diameter K&N filter was fitted to the end of each elbow. An air separation plate was fitted between the two filters to prevent interference between the airflows. With this system the power rose to 256bhp.

Whatever else you do, make sure that it's cool air that's reaching the air intake. Warm air expands and volumetric efficiency suffers as a consequence.

CHANGING & MODIFYING NEEDLES

For calibration purposes, SU needles are divided along their length into 'measuring points', which can also be called 'metering points', 0.125in/3.2mm apart, starting at the shoulder and going on down to the point of the needle. The needles used in 1.75in/44mm carburettors have 16 measuring points. However, the measuring points after the 12th are largely irrelevant because they don't meter the fuel, even at full power.

Sorting out the correct needles for an SU can be difficult and time-consuming, which is part of the reason why SUs don't enjoy a better image. There are over 800 needles available which are fine for the many standard production engines, but when it comes to modified engines, the factory needles don't always supply the correct air/fuel mixture throughout the whole rpm range. Nevertheless, for optimum performance, the needles have to be absolutely correct for the state of tune of the individual engine. The air/fuel ratio must be correct at all times so that the engine develops maximum torque, maximum power and maximum acceleration from off idle to maximum rpm under all load conditions. On a non-standard engine it means there is only one reasonable option and that's to custom modify the needles to suit the individual engine.

Another book in the Veloce SpeedPro Series *How To Build & Power Tune SU Carburettors* covers, in full, the procedures involved in working out the needle measuring points and modifying needle sizes at those points for any engine, in any state of tune. It also contains other information on

optimising SU performance.

SUs own publication the *SU Carburettor Needle Profile Charts*, published by Burlen Fuel Systems, is another important reference book.

The most commonly used standard needles are listed in this chapter, and many of them will prove to be right for modified engines. However, if they are not right at a point or points in the rpm range, the needle should be modified because the engine performance will be improved further. When the engine goes rich, for example, that fuel overdose has to be burnt off before good power is produced again; conversely, if it goes lean, the engine will slow, or hesitate, until extra fuel is supplied. If the fuel curve is correct, neither problem will occur, and this comes down to using scientific analysis to make sure that there is not the slightest richness or leanness in the fuel curve which could prevent the optimum engine performance being developed throughout the rev range. This may not seem too important, but in a race engine a slight temporary richness can be enough to prevent the car from gaining on another car out of a turn, it's that critical. There is no substitute for having the air/fuel mixture absolutely correct throughout the entire rpm range of the engine.

The scientific analysis involves checking the air/fuel mixture ratio (via Lambda or percentage CO exhaust readings) at a large number of points over the engine's rpm range to make sure that nothing has been missed. Only then can the profile of the needles be finalised to give the best overall performance. Once a pair of needles have been correctly calibrated to suit a particular engine and its state of tune it won't need to be done again, so in a sense it's a one off cost.

As an example, at wide open throttle the air/fuel mixture ratio for **any** Rover V8 engine is, on average, going to be 0.88 Lambda/13.0:1 air-fuel/3.7% CO. The acceleration phase mixture ratio will increase to 0.85 Lambda/12.5:1 air-fuel/5.0% CO. The cruise setting can be as low as 1.05 Lambda/15.4:1 air-fuel/0.15% CO. This general range applies across the board from standard road going engines to full race ones. The Rover V8 engine doesn't require a rich mixture to produce good torque and power.

Mixture ratio measurement and adjustment is best done on a rolling road to remove all possible doubt about the mixture requirements: it makes good sense to have this aspect of the engine's set up thoroughly checked.

Dynos are very accurate these days. The Dynapack chassis dyno (which requires the fitting of absorption units to the driven wheels), for example, gives extremely detailed and accurate scientific analysis and can be used on road cars or racing cars (www.dynapack.com). Alternatively, an engine could be tested on an engine dyno (more costly), which is usually what happens to racing engines.

Caution! – Too rich a mixture (too much fuel) causes power reduction as well as starting the process of 'bore-wash' (dilution of the oil film on the cylinder walls) the result of which is excessive bore wear. Too lean and the power reduces and the prospect of overheating the internal componentry and possible engine damage comes into the picture.

For most readers a trip to a rolling road/chassis dyno with an experienced operator is highly recommended to ensure that the mixture ratios are as they should be: it's just too easy to get this aspect of an engine wrong, devaluing all the other work you've carried out.

The optimum maximum power mixture setting is found by testing a range of needles with different diameters at the 11th, 12th and 13th measuring points. The 12th measuring point is the critical one for this carburettor because, in theory, it's the exact section of the needle doing the fuel metering at full power, in practice this position can be up to 0.040in/1.0mm higher (depending on the position of the jet relative to the top of the bridge), hence the need for the 11th and 13th points to be of known diameter. A 0.001in/0.025mm change in diameter (larger or smaller) at the 11th, 12th and 13th needle measuring points, will make a difference to the Lamda/CO reading. While setting the top point it's important to use needles of known uniform geometry, so there should be a 0.002in/0.05mm decrease in diameter per point from the 11th to the 13th point (for example: 11th measuring point 0.070in/1.77mm, 12th 0.068in/1.727mm and 13th 0.066in/1.676mm). The full SU range includes needles with 0.002 to 0.004in/0.05 to 0.1mm differences in diameter per point in the 11th to 13th measuring point range.

Using scientific instruments to monitor the air/fuel ratio, remove 0.001in/0.0254mm diameter from the 11th, 12th and 13th points and test the engine again. If the power increases, remove another 0.001in/0.0254mm from the diameter, or find another needle that has the

appropriate smaller sizes, and test the engine again. Carry on reducing the needle in 0.001in/0.0254mm increments until the power peaks. This is the optimum full power fuel/air ratio, and it usually corresponds to 0.88 Lambda or 3.7%CO. As a guide, if reducing the needle by another 0.001in/0.0254mm drops the power by 2-3bhp, then the previous point was the peak. If you carried on then, the power would drop by around 5 to 9bhp as the air/fuel mixture ratio becomes richer than required for top end power production. Setting the fuel/air ratio at maximum power first is important because if an engine runs lean it can be damaged internally, possibly resulting in burnt pistons.

Sorting out of the max power air/fuel mixture ratio is, perhaps, the easy bit because the carburettor pistons are at the top of their travel. The same goes for the idle speed air/fuel ratio because the piston is more or less at a known static point with the needle metering at either the 1st, 2nd or 3rd measuring point. It's the area in between these extremes that generally causes the most problems because the fuel/air ratio has to be optimised at each of the intermediate points (that's at least the 4th to the 10th points). This is time-consuming work but it's essential if the engine is to be set up correctly.

Using a rolling road and exhaust gas analysis are two key elements in obtaining an accurate picture of the fuel curve under varying conditions. With the car on the rolling road, the engine is placed under load with the throttle wide open. The dynamometer, which controls the load, is adjusted to hold the engine at a specific rpm. Typically the point tested would include the bottom of the useful torque curve (2500rpm), maximum torque (3000-4500rpm), maximum power (5800rpm), and then maximum rpm (say 6500rpm). If the exhaust gas readings go rich or lean at any point, then there's a problem with the fuel curve. The part of the needle that is metering the fuel needs to be established using calibrated rods (see *How To Build & Power Tune SU Carburettors*).

As a further guide to the kind of figures you would expect to see on a rolling road, an engine that's running too lean will hesitate and misfire. An engine that's running rich will be emitting black smoke from the exhaust and have a CO reading around 0.8 Lambda/8% CO, or more. Within reason, the fuel curves tend to be more or less linear, although they can increase in steepness from the point of maximum torque through to maximum power and maximum rpm.

In those cases where a standard needle isn't right, you have two choices: modify a standard needle to suit or accept the limitations of the closest standard needle. The complexity of setting up SUs correctly is one of the reasons for their lack of popularity. As an engineer this attitude was not

Standard needle dimensions

	KO	KL	BCP	BBG	BBV	BFW	BAK	BAC
1 -	0.099	0.099	- 0.099	0.099	0.099	0.099	0.099	0.099
2 -	0.095	0.095	- 0.095	0.095	0.095	0.0962	0.095	0.095
3 -	0.0925	0.0925	- 0.0929	0.0932	0.0932	0.0939	0.0932	0.0932
4 -	0.0895	0.0895	- 0.0905	0.0905	0.0907	0.0914	0.0907	0.0907
5 -	0.087	0.087	- 0.0881	0.0878	0.0875	0.0887	0.0875	0.0875
6 -	0.085	0.085	- 0.0858	0.0852	0.0852	0.086	0.0852	0.0852
7 -	0.0825	0.0823	- 0.0835	0.0829	0.0829	0.083	0.0823	0.0823
8 -	0.0795	0.0792	- 0.0804	0.0806	0.0805	0.0799	0.0792	0.0763
9 -	0.0765	0.076	- 0.0793	0.0783	0.0773	0.0768	0.076	
	0.0703							
10 -	0.074	0.0729	- 0.0781	0.076	0.0742	0.0736	0.0729	0.0642
11 -	0.0715	0.0697	- 0.0759	0.0737	0.071	0.0705	0.0697	0.058
12 -	0.069	0.0665	- 0.0737	0.0713	0.0679	0.0674	0.0665	0.052
13 -	0.067	0.0633	- 0.0715	0.069	0.0648	0.0643	0.0633	0.046

Alternative richer needle dimensions
(BAK included as a starting point needle)

	BAK	BAF	BBW	BDR	BAC	BCV	BCA	Special
1 -	0.099	0.099	0.099	0.099	0.099	0.099	0.099	0.099
2 -	0.095	0.095	0.095	0.095	0.095	0.0959	0.0955	0.095
3 -	0.0932	0.093	0.0923	0.092	0.0932	0.0933	0.093	0.092
4 -	0.0907	0.0905	0.090	0.0895	0.0907	0.0904	0.0897	0.089
5 -	0.0875	0.0875	0.087	0.087	0.0875	0.0875	0.0854	0.086
6 -	0.0852	0.0832	0.0832	0.0837	0.0852	0.0832	0.0795	0.083
7 -	0.0823	0.080	0.0792	0.0804	0.0823	0.0788	0.073	0.080
8 -	0.0792	0.0768	0.075	0.0758	0.0763	0.0746	0.0676	0.076
9 -	0.076	0.0738	0.0717	0.0712	0.0703	0.0687	0.0639	0.071
10 -	0.0729	0.0709	0.0682	0.0668	0.0642	0.0637	0.0575	0.065
11 -	0.0697	0.0677	0.0647	0.0623	0.058	0.0571	0.0519	0.058
12 -	0.0665	0.0646	0.061	0.0579	0.052	0.0497	0.0498	0.052
13 -	0.0633	0.0616	0.0577	0.0535	0.046	0.0445	0.045	0.048

acceptable to me, so I devised my own scheme for adjusting SU needles and then put it all into the book previously mentioned.

STANDARD NEEDLES
The needles used on the early 3.5 litre engines equipped with HS6 SU carburettors were limited to the KO & KL ranges of parallel shank needles. The later HIF6 carburettors were fitted with needles from the BBU, BAK, BBG, BGD, BFW, BCP, BBV and BAC ranges. The standard piston spring used in all of these applications was the 8oz yellow spring. The accompanying Standard Needle Dimensions table lists the diameters of all of these needles.

Only 1¾in/44mm SUs were used on these engines and so the only needle measuring points that need to be taken into consideration are the 1st to the 12th. The general trend of the HIF needles at the top end (8th to 12th points) is lean to rich going across the page. If you are using the older HS6 carburettors, the KO is richer than to KL over the same range.

The BAK is a good base line needle to start with on any road engine, but be prepared to 'jet up' immediately if it proves to be lean. **Caution!** – Don't persist with running the engine with a lean mixture.

The BAC is the richest standard needle fitted by Rover to production cars and gives considerably more top end fuel/air ratio than any of the others. This is the needle to start with for any racing engine. Note that up to the 6th metering point, all of the listed needles will give a very similar performance and fuel consumption. From the 9th to the 12th there is a significant increase in fuel richness with the BAC needle, and you will notice increased fuel consumption if a lot of accelerator pedal is being used. If even more mid-range richness is required, the BAC needle will not be right and will need to be altered or an alternative found in the *SU Needle Profile Book*.

If there is any doubt as to the

fuel/air ratio required for the degree of modification to an engine, bypass the BAK needle and go straight to BAC. The BAC needles were fitted as standard to some export model engines to reduce the potential for internal engine damage during hard use. These two needles (BAK and BAC) are identical in size up to the 7th metering point.

In many instances standard fitment needles will not be right, particularly if the engine has been modified, and the Alternative Richer Needle Dimensions table lists a richer set of needles for the HIF carburettor, going lean to richer for the 9th to 13th points from left to right. The 1st point is the same for all at 0.099in, the 2nd is from 0.095in to 0.959in, and both are a reasonable size for the engine's idle mixture requirements. Certainly the needle doesn't need to be any larger than this at the 2nd point or it can lead to sparkplug fouling. The 3rd point at 0.0925in should also about right, but if it proves to be too rich then look at 0.093in.

The 'special' needle listed is a combination of top end rich points from all of the other needles listed and is a modified original needle.

If your engine falters, (goes lean) at some point in the rpm range even with the richer needles fitted, but the top end mixture is correct, the solution is to modify your own needles using the techniques described in *How To Build & Power Tune SU Carburettors*. The lean area or areas of the needle will need to be made richer by reducing the diameter at the appropriate measuring points, while all other measuring points will remain untouched.

If the idle and mid-range air/fuel ratios prove to be correct through to, say, the 9th point, but the 10th, 11th and 12th points are too small and the engine is running rich, alternative needles will have to be found which have suitable 10th, 11th and 12th points, as well as points below the 10th which are larger than required. This may not be easy and you may have to modify lean needles by removing metal to richen them up where necessary.

Once you've learnt the techniques, it's quite easy to alter a pair of needles between tests on a rolling road and to complete the set up in one session. When altering needles, the key is to build on what you have done before and not to be disillusioned if you ruin a few needles, it isn't an exact science.

NEEDLE TUNING

Using BAC needles as a baseline, for a 3.5 litre engine that won't be lean at the top end, the 11th to 16th measuring point diameters to start with are –

11th – 0.058in
12th – 0.052in
13th – 0.046in
14th – 0.040in
15th – 0.040in
16th – 0.040in

These metering point diameters may need to be reduced to obtain maximum power, but dyno testing will help you to determine this. With the correct dimensions established for points 11 through 16, turn your attention to the 3rd metering point. All needles fitted to twin SU Rover V8s have almost identical 1st to 3rd points and they all run well at idle. Don't reduce the diameters at these points or you'll have sparkplug fouling problems. Only start to alter needles from the listed sizes **from**

above the 2nd measuring point.

This then leaves the 3rd to the 10th points. The objective is for needles to provide a mixture just rich enough to accelerate the engine as quickly as possible from idle to maximum power without hesitation. Note that the SU design inherently increases the fuel content (richness) as revs rise. To achieve this ideal progression through points 4 to 10 suitable needles may have to be made by altering standard items.

As an example, the following altered needle profile is based on a BAC original. The 1st, 2nd and 11th to 16th points remain unchanged. The only ones that are altered are the 3rd slightly and the 4th to the 10th. Each engine will be different, but this needle profile is a recommended starting point for any modified Rover V8 engine.

Starting point needle

	BAC	Altered
1 –	0.099	0.099
2 –	0.095	0.095
3 –	0.0932	0.093
4 –	0.0907	0.088
5 –	0.0875	0.082
6 –	0.0852	0.077
7 –	0.0823	0.072
8 –	0.0763	0.069
9 –	0.0703	0.066
10 –	0.0642	0.063
11 –	0.058	0.058
12 –	0.052	0.052
13 –	0.046	0.046
14 –	0.040	0.040
15 –	0.040	0.040
16 –	0.040	0.040

Note that if a needle metering point diameter is made too small there is no alternative but to start again with a new needle. The only advantage of making a needle too small for an application is that at least you can test it and learn what characteristics it produces. You'll need lots of spare needles. You'll quickly become good at making alternative needles very quickly, and should be able to modify one in 3 to 5 minutes with practice.

MODIFICATIONS FOR RACING

There are a number of areas where SUs can be further modified for racing. These changes improve the rate of acceleration, but in themselves will not increase maximum power. Briefly, they are: removal of the oil from the dashpots, removal of the piston springs (or modifying them to reduce their tension drastically), special profile needles and thinning down of the butterfly spindles. All of these mods are explained in detail the SpeedPro book *How To Build & Power Tune SU Carburettors*. Drastic modifications such as these bring a penalty which is a dramatic increase in the fuel consumption, something like 30%, or more, making these modifications suitable only for motorsport.

It sounds drastic, but a racing engine can be run with no oil in the dashpot and no piston spring in the vacuum chamber. The engine needs to be running at over 3000rpm almost all of the time for it to work, and problems can occur when the engine has to be more flexible and pull from 1000-2000rpm without hesitation. If there is a problem the spring can be retained in a modified form. Having a small amount of spring tension doesn't tend to affect the acceleration of the car and, in fact, oil in the dashpot has more of

an effect than the spring.

To fit a light piston spring, replace the existing 8oz yellow spring with a red 4.5gm spring and cut it down so that the spring is 2.0–2.0625in/51.0-52mm long. This modification applies a minimum amount of downward force to the piston which, in addition to its own weight, helps to prevent piston oscillation (the oil in the dashpot normally does this). The problem of piston oscillation is more pronounced with longer duration camshafts (ie: more than 285 degrees).

A certain amount of trial and error will be needed to establish if a spring is needed and, if so, the minimum spring rate that will work. The slight resistance of a spring, compared with no springs, can sometimes improve acceleration without needing to further richen the air/fuel mixture. Overall, most engines need to have low tension piston springs, although you should always first try to obtain optimum engine performance without piston springs fitted.

The problem with using a cut down standard 4.5oz (128gm) piston spring is that while the spring only exerts a minimum amount of pressure when the piston is in the vicinity of the bridge of the carburettor, it exerts more pressure as the piston rises (which is exactly when you don't need it).

The best combination to start with is blue/black 4.5oz (128gm) 2in SU springs cut down to 3.0in/76mm. Fitment requires some modification of the inside of the piston where the spring fits. Turn the inside

diameter of the piston on a lathe to 1.438in/36.5mm, which allows the spring plenty of side clearance in the piston.

With this spring cut down there will be 0.5oz/14gm of spring force when the piston is resting on the bridge, yet, at maximum piston lift, there will only be 4.5oz/128gm of force, which is minimal. By comparison, a standard length 1.75in 4.5oz (128gm) spring exerts at least 10oz/283gm of downward force at maximum piston lift, while a cut down one exerts 7oz/199gm. The cut end of the spring can be tidied up using two pairs of long-nosed pliers so that it looks like the uncut end. The uncut end **must** be in contact with the underside of the vacuum chamber.

The final modification is to drill a 0.125in/3mm diameter hole in the dashpot cap of the HS6 carburettor. **Caution!** – Do not do this on the later HIF carburettors with ball bearing dashpot slides; the cap has no vent to atmosphere and drilling a hole in the top results in vacuum leakage and the carburettor won't work correctly.

Just to reiterate, running an engine with no oil in the dashpot and no piston spring in the vacuum chamber should be considered a race only modification. On dual-purpose cars the best way around this limitation is to have two road going dashpot assemblies and two for racing. Second-hand SU parts are not expensive so this is hardly an outrageous idea. It takes just a few minutes to swap two dashpots.

Chapter 13

Holley carburettors

Recommended further reading for those seeking in-depth information on Holley carburettors is **How to Build & Power Tune Holley Carburetors**, by Des Hammill in the Veloce SpeedPro series.

390-CFM VACUUM SECONDARY WITH AUTOMATIC CHOKE

The most popular Holley carburettor for the Rover V8 seems to be the 390-CFM vacuum secondary with an automatic choke. However, the automatic choke tends to put too much fuel into the engine for too long, resulting in poor starting and excessive fuel consumption. The auto-choke can be replaced with a manual choke conversion (Holley List number 0-8007). The vacuum secondary version of this carburettor opens the secondary barrels more progressively and smoothly than the mechanical secondary version.

SETTING UP

As a starting point, a standard specification Rover 3.5 litre engine fitted with one of these carburettors requires the following basic jet settings for road use (final settings could be a little different once the engine has been tested) –
Primary main jets: 52
Secondary main jet (when a secondary metering block is fitted): 55
Accelerator pump discharge nozzle: 25
Accelerator pump cam (check in positions 1 & 2): Red
Power valve: 6.5
Secondary diaphragm spring (medium): standard, plain coloured

1) Float levels

Both float levels must be set to the factory specification. That is with the externally adjustable fuel bowls having fuel dribble out of the sight plug holes when the car is rocked side to side and parked on level ground.

2) Idle adjustment screw

Turn the primary idle adjustment screw so that the primary barrels are open no more than ½ a turn from the fully closed position.

If the engine runs too slow like this, remove the carburettor and adjust the secondary butterflies so that they are admitting more air. This might have to be done a few times to get it right, but with the engine idling at the required rpm and the primary barrels closed as much as they reasonably can be, the primary butterflies will sweep past the progression slots to the maximum extent possible, resulting in optimum acceleration without hesitation. This is an important adjustment that's often missed!

Vacuum secondary four barrel Holley carburettor is a very popular choice for these engines.

diagnostic equipment so that the true air/fuel mixture curve throughout the rev range can be established.

It's possible to use either a metering block or a metering plate on these particular Holley carburettors. The 4160 and the 4150 are basically the same carburettor, except that the 4150 has a metering block with removable main jets, whilst the 4160 has a pre-calibrated metering plate. There's no difference in the quality of the air/fuel mixture possible with either system, the difference is in the ease of changing the main jets as opposed to the whole metering plate.

Metering plates, although accurate, were fitted to these carburettors by Holley as a cost cutting measure.

If the metering plate you have is

3) Accelerator pump

Once the idle speed adjustment has been finalised, the accelerator pump needs to be adjusted to ensure that it works in unison with the primary throttle spindle. Any throttle movement must be matched by accelerator pump arm actuation, with the accelerator pump arm just in contact with the actuation lever. This requires some fine adjustment. The accelerator pump arm **must** be set without any slackness in the mechanism, but not so tightly that the pump arm has moved from its rest position.

4) Idle adjustment screws

Next turn the idle adjustment screws approximately 1¼ to 1½ turns out.

5) Metering block

If you're adjusting the air/fuel ratios you need proper engine analysis/

The often underrated 350-500CFM two barrel Holley carburettor is suitable for Rover V8 engines, although an adaptor will be required to make it compatible with the four barrel inlet manifolds available.

too lean or too rich, consult a Holley agent for details and availability on the next metering plates up or down the scale. The standard metering plate for this particular carburettor is a 134-34, the next richest is 134-3 followed by the 134-32, 134-40 and 134-5. Check the Holley service part listing for details. If necessary, the main jet drilling size in the metering plate can be increased using a suitably sized small drill held in a pin chuck. If the engine needs a smaller jet a new metering plate will have to be bought.

390-CFM MECHANICAL SECONDARY ('DOUBLE PUMPER') FOUR BARREL

This is a good sized carburettor for any smaller capacity (3.5-3.9 litre) Rover V8 being used for competition as well as for road use, up to its CFM limit. This carburettor was available for years under List number 0-6895, but it's now been superseded by List number 0-80507-1. Another model in the same series is List number 0-80507-2 (the same as a List 0-80507-1 but with more adjustments and developed for competition work).

Most readers should stay with the older List 0-6895, or List 0-80507-1, rather than change to the more complicated List 0-80507-2 version, in spite of the fact that the latter could give better engine response. The extra complications in its design can cause difficulties in tuning it which might result in less power.

The List 0-6895, List 0-80507-1 and List 0-80507-2 carburettors do not have a choke mechanism fitted. A half pump of the accelerator pedal is usually enough to start an engine,

followed by a series of three or four partial pumps once the engine has fired to keep it going for the first 20 seconds or so. The List 0-80507-1 and List 0-80507-2 carburettors can both be used for racing.

The List 0-6895 carburettor is the easiest of the three to set up as there are fewer adjustments to make. All three carburettors have secondary metering blocks as they are 4150 series carburettors. The List 0-6895 carburettor has a primary metering block idle adjustment only, whereas the List 0-80507 model carburettors have primary and secondary idle adjustment screws.

Start with 52-54 primary main jets and 54-56 secondary main jets and be prepared to jet up or down depending on your individual engine's requirement.

TIPS (ALL HOLLEY CARBURETTORS)
1) Float levels

The fuel float levels **must** be set first before further tuning is carried out. Make sure the car is level, remove the sight plugs from each fuel bowl and see if fuel dribbles out of the holes if the car is rocked gently. If no fuel dribbles out, the float level needs to be raised. If fuel runs out the float level is too high and needs to be lowered. In both cases undo the adjustment screw on the top and at the front of each fuel bowl and turn the adjustment nut clockwise to raise the fuel level and anti-clockwise to lower it. It's critical that the float levels be exactly right. Once adjusted, they seldom need setting again unless the car is being used off road over rough terrain, in which case they usually need frequent re-adjustment.

2) Fuel pressure

The correct fuel pressure is very important, 3.5psi/2.4 kPa is the minimum, 4.5psi/3.1kPa usual, and up to 6psi/4.1kPa acceptable. Any drop in the fuel pressure at full throttle (under full load at maximum engine rpm) needs to be investigated and remedied. Pressure can be checked by fitting a fuel pressure gauge in the fuel line at the connection point of the main fuel line to the fuel rail between the two fuel bowls. Road cars can have the gauge removed after testing, but racing engines almost always have the gauge fitted permanently so that the pressure can be monitored constantly.

3) Backfiring through the carburettor

This a sign of a weak mixture, often caused by the fuel level in the fuel bowl being too low, main jets too small, or a power valve that's not working.

4) Fuel spillage

One problem that crops up frequently when making jet changes is that the fuel has to be drained out of the fuel bowl and, in the process, goes all over the engine. This can largely be avoided if the fuel is drained into a suitably sized container fitted into the available space under one of the bottom fuel bowl screws. Undo one of the screws to let the fuel out and most of it should be caught in the container.

5) Gaskets

Only use new fuel bowl and metering block gaskets after the carburettor has been correctly jetted. Holley makes two types of gasket, a black 'one time' fitting gasket and a blue competition 'more than one time' gasket. If you're using the black 'one time' sticky-sided gaskets, these can get damaged every time the fuel bowl and metering block is removed to make a jet change. The solution to is to grease both sides of the gaskets each time the gaskets are put back on to the carburettor. Alternatively, use blue Holley competition gaskets or similar aftermarket gaskets which are re-usable. It's not necessary to ruin a pair of gaskets each time the main jets are changed.

Once the main jetting has been finalised fit new 'one time' gaskets to prevent fuel leaks. Holley carburettors only leak fuel from the gaskets or washers when there is something wrong with them, it's not usually a carburettor fault. The 'one time' sticky gaskets definitely seal best in the long term.

Caution! – It's easy to strip the threads in the carburettor body when fitting the fuel bowl and metering block. To avoid this, all four securing screws need to be fitted and screwed in evenly using light pressure before final tightening of the individual screws. The damage usually results from one screw being fitted only after the other three have been tightened, with any missalignment resulting in cross-threading of the fine threads in the carburettor body. The carburettor body can be repaired, but it's much better not to damage it in the first place.

6) Butterfly opening
Check that, when the accelerator pedal is pressed to the floor, the mechanically actuated butterflies are fully open. On vacuum secondary four barrel carburettors check that,

with the primary barrels fully open, the secondaries can be fully opened manually. This needs to be checked frequently, especially before each race day, to avoid a lack of engine performance for a very simple reason.

7) Fuel filter
Always fit a large fuel filter in the line between the fuel pump and the carburettor bowl/bowls. While some Holley carburettors come fitted with a filter in each fuel bowl inlet, they're frequently removed and a large, easy to replace aftermarket filter simply fitted into the main fuel line instead. Clogged fuel filters, such as those fitted to centre pivot fuel bowls, will cause a restriction to the fuel flow and, as they're situated after the fuel pressure gauge, the fuel level in the fuel bowls could drop but not the line pressure. Avoid this possibility by not having individual fuel filters fitted to each fuel bowl.

8) Accelerator pump
Whenever the primary barrels of a Holley carburettor are adjusted, the accelerator pump mechanism also needs to be re-adjusted so that the clearance between the accelerator pump lever and the actuating arm is correctly maintained. Failure to do this will result in delayed action of the accelerator pump action or fuel being delivered at the wrong rate.

Summary
Irrespective of which of the many possible Holley carburettors you decide to use, consult the Holley Numerical Listing for standard Holley carburettor jetting. The standard jetting, while not always perfect, will always allow an engine to start and run.

Always start with the factory recommended basic jetting for the particular carburettor and progress from there. The SpeedPro book *How To Build & Power Tune Holley Carburettors* has the Numerical Listing as an appendix, as well as covering all aspects of tuning the Holley carburettors most likely to be found on Rover V8 engines.

Tuning these Holley carburettors is a big subject in itself, which is why only the basics can be covered here. Large capacity Rover V8 engines can be fitted with larger CFM (cubic feet per minute)-sized Holley carburettors, such as 600-650CFM ones, with either vacuum or mechanical operation. Some applications might even need a 725-750 CFM carburettor. The Holley book explains how to decide on the right CFM for your application.

AIR FILTERS
Always use of one of the large diameter aftermarket air filters (air cleaners) as they do not restrict airflow significantly. Engines that draw in unfiltered air invariably wear out much quicker than those that have filters. The air filter element **must** be replaced at the recommended intervals.

Feeding the air filter with cool air is highly recommended, as is keeping the engine compartment heat away from the carburettor. Hot air has expanded and this reduces the volumetric efficiency of the engine as the temperature of the intake gas rises and the density of the incoming charge reduces. Under hood/bonnet temperatures can be quite high, so if the intake air is drawn from outside the front of the car the temperature should be much lower. The easiest way to achieve a colder inlet charge is to adapt an air filter body from a more modern engine. Ford V8 engine air filters are available for carburettors in two and four barrel configurations and suit Holley carburettors. Run a large diameter flexible tube, 2½in/64mm, or larger, from behind the grill directly to the intake of the air filter body. This will ensure that the air drawn into the engine is as cool as possible.

Conducted heat can be kept away from the carburettor by fitting a very large plate of heat resistant material under the carburettor (between the carburettor and the inlet manifold). The dimmensions of the plate being around 12in/30cm square and ¼in/6mm thick. Some form of industrial fibre being the material to use. This insulating plate will tend to reduce heat transfer from the inlet manifold and the surrounding hot components of the engine, but it isn't usually enough on its own. What is also required is a form of side shielding between the insulating plate and the underside of the bonnet (hood). Such shielding tends to keep the vast majority of engine heat away from the carburettor, but be aware that its not impossible to cause carburettor freezing if you are too thorough.

Holley makes a range of air filters, with the most common 'one size fits all' being sold under list numbers 120-101 and 120-102.

Replacement filter elements are available under list number 120-108.

FUEL FILTERS

Fit a large replaceable fuel filter in the line in between the fuel pump and the carburettor fuel bowl. Many Holley carburettors have mesh or Moraine fuel filters in them which tend to get clogged over time and need cleaning or replacing.

Most people remove the standard in-carburettor originals and fit a cheaper large capacity aftermarket filter in the fuel line. Examples of the kind of filters that can be fitted in this way are Holley list number 162-505 (plastic) or 162-511 and 162-501 (steel casing).

Use a minimum of $5/16$in/8mm inside diameter petrol/gasoline rated hosing and route it around the engine bay (**Warning!** – well away from the exhaust manifolds).

Any fuel line that is close to a heat source can be wrapped with thin aluminium sheeting or thick tinfoil to reflect the heat.

Avoid sharp bends in the hose as this could restrict fuel flow.

Use correct fitting stainless steel clamps, such as Jubilee clips, on all of the connections, and keep the number of connections to a minimum. All connectors need to be steel as opposed to cast aluminium or plastic.

Warning! – Avoid routing the fuel line adjacent to the flywheel bellhousing or, if there's no alternative, run the pipe through a piece of steel tubing. In the event of a flywheel explosion the fuel line will be afforded some protection.

FUEL PUMPS

Always fit a brand new fuel pump with a minimum $5/16$in/8mm inside diameter petrol/gasoline rated reinforced hose and make sure that all bends in the hose between the fuel tank and the fuel pump and from the fuel pump to the in-line filter and carburettor are sweeping, with no restricting sharp bends. The line from the fuel tank to the fuel pump needs to be as level as possible with a minimum of up and down deviation. Always use neat fitting, thin stainless steel hose clamps such as Jubilee clips to clamp hose connections.

Holley makes a number of electric fuel pumps to suit its carburettors and pressure regulators, as do a range of aftermarket manufacturers. In this application the correct Holley pump is list number 12-801, giving a continuous 67 gallons per hour/300 litres per hour at 5psi/3.5kPa. Other suitable pumps are made by Facet and Mallory, for example.

Chapter 14
Inlet manifolds

As with all induction systems, the inlet manifold plays a very significant part in making sure that the air/fuel mixture is distributed as efficiently and as equally as possible to each cylinder.

INLET MANIFOLDS FOR HOLLEY CARBURETTORS

The number of inlet manifolds available for the Rover V8 is quite limited, especially compared to other similar American-designed V8 engines for which the aftermarket inlet manifold manufacturers make an incredible range.

This dearth of choice is due to the lack of long term popularity of this engine in the USA compared to the small block Chevrolet and Ford engines. In past years the range of aftermarket four barrel manifolds available included the Harcourt 360 degree, the Offenhauser 360 degree 'Dual Port' (there was a JWR version of the same manifold) and the Huffaker 360 degree; of these older 360 degree units only the Offenhauser manifolds are available new today.

The only other four barrel manifolds available new today are the Edelbrock 180 degree and the Wildcat 'Spider' 360 degree.

The original standard Buick/Oldsmobile inlet manifold was a 180 degree/dual plane unit. Each side of the carburettor fed two cylinders on one side of the engine and two on the other side. With this configuration, one side of the carburettor feeds the two outer cylinders of each bank of cylinders and the two middle cylinders of the opposing bank. It ensures that the induction pulses from the eight cylinders are spaced as evenly as possible over two complete revolutions of the engine. The original inlet manifold was also made as low as possible to keep the engine as compact as possible.

The Australian Leyland P76 engine had a very similar design of inlet manifold to the original Oldsmobile/Buick type and it was fitted with a downdraught, twin barrel Stromberg carburettor.

If you look at the standard Rover V8 inlet manifold you'll see the firing order '18436572' cast in it and, if you look further around the top surface, where each inlet manifold runner feeds into the cylinder head ports, you'll also see the individual cylinder numbers '1' to '8' cast in. This was done to help with servicing and to eliminate ignition lead/firing order problems. These numbers also help in understanding the inlet manifold's 'runner' configuration. When standing in front of the engine block, the cylinders are numbered 2, 4, 6, and 8 on the right hand side

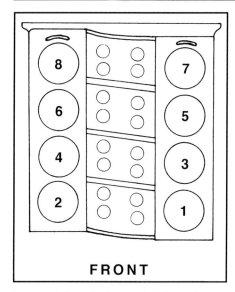

FRONT

Layout of the cylinders and their numbers.

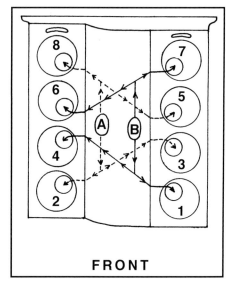

FRONT

Schematic of the standard inlet manifold configuration. Carburettor butterflies are at 'A' and 'B'.

and numbered 1, 3, 5 and 7 on the left hand side.

While not necessarily easy to see at a glance, there are differences in some of the inlet manifold configurations and you need to be aware of these before buying.

On the standard Rover V8 manifold, the right hand SU feeds cylinders 1, 7, 4 and 6 while the left hand SU feeds cylinders 2, 8, 3 and 5. If you correlate this to the firing order you'll see that it has been designed so that each carburettor venturi feeds alternate cylinders in the firing sequence. The induction pulses are spaced as wide as possible within the V8 engine configuration, apart from cylinders 5 and 7 which are adjacent, and which fire consecutively. However, the manifold design gets around this and ensures that 5 and 7 are not fed from the same carburettor venturi. This is not the only configuration possible for this engine, and neither is it the most desirable.

180 degree manifolds
The 180 degree/dual plane inlet manifolds are divided into two distinct groups, 'low rise' and 'high rise'.

Low rise
The factory standard for SU carburettors is a 'low rise' type, which means that half of each bank of cylinders are fed by inlet manifold runners that come from the opposite side, across the lowest part of the inlet manifold and then intersect with the four inlet ports at about 45 degrees. It's a rather tortuous path with a sharp entry into the inlet port, resulting in a less than smooth flow for the air/fuel mixture. The top tier of runners on the other hand take a relatively straight path, with only a slight angle downwards into their respective four ports. The 'low rise'-type manifold works well, but not as well as a the 'high rise' equivalent. American engine manufacturers have used the 'low rise' type across the board for decades on their standard

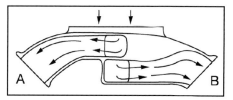

Top tier of individual inlet manifold runners are representative of 'A' (angled down into each inlet port). Lower tier of individual manifold runners are representative of 'B' and they do not turn down into the port like those of 'A'.

engines because the design allows the carburettor to be situated as low as possible in the valley of the block, keeping the overall height of the engine to a minimum.

The inlet manifold used by Rover from 1967 onwards with SU or Zenith carburettors follows the same basic configuration and style as the original Buick/Oldsmobile manifold, except for the changes necessary to accommodate the different carburettors.

An aspect of the standard inlet manifold that is not always appreciated is the way that the air/fuel mixture has to turn left or right to go to each individual inlet port at the end of its primary runner. The turns are tight, and while they're acceptable for standard engines, they're too tight for high performance engines running at high rpm with high flow rates through the manifold.

High rise
On a 'high rise' 180 degree/dual plane manifold, all of the runners curve down into the inlet ports of the cylinder heads. The top tier of runners are angled down more steeply into the inlet ports than the lower tier but, nevertheless, it's a significant improvement in terms of reduced losses and more even air/fuel distribution than the 'low rise'

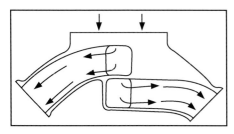

Typical aftermarket dual plane 'high rise' inlet manifold in cross-section, front on. It has both tiers angling downwards into the cylinder heads. The cross-sectional shape of the runners tends to be more consistent on aftermarket inlet manifolds.

The highly favoured 180 degree/dual plane Edelbrock Performer 3.5l 'high rise' inlet manifold is ideal for up to 6500rpm for all general road use and racing.

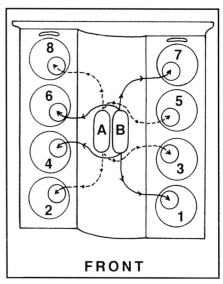

FRONT

Schematic of the Edelbrock inlet manifold configuration. It's quite different to the standard one. Carburettor butterflies are at 'A' and 'B'.

type. 'High rise' inlet manifolds have been a well established technology since the early 1960s.

Aftermarket 180 degree manifolds

The aftermarket range of 180 degree type inlet manifolds is very small with only one being currently readily available: the Edelbrock Performer 3.5l. It's very difficult to improve on this manifold for all round general use from off idle to 6500rpm. The Edelbrock's configuration is not the same as the standard Rover V8 type, even though it looks similar.
One of the earliest examples (if not the earliest) of the design configuration used by Edelbrock appears to have come from Buick in the early 1960s when it was used on its large capacity engines in 'low rise' form. Chevrolet realised the design's potential too and used it in the late 1960s on its 302ci Camaro Z28 engine in aluminium 'high rise' form. At the time it out-performed all other 180 degree manifold configurations up to 6500rpm.

This design of manifold uses equal length runners within the confines of the usual inlet manifold space. It retains the principle of two inlet manifolds in one, like all other 180 degree/dual plane manifolds, with the same even induction pulse

system. The difference is in the near-equal length of the individual runners. They start as close to the carburettor as possible and all are of a sweeping curve configuration. The Edelbrock manifold is classed as a 'high rise' type and is a very good road/race inlet manifold, provided there are no conflicting limitations on engine height.

One aspect of the Edelbrock manifold that readers need to be aware of is that the cross-section area of the individual runners is sized to suit the standard inlet port size of 0.950in/24.0mm wide by 1.575in/40.0mm high at the cylinder head/inlet manifold interface. If the cylinder heads have been extensively ported, the inlet manifold runners could well limit the engine's performance by restricting gasflow. In theory, the solution is to have the inlet manifold ported to match the cylinder head, but this is not an easy task, nor a very practical one. The Edelbrock manifolds were essentially designed to suit standard port cylinder heads.

360 degree manifold

The widespread use of 360 degree inlet manifolds became common in the USA in the late 1960s and

early 1970s for high rpm racing applications, where they proved to be more efficient than the more common 180 degree/dual plane 'high rise' inlet manifolds. With these 360 manifolds, all of the carburettor barrels feed into a plenum chamber in the centre of the manifold and the eight cylinder head ports are all fed from here. The inlet runners within the manifold are shaped as smoothly in contour as possible while taking the most direct route possible from the plenum chamber to the cylinder head ports. The positioning of the inlet ports in the cylinder heads makes for quite a compact inlet manifold because of their spacing. The two inner ports of a cylinder head are centrally positioned adjacent to each other, and the two outer ports are as close as possible to the ends of the cylinder head.

The first 360 degree aftermarket inlet manifold is the one from Offenhauser (dual port). This manifold is different from all other

360 degree types because of its very low carburettor fitting height. You can't get a more compact heightwise combination. Consequently, it's an ideal manifold and sometimes is the only manifold that can be fitted in an engine installation that is height sensitive. Its low height means it's considered to be a 'low rise' manifold. It's pre-drilled to accept four barrel Holley and Edelbrock carburettors and is readily available from all Rover V8 engine specialists. The working range is from off idle to 6000rpm, making it ideal for all road going applications and for some racing engines.

Other 360 degree manifolds to consider include the Harcourt & Huffaker ones, although neither are now in production. They're still available second-hand, albeit very difficult to find. Despite being very good manifolds, these items went out of production through a lack of sufficient demand and, in one case, destruction of the patterns.

A similar inlet manifold to the Harcourt & Huffaker one is that currently made by Wildcat Engineering. The large runners of this inlet manifold are better suited to the higher gasflow rates of larger capacity engines (3.9 litre and above) or high performance engines with larger inlet ports. This manifold can be ported out reasonably easily.

In many instances the best way to find out which inlet manifold is best for your engine is to try those that are available to you. There are plenty of second-hand manifolds available to try out and it doesn't take all that long to change one: test a few and make the comparisons.

Summary

• As a general rule, take it that the

Offenhauser 360 inlet manifold is the one that gives the lowest carburettor fitted height, and will give bonnet (hood) clearance where all of the others might not. These manifolds have been designed to suit the standard port sizes.

• The Edelbrock 3.5l raises the carburettor but is an extremely efficient type of inlet manifold from off idle to 6500rpm. These manifolds have been designed to suit the standard port sizes.

• The Wildcat Engineering 360 degree 'spider' inlet manifold is a 'medium rise' item, yet is not so high that it creates carburettor installed height problems in the usual applications. The runner size is slightly larger than the standard inlet port size, with the clear implication that it's more suited to larger capacity engines (3.9 litre and more).

OTHER DOWNDRAUGHT CARBURETTOR OPTIONS/ADAPTORS

The vast majority of four barrel carburettor inlet manifolds are suitable for use with Holley/Ford four barrel carburettors as a straight bolt on. If the bolt pattern of the manifold is to suit a Holley/Ford carburettor an adaptor plate will have to be used in order to fit a Carter Thermoquad, Edelbrock or Weber-type four barrel carburettor (actually all the same basic carburettor).

Some four barrel inlet manifolds are designed to suit these types of carburettor rather than the Holley. In such cases an adapter will be required to fit a Holley carburettor on such an inlet manifold.

Holley makes an adaptor plate to fit a 2300 two barrel Holley carburettor on to a four barrel inlet manifold. These two barrel Holley

Aftermarket adapter plate which allows the fitting of a 350-500CFM 2300 twin barrel Holley carburettor onto a Holley/Ford bolt pattern four barrel inlet manifold. It can also be used to fit a four barrel Holley, Carter Thermoquad, Edelbrock or Weber on to a two barrel Holley/Ford carburettor inlet manifold.

carburettors are excellent and highly suited to the Rover V8, but very underrated for this application.

STANDARD & AFTERMARKET INLET MANIFOLDS FOR SU CARBURETTORS

There have been two standard inlet manifolds for the Rover V8. The first was used until 1973 for the HS6 carburettors with side mounted fuel bowls. These are quite easy to identify by the hump of the water jacket at the back of the carburettor mounting tower. The later inlet manifolds have slightly better flow characteristics.

The original Buick/Oldsmobile inlet manifold forms the basis of the standard Rover-manufactured inlet manifold which features a very distinctive tower to take the twin SU or Zenith carburettors. While this induction system allows the engine to rev to quite high rpm, it is not very efficient when it comes to acceleration. Designed for road use, the Rover manifold is very good for that application, but change the application and it has shortcomings.

The standard inlet manifold configuration can be modified to a certain extent to improve airflow. The equipment needed is a 0.375in/10mm diameter parallel sided rotary file about 0.625in/15mm long. The inlet runners should be smoothed and enlarged, using the manifold gasket as a template for runner dimensions. The runners can be opened up back into the manifold for about 2in/50mm, or so. The production standard does vary and some runners will be worse than others to clean up.

The plenum chambers are other areas that benefit from attention.

The two factory machined 1.75in/44.5mm diameter holes in the manifold do not blend into the casting all that well and can be smoothed using a 0.5in/12mm diameter ball-nosed rotary file. With the inlet manifold runners opened out and aligned with the inlet ports of the cylinder heads, the improved airflow will give better performance between 4000-6000rpm.

Not much else can be done to improve the standard inlet manifolds without a major rework. In the past, standard inlet manifolds have been cut in half to enable the cross-sectional area of the internal passageways to be opened up and reshaped, then welded back together again, yet still keeping within the racing rules. While there was some improvement, the amount of re-work involved didn't warrant the effort and no matter what you did to these 180 degree manifolds they would never match a 180 degree Edelbrock Performer or a 360 degree Huffaker manifold above 4500rpm.

In racing classes where twin SUs have to be retained, but the inlet manifold is not mentioned, the carburettor mounting tower from a standard inlet manifold can be cut off and grafted onto a Huffaker 360 degree inlet manifold with spectacular results. The maximum power you can expect from a 3.9 litre V8 equipped with twin SUs on a standard manifold is 260bhp. Change to a Huffaker 360 degree with a standard inlet manifold tower grafted on to it and the maximum power jumps to 300bhp. Clearly the carburettors are not the limiting factor, it's the manifold that holds back both the maximum power and the engine's ability to accelerate. As an indication a modified standard manifold limits 3.9 litre engines to about 67bhp per litre.

Chapter 15
Fuel injection & engine management systems

This chapter has been put together with information received from ex-Lucas engineers Albert Tingey, Drew Selvey, Brian Hall, Phil Blay and Norman Jukes. The information about the modification of the Lucas systems for racing purposes and all other non-standard applications, and some of the standard information, has come from Mark Adams of Tornado Engine Management Systems <mark.adams@bjds.com> or telephone (UK) 01694 720 144.

Note that in the context of electronically-controlled fuel injection systems, the term 'hardware' applies to the mechanical aspects of the injection system (eg: inlet manifold, plenum chamber, and so on) while 'software' applies to the actual electronic componentry involved.

L-JETRONIC 4CU FUEL INJECTION SYSTEM (USA & AUSTRALIAN TYPES 1974-1990): OVERVIEW

Rover V8 engines were first fitted with the Lucas 4CU L-Jetronic fuel injection in 1974. This fuel injection system was actually a Bosch system made under license by Lucas (Bosch and Lucas having had close ties for over 60 years). The system was fitted to Triumph TR8s and SD1 Rovers for the North American market: a measure to make the engine suitable for the rigorous exhaust gas emission laws of North America.

There were in fact two early systems (1974-1982) and they are easily recogniseable because the eight individual inlet tracts are in a line in the centre of the 'Federal Specification' plenum chamber. This plenum chamber's volume and the throttle butterfly were quite small compared to the later systems (1982 on). One version of this early system was for the North American market, the other for Australia.

On the North American system there is an unheated 1 volt Lambda sensor in each exhaust manifold and the cars are fitted with catalytic converters. Lambda is a feedback system, meaning that information is sent to the ECU (Electronic/Engine Control Unit) from the exhaust manifold mounted sensors which measure the oxygen content of the exhaust gases from each bank of cylinders. The air/fuel mixture ratio is altered by the ECU accordingly.

There is no 'full loading enrichment' programmed into the

ECU (Lucas part number 83617) and the injection system, as a consequence, will only supply fuel at the rate of 'Lambda One'/14.7:1 air/fuel ratio under *all* circumstances. These engines are set with very low ignition advance allowing only 20 degrees of total advance. Because of this factor and the poor fuelling over 4000rpm, these engines don't perform well: a case of low emissions **and** low power.

Lambda 1 is equivalent to 14.7:1 because 14.7 parts of air to 1 part of fuel, by weight, is the chemically correct air fuel mixture ratio for the most efficient burning of fuel: this ratio is termed 'stoichiometric'. In reality, there's always some variation between designs of engines and, in the case of the Rover V8, a slightly richer mixture is needed to achieve optimum efficiency so for these units the best mixture ratio is 14.35:1. At this setting the CO (carbon monoxide) and the HC (hydrocarbrons) in the exhaust are at the lowest level it is possible to have them both at near equal parts per million (exhaust gas analysed **before** going through a catalytic converter).

Note that when it comes to measuring constituents of exhaust gases from car engines, C6 H14, which is one of many hundreds of hydrocarbons found in exhaust gases, is the one that environmental agencies have chosen to combat. Therefore, automobile manufacturers have geared up to test, monitor and, ultimately, reduce this one HC only. What this means is that the other hydrocarbons are not taken into consideration.

The Australian version of the 'Federal Specification' L-Jetronic fuel injection system introduced in 1977 is slightly different from the North American version. It doesn't have Lambda sensors (or the circuitry to suit them in the ECU) and the cars don't have catalytic converters. This EFI also had no 'full loading enrichment,' just like the USA system and, therefore, similarly poor fuelling over 4000rpm. These engines also don't perform well in terms of power production.

These two particular models of L-Jetronic injection system are not as suitable for any high performance application as the later 4CU systems, but ultimately only because of their smaller and less efficient plenum chambers. The ECUs of both of these early fuel injection systems can be altered to be similar to the later model European specification ECUs and have full power enrichment and high rpm fuelling. These ECUs have to have the technology added to them. The circuitry is essentially all there it's just a few vital components that are missing. With the technology added, these ECUs are as good as the others for many applications.

Replacing either of the above type of fuel injection systems with a 1983-1990 UK engine European specification L-Jetronic injection system in its entirety will result in an increase of about 30bhp, even with no other changes. The ECU of the 1983-1990 UK system is easily recogniseable by its Lucas serial number 83986.

The L-Jetronic system is an intermittent flow fuel injection system which opens and closes the four injectors on one bank of cylinders and 180 degrees of crankshaft rotation later opens and closes the four injectors on the other bank of cylinders. This means that all eight individual electronic fuel injectors open and close once in every revolution of the engine and because the Rover V8 is a four stroke engine (two revolutions of the engine between ignition firings) that means that there are two injection pulses by each injector between each cylinder firing.

L-JETRONIC 4CU FUEL INJECTION SYSTEM (UK TYPE 1983 TO 1990): OVERVIEW

The Lucas L-Jetronic 4CU fuel injection system was first used by Rover for its performance enhancing capability, as opposed to emission control capability, on the marque's 3500 Rover Vitesse EFI from 1983-1986, on 3500 Vanden Plas EFI 1984-1986 and on Range Rover EFI cars from 1985-1990. The main visual difference is the fact that the eight air inlets are staggered in the plenum chamber of these later L-Jetronic systems.

There is no exhaust gas monitoring on these 1983-1989 UK market 4CU fuel injection systems and, as a consequence, no Lambda sensor in each exhaust manifold. The ECUs for these engines did not have the 'tile' of resistors (series of resistors) fitted like the earlier ECU of the emission controlled North American engined cars and, therefore, cannot be used in conjunction with Lambda sensors without modification.

The 1983-1989 4CU fuel injection systems came in three versions: two types of single throttle (single butterfly) plenum and a twin throttle (twin butterfly) plenum. The twin-throttle plenum was introduced for racing purposes in the mid 1980s to increase the total air volume that could be supplied to the engine: it was fitted in small numbers to road going vehicles for homologation purposes. The twin-throttle plenum did increase the total amount of air that could be fed into the engine but, except for full race engines, the single throttle plenum ended up being the most favoured unit to use through being more common.

The most usual of these fuel injection systems that will be encountered these days is the single-throttle plenum type, with all parts still being available. To all intents and purposes, the general workings of single and twin plenum systems can be considered identical.

L-JETRONIC 4CU FUEL INJECTION SYSTEM: OPERATION
ECU (Electronic/Engine Control Unit)

The ECU is the electronic 'computer' that receives the information ('feedback') from various sensors fitted to the engine and processes this information. It then 'decides' on the ideal injector pulse time that will run the engine most efficiently for the set of circumstances prevailing at that instant.

'Feedback' comes from sensors such as the air speed sensor ('airflow meter' in the case of the Lucas 4CU L-Jetronic), the throttle's butterfly position potentiometer, the air temperature sensor, the water temperature sensor and Lambda sensors (one in each exhaust manifold, when fitted). The parameters of what amount of injector time will be required to successfully run the engine under every conceivable condition were found by Lucas engineers when laboratory testing a standard engine and were programmed into the ECU

during manufacture.

For fuelling control purposes the ECU receives information from several sources on a constant basis as already mentioned, however, the one thing that this system does not have is any air temperature sensing device. This means that the ECU cannot compensate for changes in the density of the air drawn into the engine. (On a cold day air is denser than on a warmer day, and less fuel is required when the air is warm. Also, air is denser at sea level than at high altitude, and less fuel is required at high altitude.) The ECU can't tell the difference between cold air and hot air, or whether the engine is operating at sea level or high altitude (anything above 5000 feet above sea level). Therefore, on a very hot day, or at high altitude, or both, the engine will be running with an unnecessarily rich mixture (using extra fuel and not necessarily performing as well as it should).

With the L-Jetronic fuel injection system, the injection of fuel into the inlet ports is at random: ie, two sets of four individual inlet ports have fuel injected into them, **irrespective** of what the position of the inlet valve is at the time (open or closed, opening or closing).

The distributor is connected to the ECU as an engine speed sensor with eight ignition pulses, per two revolutions of the engine, being fed to the ECU which has an electronic clock which 'times' the gaps between the individual pulses. Once the engine is turning over at 90rpm on the starter, the ECU clock is able to measure the time between the firings and starts to inject fuel into the right hand bank of cylinders ('A' bank) and 180 crankshaft degrees later injects fuel into the left

hand bank of cylinders ('B' bank). The process is then repeated every subsequent revolution of the engine. The electronic clock in the ECU doesn't know which cylinder is being fired at any particular time (there's no number one cylinder recognition), it's simply that as soon as there is a recognisable firing interval the ECU starts the fuel injection cycle.

The electronic clock in the ECU won't time the gaps between the firings at any speed below 90rpm because it is all happening too slowly and the ECU can't 'remember' when it started timing by the time it gets to the next ignition pulse. This happens because this electronic clock is a high speed device designed to time the gaps between the individual ignition firings of an 8 cylinder engine revving to a maximum of 5800rpm (hydraulic lifters start to pump up at 5800rpm), which is 386 individual ignition pulses per second!

Airflow meter

Air enters the induction system via the air cleaner unit and is routed directly through the 'airflow meter' (referred to as an 'air sensor' in some workshop manuals).

When the engine is idling the air flap in the airflow meter is in the near closed position as the speed of the air going into the engine is too slow to lift the flap. When the engine is at wide open throttle, under high load and at maximum rpm, the speed of the air drawn into the engine is high and the air flap will be in the near fully open position.

The air flap inside the airflow meter is mechanically connected to a potentiometer, a unit which varies the amount of electrical current passing through it commensurate with the position of the air flap. The potentiometer current is read by the ECU which therefore knows how much air is being drawn into the engine.

Note that the voltage output from the position of the air flap is **not** directly proportional to the air flap's position between 0 and 10 degrees. The voltage output is designed to 'map' the fuelling requirements of the engine. These requirements were established by extensive engine testing in a laboratory and then built into the potentiometer's 'voltage track' by Bosch and, subsequently, is not alterable by any means available to anyone outside of Bosch. The potentiometer of the airflow meter is the main fuel requirement sensor in the ECU system and controls the majority of the fuelling of the engine, especially once the engine is up to operating temperature (water temperature).

Maximum torque would have the air flap at about 60-70 degrees which would send more voltage to the ECU than when the air flap was on maximum airflow (110 degrees of air flap opening). This is because more fuel and the longest injection time in milliseconds is required to develop maximum torque than is needed for maximum brake horse power (bhp) at maximum engine rpm.

There are four basic L-Jetronic airflow meters available from Lucas for the Rover V8, with four different built in 'voltage tracks' in their potentiometers. The leanest airflow meter is the one fitted to the Triumph TR8, then getting ever richer are meters from the USA market SD1 engines, Range Rover and UK market SD1 engines: the latter (Lucas serial number 7324A) is the one to use for all high performance applications.

The L-Jetronic fuel injection system is an 'analogue' type system because it uses the sweeping arm action of the airflow meter to measure airflow. The actual air flap sweeps through a 110 degree arc of travel and responds positionally to the speed of the air passing through it (**not** the mass of air passing through it).

The arm of the potentiometer mechanism sweeps over a conductive ceramic material and, dependant on its position, picks up a given amount of voltage from the 'voltage track' built into the surface of the potentiometer. The 'voltage track' of any particular model of airflow meter is not alterable by any means but the 'voltage tracks' as made or these 4CU L-Jetronic fuel injection systems do vary depending on the particular model of airflow meter (that's the four types listed previously).

These airflow meters operate on 4.5 volts maximum with the voltage dropping to richen the fuelling to the engine. This means that at idle with the least amount of fuel being injected into the engine the voltage will be at its highest. At the point of maximum torque the fuelling will be at its highest and the voltage output will be at its lowest value.

Airflow meter: setting

The amount of voltage that operates the ECU is 5.0 volts which gets reduced to 4.5 volts in certain circuits due to the unit protection circuitry housed within the ECU (there is a loss in the system of 0.5 volts). The amount of voltage that operates the airflow meter is 4.5 volts (the circuitry of resistors and diodes in the ECU protect it from incorrect wiring and high voltages that would otherwise ruin it). These ECUs are very well protected in this sense. Assuming the airflow meter is in 100% serviceable condition and with its flap closed, the voltage as measured with a multimeter will be 3.5 volts. With the meter's flap manually held fully open the voltage will drop to 1.6 volts.

Setting the airflow meter can be done by anyone who has a multimeter with sharp pointed probes that can be pressed through the insulation into the relevant wires to make electrical contact. The best time to set these meters is when the ambient air temperature is that of a cold clear night. Everyone knows that their car seems to go much better in these circumstances than at any other time, and with very good reason: air density is highest in these conditions.

Setting the airflow meter requires the engine to be under maximum loading and at high rpm (like when going up a long steep hill in a lower gear, for example) with a multimeter connected to the wires of the airflow meter. The multimeter needs to be inside the car and the probe leads firmly connected at the meter, so extension leads will need to be made in some cases. On a test like this, in these ideal conditions, the reading seen on the multimeter can be seen to be as low as 1.63 volts if the conditions are as cold as they ever get in your area. This still leaves some slight latitude before absolute maximum possible flap opening is achieved (0.03 volts worth).

If the airflow meter was set like this to 1.63 volts on a very hot day (less dense air) the engine would run lean on a very cold night. This is one of the problems compared to the later 14CUX fuel injections systems in that L-Jetronic 4CU fuel injection system measures the air speed and not the air density. This factor is not really a problem provided the system is set correctly for cold clear night maximum air density conditions at 1.63 volts.

Throttle body potentiometer

Acceleration fuelling was insufficient when the ECU/injection system was originally trailed by Lucas. This was because the airflow meter was the only device that controlled fuelling during the acceleration phase, but the engine required more fuel in this phase than most other engines fitted with this type of fuel injection system. To avoid the lean condition which prevailed when the throttle was quickly opened, a throttle body potentiometer was fitted to the butterfly.

With the potentiometer fitted to the throttle body (butterfly) and sending its positional information to the ECU, the instant the accelerator pedal was depressed the ECU 'knew' that more air was being admitted to the engine and that more fuel was required. Prior to this the throttle body butterfly would be opened but the airflow meter would only be registering the air speed of the moment and this was an insufficient criteria for successfully accelerating this particular engine (giving a flat spot in the acceleration phase). Adding the throttle body potentiometer solved the problem because, as soon as the accelerator pedal was depressed, the ECU 'knew' it and commenced 'full load enrichment'.

The incorporation of a throttle body potentiometer can be likened to the action of an accelerator pump in a carburettor. The correct amounts of extra fuel that needed to be injected into the engine were found by testing the engine in laboratory conditions and the fuelling requirements to do this built into the ECU.

Another benefit of having a potentiometer fitted to the throttle body is that the instant the accelerator pedal is released the butterfly shuts and the voltage output of the potentiometer drops to next to nothing. The ECU 'knows' what has happened and shuts the fuel off. The ECU selects position 0 on the fuel map at any engine speed above about 1200rpm while the accelerator pedal is in the released position and does not reinstate injection until the engine needs to idle (starts to inject fuel at about 1200rpm). This causes a smooth transition to the engine idle speed of 600-800rpm.

Throttle body potentiometer: setting

The throttle body potentiometer, like that of the airflow meter operates on 4.5 volts maximum.

With the throttle body butterfly shut at the engine's idle setting, the voltage being passed through the potentiometer must measure 0.3 to 0.32 volts. The securing screws of the potentiometer (later ones have two as opposed to three) are loosened and the potentiometer swiveled until the required voltage reading is realised. The securing screws are then tightened. There are three wires coming out of the potentiometer: green (earth), red (signal) and yellow (power feed). The negative probe of a multimeter goes to the green wire, the positive probe to the yellow one.

Fuel delivery control

Note that one millisecond is one thousandth of a second: derived from the Latin word 'mille'. This measurement is, in turn, taken to five decimal places.

There are 256 individual fuelling level positions in the Ferranti 'read only' silicon chip fitted in the L-Jetronic ECU. This chip governs fuel delivery by timing, in milliseconds, the period each injector is open. The amounts of fuel delivery in the individual positions are not alterable by any means, they're all 'burnt' into the 'chip' by Ferranti during manufacture.

The injector gets a pulse of electricity of a certain length which opens it and keeps it open for the desired period of time. The chip's control steps are in milliseconds and are binary, this means there are approximately 0.03925 milliseconds between each 'step'. Position 0 being 'fuel cut off' (no fuel flowing) and position 1 offering an opening time for an injector of 0.03925 milliseconds, position 2 0.07850 milliseconds and so on, up to position 255 which gives 10.00000 milliseconds of injection: position 256 giving continuous injection (injector held in the open position).

When laboratory testing in controlled conditions, such as with a barometric pressure of 30.0 and 20 degrees C/68F of air temperature, with a standard Rover V8 idling, the engine is operating on approximately 0.78500 milliseconds of injector 'pulse time,' and at about position 20 of the chip's fuelling ramp.

At wide open throttle, with

the engine at maximum torque, a standard Rover V8 engine will be operating at a maximum of approximately 9.20 milliseconds of injector 'pulse time' and at about position 235 of the chip's fuelling ramp.

At maximum rpm and on wide open throttle, the engine will be operating at a maximum of approximately 7.80 milliseconds and at about position 200 of the chip's fuelling ramp.

The maximum controlled 'pulse time' possible in this system is 10.000 milliseconds (position 255). With position 255 of the 'fuel map' selected and the engine turning 6000rpm the injection would be continuous on the basis of the engine speed. That's 6000rpm divided by 60 seconds which means that it takes 10.0000 milliseconds for the crankshaft of the engine to do one complete revolution which is the maximum injector pulse time.

Note that maximum torque is developed at the point of maximum charge density and requires the richest air/fuel mixture ratio which is 9.2 milliseconds of pulse time in the case of a standard SD1 Rover V8 equipped with a 4CU L-Jetronic fuel injection system.

Under cold test conditions the ECU was programmed to pulse the injectors continuously (position 256) when the air temperature is at zero degrees C/32F, the barometric pressure at 30.6 and the engine turning 3000rpm (maximum torque and maximum charge density). In this severe cold test situation all eight injectors were open constantly delivering 1440ml of fuel per minute. Standard 3.5 litre Rover V8 engines were tested right down to –30 degrees C/-54F.

The air temperature sensor information sent to the ECU in these extreme cold conditions overrides the airflow meter feedback and 'tells' the ECU to pulse the injectors constantly.

Originally, the test Rover V8 engines equipped with L-Jetronic 4CU fuel injection had the ECU programmed to electronically limit engine speed to 5500rpm. However, Rover engineers advised Lucas that this would not be necessary as the engines were equipped with hydraulic lifters and that the lifters tended to pump up at approximately 5800rpm, which limited the rpm anyway. Lucas removed the rev limiting circuitry from the production L-Jetronic ECUs.

The electro-magnetic injectors receive a 12 volt pulse from the ECU when they're required to open. Once open the voltage is reduced to 8 volts which maintains the injector in the open position. Once the appropriate amount of milliseconds of open time has elapsed, the ECU reduces the voltage to zero and the small coil spring inside the injector returns the 'pintle' to its seat. There are two wires going to each injector, one takes the current from the ECU to the injector and the other wire completes the circuit back to the ECU, making both wires 'live' when the injector is open.

The injectors are also affected by the actual voltage that is fed to them: the higher the voltage the longer the injectors will remain open, the lower the voltage, the quicker they'll close. The ECU compensates for this factor by altering the pulse time according to the actual voltage generated by the battery at any given time. For example, if battery voltage is 11.8 the ECU will increase

the 'pulse' time of the injectors so that they deliver the same amount of fuel that they would if there was 12.0 volts going to the injectors. Conversely, if the battery voltage is 13.8 (the usual voltage for a correctly set up charging system), the ECU will reduce the injector time to match the amount of fuel that would be delivered to the engine if there were 12.0 volts going to the injectors. The variable battery voltage factor has to be included in the ECU's controls to take into account the various battery and alternator conditions that could apply to an engine at any time. For example, even if the battery is slowly failing, or the alternator is no longer putting out the specified voltage, the engine still has to run correctly during this process. Allowances have to be made for non-perfect operating conditions.

Note that the times, in milliseconds, of the opening and closing of the injectors are electrical 'pulse' times and are not the true times that the injectors are in fact fully open. There is a reduction of approximately 1.5 milliseconds for the opening and closing of the injector.

Fuel supply system

Fuel is pumped from the fuel tank to the injector 'rail' by an electric fuel pump at a factory-rated constant pressure of 70-74 pounds per sq.in (psi) or 5 Bar. At the back of the fuel rail there is a fuel pressure regulator with a feed back to the tank, this regulator is set at 36psi/2.5 Bar. This means that fuel is always being returned to the fuel tank from the pressure regulator. There is also a large fuel filter in the line between the fuel pump and the injectors. The filter is located in the engine compartment close to the injector rail. While the factory rated working fuel pressure is 36psi, readings as low as 34psi and as high as 38psi have been known.

Cold start controls

When the engine is cold, the coolant temperature is low and the ECU will 'know' this because it constantly monitors the water temperature through a coolant temperature sensor. For cold starting purposes, there is a ninth injector, or cold start injector, fitted into the plenum chamber housing. When appropriate (coolant temperature below 20 degrees C/50F), this injector operates on a continuous basis (no pulsing). Further to this, when the engine is initially cranked on the starter, the injector is opened and flows fuel but, as soon as the engine is revving at over 120rpm, or more, the injector closes.

After cold starting, the extra fuel supplied to the engine by the eight injectors is reduced in three threshold reducing steps. These reduction points are at coolant temperatures of 32 degrees C/90F, 50 degrees C/122F and finally at 80 degrees C/176F. At this point the ECU defaults to normal operating temperature fuelling settings.

Lambda sensors

The word Lambda comes from Latin and means 'one function,' and, in this case, that one function is to keep the air/fuel ratio of the engine at the chemically correct ratio of 14.7:1. There have been two types of Lambda sensor used on Rover V8 engines: the 'Zirconia' type as used on the 4CUs and the later 'Titania' type as used on later Rover V8 engines such as the 13CU,

14CU, 14CUX and GEMS 8. Both types measure the oxygen content in the exhaust gases and both types generate a voltage dependant on the amount of oxygen: this voltage is read by the ECU, allowing it to 'know' what the oxygen content of the exhaust gases is at any given time.

The early non-heated 1 volt type 'Zirconia' Lambda sensors (1974-1982 USA specification Rover V8 engines) are calibrated to 'tell' the ECU when the engine is rich or lean when it is running 'closed loop'. The optimum voltage for the optimum 14.7:1 air to fuel ratio (actually 14.35:1 for the Rover V8) is 0.54 volts. These Lambda sensors take time to warm up, which means that the engine cannot be run under Lambda control (or 'closed loop') until the sensors are up to temperature. Once the Lambda sensors are up to temperature, any voltage reading of 0.54 and above (up to 1 volt) will cause the ECU to add fuel (because the fuel mix is lean as there's too much oxygen in the exhaust gas); conversely, any voltage under 0.54 (down to zero) volts will cause the ECU to reduce the amount of fuel being injected into the engine (the mix is rich as there's not enough oxygen in the exhaust gas). It's never a stable situation, the ECU is constantly adjusting the fuelling by switching abruptly from increasing the fuel to reducing it in order to try to maintain the optimum ratio.

Note that 'closed loop' means that the engine is being controlled to run at Lambda 1, the stoichiometrically correct mixture ratio for best possible burning of petrol/gasoline and air as a mixture (complete combustion), while 'open

loop' means that the engine is running uncontrolled and could have an air/fuel mixture ratio of anything from 11:1 to 16:1, depending on the loading.

The instant the ECU learns that the mixture is lean, the ECU adds 5% more fuel immediately; conversely the instant the ECU learns that the mixture is rich it removes 5% of the fuel immediately. Because of the comparative slowness of the readings of the Lambda sensor compared to the speed that the ECU can do things, nothing is changed dramatically and instantly. The ECU 'moves' towards richness or leaness in a series of 5% increments guided by the Lambda sensors which prevent over-richness or over-leaness which, ultimately, would cause the engine to hesitate if taken too far too quickly in either direction. The maximum amount of deviation in the fuelling by this means, in any direction, in a series of steps, is 22%.

Early Rover V8 engines of 1974-1982 have two Lambda sensors because there are two exhaust manifolds and two sets of injectors (working independently of each other). The eight injectors are all on the same fuel feed system. Each Lambda sensor supplies a voltage to the ECU, and the ECU 'reads' each voltage independently of the other and will therefore fuel each cylinder bank of the engine differently by up to a maximum range of 22%.

Ignition system

The ignition system used on most engines equipped with the Lucas L-Jetronic fuel injection system was of 'electronic'-type (ie: no contact breaker points). The rate of ignition advance and the general workings of he distributor were much the same s on earlier Rover V8 engines that sed contact breaker points. While he ECU enabled the ignition system, nd received firing signals from it, he ignition system was effectively ndependent from the ECU. It was ot until 1994 that the ignition and uel injection control were integrated to the ECU of Rover V8 engines.

L-JETRONIC 4CU FUEL INJECTION SYSTEM: EARLY METHODS OF MODIFICATION FOR HIGH PERFORMANCE

Vhile this fuel injection system was he leading edge of the technology in s day, it doesn't lend itself to being nodified or adjusted far enough from tandard for racing applications.

The crux of the problem is he non-adjustable Ferranti chip the ECU and the airflow meter's otentiometer track which also annot be altered.

Obtaining the optimum fuel jection settings for standard ngines took Lucas engineers onths of testing in laboratory onditions. Only after all this esearch work could the correct rack' details be finalised for the irflow meter potentiometer and the osch manufacturing plant start naking them by the thousand. The arts were relatively cheap to make hen mass produced, but most ertainly don't lend themselves to eing made in limited numbers (quite npossible, in fact). This factor is hat originally limited the application f this particular fuel injection system r use on modified engines. If the irflow meter's voltage output had een easy to adjust (new track) this ystem would have been infinitely djustable, via the airflow meter,

from day one, but this is not the case and only one airflow meter (Lucas serial number 7324A) is used when an L-Jetronic fuel injection system is upgraded.

The unalterable airflow meter and Ferranti ECU chip controlling the engine's fuel profile originally limited alteration to the fuel injection system by aftermarket modifiers to overall fuel enrichment throughout the entire rpm range. Unfortunately this meant that if the amount of fuel being injected into the engine at maximum torque was correct, it would automatically be far too rich at idle and low rpm and too rich at maximum rpm. The engine would perform well enough in a racing situation, but this is hardly optimum fuelling of an engine and represents rather a waste of a sophisticated fuel injection system.

Fuelling has often been altered rather crudely for high performance applications by the following means: change the injectors for higher flowing ones, alter the position of the potentiometer in the airflow meter to give lower voltage outputs, put a resistor in the line between the water temperature sensor and the ECU to 'fool' the ECU into thinking the water temperature is lower than it really is and, finally, to increase the fuel pressure. This works in a fashion but, realistically, just wasn't good enough and didn't match well set up carburettors in the performance stakes.

Airflow meter: altering setting

The cover is removed and the position of the potentiometer mechanism in relation to the actual air flap is altered. This is quite easy to achieve because it's adjustable

via the standard ratcheting system in the airflow meter used to calibrate the injection system. The spring tension can be reduced, or increased, by moving the ratcheting mechanism left or right.

This change has the effect of increasing or reducing the flap's resistance to opening. The higher the spring tension the more resistant the flap is to opening (leaner mixture) and vice versa. All that is being done by reducing the spring tension is to fool the standard mechanism into increasing the overall richness factor throughout the entire rpm and load range within the confines of the original airflow meter's fuel track control. The lower the voltage being sent from the potentiometer of the airflow meter to the ECU, the larger the amount of fuel injected into the engine at **any** given time under **any** load. There are limits to how far the ratchet can be adjusted. Excessive low rpm richness being the first problem encountered. To increase the overall richness, start by decreasing the ratchet setting by one tooth at a time and test the engine after each move.

Note, before starting to alter the ratchet of an airflow meter, mark the original position of the ratchet wheel in relation to the body using a felt-tipped pen so that you can always go back to the original setting.

Note that it's just as easy to increase the spring tension; a factor which can be used to improve overall fuel economy, without detriment to all round general road going engine performance. Many a Rover V8 has been found to have an insufficient spring tension in its airflow meter and, consequently, guzzles fuel at an alarming rate. The solution is very simple, increase the spring tension. You've gone too far if the engine performance starts to drop off (lean). The safest way to make this adjustment is to put the car on a rolling road dyno and set the mixture. This way there will not be any possibility of setting the mixture too lean and possibly damaging the engine.

Note that when it is stated that an engine is running 'open loop,' it means the air/fuel regime is not under Lambda control. When an engine is running 'closed loop,' it means the air/fuel mixture ratio is being controlled at Lambda 1 or a 14.7:1 air/fuel mixture ratio via the feed back from the two Lambda sensors in the exhaust manifolds.

The point at which the maximum amount of fuel (longest pulse time) will need to be injected into the engine is at maximum torque, which could be anything from 3000 to 5500rpm. The standard engine uses up to 9.2 milliseconds of injector pulse at maximum torque, but this value should be anything between 9.4 and 9.7 milliseconds for a modified engine.

The potentiometer is set in such a position that at maximum torque the air/fuel ratio will be correct without exceeding 10.000 milliseconds of pulse so that the fuel injection rate is not continuous or uncontrolled. This setting can be achieved using a rolling road dyno and an airflow meter or an exhaust gas analyser monitoring the CO of the exhaust gas: the airflow meter gives an instant reading and is the preferred method.

Fuel pressure: increasing

Fuel pressure may also have to be increased quite considerably on

some engines to get that little bit of extra fuel into the engine during each injector's open period. The fuel consumption will be much heavier than normal as there will be excessive low rpm/mid-range low load fuelling.

Temperature feedback: altering

Another way of increasing the overall fuelling is to fit a resistor in the wire from the water temperature sensor. This will have the effect of fooling the ECU into 'thinking' that the engine is still in its warm up phase and cause the ECU to increase fuel supply to the engine across the board. The resistor limits the amount of voltage going to the ECU and, even if the engine is at 80 degrees C/176F, the ECU is getting an amount of voltage commensurate with running the engine under the 50 degree or 32 degree water temperature thresholds.

Conclusion

The three methods of enrichment just described are not generally satisfactory because they all provide a crude across the board enrichment of fuel supply which will often be at odds with the engine's actual needs, and will not result in good crisp performance throughout the rpm range. In the past, the Lucas L-Jetronic fuel injection system has not enjoyed a good a reputation amongst those seeking higher performance because of its apparent lack of tuneability. Frequently, the whole system has been replaced by a later 14CUX fuel injection system.

L-JETRONIC 4CU FUEL INJECTION SYSTEM: CURRENT METHODS OF MODIFICATION FOR HIGH PERFORMANCE

Nowadays, the early original Lucas L-Jetronic fuel injection system has been fully sorted by aftermarket specialists, so what follows is the sequence of modifications that leads to obtaining optimum fuelling for high performance with one of these early fuel injection systems. The methods described all come from Tornado Engine Management Systems.

The L-Jetronic is an excellent system and enjoying a considerable renaissance with enthusiasts because, now, they can be recalibrated to suit **any** application. The method of getting the engine to run correctly with this system is to make sure that the **right** upgraded parts are fitted: an altered ECU being the key factor to making the L-Jetronic system excellent for use on modified Rover V8 engines. The L-Jetronic fuel injection system can now be set up and used with total confidence.

Injectors

The standard injector for L-Jetronic Rover V8s is a 'pintle' type and is termed a 'grey' injector (so named because of the grey colour plastic body). The Lucas injectors are low impedance (resistance) 2.5kV Ohm type injectors.

Grey injectors are rated to inject 185cc of fuel per minute and should always be used until it is proven that the maximum amount of fuel that they can supply is not enough.

All injectors take, on average, 1.5 milliseconds to open and close. At idle the pulse time will e, on average, 2.5 milliseconds which means that there is only 1 millisecond of controlled injection nd 1.5 milliseconds of uncontrolled ow. At maximum torque the ulse time will be, on average, 9.2 milliseconds with 1.5 milliseconds of hat time being taken up by opening nd closing , so there is, on average, .7 milliseconds of controlled fully oen flow and 1.5 milliseconds of ncontrolled flow. The uncontrolled jector opening and closing flow me being the pertinent point here, ecause it is not possible to know ow much fuel will be flowing out f each individual injector during his time. The smaller the injector e less the fuel flow that can take ace during opening and closing ompared to that of a larger injector.

The point of change over to rger injectors than the grey units usually when 270 foot pounds of rque, or more, is being generated y the particular engine. The andard grey injectors are then eplaced with 'black' injectors, uch as those fitted to a L-Jetronic quipped Jaguar XJ6 engine hich flow 200cc per minute, or oproximately 7% more than grey jectors for the same amount of jector pulse time. The 7% increase fuel injected into the engine is cross the board. The decision to se either grey or black injectors hould be made at the time the CU is remanufactured and the 'fuel rofile' altered so that low rpm/ w load fuelling can be reduced ccordingly.

These early type injectors are ebuildable and anyone going to e trouble of having their 4CU -Jetronic fuel injection system tered for optimum all round engine erformance must have the injectors

rebuilt to very precise criteria. It is vital that each of the eight injectors are matched for flow rate and spray pattern. Failure to do this can result in a serious reduction in engine efficiency. It is a proven fact that there is a 35% difference in the flow rate and the spray pattern of the standard injectors. Any road going engine needs to have a set of injectors that are within 5% of each other in terms of flow rate and spray pattern: any race engine needs to have the injectors within 2% of each other.

There are companies which specialise in rebuilding these particular injectors and offer matched sets. Two of them are Mech Motorsport (UK 01242-243-385/www.rollingroad.co.uk) or Power Engineering (UK 01895-243-699/www.powerengineering.co.uk). You can send your original set of injectors to them and they'll rebuild them and, if necessary, after checking the flow rate and spray pattern, will substitute rebuilt injectors from their own stocks to make up a well matched set.

At least 20% of engines will have fuel injector problems which are directly related to flow rate and spray pattern mismatching. The difference in performance between an engine fitted with a matched set of injectors and one that is not can be massive. Don't ignore this vital factor and don't assume that all injectors of one colour code are identical, this is not the case at all.

Note that this problem with variable injector performance is what caused engineers to build in technology to modern aftermarket racing engine electronic fuel injection systems that takes this factor into consideration. The flow rate of each

individual injector is measured and the spray pattern checked. With the spray patterns identical, but the flow rates different, the injectors can be used in any engine because the ECUs are specially built to be able to compensate for different flow rate injectors. They are programmed with the flow rate information of each injector and which cylinder each injector is for, then each injector is pulsed for a different amount of time to ensure that each cylinder receives exactly the same amount fuel per engine cycle. This technology removes the problem of having to have matched sets of injectors in terms of fuel flow. GEMS 8 does **not** have this facility.

ECU upgrade

Tornado Engine Management Technology, for example, remanufacture 4CU L-Jetronic ECUs. Upgraded new components are fitted to replace original components known to be trouble prone wherever it's possible to do so. As a result of the extensive remanufacturing process that all of these ECUs go through, all come with a 2 or 3 year warranty.

Once the basic units are sound, they're subjected to 'fuel profile' upgrading to suit the individual application. Consultation is required with Tornado Engine Management Systems so that the correct fuel profile is built into **your** ECU. The full details of the level of modification of your engine have to be compared against known data for the right choice of fuel profile to be made. All L-Jetronic equipped Rover V8 engines rebuilt from standard to all out racing engine will respond to the specialist tuning/ECU recalibration detailed in this section.

Tornado Engine Management Technology remanufactures the five types of ECU used on the 4CU L-Jetronic, but the USA federal specification ECU and the Australian specification ECU are not normally rebuilt for high performance applications because the Ferranti chip in each of them has low fuelling capability over 4000rpm. In recent times there has been some demand for upgraded USA and Australian ECUs and T.E.M.T. has put the necessary componentry into these ECUs, as well as blanking out the Lambda sensor if necessary. This is all quite legal to do as it does not affect the emission control status of the fuel injection system. That leaves the three other ECUs: serial number 83986 (3.5 litre Rover Vittesse cars 1983 and 1986), serial number 84477 (3.5 litre Range Rovers 1985 and 1987) and serial number 84941 (3.5 litre Range Rovers 1987 and 1990).

The three ECUs are then further categorised by the known fuel profiles of the Ferranti chips fitted to them –

A serial number 83986 ECU from a Rover Vitesse has a flat fuelling profile that goes right across the rpm range, making it ideal for all racing applications.

A serial number 84477 ECU has very good low and mid-range fuelling profile, but is not as good as the 83986 chip at high rpm, making this ECU ideal and better than the other two for small and large capacity road going engines which do not rev to more than 5000rpm on a regular basis. There are also some applications where this ECU is used for racing purposes.

A serial number 84941 ECU is a good all round unit which has a good basic mid-range and high rpm fuelling profile.

Note that if the ECU that you have has been rebuilt, it could have one of five unalterable Ferranti chips installed, and not necessarily the same type that it would have had originally! There are no visible marks on these chips to distinguish them one from another. The only way to tell for sure what chip is in a rebuilt ECU is to test the chip and 'read' its profile. The five chips are very easy to distinguish during testing because they are all quite different in fuel profile. An original non-rebuilt ECU will definitely have the correct Ferranti chip in it and its serial numbers used with confidence to identify what chip is in the unit. All chips are identified by T.E.M.T. when an ECU is dismantled and are then colour coded.

With the three popular ECUs categorised, the most suitable of the three ECUs is chosen for each individual application and the fuel profile modified within the limits. T.E.M.T. has 30 basic recalibrating 'fuel profiles' based around the three ECUs and has an extra 5 fuel profiles for very specialist applications. The 30 basic fuel profiles have been arrived at over the past 15 years of working experience with the 4CU L-Jetronic fuel injection systems and involve the removal and replacement of on average of 10 to 20 resistors and 6 to 12 capacitors out of the mass of resistors and capacitors fitted in the ECU.

Changing various resistor and capacitor values allows the original fuel profile of the Ferranti chip to be distorted and made richer where the fuel profile needs to be richer for the particular application, and also leaner when required. Expert modification of the ECU in this manner is the secret to making the 4CU L-Jetronic fuel injection system work. Mark Adams of Tornado Engine Management Technology regards the 4CU L-Jetronic fuel injection system as a very clever piece of engineering for its time, and it still has it's place today.

Airflow meter

Whenever a Tornado Engine Management Technology remanufactured ECU is going to be fitted, the airflow meter (serial number 7324A European specification airflow meter only) should be one of its remanufactured ones or, at the very least, your own original airflow meter sent to T.E.M.T. to be checked out. About 50% of used airflow meters will be found to be faulty ... If an airflow meter which is not 100% serviceable is used in conjunction with a remanufactured ECU the result will be less than it should be. Tornado Engine Management Technology stocks used and tested airflow meters to suit its ECUs, and all are guaranteed for 1 year.

Note: be aware of the fact that 4CU flap type airflow meters are no longer available new and that finding second-hand ones is becoming a problem. No airflow meter for an L-Jetronic fuel injection system should be thrown away, they can usually be rebuilt.

Rising rate fuel pressure regulator

The F.S.E. fuel pressure regulator as made by Malpassi in Italy has been available since the late 1980s. They are available for the Rover V8 in three rated pressures 2.0, 2.5 and 3.0 Bar/39, 36 and 43.5psi. Tornado

Engine Management Technology only uses one of them and that's the 2.5 Bar/36psi unit. It's recommended that the regulator be mounted away from engine heat and vibration.

Under maximum wide open throttle acceleration (zero vacuum being generated) the pressure regulator increases the fuel rail pressure by a maximum factor of 1.75 Bar/25psi. This means that a pressure regulator rated at 2.5 Bar/36psi pressure will increase the fuel rail pressure to a maximum of 4.2 Bar/61psi. The instant the acceleration phase is over (the throttle not wide open and the engine generating vacuum) the fuel pressure reverts to its rated amount of 2.5 Bar/36psi or the standard amount of fuel pressure. When an engine is idling (high vacuum) each standard rated fuel pressure amount is reduced by 0.5 Bar/7.25psi: this is to prevent low rpm injector leakage.

The reason for fitting a rising rate fuel pressure regulator is to gain increased fuelling during acceleration (wide open throttle) and top end work (again, wide open throttle). The principle being that the injectors are open for a specific amount of time and the higher the fuel pressure the greater the amount of fuel that will be injected into the engine.

F.S.E. rising rate fuel pressure regulators are also adjustable for base pressure. While being standard rated at a basic 2.5 Bar/36 psi there is an adjustment screw on the unit that will allow the base fuel pressure to be increased. This adjustment can be used to trim the amount of fuel going into the engine with 3.1 Bar/45psi being the absolute maximum ever used by Tornado Engine Management Systems. This means that while the ECU will have

had its fuel profile recalibrated to suit the application and be extremely near; adjusting the fuel pressure can be used to fine tune the amount of fuel being injected into the engine. If more than 3.05 Bar/44psi is required, it indicates that the ECU is not right for the particular engine application and should be returned to Tornado Engine Management Systems for an alternative one.

Raising the injection pressure by 0.07 Bar/1psi, for example, gives, on average, a 2% increase in the volume of fuel being injected into the engine. An increase of 0.5 Bar/8psi gives, on average, an increase in volume of fuel being injected into the engine of 4%. All T.E.M.T. ECUs are designed to provide fuelling which is on the lean side for the particular engine capacity and state of tune, meaning that an increase in fuel pressure from 2.5 Bar/36psi will likely be required to get the engine to perform spot on.

Note that no engine should ever be run with less than the standard rated 2.35-2.5 Bar/34-36psi of fuel pressure as the spray pattern of the injector is adversely affected. Having the fuel pressure set anywhere between 2.5 Bar/36psi and 3.05 Bar/44psi is acceptable. If, for example, the particular ECU fitted caused the engine to run rich and the fuel pressure was at 2.5 Bar/36psi it would be impossible to fine tune the fuel curve (lean it off slightly) and the engine would be forever over-rich, indicating that the ECU has not been recalibrated correctly to suit the particular engine. If the fuel pressure has to be raised above 3.05 Bar/44psi to get the engine to run correctly, realistically the particular ECU being used is not suitable.

Caution! – In many instances in

the past the fuel pressure was set to 4.2-4.8 Bar/60-70psi on a constant basis by various means. This was in the days before modified ECUs were available and, while engines would run like this, the ultimate problem was that the fuel pump would burn out as it was not made to run at this sort of pressure on a constant basis. T.E.M.T never sets the constant pressure to more than 44psi; if there's not enough fuel flowing into the engine with a maximum of 44psi the ECU is not correct for the application (injectors need more open time as opposed to higher fuel pressure), it's as simple as that. This is why T.E.M.T requires the details of the engine for which it's been asked to supply modified equipment so that it can accurately match **your** engine's individual requirements to one of the 34 modified ECU types that it supplies.

4.2 litre upgrade

There is also a very good upgrade option for 4.2 litre Rover V8 engines fitted with the 1983-1990 UK market Lucas L-Jetronic 4CU fuel injection system and a 1983-1986 part numbered 83986 ECU. This upgrade involves using standard Lucas L-Jetronic componentry from other engines.

Tornado Engine Management Technology has found through experience that fitting the Jaguar XJ6 4.2 litre engine's airflow meter (part number 73171B) and the 'black' Lucas injectors from the same engine, that the 4.2 litre capacity V8 will go extremely well with no other modifications except standard recommended adjustments and an F.S.E. rising rate fuel pressure regulator fine tuned by testing for optimum engine performance to between 2.9-3.1 Bar/42-45psi. The only problem with this arrangement is that the cruise condition fuelling is richer than it needs to be and, as a consequence, the cruising speed fuel economy is less than it could be.

Fitting the Jaguar XJ6 L-Jetronic 4CU airflow meter is not quite a simple bolt on exercise as the Rover V8 airflow meter is side bolted into position, whereas the XJ6 airflow meter is top bolted. A bracket will have to be custom made to fit the XJ6 airflow meter to the engine. There were 5 types of airflow meter fitted to XJ6 Jaguar Series III saloon car engines, but the 73171B is the **only** one that will work correctly in this Rover V8 application. The airflow meter needs to be tested and, if necessary, rebuilt to standard Lucas specifications to guarantee that the mechanical performance of the airflow meter is correct for this application.

Twin plenum L-Jetronic 4CU fuel injection system

In the mid-1980s the twin plenum system was introduced, with 500 examples fitted to road cars for homologation purposes. About 200 were fitted to road cars on a random basis on the engine assembly line meaning that a purchaser of an new SD1 car could have ended up with a twin plenum L-Jetronic fuel injection system and not even know it. There was no code number sequence to indicate that the engine was fitted with a twin plenum.

Some of the 1985-1986 made engines fitted with a twin plenum system were also fitted with forged steel rocker arms, which had their adjusting nuts welded to prevent any movement. All SD1 cars fitted with a twin plenum system were also fitted with a fuel tank guard (no Rover part number for the fuel tank guard either). Some twin plenum engines were also equipped with Nykasil linered racing engine blocks. The main caps of Nykasil blocks were of the four bolt type, although only the two vertical bolts were fitted. These blocks require reworking to have the extra two bolts per main cap fitted, but the basics are all there. The Nykasil blocks are easily recogniseable via the noughts and crosses patterning on the side of the block casting.

The twin plenum system had two throttle bodies which were joined to a single standard airflow meter by an aluminium Y-piece and associated rubber piping. The ECU and the airflow meter were of exactly the same type (serial number) as fitted to all standard production single throttle body engines, and this resulted in the engines fitted with the twin plenum system producing identical power to the standard single throttle body equipped engines. The twin plenum fuel injection system flowed more air than the single throttle body system but, because the same ECU and the airflow meter were fitted, the engine tended to run lean resulting in no gain in power.

When these twin plenum systems were being prepared for racing use it was found that the standard Y-piece didn't distribute the air equally, and favoured the rear throttle body, causing the front cylinders to run weak. For racing purposes an all new Y-piece had to be made to remedy this situation.

The two butterflies have to be very accurately synchronised which is not necessarily an easy task.

There is a joining linkage between them which has an adjustment mechanism which allows each butterfly to be adjusted so that it is shutting off against the throttle body bore wall. There is no throttle stop for example. Idle is effected by having the two butterflies adjusted identically for maximum shut off, with the amount of air that can pass around each virtually closed butterfly being what effects the idle. The usual method of making sure that the butterflies are closed as far as possible is to measure the gap around the edge of each butterfly to throttle bore with a 0.001in feeler gauge. If one or other butterfly is not shutting off completely the idle speed will be high. Optimum overall engine performance is only possible when the two butterflies are perfectly synchronised. There is only one throttle position potentiometer and it is set the same as for a single plenum L-Jetronic 4CU system (ie: 0.3 to 0.32 volts).

Note that failure to have the two throttles correctly synchronised, and the throttle body potentiometer set correctly to the specified voltage, means that optimum power cannot be generated.

The standard airflow meter is ultimately the restriction on these twin plenum systems and, to make any improvement, it has to be changed for a larger one. The one to use is the 73171B airflow meter from an XJ6 Jaguar Series III saloon car. The ECU has to be a rebuilt and modified one with a fuel profile to suit the modifications to the particular engine. Tornado Engine Management Systems can provide all of the necessary correctly recalibrated componentry. Depending on the condition of the

3.5 litre engine, the power will be increased, on average, from the standard 185bhp to 205bhp. Slightly modified engines will produce up to 225bhp. The best modified, but still road going, 3.5 litre engines will produce up to 250bhp. Racing engines of days gone by were reported to produce 300bhp using the twin plenum system.

Twin plenum L-Jetronic 4CU fuel injection system: twin airflow meters

To cure the airflow distribution problem, two standard 7324A European specification airflow meters can be fitted to the twin plenum system. The two airflow meters have to be perfectly matched electrically and mechanically, which means that the voltages at minimum and maximum flap movement have to be identical (1.6 volts fully open, 4.5 volts fully closed). The springs in the two airflow meters must also be perfectly matched throughout the rpm range so that the flap movement and the voltage outputs are always identical. Tornado Engine Management Systems can supply identical – in every respect – airflow meters from its stock.

The cold start is taken off the front airflow meter and the idle air is drawn out of the airflow meter fitted at the rear. One airflow meter is the 'master' and the other is the 'slave'. With the two airflow meters being identical electrically and mechanically in every respect only one is required to generate a signal for the ECU and because, and only because, the airflow meters are identical the system works.

The remanufactured and re-calibrated ECU that Tornado Engine Management Systems supplies for these twin airflow meter twin plenum systems will be one of the 30 ECUs that it regularly supplies, with the choice of ECU being based on the particular engine modification information supplied by the customer. In all cases, the ECU will be set slightly lean so that the fuel curve can be fine tuned by increasing the fuel pressure above the standard 2.5 Bar/36psi, but not over the maximum of 3,05 Bar/44psi.

The air distribution into the plenum chamber is what is being optimised in this instance. With this L-Jetronic 4CU system fitted, many high performance 4.2 litre engines have registered 320bhp, while a J. E. Developments 3.9 litre racing engine has registered 340bhp.

Tornado Engine Mangement Systems also makes a fully adjustable L-Jetronic ECU but, while it's a good idea in principle, it's not good value for money compared with the cost of a rebuilt and recalibrated standard type ECU which will do exactly the same thing.

In conclusion, the Lucas L-Jetronic 4CU fuel injection system is an extremely good system and can be used with absolute confidence on any engine provided various parts are recalibrated to suit the particular application. There are limitations with this system compared to the later systems but, nevertheless, getting the right bits and the right specialist assistance gives an excellent result.

L-JETRONIC 13CU AND 14CU ELECTRONIC FUEL INJECTION SYSTEM: OVERVIEW

These two 'Federal Specification' versions of the Lucas system were fitted to 3.5 litre Range Rovers and Land Rovers destined for the North American market from the mid 1980s up until 1989. They were the first of the micro-processor, or EPROM (Electronically Programmable Read Only Memory), silicon chip type ECUs. They use only 2K of memory to run the fuel injection system.

The reason for the introduction of these two versions of the L-Jetronic fuel injection system was that the California Air Resource Board specification 'OBD1' (On Board Diagnostics, with 1 being the first stage of the specification) required that cars had to have on board diagnostics and, as the 4CU L-Jetronic had no micro-processor, it couldn't possibly comply with the new legislation. These two systems were devised by Lucas for Rover so it could continue to sell its cars in the USA.

13CU and 14CU are very similar systems, with 14CU being just an evolutionary version of the earlier 13CU. The 14CU has an ECU that uses better hardware and is more physically compact than the 13CU equivalent. The ECU of the 13CU is actually quite large and uses less sophisticated internal componentry compared to the later 14CU with its compact cast alloy casing. The two ECUs are interchangeable via their pin plug connectors and the ECU of the 14CU is the direct forerunner of the ECU of the 14CUX fuel injection system.

These ECUs also both came fitted with a 'hot wire' airflow meter instead of the 'air flap' type. With this new system there were no moving parts and this form of airflow meter takes into consideration the air temperature/air density (a requirement of the California Air Resource Boards OBD1 specification) and something the air flap system could not do.

These two fuel injection systems had a 1 volt heated 'Titania' type of Lambda sensor in each exhaust manifold. These early Titania Lambda units, as used on Land Rovers with the 13CU, 14CU and 14CUX Lucas fuel injection systems, had a maximum output of 1 volt with zero to 0.54 volts indicating a rich mix and anything over 0.54 volts a lean mix, meaning that 0.54 volts corresponds with a 14.35 to 1 air/fuel ratio (the most efficient for the Rover V8).

With these 13CU and 14CU as well as the 14CUX fuel injection system, the fuel injection system's ECU is either adding fuel or removing fuel on a constantly changing basis dependant on the voltage being generated by the Lambda sensors, it's never a stable situation.

These injection systems are used in conjunction with 'air rail' cylinder heads, which used an air pump to pump air into the exhaust manifold to assist in the reduction of exhaust emissions. Both systems run the engine at Lambda one under all circumstances and have no 'power enrichment' so engine performance is hardly startling. There has never been any call for high performance upgrading of these 13CU and 14CU systems and they're only suitable for 3.5 litre engines.

L-JETRONIC 14CUX ELECTRONIC FUEL INJECTION SYSTEM: OVERVIEW

The third type of fuel injection system is the 'hot wire' 14CUX fuel injection system, introduced in 1988 and continued until 1998. This system differs from its forerunners the 13CU and 14CU systems, in that it has 'power enrichment' and yet still complies with the OBD1 specification of the California Air Resource Board in that it has on board diagnostics. This system runs with 4K of memory and was fitted to Range Rover Classics, Land Rover Discovery 200 and 300s, some export Land Rover Defenders, Morgans, TVRs and Marcos sportscars.

The 14CUX Lucas electronic fuel injection can be altered to suit many Rover engines, from the small destroked 3.5 litre racing engines which have been used in past years, to 4.6 litre, or larger capacity, turbocharged engines.

The 'hot wire' fuel injection system is a better system than the 'air flap' system' because of its greater sophistication. Also the fact that it can have its fuel curve completely altered to suit any specification of engine at a very reasonable cost by changing one basic component. This process is commonly referred to as 'chipping,' and involves changing the EPROM for another one that has been programmed with different criteria. That said, if an engine is fitted with a 4CU L-Jetronic fuel injection system with everything optimised for best all round engine performance, then that fuel injection system was changed for a 14CUX fuel injection system with everything optimised for best all round engine performance, you'd be hard pressed to tell the difference.

Injectors

The injectors of the Lucas 14CUX are 'disc' type as opposed to being 'pintle' type and they're also high impedence (resistance) 14.5 kV Ohm ones. The standard fuel pressure is still 2.5 Bar/36psi on the 14 CUX fuel injection system and, while the fuel pressure can be increased, it has to be limited to 3.05 Bar/44psi because at 3.25-3.4 Bar/47-48psi, and above, this type of injector is incapable of opening. These injectors have a metal lower body and a black plastic upper body which has a green band around it.

Dirty injectors can be a problem, which is why all injectors used on any engine must be serviced/rebuilt or new ones and have had their spray patterns and rated amounts of fuel delivery checked. An advantage of disc type injectors over pintle type injectors is that they are very quiet in operation.

25% of well used disc injectors will be found to be faulty. The original Lucas part numbered injectors are no longer available, but these injectors can be substituted with Bosch or Weber pintle type replacement part injectors.

ECU

The ECU of the 14CUX is more modern than the 4CU L-Jetronic type and is run by a micro-processor or EPROM chip.

For high performance applications Tornado Engine Management Systems alters the programme that runs the engine to suit the particular application. For example –

The rev limiter is made 'soft cut' compared to the standard rev limiting, which is very severe.

The road speed limiter, which gets its input from the speedometer transducer, is removed (with standard ECUs fitted, the maximum road speed is limited to 90mph/144kph or 112mph/179kph, depending on the vehicle).

Cold start fuelling is also reduced, as is warm up period fuelling.

Cranking speed fuelling is reduced (often by as much as 20% to prevent engine flooding). Note that in many instances standard engines that won't start will be found to have fuel fouled sparkplugs.

Engine braking is altered so that gear changing is smoother. This is achieved by altering the idle valve setting (reducing the amount the idle valve opens).

An engine firing delay is also built into the ECU so that a cold engine cranks two or three times before the ignition is switched on.

The fuelling data is changed to suit the individual application.

Tornado Engine Management Systems has 200 basic fuelling curves on record, but with the minor adjustments that are able to be made the number of individual fuelling curves could be limitless. What T.E.M.S. requires before supplying an uprated ECU is the **precise** specification of the engine and a full description of what the application is. For some specialist applications T.E.M.S. will supply three ECUs, the customer being required to test the engine with each in turn and to decide which ECU causes the engine to perform the best.

There are 16 'engine speed sites' and 8 'engine load sites,' in the ECU with each 'load site' in turn being subdivided into 8 further separate parts, making a total of over 1024 individual fuelling points. The division of each individual load site into 8 further parts is in the original programming.

There are also a few types of EPROM that can be used in these ECUs but Tornado Engine Mangement Systems only uses the industrial quality EPROM which has a temperature tolerance from –20 degrees C/-6F to 80 degrees C/176F. When available, T.E.M.S. will use military specification EPROMs which have a temperature range from –40 degrees C/-42F to 30 degrees C/86F. The industrial quality EPROM is quite adequate for all applications. T.E.M.S. does not use the general commercial EPROM which is rated from 0 degrees C to 60 degrees C.

Airflow meter

There are two standard airflow meters. The early one is the 3AM type (a Hitachi labelled component) which was superseded by the 5AM type (a Lucas labelled one, part number ERR5198). Both are interchangeable and neither are available new today so, whichever one you have, it needs to be checked to make sure it is working correctly. This can be done by sending it to Tornado Engine Management Systems to be checked and, if necessary, rebuilt. All airflow meters checked or supplied by Tornado Engine Management Systems come with a one year guarantee.

There is a range of checks that anyone can do to determine whether or not their airflow meter is serviceable and acceptable for further use without removing it from the engine. All that is required for these tests is an accurate digital volt meter. The procedure is as follows –

There are four wires coming out of the airflow meter. The red wire with the black trace is the ground wire. The blue wire with the green trace is the airflow signal. The brown wire with the orange trace is the 12 volt feed to the unit. The blue wire with the red trace is the idle CO trim. All testing is done with the multimeter's negative probe in the red and black trace wire.

Firstly, set the voltmeter to 5 volts, switch the ignition on, but don't start the engine. The 'CO trim' is checked and set by probing the blue and red wire trace wire with the positive probe to see what the voltage is. Expect, on a non catalytic converter equipped engine, to see 1.0 volts and on a catalytic converter equipped unit a 1.8 volt reading. The setting can be altered by turning the adjuster through its range until the require voltage is registering. The adjuster goes from 0.0 volts to 3.5 volts through its whole range of twenty two turns. More volts means a higher percentage of CO at idle (a richer idle mixture).

Next, with the positive probe, probe the brown and orange trace wire with the ignition switched on (engine not started) to check that battery voltage is read. The voltage could be anything from 12.0 volts to 12.4 volts, perhaps as much as 12.5 volts, depending on the condition and charge state of the battery.

Next probe the blue and green trace airflow signal wire with the ignition switched on (engine not started) and expect to see 0.3 volts. Now turn ignition off for ten seconds and then turn it back on. The voltage should jump up to 0.3 volts. If the reading jumps up to between 0.5 and 0.8 volts and takes 3 to 5 seconds to come down to 0.3 volts, the airflow meter needs replacement as it is failing.

Finally, start engine and let it idle and then use the negative probe to on the red and black trace wire and the positive probe on the blue and green trace wire. The voltage on a 3.9 litre engine should be 1.7 to 1.8 volts with the engine completely cold but, when the engine warms up, it should settle down to 1.5 to 1.6 volts.

The standard 3AM and 5AM airflow meter has an aperture of 55mm diameter through which all air drawn into the engine has to pass: this can be bored out to a maximum of 60mm in diameter. An alternative to using a bored out 3AM or 5AM airflow meter is to use a 20AM airflow meter from a 4.6 litre Rover engine, however, no engine smaller than 4.5 litres needs a 20AM airflow meter. The 20AM airflow meter is the later GEMS system airflow meter and it flows 30% more air than a bored out standard Lucas 14CUX airflow meter. When this airflow meter is fitted, the 14CUX fuel injection system is capable of being used on larger than stock capacity engines which are developing 400 foot pounds/547Nm of torque.

Note that all engines must be fitted with an airflow meter which is large enough; but avoid using an airflow meter that is too big, as this can cause a flat spot in the acceleration phase. The engine will rev through the flat spot, but this is not efficient: use the smallest airflow meter that allows maximum power to be developed.

In terms of performance tuning, the main difference between the Lucas L-Jetronic 4CU flap type airflow meter system and the Lucas L-Jetronic 14CUX hot wire airflow meter system is that the earlier system uses a Ferranti (read only) silicon chip to control fuelling, while the later system uses a readily available micro-processing EPROM

silicon chip in its ECU. The latter is the same sort of silicon chip as used in the radio and television industry, for example, as well as the household appliance industry.

In order to re-chip to improve fuelling for high performance applications, the ECU is removed from the car and partially dismantled to get at the appropriate chip. The Lucas 14CUX fuel injection system has a 4K silicon chip and uses 3.998K of it's capacity to run the engine.

When Rover V8 engine specialist companies started to work with the hot wire fuel injection systems it was soon realised that the EPROM of the ECU controlled the engine fuelling. Better still, the EPROM was, in many cases, a plug in device (some were soldered into position and had to be unsoldered to remove them ... tricky). Only the early European/UK ECUs had the soldered in EPROMs: USA ones had plug in EPROMs which are easily removable. They were designed to be removable in case of problems complying with the USA emissions legislation and, in fact, originally 70% of new cars failed the end of line test at the factory. Their ECUs had to be removed and be replaced with ones which had wider tolerances.

GEMS 8 INTEGRATED ENGINE MANAGEMENT SYSTEM: OVERVIEW

The 'Generic Engine Management System' (GEMS) was a wholly Lucas-designed and built system, which was first fitted to the Rover V8 in 1994. GEMS was created by Lucas engineer Dr David Williams (Project Engineer) and his colleagues. The software was designed and developed by Jim

Samuels (Chief Engineer Software). Work first started on the GEMS system in early 1991 and it took three years to develop it fully to production level.

GEMS came into being when Lucas approached Rover and Jaguar telling them that it would develop a new hot wire, integrated engine management system which would comply with the rigid OBDII requirements of the California Air Resources Board (the full requirements of the new standard were not known at this time). Both Rover and Jaguar knew that to sell their cars in the USA after a certain date they'd have to have such a system. Both companies agreed to buy the Lucas GEMS system for a certain number of years so that it would all be worthwhile for Lucas to develop such a system and then gear up to mass produce it.

The OBDII specification was actually published in 1989 and all vehicles sold in California had to comply generally by 1994, and totally by 1996. GEMS 8 complied with the legislation in 1997 (having been given dispensation to exceed the compliance date) and was discontinued by Rover in 2001.

The first forty cars sent to the USA had their ECUs reworked twice before being sold to the general public. While the cars were being demonstrated to Rover dealers, there were a few driveabilitiy problems. These were mainly cold running problems, so the calibration was altered. Ultimately, two 'tunes' were used in USA Range Rovers. If an early model car started to have running problems in later years, two new chips would be installed in the original ECU by the main dealer to upgrade the ECU to the 2nd 'tune' which would cure the problems.

When it was first checked by the California Air Resources Board in 1994/1995 the system only failed on 'engine backfire'. This didn't stop the GEMS 8 system being accepted at the time because the problem was a very minor consideration and the rest of the system complied perfectly.

With regard to the backfire issue, on a manual transmission car the throttle can be blipped and, depending on how quickly the accelerator pedal is moved, the engine responds in one of two ways. At the average 100 milliseconds that it takes a driver to floor the accelerator pedal, GEMS 8 coped. However, if the accelerator pedal was depressed quicker than this, the air/fuel mixture would be lean and the engine would likely backfire. The ECU by now realises the mixture is lean and richens it by too much as this leaness is only a momentary situation, the air/fuel goes rich (high CO and HC readings). It takes two or three seconds for it all to settle down, but this behaviour is not acceptable to comply precisely with OBDII. The software was altered to eradicate the backfire problem and then complied fully with OBDII.

The GEMS 8 system was first introduced in 1994 on Land Rover Defenders that went to North America with 4.0 litre V8 engines, this was followed by Land Rover 300 Series Discovery for North America also with the 4.0 litre V8, then, in 1998, all Range Rovers made in the UK with either the 4.0 and 4.6 litre versions of the Rover V8 engine were given the new system. The GEMS 8 system was phased out in 2001, replaced by a Bosch engine management system which will remain the current until the engine is phased out of production.

The GEMS 8-equipped vehicles sent to North America had four Lambda sensors fitted. In each of the two exhaust manifolds there is one Lambda sensor fitted before the catalytic converter and one after (both sensors are electrically heated). The Lambda sensors fitted before the catalytic converters measure the oxygen in the exhaust gas in their vicinities and relay the information to the ECU to control the fuelling. The two Lambda sensors fitted after each catalytic converter measure the oxygen content of the exhaust gases after the exhaust gases have been through the catalytic converters. If the second pair of Lambda sensors detect that there is too much or too little oxygen in the exhaust gases they initiate the 'fault code' and the MIL (Malfunction Indicator Light) dash light will come on.

Note that the term 'fault code' means that a light in the dashboard of a car is switched on and that the diagnostics of the ECU have located a fault in the system. In the USA it is illegal to drive a car with the 'fault code' or the MIL illuminated on the dashboard.

The Lambda sensors behind the catalytic converters only activate the 'fault code' and do not play any part in controlling the fuelling. The engine will run as before the light came on, unless the fault (excessive richness) is one which won't allow the engine to run at all. Also these Lambda sensors operate independently of each other and it only takes one cylinder on one side of the engine to develop a fault for the Lambda sensor on that side of the engine to activate the 'fault code.'

The flywheels and flexplates (auto trans) of GEMS 8-equipped Rover V8 engines have 36 individual segments for 10 degree readings of crankshaft position by the ECU sensor. There's also a wide space, by way of a missing tooth, to indicate a piston position of 20 degrees before top dead center (BTDC) in number one cylinder. When the engine is first cranked by the starter, it takes three teeth to pass the sensor before the ECU starts 'looking' for the missing tooth. Once the ECU locates the missing tooth it then 'knows' where TDC of number one cylinder or number six cylinder is, but not which one is on a firing stroke on the first revolution of the engine.

The detection of the missing tooth causes the fuel injection system to start injecting fuel in both banks of cylinders in a non-sequential manner (all together) and also to fire the ignition system at the correct number of degrees before top dead centre (BTDC). The initial advance for starting is 6 degrees. The engine starts and, as the camshaft position lobe passes its sensor, the ECU 'knows' exactly which cylinder is on the compression (firing) stroke and will then start the correct sequential fuel injection within two complete revolutions of the engine.

The positioning of the missing tooth 20 degrees BTDC means that the engine starts on average one third of second quicker than it otherwise would as this creates enough time to process the engine positional information and commence fuel injection and ignition for the number one and six cylinders, as opposed to finding true TDC immediately and firing the next cylinder in the firing order. The least possible emissions at start up are also realised.

There are two knock sensors on these Rover V8 engines: they're of the 'Piezo-electric accelerometer' type. The knock sensors are fitted into cast in bosses on each side of the block, which means that the GEMS 8 system is, in a sense, block specific. The knock sensors produce a voltage which is calibrated proportionally to the mechanical vibration and noise being produced by the engine. The information by way of a variable voltage, is sent to the ECU and, if the engine is above the designated vibration and noise level, the ECU retards its ignition timing, the ECU does not alter (increase) the fuelling.

The ECU has two 'base knock maps.' One measuring the even firing number cylinders, the other the odd firing cylinders. The 4.0 litre engine also generates a different amount of vibration and noise compared to the 4.6 litre engine, so both engines' ECUs have different base knock maps. From knock sensor feedback, the ECU recognises normal running and abnormal running. When a certain voltage output is reached by the knock sensor, the ignition is retarded. The bigger the voltage reading, the larger the amount of ignition retard within the parameters of the programming of the ECU.

Note that if the camshaft sensor fails, the knock sensing ability of the ECU stops because the ECU relies on the camshaft position sensor to 'know' which cylinder is which.

There have been four different ECUs for the GEMS 8 system and thirty one versions of these four. The major differences between the ECUs are related to their applications. For example, there are between one and six different states of tune programmed into the ECUs and the state of tune to be used in a particular standard application is selected by the resistance in the wiring loom. These various states of tune are for the various octane ratings of fuel used around the world, the particular market the car is going to (on the basis of the emission control and legislation requirements of the region), engine size, engine accessories and transmission type. Each ECU has two micro-processor chips (EPROMs). One is made by Intel, the other by TMS. Both store the data and the programmes which run the engine management system and both chips are matched.

For engines fitted to cars being sold to countries which do not have unleaded fuel, such as India, Africa and the Gulf States, the version of GEMS 8 that they use run 'open loop'. These versions of GEMS 8 do not have knock sensors and no Lambda sensors (catalytic converters are not used on these vehicles). The ECUs for these markets are not 'self learning' as there is no useful feedback for the ECU to learn anything from. As a consequence, these particular ECUs are not upgraded by Tornado Engine Management Technology as the software is completely different.

GEMS 8: METHODS OF MODIFICATION FOR HIGH PERFORMANCE

What Tornado Engine Management Systems does with a GEMS 8 is mainly confined the ECU into which the company can reprogramme the engine performance 'targets' for fuelling, ignition timing, knock, idle stability, idle speed and cold start fuelling.

Some ECUs for roadgoing cars have further alterations made such as removal of the 115mph/184kph max speed limit if required. T.E.M.S. is always reluctant to remove the maximum speed technology on road vehicles because modified engines used in Range Rovers would be quite capable of exceeding 115mph with ease and these vehicles are just not stable over this speed.

The 'self learning' capability of the GEMS 8 system, via the very clever use of two wide band heated 5 volt Lambda sensors, ensures that all of the engines operating requirements are optimised for perfect running under all conditions.

T.E.M.S. requires the exact specifications of the engine and the application, then the ECU (your own, or one of theirs) will be custom rebuilt to suit. The company has a database which allows it to make sensible component choices which means your ECU will be correct when you receive it.

As usual with modified ECUs, the fuel pressure will require fine tuning from the standard amount of 2.6 Bar/38psi through to 3.05 Bar 44psi (3.1 Bar/45psi being the absolute maximum). Matched injectors (spray pattern and flow capacity) are required, with racing engines requiring the tightest tolerance (within 2% of each other) to ensure even fuel distribution to each cylinder.

For road going use a significant improvement in cruising speed/partial load fuel economy is possible by the leaning out the air/fuel mix for these conditions. To prevent the production of NOx, the air/fuel mixture ratio is deliberately kept richer than it needs to be. For cruising along a motorway/freeway the mixture only needs to have a strength factor of 15.5 to 16.5:1. The downside to this is, of course, that NOx (a poisonous gas) is being produced in the largest possible amounts and is going into the atmosphere while you're making a fuel saving.

With heated 'wideband' Titania Lambda sensors fitted to GEMS 8-equipped Rover V8 engines, the ECU is fed information instantly about air/fuel mixture ratios (between 16.5:1 to 11.0:1 – as wide a range as any engine would ever operate under). The later type Titania wideband TO17 Lambda sensor works the opposite way to the earlier 1 volt Zirconia-type. The higher the voltage reading from the Lambda sensor, the leaner the air/fuel mixture ratio is and, conversely, the lower the voltage, the richer the mixture. The electrical resistance of the Lambda sensor is proportional to the oxygen level in the exhaust gases. At Lambda one/14.7:1 air fuel mixture ratio/0.5 CO, the voltage feedback from the Lambda sensor is between 2.5 and 3.0 volts.

Note that one of the biggest wreckers of oxygen sensors on Rover V8s, fitted with GEMS 8, is the block cracking problem. The coolant that gets into the exhaust gases affects the Lambda sensor and the chemicals in the antifreeze contaminate the ceramic surface of the sensor.

The Range Rover's ECU is much more sophisticated than the Land Rover's 'alarm only' unit in that it operates the central locking, the security system, the control of every light on the vehicle and every other electrical circuit in conjunction with the 'Body Controlled Module', or 'BCM' as it is commonly called. An

example of the BCM's role is that when the key fob is used to open the door on a Range Rover, the EPROM in the BCM checks to see if it is the right key fob accessing the car: if not the doors will not be allowed to unlock.

To get GEMS 8-equipped Rover V8 engines to run in other cars, such as racing cars, and in other engine transplant situations, the Land Rover 'alarm only' ECU is used which only requires special programming to block the alarm part of the ECU out. With the alarm component blocked out (no BCM component), the Land Rover alarm unit ECU still has the Lambda sensor and knock sensor feedback technology, all that's required for the optimum running efficiency of an engine.

GEMS 8 systems, as prepared by Tornado Engine Management Systems for racing engines, always retain the knock sensors and Lambda sensors, as this is how they provide the feedback which controls the self-learning aspect of the ECU and, ultimately, delivers excellent engine performance. It can also can save an engine from a very expensive failure if something goes wrong because the ECU will retard the ignition timing in one 10 millionth part of a second the instant it detects that something out of the ordinary.

If a GEMS 8 system is being used on an engine for pure racing purposes, in some instances the standard knock sensors will be found to be a bit bulky when tubular exhaust manifolds are fitted. The standard Lucas sensors can be changed for Bosch ones and the ECU reprogrammed to work with them instead. This, of course, has to be decided on before the

ECU is prepared for the particular engine. Also, the later 'Titania' 5 volt Lambda sensors are not always a straightforward fit into a set of tubular extractor type of exhaust manifolds, because they have an unusual thread size at 12mm by 1.25mm pitch with a fairly short thread. The earlier Lambda sensors had a sparkplug size 14mm by 1.5mm pitch thread and a longer thread. The problem here is that if a nut of the right thread size is brazed or mig welded onto the exhaust pipe collector, the probe of the Lambda sensor will not protrude into the exhaust gas stream far enough. The nut will either have to be turned down so it is shallower, or a 8mm thick plate brazed or mig welded onto the exhaust collector (transition piece, where the four pipes merge) and then the Lambda sensor will protrude a suitable amount into the exhaust gas stream. About 8mm of thread length is required for the Lambda sensor.

In an effort to get the most out of the GEMS 8 system, J.E. Developments has increased the diameter of the standard inlet manifold runner holes from 38mm to 45mm diameter and then ported the rest of the inlet tract to the cylinder heads to suit: new inlet trumpets/ram tubes are made to suit this new diameter. It all fits inside the plenum as per original. The increase in mid-range power is noticeably improved but the top end power, with either the standard 20AM airflow meter (65mm diameter butterfly) or an enlarged one (72mm diameter butterfly) does not result in increased top end power (except for 1 or 2bhp).

J.E. Developments uses the standard sized GEMS 8 airflow

meter (20AM) on all of its engines with the standard 38mm diameter inlet manifold, or the 45mm diameter ported out inlet manifold, as it finds the fitting of a larger diameter butterfly to be less effective overall (reduction in mid-range engine response). The increased size inlet manifold allows significant gains in mid-range power for large capacity engines.

The size of the butterfly isn't the problem when it comes to airflow, rather it's the design of the 'hot wire' part of the airflow meter unit. The limit to the use of the Lucas GEMS 8 fuel injection system is the amount of air that the airflow meter can pass. There is an unrecoverable loss (pressure loss) in the meter via the hot wire and bracket which is in the airstream. The advantage of using an airflow meter of this type on the standard engine is that it makes the overall system easy to calibrate. However, with a change of application requiring much higher airflow requirements (eg: a high rpm racing engine) the airflow meter becomes a limiting factor. To all intents and purposes there is no easy way around this problem if the cost of the performance improvement is to be kept reasonable: this is a well known problem in fuel injection circles. The difference in maximum power of an engine equipped with an individual induction tract-type of aftermarket fuel injection system, and the same engine equipped with a modified GEMS 8, will be in the order of 15-20bhp.

GEMS 8: IGNITION SYSTEM

The GEMS 8 ignition component of the engine management system uses four individual ignition coils, with each coil having two HT leads (ignition wires) going to two spark plugs. The ignition system is a Direct Ignition System (DIS) type which operates on the 'wasted spark' principle so that when the circuit is activated and the ignition coil discharges, two cylinders' spark plugs receive HT voltage. This whole system was devised to save money on the basis that four coils are cheaper than eight, while still maintaining acceptable electrical efficiency.

The first ignition coil fires cylinders 1 and 6, the second coil fires cylinders 5 and 8, the third coil fires cylinders 7 and 4 and the fourth coil fires cylinders 3 and 2. The four coils also discharge once in every revolution of the engine. When coil one, for example, fires cylinder 1 on the compression stroke, it also fires cylinder 6 which is on its exhaust stroke. On the very next revolution of the engine, when coil one discharges again, it fires number 6 cylinder which is on its compression stroke while number 1 cylinder is on its exhaust stroke. The wasted spark principle revolves around the fact that the cylinder on the compression stroke receives more electrical energy because the air/fuel mixture in the cylinder under compression is easier to ionize and the coil will dissipate vastly more energy into that cylinder. 20-22kV has been found to be quite adequate for complete combustion on these engines, although vastly higher voltages were tried when the system was being trialed which resulted in spark plugs lasting little more than 1000 miles!

One of the factors resulting from using one coil to fire two cylinders in this manner is that one cylinder gets positive EMF (Electro-Motive Force) while the other gets negative EMF. This is the difference between positive EMF jumping from the cylinder head to the sparkplug electrode and negative EMF jumping from the spark plug electrode to the cylinder head when the sparkplug fires. While negative EMF is not strictly speaking correct, ignition performance is not noticeably reduced because of it.

GEMS 8 is rated as a "simply brilliant system and currently in a class of its own for what it is" by Mark Adams of Tornado Engine Management Systems and the ultimate all round Rover V8 engine management system for the following reasons –

Its overall level of sophistication is virtually unrivalled by any other standard type system, it has excellent diagnostics and can tailor optimum fuel levels and optimum ignition requirements to an individual engine, irrespective of the engine's level of modification once the ECU has had its targets altered. The only problem with GEMS 8 being the slight reduction in top end power due to airflow restriction in the airflow meter compared to an aftermarket individual inlet tract-type of fuel injection system. Everywhere else in the rpm/load range, GEMS 8 matches virtually any other system on the basis of response, economy, smoothness of power application (ideal mixture strength being supplied to the engine under all circumstances). The cost of altering the standard GEMS 8, versus the cost of an all new aftermarket individual runner fuel injection system, offers excellent value for money.

Drew Selvey (ex Lucas engineer) says that GEMS 8 was "Well ahead of the game when it first came out, and now all current engine management systems use similar operating criteria." The sophistication of the system also caused problems for Rover service engineers around the world which resulted in *Don't Panic*, an internal publication, being written by Peter Tibbles and Jon Caine who worked at Land Rover: a booklet which neatly solved most fault diagnosis situations.

BOSCH MOTRONIC ML.2.1 ENGINE MANAGEMENT SYSTEM: OVERVIEW

Bosch Motronic ML.2.1 fuel injection system was fitted to Rover V8 engines from the year 2000 and is still the current engine management system for the Rover V8. This system uses a 'hot film' airflow meter. It does not currently have a particularly good high performance image as experiments carried out on engines fitted with this engine management system resulted in the following conclusions –

Engine performance was down overall compared to any of the three Lucas systems used previously (all of which have at the present been successfully altered to suit mild to wild engines).

For all round general road use with a standard engine the Bosch system is excellent, with extremely good mid-range torque being produced just as you require for a road going vehicle.

The Bosch system has proved successful up to a maximum of 270bhp.

Engines equipped with this system are Lambda 1 controlled under all conditions. Meaning that a 14.7:1 air/fuel mixture is maintained at all times.

The Bosch system is 'focused' on low emissions and diagnostics, as opposed to the best possible accelerative engine performance and can't easily be changed. The diagnostics are so sophisticated they can, for example, identify a cylinder which is not firing via the momentary speed differential of the flywheel.

Tornado Engine Management Systems may look more seriously at reworking these systems in the future, but at the time of writing this system is being bypassed in favour of the older systems.

HT (HIGH TENSION) LEAD/WIRE REQUIREMENTS (ALL SYSTEMS)

All of these electronic fuel injection systems require the use of top quality suppression-type HT leads/sparkplug wires to be used to prevent electro magnetic induction (EMI). When EMI occurs it causes a voltage signal (spike) to be sent to the ECU which will result in an engine misfire as the sparkplugs will be fired at the wrong time.

On new engine installations the ECU should be checked to see that there are no ignition pulse induced voltage spikes being fed into the ECU's circuitry. This is done by checking to see if there are any voltage spikes in the ECU which coincide with ignition firings. A sensitive oscilloscope is used to check this where the wires go into the ECU. The greatest amount of interference, if there is any, will be found at highest engine loading/maximum torque. The ideal place to carry out this check is on a rolling road dyno (complete engine installation with all wires in place exactly as the engine will be running in its application).

Even when using top quality suppression high tension wire, the sparkplug wires should never be placed within 2in/50mm of each other, and they should not be within 3in/75mm of any part of the injector wiring loom. The sparkplug wires can be crossed at 90 degrees to each other.

One of the best sparkplug wires is made by Magnecor and there are two types that suit these engines. The first is the 8mm 'blue' wire ('Magnecor Electrosports 80 – Ignition Cable') which has a spiral wound stainless steel conductor; the second is the 8.5mm 'red' wire ('Magnecor V85 Competition – Pure Silicone Ignition Cable') which has a pure silicon covering. These V85 brand name wires require careful handling when fitting the boots to the distributor cap/coils and the sparkplugs as the material is easy to damage. That's not to say that they're weak, just that they require careful handling to avoid any possibility of damage. The V85 wire insulation is the best available.

Similar high quality HT wires are manufactured by Moroso, MSD, Taylor, Mallory and Accel, for example.

Note: failure to fit good quality, well insulated sparkplug wires can result in stray impulses being picked up by the ECU: this will cause erratic engine performance (misfiring).

CATALYTIC CONVERTERS (ALL SYSTEMS)

There have been two types of

catalytic converters used on Rover V8 engines: 'two way' and 'three way.' The older 'two way' catalytic converters deal with two pollutants, CO (carbon monoxide) and HC (hydrocarbons). The catalytic converters that can deal with these two pollutants are those that use platinum as a catalyst. This was fine until environmental agencies realized that the poison NOx (oxides of nitrogen) was also being produced in quite large amounts and they decided to deal with this as well. Consequently, a new type of 'cat' was required and this was called a 'three way' catalytic converter.

The later 'three way' catalytic converters use platinum and rhodium as catalysts and are able to deal with three pollutants : CO, HC and NOx. The platinum deals with the CO and HC and the rhodium the NOx.

NOx is only formed at elevated combustion chamber temperatures such as 2500 degrees C/4532F and above. The leaner the mixture the engine is running at, the higher the amount of NOx the combustion process will produce. The minimum levels of NOx production are at between 11:1 and, approximately, 14.7:1 air /fuel mixture ratios. From 14.7:1 and weaker, the production of NOx rises very steeply and the maximum production of NOx is at about 16.5:1 air/fuel ratio. The

Rover V8 engine won't run on partial throttle loading at much more than 16.0:1 so this is the range under consideration. So, while an engine will be returning maximum fuel economy operating between 15.5:1 and 16.0:1 air/fuel ratios, unacceptable levels of NOx are produced. The air/fuel ratio which sees all three pollutants reduced to the minimum possible is 14.7:1 (Lambda/stoichiometric). If NOx was not included in the emission control regime, Rover V8 engines could be set to run at 15.8 to 16.3:1 air/fuel mixes for all partial load/cruise conditions.

Lucas set the cruise mixture at 14.35:1 for three reasons. First, even though the Rover V8 engine will run perfectly with a 15.8-16.3:1 air/fuel ratio, the air/fuel ratio is set at 14.35:1 to keep NOx emmissions down: a richer mixture and which uses slightly more fuel than the engine actually needs. Second, an air/fuel mixture ratio that averages 14.7:1 suits catalytic converters in that they work best (do not get overloaded) dealing with exhaust gases that have been burnt at the chemically correct mix ratio. Third, the Rover V8 tends to run hot at 14.7:1, the slightly richer mixture reduces temperatures.

While the production of NOx is starting to increase when the CO and HC are at their lowest possible

levels, there isn't really any other way of getting around it. Therefore, the NOx is simply dealt with by the use of a 'three way' catalytic converters and, in more recent years, the amount of rhodium in catalytic converters has doubled (up from 6% to 12%).

While catalytic converters start to operate at about 380 degrees C/716F, with air/fuel mixtures of 14.7:1, the average operating temperature of the later type catalytic converters can be in the region of 930-950 degrees C/1706-1742F. During engine testing by Lucas engineers, the temperatures of the catalytic converters would on occasion, for very short periods, hit 1100-1150 degrees C/2012-2107F. Continuous use at these elevated temperatures would result in premature failure of the catalytic converters, so to prevent this sort of overheating the mixture strength is increased (engine run 'open loop').

For instance, at 5000rpm under wide open throttle conditions the ECU of the later GEMS 8 system sets the air/fuel mixture ratio to 11:1 to keep the internal engine componentry cool (pistons, for instance). Fuel consumption under these extreme heat conditions drops away to a very low figure indeed – 5 miles to the gallon is not impossible!

Chapter 16
Exhaust system

ORIGINAL EXHAUST MANIFOLDS

Rover's range of original standard cast iron exhaust manifolds varies, with some being better than others. The cast iron manifolds fitted to the early engines are quite good and are still fine for road applications, and their efficiency is better than many American-made standard cast iron V8 manifolds of the time. The later factory manifolds were compromised to suit particular engine installations and sometimes were more functional than smooth flowing. Nevertheless, they are all reasonably efficient and certainly very acceptable for road going applications.

The configuration of the early exhaust manifolds was a four into one system for each side of the engine. In later designs the four primary pipes from each cylinder head were grouped into pairs in the cast iron exhaust manifolds, leading

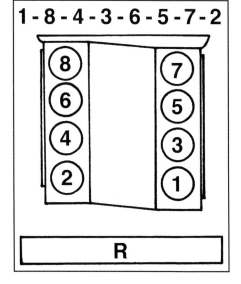

into two tubular exhaust pipes and then into one pipe at a bifurcated joint. Finally, the two primary main pipes (one from each bank of cylinders) were joined into one main pipe, again via a bifurcated joint, and this single pipe went to atmosphere.

The firing order of a Rover V8 is 1-8-4-3-6-5-7-2. The right hand side of the engine, looking from the front, comprises cylinders 1-3-5-7, while the left hand side of the engine comprises cylinders 2-4-6-8. The diagram gives the individual cylinder positions by number ('R' being the radiator in front of the cylinder block). As can be seen, cylinders 5 & 7 are adjacent consecutive firing cylinders. On the standard 4 into 1 manifolds, two exhaust pulses follow each other into the same exhaust manifold. On the later standard 4 into 2 into 1 manifolds the configuration ensures that the primary exhaust pulses are separated nearly equally.

The principle of this design was to group the exhaust firing pulses as advantageously as possible for low rpm torque and to produce as compact a system as possible.

A key principle in designing exhausts for V8s is the way that the engine's firing order and the resultant exhaust gas pulses are dealt with. The aim is to produce an efficient design that ensures a even flow of exhaust gas pulses and avoids consecutive exhaust pulses in the secondary pipes. The two factory configurations of cast iron manifold approach the problem from different perspectives. The early manifolds have a simple 4 into 1 layout, while the later manifolds have a 4 into 2 into 1 layout that sought to take advantage of the engine's firing order and to avoid the consecutive pulse problem. This aspect of exhaust system design is one of several that are not widely appreciated, ignorance or confusion leading to poor system design.

Both basic configurations are commonly used by car makers and aftermarket suppliers, and both are efficient. The four into two into one configuration tends to produce better low/mid range engine performance, while the four into one is better for top end performance and is generally a simpler design.

All standard production cast iron manifolds have relatively small diameter internal passageways commensurate with the exhaust port sizing and with the flow rate of exhaust gas from a standard engine. There is some benefit to be had by changing the original cast iron exhaust manifold for a tubular extractor-type manifold, especially if the exhaust ports have been enlarged and the camshaft duration and lift have been increased, resulting in a higher exhaust gas flow. The scope for improvement will depend largely on the engine installation and the space available in the engine compartment for larger diameter primary pipes that may not be as compact in design as the cast iron originals. In some instances the cost of a set of tubular exhaust manifolds may be very high

in relation to the improvement they'll bring, if any, over a set of standard cast iron exhaust manifolds.

The standard exhaust manifolds and the standard exhaust systems should not be regarded as inefficient items best discarded at the first opportunity. However, the standard system's flow capability can be exceeded by modified engines and, when this happens, worthwhile gains can be made by using alternative manifolds with larger diameter pipes.

One set of factory cast iron exhaust manifolds stands out from all other similar looking ones. This is the 'Dakar Rally' manifold, which is of the four into two into one-type configuration. This manifold is particularly efficient and, with suitably sized piping from the exhaust manifolds on, is part of an extremely efficient exhaust system. The major difference between this exhaust manifold and the standard ones is the diameter of the internal passageways: 1.75in/44mm right up to the exhaust port, which is much larger than standard. However only a limited number of these manifolds were ever made.

TUBULAR EXHAUST MANIFOLDS (HEADERS)
There are three main exhaust system configurations that can be used on Rover V8 engines. Two of them reflect the essential design of the original factory cast iron items, but one is entirely different.

Note that all exhaust pipe diameters for tubular manifolds refer to the **outside** diameters as measured with a vernier caliper.

4 into 1
This manifold (header) design has the four individual primary pipes,

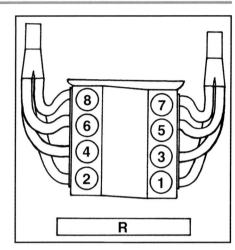

Four into one configuration for a tubular exhaust manifold. The original cast iron exhaust manifolds have the same configuration, but with much shorter primary tracts. Note the grouping of the cylinders.

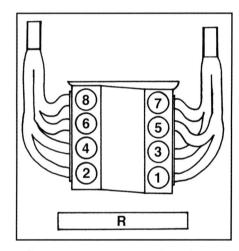

Four into two into one configuration for a tubular exhaust manifold. The original cast iron exhaust manifolds have the same configuration, but with very much shorter primary tracts. Note the grouping of the cylinders and the different layout for the two banks of cylinders to overcome the problem of cylinders 5 & 7 firing consecutively.

typically 1½in/38mm diameter, coming from each cylinder head, which all turn downward to run down the side of the engine. At about the level of the bottom of the engine

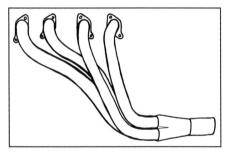

Typical, easy to fit, four into one tubular exhaust extractor manifold (header), which uses 1.5in/38mm primary pipes and a 2.0in/50mm main pipe. Both sides of the engine use a similar configuration.

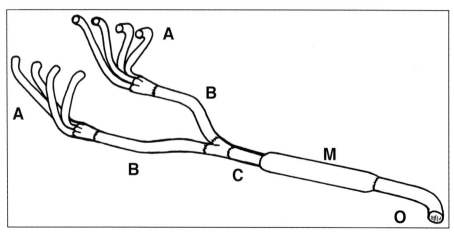

The eight 1½in/38mm primary pipes are at 'A' & 'A', the two 2in/50mm 'primary main' pipes are at 'B' & 'B', these two pipes merge at a bifurcated joint into a 2½in/63mm main pipe at 'C' which feeds a silencer (muffler) 'M' before the gas is released to atmosphere through a 2½in/63mm tail pipe/side pipe at 'O'.

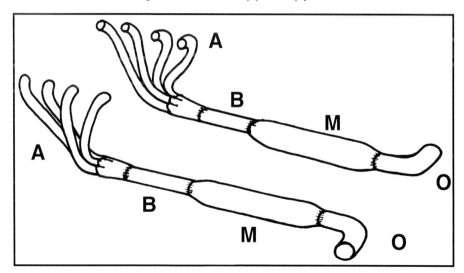

Independent main pipes have the same 1½in/38mm diameter primary pipes as the previous example at 'A' & 'A' but, the two 2in/50mm main pipes 'B' & 'B' do not merge, instead they go into separate silencers (mufflers) at 'M' & 'M' and exit at 'O' & 'O' having maintained the 2in/50mm main pipe sizes.

the pipes turn towards the rear of the car, and then all four primary pipes are joined together into a single 2in/50mm main pipe. The individual primary pipes are not of equal length, but this is not critical until used with high rpm engines. All engines equipped with standard cylinder heads can use this design of exhaust manifold.

The two 2in/50mm 'primary main' pipes (one for each cylinder bank) join into a single 2½in/63mm pipe after the gearbox, wherever it's convenient to join them. This pipe then feeds the exhaust gases through a suitable silencer (muffler) after which a pipe of the same diameter releases them to the atmosphere. Today, even racing cars have silencers (generally absorption type) that reduce exhaust noise to 90-95 decibels.

Joining the two primary main pipes is a good thing to do as it improves the scavenge effect, but it's not absolutely necessary. In fact, in some instances, it's just not possible to join the two pipes because of space constraints, and in such cases each primary main pipe feeds directly into its own main pipe/ silencer and then to atmosphere.

Pipe dimensions

For lightly modified or standard cylinder heads, whether fitted to a standard capacity 3.5 to 4.6 litre engines, or aftermarket stroker versions of these capacities, the smallest primary pipes to use are 1½in/38mm diameter and the largest 1⅝in/41mm. These larger 1⅝in/ 41mm primary pipes would typically feed into a 2⅛in/54mm main pipe.

Racing engines of 3.5 to 4.5 litres, using gasflowed heads with larger ports, will always use a minimum of 1⅝in/41mm diameter primary pipes, with up to 1¾in/ 44mm feeding into 3in/75mm main pipe being usual for 4.0 to 4.5 litre engines.

4.5 to 6 litre racing engines

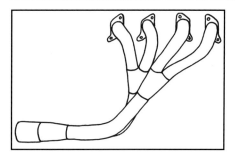

Right hand fitting 4-2-1 tubular exhaust manifold. The four primary pipes are 1¹/₂in/38mm in diameter, the secondary pipes are 1³/₄in/44mm and the main pipe is 2in/50mm. Adjacent primary pipes are paired (the rear two pipes are paired as are the front two).

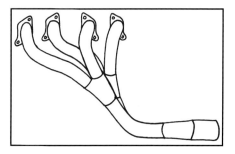

Left hand fitting 4-2-1 tubular exhaust manifold. The pipe sizes are the same as those for the right hand manifold (header). The first and third primary pipes are paired as are the second and fourth primary pipes. This is a different arrangement from the right hand side manifold.

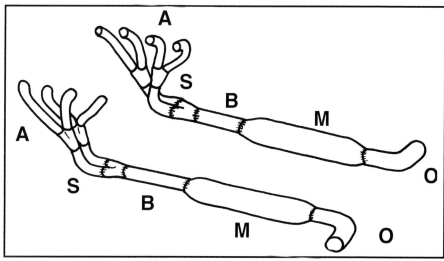

These 4-2-1 exhaust manifolds can be kept separate in a twin system. The four primary pipes at 'A' & 'A' feed into two secondary pipes at 'S' & 'S', go into main pipes at 'B' & 'B', then through the mufflers/silencers at 'M' & 'M' and, finally, the main pipe outlets at 'O' & 'O'.

could feature 1³/₄-1⁷/₈-2in/44-47-50mm primary pipes feeding into a 3¹/₂in/90mm main pipe through a four pipe joint. Often after the downpipes, the exhausts from each cylinder bank remain independent due to lack of space to join them. This independence makes the overall system simple to make and fit. Front-engined sprint cars feature this sort of system, for which it's known as a 'down swept primary pipe' system. It's similar to the 'up swept primary pipe' system fitted years ago to rear-engined Formula A/Formula 5000 cars. In both cases it works extremely well when

designed and made correctly. On some front-engined saloon (sedan) cars it's possible to link the two main pipes by taking one of them across the back of the engine or across the driveline after the gearbox (transmission). Depending on the car and the available room, the single large diameter 4.0in/100mm main pipe would go into a large silencer and then exit to atmosphere. The silencer could be positioned more or less in the centre of the car, but to one side, and the tailpipe could exit just before the rear wheel arch in a typical racing saloon (sedan) set up. This is a top-performing configuration, but it can be difficult to fit and remove.

The primary pipes of racing engines running in the 7000-7400rpm region are likely be 34-38in/87-97cm long, and the main pipes anything from 24-30ines/61-76cm long. In both cases the exact lengths can only be established by dyno testing of the individual engine. The primary pipes would need to be

of equal length on such an engine to gain the maximum extractor effect, giving optimum scavenging and therefore better cylinder filling.

4 into 2 into 1

This type of manifold (header) design is commonly known as the 'Try-Wy' system in the USA. It was devised to remove the adverse effect of the consecutive firing of cylinders 5 and 7, and to gain from the scavenge/extractor effect. This design is equivalent to the later standard configuration used by the factory for the original cast iron items. The tubular manifolds for each side or the engine will look very similar overall but, in fact, are quite different because of the different pairings of the cylinders of each bank.

The primary pipes of these manifolds start at 1¹/₂in/38mm diameter for standard engines and feed into 1⁵/₈in/41mm secondary pipes through bifurcated joints. The two secondary pipes then feed into a 2in/50mm main pipe, again through

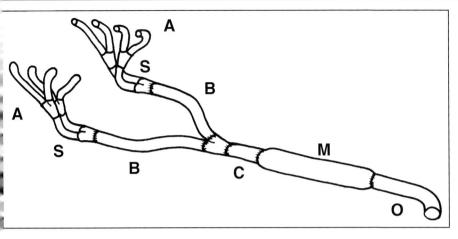

These 4-2-1 exhaust manifolds have their primary main pipes joining into one large main pipe. With this system the four primary pipes per manifold at 'A' & 'A' feed into two secondary pipes per manifold at 'S' & 'S', the primary main pipes at 'B' & 'B' then feed into a main pipe at 'C', through the silencer (muffler) at 'M' and, finally, to the outlet pipe at 'O'.

bifurcated joints.

For a higher performance engine the primary pipes would be 1⁵/₈in/41mm feeding into 1³/₄in/44m secondary pipes and then into 2¹/₈in/54mm main pipes.

The largest primary pipes sizes used for any Rover V8 engine are 1³/₄in/44mm going into 2in/50mm secondary pipes and then into 2¹/₂in/63mm main pipes.

For cars where space around the engine/gearbox (transmission) and under the car is limited, such as the Westfield or a Cobra replica, the two main pipes can then go via independent silencers (mufflers) and tailpipes to atmosphere.

The main pipe sizes determine the silencer (muffler) size because the main pipe diameter is maintained throughout the remainder of the system. In most cases the silencers (mufflers) are of the tubular absorption-type, in which perforated tubing passes through glassfibre wool packing inside an outer casing). Silencers for this sort of application come in a wide range of diameters, lengths and constructions.

Where space permits, the better alternative to a twin system is to pair the main pipes of the manifolds into a large single main pipe. This then feeds into a large single silencer (muffler) of either the absorption-type, or interference-type (in which there are an number of chambers inside a large oval casing). The advantage of the single main pipe system is that all of the exhaust pulses are linked together using a reasonably compact configuration that gives good overall scavenging, and hence good cylinder filling.

Pipe dimensions

As with the four into one arrangement, the minimum primary pipes for standard engines would be 1¹/₂in/38mm diameter, feeding into 1⁵/₈in/41mm diameter secondary pipes, and then on to 1⁷/₈in/47mm main pipes. If the two main pipes remain separate the 1⁷/₈in/47mm pipe diameter size is maintained all the way to atmosphere.

If, on the other hand the two main pipes are merged, they're joined via a bifurcated joint into a

2in/50mm diameter main pipe, and this diameter is maintained all the way to atmosphere.

If it's a higher performance engine than the standard unit, the primary pipes would be 1⁵/₈in/41mm diameter, feeding to 1³/₄in/44mm secondary pipes and then to 2in/50mm main pipes. If a twin system is to be used the 2in/50mm main pipe size is maintained all the way to atmosphere. If it's to be a single system, the two main pipes merge into one main which is 2¹/₈-2¹/₄in/54-57mm in diameter, this size then being maintained all the way to atmosphere.

The smallest 1¹/₂in/37mm primary pipe system will suit all Rover V8s being used on the road, irrespective of their capacity. Any larger capacity road going Rover would normally be fitted with a 1⁵/₈in/41mm diameter primary pipe system. Any road going Rover V8 can have a 1⁵/₈in/41mm diameter primary pipes system fitted to it without detriment, although 1¹/₂in/38mm seems to be more readily available.

For racing, the minimum primary pipe size to use is 1⁵/₈in/41mm diameter which works very well for any 3.5-4.6 litre engine, including longer stroke versions. For larger racing engines consider using 1³/₄in/44mm primary pipes which feed into 2in/50mm secondary pipes, followed by 2¹/₂in/63mm 'primary main pipes' and finally into a 3in/75mm main pipe.

A 1³/₄in/44mm primary pipe system is normally the largest you would ever use on a Rover V8 although, in exceptional circumstances, even larger ones, such as 1⁷/₈-2in/48-50mm primary pipes can be used.

Crossover

The third manifold (header) design is the complicated crossover system as used on the Ford GT40 in the 1960s. It's a well established design that is known to work, but it has a drawback: the installation is complicated to say the least. The 'plumbers nightmare' tag is still firmly attached to this design and is the main reason why it's not used more frequently, except when there is a need for authentic replication.

The system has mainly been used for rear-engined cars because they generally have the space across the back of the engine to accommodate it. However, space limitations have not stopped many engineers from fitting such systems to front-engined cars for Trans Am & Speedway, with the primary pipes going either over the back of the top of the engine or crossing over under the car just behind the engine. The latter arrangement has fallen out of favour through being prone to track damage. While these systems produce optimum power because of their even firing regime, other less complicated systems are now within 2 to 3bhp of equal performance.

The design works by linking the eight equal length primary pipes into two main pipes as evenly as possible, thus providing perfectly equally spaced exhaust pulses. With the firing order of 1-8-4-3-6-5-7-2 the four primary exhaust pipes 1-4 6-7 are linked together as are pipes 8-3 5-2, so that there is exactly 180 degrees of crankshaft rotation between any of the primary pipes' exhaust pulses. These primary pipes are joined into the two groups of four

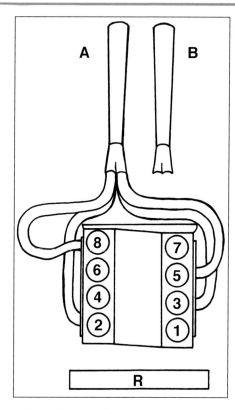

This schematic diagram shows the two pipes from cylinders 3 & 5 (centre two cylinders) of the left hand bank going around the back of the engine and linking up with cylinders 2 & 8 of the right hand bank, with these four primary pipes going into main pipe 'A'. The primary pipe configuration for main pipe 'B' is the exact opposite to the one shown for 'A' but is not shown for the sake of clarity.

at their junction with the two main pipes. The front and rear cylinders of the right hand bank are linked to the two centre cylinders of the left hand bank, and the front and rear cylinders of the left hand bank are linked to the two centre cylinders of the right hand bank.

This looks to be a complicated exhaust system, but in some installations it's really not all that difficult to achieve, although you

should never underestimate the task. Today, you are only likely to see such an exhaust system when it's fitted to a Rover V8 in the back of a replica GT40, and the exhaust has been made to look and sound identical to the original Ford GT40.

Pipe dimensions

The minimum primary pipe diameter size you would ever consider using for one of these systems is 1½in/38mm, which would feed into 2in/50mm main pipes. Depending on the engine performance the sizes would progress on to 1⅝in/41mm primary pipes feeding into 2¼in/57mm main pipes for a moderately modified engine of any capacity, followed by 1¾in/44mm primary pipes feeding into 2½in/63mm main pipes for a racing engine. The primary pipes are all going to be of equal length, in the region of 38-40in/97cm.

SEALING EXHAUST MANIFOLDS

Sealing the exhaust manifolds to the cylinder heads can be difficult. ADOS makes an adhesive sealant called 'Galvseal' which is very good. Avoid applying too much or the excess will squeeze out into the exhaust ports. Try to keep the sealant at least 0.125in/3mm away from the exhaust ports of the cylinder head and manifold. Apply to clean components and get the exhaust manifolds bolted up as quickly as possible once the sealant has been applied. The manifold flanges must be flat: Galvseal is not a filler.

Chapter 17
Cooling system

Over the years, standard road going Rover V8 powered cars have run at a range of thermostatically controlled cooling system temperatures. The early cars ran at about 80 degrees C/175F, while the later 38As of the mid-1990s onwards ran at 96 degrees C/204F (for emissions control reasons).

The engines fitted to HSE Range Rovers ran at 96 degrees C/204F, but there were substantial differences in the reliability of the 3.9 & 4.2 litre 'interim' engines fitted to the Classic Range Rovers compared with the 38A engines (the same basic block) fitted to the HSE Range Rover. The Classic Range Rovers have some cylinder block cracking problems, but nothing like those of the 4.0 litre 38A engine and, to a lesser extent, those of the 4.6 litre 38A engine.

The one noticeable difference between these two engine installations is the cooling system configuration. The Classic Range Rover uses a large crossflow radiator with a conventional radiator hose layout, and with the thermostat positioned in the inlet manifold (as on all previous engines). If required, the thermostat can be changed for one with a lower setting in line with most other engines, for example, 72-74 degrees C/162-165F.

The HSE engine uses a conventional vertical flow radiator, with a very high rise top hose and a very different thermostat arrangement in which the thermostat is near the bottom of the radiator's outlet connection. With the thermostat shut the coolant circulates through the engine, then through the heater matrix via external pipes, and then back to the thermostat housing through a small pipe at the rear. The coolant also flows from the inlet manifold through a small pipe to the rear of the thermostat housing, making a total now of two pipes feeding hot coolant to the back of the thermostat housing. There is a third pipe on the thermostat housing which takes coolant from the back of the thermostat housing to the inlet side of the water pump, so that when the thermostat is shut there is a pumped bypass of coolant. The advantage of this system is that, within 20-30 seconds of starting the engine, hot coolant is going through the heater matrix and heating the inside of the car. Once the thermostat opens at its 96 degrees C/204F rating the coolant circulates through the radiator in the normal fashion. The drawback is that the thermostat is permanently fitted inside the plastic thermostat housing, and cannot be changed for a lower rated unit. The system also has a header tank with two bleed pipes going to it, one from the top of the radiator and one from the fuel injection manifold.

As soon as the HSE was launched, Rover was inundated with top radiator hose failures. As a consequence of top hose failure the engine would lose all of its coolant and would overheat seriously. A new radiator hose would be fitted and the same thing would happen again, in some instances three or four times, with the end result of cracked blocks and, sometimes, dropped cylinder liners. Certainly a 4.0 litre engine will only stand three major overheats before the block cracks.

Rover has been through three different designs of top hose for these later engines in an attempt to cure the problem. While the latest top hose doesn't fail, thousands of engines have had failures in the past, and it's anybody's guess as to how may engines have suffered from severe overheating at some point in their past lives. In addition, many blocks didn't overheat severely but still cracked, so it wasn't just the top hose failures that were to blame. **Caution!** – Checking and replacement of the top hose at regular intervals is still an **essential** requirement for **all** HSE engines, in spite of the latest standard of top hose. If you're buying one of these engines second-hand check its provenance very carefully ...

KIT CARS
Radiator
If you are using a Rover V8 in a kit car, the cooling system needs to be based on the large capacity crossflow radiator from a Range Rover Classic, or similar. **Caution!** – The top radiator hose **must** be routed so that it is parallel to the ground, or inclined upward to the top radiator connection.

Thermostat
Fit a 78 degree C/172 degree F thermostat, so that the engine will run at about 80 degrees C/175F (fuel enrichment will be turned off if engine has EFI), assuming the radiator has enough capacity and cooling air passing through it.

Most thermostats do not have bleed holes in them for self-bleeding of the system when the coolant is first added or refilled, so three 0.125in/3mm holes drilled into the thermostat flange are recommended. This modification has the added benefit that if the thermostat jams in the shut position, you'll have slightly more warning of what has happened because some coolant will still be able to circulate. Some thermostats are available with a single bleed hole in them if you don't want to start drilling holes yourself. You'll need to use a header tank with bleeds or fit a radiator cap into one of the side tanks.

Fan
Front-engined cars can have an engine-driven fan fixed to the water pump pulley, or a large electric fan fitted in front of the radiator with thermostatic control or manual control via a switch mounted on the dashboard. Electric fans are normally mounted behind the radiator on standard cars because of space limitations, however this restriction doesn't usually apply to a front-engined kit car. The important point is to fit as large a fan as possible. If the fan is to be engine driven, it needs to be shrouded from the back of the radiator to enclose the fan, with a minimum clearance between the tips of the fan blades and the shroud of about 0.25in/6mm. This ensures that the fan is only drawing air through the radiator for maximum efficiency. Large engine-driven aftermarket fans are available which have blades that feather as the engine speed rises, so reducing the power required to drive them. Such fans can shift a serious amount of air, even without shrouds. **Warning!** – These fans frequently have thin stainless steel blades. Avoid bodily contact with the tips of the blades when the engine is running. Serious injury is possible. Shrouding is recommended on the basis of safety and efficiency.

Pipework
If you're building a rear-engined car with a front mounted radiator, keep the coolant pipes running from front to rear of the car as high as possible **Do not** run the pipes underneath the car if you can avoid it, hot coolant doesn't like to be pumped downwards. There are numerous instances of this contradiction of the natural laws of physics resulting in endless cooling problems and leading, ultimately, to engine failures. The principles surrounding this are well established, and while it might be necessary to pump the coolant downwards to a small degree, it should be minimised. Extra pump capacity is likely to be required and you should expect to have to use a 1:1 drive to the water pump.

Caution! – All Rover V8 engines **must** have the proper inhibiter in the coolant. Failure to comply will result in serious deterioration of the internal waterways of the head and block, which can be bad enough to cause the engine to be scrapped.

RACING CARS
Optimum temperature range

All competition engines should have a large enough radiator to keep the coolant temperature down to between 60 and 80 degrees C/140 and 175F, **irrespective of the ambient air temperature**. This is because maximum power is generated when the coolant temperature is not more than 80 degrees C/175F, with 65-75 degrees C/150-165F being the optimum. For example, if an engine develops 200bhp with the coolant at 80 degrees C/175F, it'll only develop 170bhp if the coolant temperature is 100 degrees C/212F: a 10% reduction in power.

With a pressurised cooling system it's quite possible to see 115 degrees C /240F on a temperature gauge, which is much too high. Adhering to these lower temperatures will result in consistent lap times for racing cars instead of increasing lap times as the coolant temperature rises. If the temperature goes over 80 degrees C/175F, then there is a problem with the cooling system that needs to be addressed.

It's almost always possible to get the coolant temperature down to 55-65 degrees C/130-150F in a country with a temperate climate, for example 20-30 degrees C/65-85F in the summer. If you live in a hotter country, your car's cooling system needs to be able to cope with the high ambient air temperatures and a lot more effort will be needed to maximise its efficiency.

Radiator

The first task is to fit the largest aluminium crossflow radiator that can be accommodated in the car. In some cases you may need to modify the car to fit a big enough radiator, but it's better to do this than to persevere with an undersized radiator.

Restrictor plate

Ideally, the cooling system should be designed to overcool the engine, with a restrictor plate fitted in place of a thermostat to control the coolant flow rate around the system and hence control the coolant temperature. Thermostats are not normally used in racing engines because, if they jam in the shut position, the engine can quickly be ruined. Restrictor plates are available from aftermarket suppliers with a range of holes sizes, for example: 0.625in/16mm, 0.75in/19mm, 0.875in/22mm or 1.0in/25mm. Alternatively, you can make your own out of some steel or aluminium sheet and use a different sized hole to achieve exactly the correct flow rate and coolant temperature for your application.

SELECTING & FITTING A RADIATOR

The Range Rover crossflow radiator is a good choice for most high performance applications. This is a large conventional crossflow radiator, measuring 33in/84cm over the tops of the two header tanks, which is quite wide. The actual core is 29in/74cm wide by 17in/43cm high and 2in/50m thick. This is a good example of the usual size of radiator for a V8 engine, and in most cases it be accommodated in a car and will provide sufficient cooling capacity.

Caution! – The radiator should be fitted in the car so that the coolant outlet from the engine is either lower than, or at the same height, as the top hose inlet of the radiator. If the radiator has a top hose connection that is much lower than the engine's coolant outlet, move it to the highest possible point on the side tank and blank the original. This will involve tig welding or soldering a new hose connection, or the original if it can be moved. Some outlets from engines are much higher than they need to be and can be moved by cutting the original and tig welding it into a new lower location. The outlet should still be at the highest point of the engine's coolant level.

Good sources of large aluminium crossflow radiators are USA/Australian made cars, such as Ford Falcons and Mustangs. These radiators can be 30-35in/76-89cm wide by 20-22in/51-56cm deep and up to 3in/75mm thick, with a single row core.

RADIATOR CAPS & HEADER TANKS

Most modern engines feature a header tank system which is continuously self-bleeding with at least two small bleed pipes, one coming from the top of the radiator and the other from the highest point of the top radiator hose. These bleed-off systems are quite efficient in standard engine installations, but when racing they can result in higher than desirable coolant temperatures.

The problem with the header tank system is the continuous bleed-off (from the top of the top radiator hose and from the top of the radiator) of a small amount of hot coolant directly back to the header tank when it's at its hottest. This results in a slight loss in cooling efficiency that many engines can do without. The problem can be

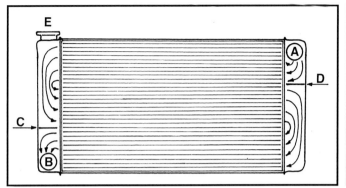

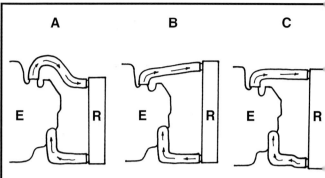

Large aluminium crossflow radiator with the top radiator hose connecting at 'A' and the bottom radiator hose connecting at 'B'. The radiator header tanks have had partitions fitted to them at 'C' and 'D'. The tank has been cut and 2mm thick pieces of sheet aluminium fitted and 'Tig' welded into place. The partitions do not have to be a neat fit in the header tanks, but should be as neat as you can reasonably make them. The hot coolant from the engine enters the radiator at 'A', drops down as far as partition 'D' and then goes across the radiator core to the other header tank. Next it drops down as far as partition 'C' and then crosses back to the other side of the radiator. Finally it drops down as far as the base of the header tank and then crosses the radiator core again to exit at 'B', and goes back into the lower part of the engine. It's important that the radiator is installed level in the car.

The three diagrams show three arrangements of top hoses to su the various radiator installations. Diagram A shows the coolan coming out of the engine (E) and going up and then down to the radiator (R). This is not desirable at all and is to be avoided: it's very difficult to pump hot coolant downward. Diagrams B & C show acceptable top hose arrangements. The hot coolant trave upwards slightly in diagram B and flows on the level in diagram

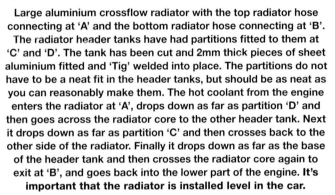

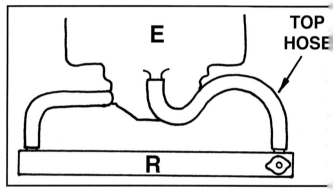

Looking from the top onto an engine and radiator installation, th top and bottom hoses can have full, constant cross-sectional are sweeping curves in them if necessary between the engine (E) an radiator (R) to avoid obstacles without detriment to the cooling The ducting of clean undisturbed air to the front of the radiator is another factor that can make or break an engine/radiator installation. It's important to ensure that the air taken from the fro of the car to the radiator core is directed as much as possible to through the core and not around it. To achieve this the ducting is close as possible to the radiator core but obviously not touching ¼in ID rubber piping split along its length can be used as beadin to create an effective seal between the duct and the radiator cor

reduced by restricting the bore of the pipes going back to the header tank, forcing virtually all of the hot coolant to go through the radiator. A 0.0625in/1.5mm restrictor in the pipe to the header tank will still allow the system to self-bleed and function more or less as standard.

The header tank system works, but it can be dispensed with by fitting a pressure cap in the top of the radiator. **Caution!** – ensure that it's at the highest point in the whole system. Most modern radiators do not have filler caps or pressure caps, although it's quite possible to fit one to the top of one of the side tanks if they're metal (so that they can be tig welded if aluminium or soldered if brass). It's not really practical to do this if the side tanks are made of plastic. Fitting a pressure cap in the top of the radiator's side tanks is a good option because it alleviates

the need for a separate header tank and bleed-off system, with the result that all of the hot coolant from the engine goes through the radiator core.

Some top radiator hoses are designed to bend around or over things like alternators, power steering pumps and air conditioning units and, in some instances, to rise up 6-9in/150-230mm above the coolant outlet of the engine. This is just no good at all, and such hose arrangements have no place on a high performance engine, especially

a racing one. The top radiator hose needs to go directly from the coola outlet on the engine to the top radiator connection in a horizontal plane parallel to the ground, or an upward slope, but it can do so in a series of curves if necessary.

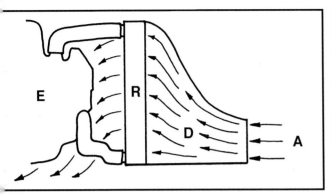

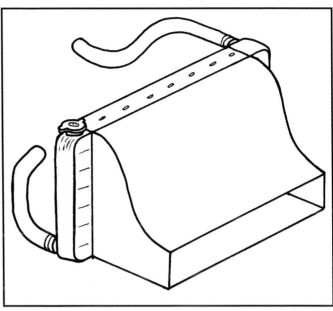

r enters the front of the main air duct (A) which is about one third of the height of the radiator (R) and is directed to the core. The edges of the aluminium/glass fibre duct are within 0.125in/3mm of the radiator so that a minimum of air can escape through the ap. The edges of the ducting are often fitted with purposely split rubber piping to reduce the potential for crash damage to the adiator. Ducts are also designed to crush down in an accident to inimise damage to the radiator. Once the air has passed through the radiator core it usually goes around the engine (E) and out nderneath the car, but the flow depends on the design of the car.

General view of an assembled radiator and air shroud (duct).

WATER PUMP SPEED

ne next step in achieving optimum ooling is the speed of the water imp. The requirement is to rculate the coolant around the igine at such a rate that it has ne to transfer the heat from the ombustion process in the engine, id then has time to transfer it to the r passing through the radiator. The oolant circulation rate through the igine is essentially fixed because s determined by the engine's rate ' heat generation. The radiator the major variable: the system ficiency can be changed by fitting different radiator (and/or, perhaps, / changing the rate that coolant is imped around the engine).

If the coolant travels too fast rough the engine there won't be ifficient time for the heat being enerated by the combustion ocess to be transferred to it. If the oolant travels too slowly through e engine, the coolant temperature ill increase dramatically because e amount of heat being transferred

is too much for the flow rate, and boiling will result.

If the coolant travels through the radiator too quickly, because it's too small, there won't be enough time for the heat to transfer to the air via the cores. Fitting a larger radiator is seldom a bad thing.

If the water pump is turning too fast, then the impeller will cause cavitation of the coolant in the water pump housing and the coolant will stop moving, resulting in a rapid rise in the temperature of the engine.

If the pump is turning fast but without causing cavitation, then the coolant may be circulating around the engine faster than required and the water pump will be taking more power than is necessary.

Increasing the pump speed above standard also requires a close look at the pulley and belt arrangement to avoid the belt being thrown off.

Clearly a happy medium has to be struck here.

Rover has used a range of water

pump drive ratios over the years, but a simple tape measure is all that is needed to work out the drive ratio. Just measure the diameters of the crankshaft pulley and the water pump pulley and divide the crankshaft pulley diameter by the water pump pulley diameter.

Example 1: If the crankshaft pulley is 6in/152mm diameter and the water pump pulley is 7in/178mm diameter: 6 ÷ 7 = 0.85, or 152 ÷ 178 = 0.85. In this case the water pump pulley is under-driven.

Example 2: If the crankshaft pulley is 7in/178mm diameter and the water pump pulley is 6in/152mm diameter: 7 ÷ 6 = 1.17 or 178 ÷ 152 = 1.17. In this case the water pump pulley is over-driven.

No high rpm Rover V8 needs to have the water pump running faster than the crankshaft, meaning a 1:1 ratio is required (same diameter pulleys). Some standard engines have the water pump turning faster than crankshaft speed, but this is mainly in low revving road going applications with no possibility of over speeding the pump. Some Range Rovers, for example, have a 7in/178mm diameter drive pulley on the crankshaft and a 5in/104mm diameter water pump pulley, which means that the water pump is approximately 1.25:1 over-driven. If such an engine is run at over 6000rpm, then you'd expect pump cavitation. In this case the solution to the problem would be a second-hand but similar shaped 7in/180mm pressed steel pulley, which might need slight modification to the locating hole and the securing bolt holes to fit. This pulley will reduce the drive ratio to 1:1.

With the firm knowledge that 1:1 is good starting point, it's now a question of how much slower the pump should be turned. If the pump is being turned too slowly, the engine temperature will rise at low rpm and yet be normal at higher rpm. For an engine revving between 6000 and 6500rpm a 1:1 ratio is about right and would be a safe choice. If the engine is revving higher than this, say to 7000rpm, then a 0.9:1 ratio is more appropriate. You may need to experiment with different pulley diameters before finding one that gives the best overall performance.

There is no point in running the pump so slowly just to save a bit

of power that the engine starts to overheat below 4000rpm.

If you require an under-driven arrangement, a 1in/25mm difference between the pulley diameters will normally be about right. An under-driven ratio of 0.8 is marginal and likely to be too slow. It might well be possible, provided everything else is working to maximum efficiency, but it would all need to be thoroughly tested to make sure that the engine is not going to overheat. Reliability has to be the priority.

Swapping pulleys

Early engines had the belt drive groove machined directly into the crankshaft damper rim and, as a consequence, it's much more convenient to change the water pump pulley. Find an appropriate pressed steel water pump pulley from another Rover V8, or even from a totally different engine, and mount that on the water pump, making sure that the two pulleys are perfectly in line with each other. **Caution!** – Pulley alignment is essential, but is often overlooked, leading to lost belts. The alternative pulley must also run concentric with the water pump shaft. Like all of these things, whatever you do has to be done correctly if the alterations are to be successful and reliable.

OTHER OPTIONS

Despite all of your efforts, some very simple things can be the cause of major overheating problems on competition engines.

In the vast majority of racing cars no fan will be used, especially for circuit cars. In this case, when overheating does become a problem, an engine-driven or an electric fan may well have to be used. A larger front duct opening might be needed in conjunction with the fan and the fan should be well shrouded (to minimise losses between the back of the radiator core and the tips of the fan blades). The air that is drawn in through the radiator must pass through the fan blades and into the engine compartment and then go out underneath the car. Avoid over speeding the fan by taking note of the manufacturer's recommended maximum fan rpm.

Consider using an additive like Wynn's 'Water Wetter' in your engine; it tends to reduce the amount of air bubbles that are produced during the boiling process meaning that the coolant is still liquid and not a mass of air bubbles. It may help to save your engine.

Chapter 18
Flywheel & clutch

FLYWHEEL

The standard cast iron flywheel can be used in any engine which will not rev at more than 7000rpm. Failures of cast iron flywheels are very rare.

The original equipment cast iron flywheels can also be lightened, but only so much. If you intend to have a standard cast iron flywheel lightened, send it to a Rover V8 specialist like J.E. Developments which will have the experience to reduce the weight without significantly reducing the strength. **Warning!** – Standard flywheels can only be lightened so much before dangerous failure becomes likely, even though they might look all right: it is **essential** that lightening is carried out by an expert.

John Eales uses standard, but lightened, cast iron flywheels with organic clutch plates for most high performance applications. The choice of clutch cover being determined by the power output of the particular engine, but usually confined to two ratings: AP Racing brand 'brown spring' or 'green spring'.

Amongst the specialists, J.E. Developments, for example, makes two sizes of steel flywheel. The first is a direct replacement for the standard cast iron-type. Steel is a better material for racing purposes because, irrespective of what happens to it in terms of revs or abuse, the flywheel is much less likely to fail (shatter, break or crack). Steel flywheels are also far more resistant to surface cracking of the friction matching surface when the clutch is subject to hard use, especially if a cerametalic clutch plate is used. This direct replacement flywheel is drilled and dowelled to take the standard single plate type clutch arrangement, although it can be drilled and dowelled to take a triple plate clutch if required. The second, smaller diameter, steel flywheel is intended for use with the J.E. Developments dry sump system.

The standard starter motor is perfectly adequate for all standard size flywheel applications.

J.E. Developments' dry sump system flywheel

This dry sump (oil pan) system uses Pace BG-type pumps (one pressure, two scavenge) in conjunction with a specially manufactured cast aluminium sump which has two scavenge take off fittings in the base. All mounting brackets, drivebelts and cogs are supplied in the kit, as is the pipework if the exact lengths are given. A J.E.D.-manfactured smaller than standard diameter steel flywheel is used in conjunction with the dry sump system to enable the engine to be fitted as

Tilton brand triple plate clutch mounted on a flywheel.

low in the chassis as possible. The smaller flywheel requires an offset starter motor. The clutch used with this flywheel system is an AP 7¼ inch, triple plate, cerametalic type unit. The steel flywheel is as light as possible, conducive to good strength.

You could use this small diameter steel flywheel and triple plate clutch system in conjunction with an offset starter on a non dry sump engine if you wanted to get the rotating mass weight as low

as possible. Normally, though, the direct replacement steel flywheel and single uprated clutch with either an organic clutch plate or a cerametalic clutch plate is used.

CLUTCH
The standard 9½ inch SD1-type Rover clutch plate & pressure plate/clutch cover is capable of transmitting approximately 250 foot pounds of engine torque. The next step up from this, the AP Racing 'brown spring' pressure plate, will transmit approximately 270 foot pounds of engine torque. The AP Racing 'green spring' pressure plate will transmit approximately 340 foot pounds of engine torque. There is a further uprated version of this last mentioned pressure plate which is capable of transmitting 400 foot pounds of engine torque.

AP Racing supplies organic material and cerametalic clutch plates. The company also supplies clutch covers with steel pressure pads for use with cerametalic clutch plates and iron pressure pads for

use with organic lined clutch plates. **Caution!** – While cerametalic clutch plates can be used with cast iron flywheels and clutch covers which have iron pressure pads fitted to them, they tend to cause the friction matching surfaces of the flywheel and the clutch cover to wear out prematurely. For severe abuse applications, such as racing, the use of a cast iron flywheel and a clutch cover which has an iron pressure pad together with a cerametalic clutch plate is not a good idea.

Cerametalic clutch plates are available in 3, 4 and 6 'puck'-types. The 3 puck-type is the lightest but has the severest 'take up' when the clutch is let in. The 6 puck-type, which is the heaviest, has a less severe 'take up'. For all out racing purposes the three puck-type is favoured for it's lightness, but all three seem to work extremely well. If you were to use one in a road going application (which is quite possible), the 6 puck-type would be the best choice.

Chapter 19
Rolling road dyno

While it's quite possible to tune an engine's carburation or fuel injection yourself and think that you have it 'dead right,' it's all too easy to get this aspect of your engine's tune a little wrong and not know how much potential engine efficiency is not being realised. It really is difficult to assess the exact quality of the fuelling system tune simply by driving the vehicle: it always pays to have carburettor performance checked using scientific diagnostics so that you can be sure that the air/fuel ratio mixture is as correct as possible.

For most readers this optimisation of settings will normally mean conventional 'rolling road' (dynomometer) testing to determine what the air/fuel ratios are at cruise (light load) and under wide open throttle conditions through the gears (maximum loading). The beauty of a rolling road is that the car is 'driven' by the operator, just as it would be on the road or track but with diagnostic gear attached. Conventional rolling road dynos are excellent devices for gaining baseline jetting at the very least and, very often, exact jetting very quickly. The facility of being able to run the engine under all load conditions while the car remains stationary and plugged into diagnostics is sound. Accelerating through the gears with a quick acting wideband Lambda sensor or CO exhaust gas sampling meter connected, allows you to see exactly what the fuel mixture is through the engine's rev range and under load. Any excessive richness or leanness is easy to spot on a diagnostics screen or a printout.

The limitation of a conventional rolling road (one that you drive a two wheel-drive car into) is the fact that, depending on the weight of the car and the power being generated by the engine, there can be a problem with keeping the car's drive wheels in correct contact with the rolling road's rollers. As a general rule, the top power limit for these machines is between 350 and 375bhp for a 1500kg (3307lb) saloon, for example. You know you're getting near the machine's limit when the drive wheels start to spin on the rollers. When this happens, the tyres need to be sprayed with something like CRC 'Belt Grip' to make them a bit more tacky. Unfortunately, if the engine is too powerful for the rolling road, the results for comparison purposes are not accurate. Various things are done to improve tyre grip like loading the boot (trunk) or using chains to prevent the rear axle from moving away from the rollers but if it all gets to this stage distortions are creeping into the test regime: nevertheless, these sorts of rolling road are very good up until the traction limit is reached.

There are other sorts of rolling roads such as the Dynapack type for example (<www.dynapack.com> or e-mail <sales@dynapack.com>). This system requires the drive wheels to be removed, hub adapters bolted on in place of the wheels and connected (inserted) into hydraulic absorption units (one unit per driven wheel). This type of dyno can take any amount of horsepower, and each test run can have a separate print out (or up to five consecutive test runs printed out on the same sheet for comparison purposes). These dynos are sold as either two or four wheel-drive systems: two wheel-drive systems have two absorption units and four wheel-drive units, four. If a two wheel-drive car is to be tested on a four wheel drive unit, only two of the four absorption units are used and the computer set to suit.

In each case with a rolling road type of dynomometer the engine has to be provided with large capacity external fan cooling; the trend these days is to use one very large fan to cool the engine and, even then, cooling breaks will have to be taken. A careful watch has to be kept on the engine temperature when testing because once the engine temperature gets up to 85 degrees C/184F, testing needs to stop until it's back down to 70 degrees C/158F. The way this is done is to keep the fans on and have the engine running at between 1000-1800rpm (varying between these revs) with no load (out of gear) and the temperature will drop off in about 5 minutes. Testing can resume once the engine temperature is down to this level. Many rolling road dyno cells have a large fan feeding air from outside

of the cell to the front of the car to make sure there is a good steady supply of cool air coming in. Some dyno cells route the exhaust gases outside while some don't.

All modern diagnostic machines now give print outs (something older machines didn't), which means that after the test runs the results can be looked at and used for comparison with known values. Further to this, power readings can be taken with various carburettor jetting set ups. The print outs can then be compared against each other; The object of the exercise being to obtain the optimum air/fuel mixture ratio to give the best possible power throughout the engine's effective rpm range, and which also allows the fastest acceleration rate possible.

For example, if the mixture goes rich between 3500 and 4500rpm, you'll actually see this on the diagnostics screen or on the print out. The CO reading might go to 8% or 0.88 Lambda during this rpm range, in which case the power output will be down, as will the engine response. The diagnostics are 'telling' you that the mixture is too rich. The operator/mechanic now has to decide what's causing the excess richness and change the jetting/fuel injection settings accordingly and then retest, repeating the process until optimum power and engine response is achieved. This can take a lot of time! The results are always worthwhile if testing and adjustment are taken to conclusion.

It's a pointless exercise to check an engine's air/fuel mixture and say 'its about right' and then leave it as it is because either the cost to alter it is high, or the route to optimum performance is not known. This

happens all the time and is a part of the reason why carburettors/injection systems don't get optimised and a huge number of engines don't get tuned correctly. The diagnostic machines virtually always give correct readings and can be relied upon to do so (if they are calibrated correctly). Choosing a rolling road dyno facility whose operators are very familiar with the type of induction system you are using is a really vital requirement.

The most current diagnostic regime is an exhaust gas Lambda reading which measures the gas's oxygen content continuously: the reading is instantaneous. The main factors for the change to the Lambda sensing system are the need to measure air/fuel ratios very accurately and very quickly over a wider band (17:1 through to 10:1) than was previously possible.

The previously widely-used diagnostic system was the exhaust gas analysed percentage CO (carbon monoxide) and, going further back, air/fuel ratio meters were used (slow reading). Percentage CO readings were not as wide in band, although they were wide enough for most applications. For example, with the advent of engines being fitted with electronic fuel injection, idle emissions came down to 1.5 to 2.0% CO (no catalytic converter fitted). By comparison, carburettor-equipped engines were normally anything from 2.5% CO to 3.5% CO, with 3.5% CO readings being more normal than 2.5%. A further reason for the change from percentage CO readings to Lambda readings was the need to be able to ascertain the air/fuel ratios when cars started getting fitted with catalytic converters. Clearly once catalytic converters were in use there would not be constant and accurate CO readings as the catalytic converters would be removing this poisonous gas in varying degrees.

CO reading equipment represents an old system which is outmoded these days, but still very much in use. It doesn't matter what scientific diagnostic mixture testing regime is used, provided the true mixture requirements are ultimately defined. CO and Lamda based equipment is effective in the hands of good technicians.

All modern diagnostic machines give printouts showing the levels of all values from one adjustment, and subsequent dyno run, to another, and these print outs can be compared. All you have to do is record what jetting was used for each test. Under these circumstances an extremely good picture of what does what can be built up and everything narrowed down to the ideal settings. It does take time and it does cost money to do this, but it really is the quickest, easiest and most convenient way to make sure that your engine is set up correctly to give maximum power/ accelerative efficiency.

Often the top end maximum power of the engine will not be improved after dyno testing, but very often the mid-range engine performance and the acceleration rate can be seriously improved. The bottom line here is that an ideal fuel curve is something that definitely needs to be attained. If you know what the correct sort of fuel curve looks like for an engine, it is very easy to see if the tuning company has got the mixture correct by comparing its figures to known general figures. Obtaining suitable

base values has always been something that has been relatively difficult, but his book lists suitable values for virtually all engines.

Note that you are looking for the air/fuel mixture ratio which gives the best power under load at every 250rpm point from idle to the point of maximum power.

Important! – Too rich an air/fuel mixture causes the engine to be slower accelerating and produces less than optimum power while doing so. A lean air/fuel mixture causes similar engine response as well as hesitation. An optimum air/fuel mixture allows the best possible rate of acceleration. The optimum acceleration rate and maximum power air/fuel mixture is going to vary engine to engine, and rpm to rpm, although the pattern for all engines is similar.

If an engine performs well on the rolling road, it will always go well on road or track provided the temperature and the barometric pressure inside the dyno cell were similar to the general conditions that the engine has to operate in normally. A potential problem here is that there can be quite a differential in these atmospheric factors outside the dyno cell. This could mean that at times an engine ends up slightly lean or rich on the road or track, and will not perform as well as it might. Engines definitely need to be tuned for the prevailing atmospheric conditions in which they'll operate. The division between being dead right and not quite right can be small.

Another significant factor is that the car is moving through the air on the road or track, whereas it was stationary on the rolling road. The movement of air over the vehicle and

through the engine compartment can play a part in causing slight mixture alterations. However, by and large, provided the air temperature and the barometric pressure at the dyno were similar to those prevailing, all will be well. Certainly for a racing engine, dyno generated jetting will very likely be exactly right outside in spite of the possible exhaust recycling going on in the dyno cell. This is because racing engines are set for maximum power, with no consideration given to economy.

Many people who set up cars in a dyno cell for racing purposes use a 'density meter' reading (see www.longacre.com, for example, as a supplier of these meters) taken during dyno testing as a datum and always carry plus and minus jetting to cover air density/temperature changes from the original test conditions. For example, this means for a conventional carburettor (eg: Holley) with main jets carrying spare jets which are typically 0.001in/0.025mm smaller and 0.001-0.002in/0.025-0.051mm larger. A 0.001in/0.025mm hole size in a main jet makes quite a difference. For an SU or Zenith-equipped engine, consider a 0.001in/0.025mm needle measuring point size to be enough to make a difference.

Many racers monitor the atmospheric conditions at each track they go to using a density meter and, if necessary, try different jetting based on the meter reading if it's higher or lower than that recorded in the dyno cell when the engine was setup. Lap times and driver feedback, in conjunction with the density reading, are used to guide the jetting changes. With the density meter reading and the jetting/fuelling settings recorded, the engine jetting/

USA-made, Longacre density meter. Density meters read a combination of air temperature and barometric pressure, which are then presented as an air density percentage reading on the dial. It's a good tool to have if you intend to maintain absolutely correct air/fuel ratios in the majority of climatic conditions. Whatever the percentage density reading is becomes the baseline figure from which all subsequent adjustments are made in the dyno room. With the engine producing optimum power and efficiency on a rolling road and the percentage reading known, correct adjustments to take into account the changing conditions can be made.

Conversion chart

Lambda	Air/Fuel	%CO
0.80	11.8	8.0
0.81	11.9	7.3
0.82	12.0	6.5
0.83	12.2	5.9
0.84	12.4	5.4
0.85	12.5	5.0
0.86	12.6	4.85
0.87	12.8	4.35
0.88	13.0	3.8
0.90	13.2	3.3
0.91	13.4	2.85
0.92	13.5	2.6
0.93	13.7	2.15
0.94	13.8	1.9
0.95	14.0	1.6
0.96	14.1	1.4
0.97	14.3	1.0
0.98	14.4	0.8
0.99	14.6	0.6
1.00	14.7	0.5
1.01	14.8	0.6
1.02	15.0	0.3
1.03	15.1	0.15
1.04	15.2	0.2
1.05	15.4	0.15

Conversion chart for Lambda & percentage CO measured air/fuel ratios. The percentage CO scale does not cover the extensive range that air/fuel or Lambda does, therefore it's not possible to cross-reference the figures exactly. Furthermore, any comparison is not an exact science, so the figures given should be regarded as close approximations.

fuelling setting requirements can be narrowed down to a point where a certain jet combination is used with a certain air density reading. This takes work but it's necessary if top engine performance is required.

Road cars don't need this sort of treatment, even though if an engine was dyno tested on a very hot day it might end up being slightly lean for a cold mid-winter day. Very cold clear days or nights lead to best possible power outputs being developed by engines, provided they are jetted/fueled correctly for those conditions.

The accompanying two Lambda charts detail the fuelling requirements for both a standard engine (A) and a racing engine (B).

The actual Lambda/air/fuel/% CO requirements for either specification of naturally aspirated engine – and all engines in between – are remarkably similar. **All** Rover V8 engines seem to require, on average, to have a 0.92 Lambda/13.5:1 air/fuel mixture ratio/2.6% CO to achieve a suitable idle.

When accelerating from a standstill using maximum throttle, **all** engines will require fuelling (fuel enrichment) in the vicinity of 0.85 Lambda/12.5:1 air/fuel mixture ratio/5.0% CO to achieve the best possible rate of acceleration. Note that going too rich will cause the car to accelerate slower.

With the acceleration phase over and the engine at wide open throttle, anywhere from the point of maximum torque through to the point of maximum power, the fuelling requirement will be in the vicinity of 0.88 Lambda/13.0:1 air/fuel ratio/3.8% CO. These values are proven.

Chart A

On road going engines which are required to give the best economy the fuelling can be set as low as 1.05 Lambda/15.4 air/fuel ratio/0.15% CO. However, the factory will not have set the mixture this lean because of the excessive production of oxides of nitrogen (a poisonous gas) it causes. The factory set the engine to run at 1.00 Lambda/14.7 to 1 air/fuel mixture ratio/0.5% CO because this mixture will ensure that only low amounts of oxides of nitrogen are produced and that the 'three way' catalytic converters (rhodium) deal with the oxides of nitrogen that are produced. The cost of preventing the production of excessive oxides of nitrogen is a slight increase in fuel consumption at cruising speeds. Aftermarket fuel injection systems, ECUs and engine management systems can be altered to give a lean setting, but it isn't good for the environment.

Chart B

On both charts the A and B the line 'A' is the acceleration phase mixture strength requirement and represents the richest mixture the engine would

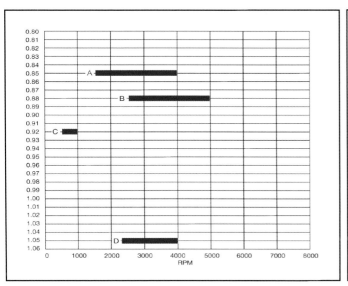

Lambda chart A: Road going engines (see text).

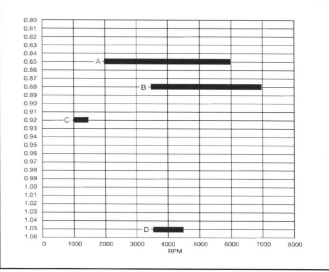

Lambda chart B: Racing engines (see text).

ever be provided with.

Line 'B' is the mixture strength required to produce maximum torque and maximum power. Line 'C' is the mixture strength required for idling purposes. Line 'D' is the leanest mixture strength for high speed cruising: **Caution!** – Don't go leaner than this.

Maximum torque is that point in the rpm range of 'maximum induction charge density', which means that point in the rpm range where the maximum amount of air is being inducted into the cylinder per revolution and the cylinder is as full of air as it is possible to get it in the particular engine. The induction charge density slowly reduces after this point which is why the torque value reduces as the revs rise. The brake horsepower (bhp), on the other hand, increases due to the number of power strokes per minute. When the point of maximum power is reached, which is the maximum number of 'efficient' power strokes possible per minute, and is then exceeded, the bhp starts to reduce

as rpm rises further.

There really is little point in taking an engine past the point of maximum power, although in a racing situation there are reasons why you might do this. You might, for example, let the rpm rise above the point of maximum power because you are between two corners and changing gear is just not worthwhile. Vehicle speed is maintained, but you know when you are in this rpm range because the engine isn't really doing anything except revving (it is no longer propelling the car forward with the usual 'accelerative push').

Conversion chart
Each engine needs to be individualised for optimum performance, and they can be with the use of scientific diagnostic equipment. The optimum fuelling, and the optimum ignition advance, can both be found by testing on a rolling road. With, in the first instance, the ignition advance set as recommended in this book for the particular capacity range of the

subject engine and basic fuelling set into the engine, test runs are done, power readings taken, and adjustments made to either increase or decrease the amount of ignition advance and fuelling. You test the engine with plus and minus settings for both the fuelling and the ignition advance to obtain the optimum. The fuelling is done first.

For example, if you have an engine registering 240 foot pounds of torque, and it takes 36 degrees of total advance and a 0.88 Lambda to do it, during testing the mixture will have been taken to a point where a power loss was registered (say 0.85 Lambda) in order to prove that 0.88 Lambda is right. Look to the rich side first, as opposed to the lean side, but registering a power loss after going richer means the mixture is too rich.

If the ignition advance is settled at 36 degrees before top dead centre you will have tried 38 and found there to be no improvement, you will also have tried 34 degrees with a similar result. **Caution!** – No real testing of any description should be done until it is positively proven that the mixture is not lean. Lean mixtures can burn pistons/cause seizures and an engine can very quickly be ruined.

On an older rolling road such as a Sun Road-A-Matic, the bhp at various revs is registered on dials as are the diagnostics: these figures must be noted after each run. Despite this shortcoming, a very accurate picture of engine performance can be ascertained using these older machines.

With a modern dyno like a Dynapack (see earlier) you get an accurate print out of each run. If you make a change you can see at a glance if there is an improvement or a reduction in efficiency. Any new machine of any type gives an accurate print out instead of dial measurements alone.

With the fuelling set to a minimum of 0.88 Lambda, the ignition advance is set at maximum torque. This is because if the engine is going to knock or 'pink'/'ping' it will do it at maximum charge density. As the rpm increases above the maximum torque the prospect of knock or 'pinking'/'pinging' reduces and, as a consequence, the amount of spark advance required is largely academic from the point of maximum torque onward.

Now, after all these years, Rover V8 engine optimum amounts of spark advance are largely set in concrete at 34-36 degrees before top dead centre (BTDC) for 3.5 litre engines, 32-34 BTDC for 3.9 to 4.2 litre engines, and 28-30 degrees BTDC for 4.6 litre or larger engines. The range of total amounts of advance for any Rover V8 is between 28 and 36 degrees. A setting in this range is going to extract optimum power from your engine even though the optimum total ignition advance for any Rover V8 engine is found by test it will be within the given range. **Caution!** – During testing, don't exceed 38 degrees under any circumstances unless you are using alcohol fuel in which case you will require about 42-44 degrees of total advance and about 20-22 degrees of static/idle speed advance.

In fact, you don't actually need to know the precise number of degrees of advance that produce maximum torque: whatever setting it takes to achieve it is all that really matters. Effectively you position the distributor to the advance position where maximum torque is produced. However, it's convenient to know what the figure is, of course, so that the distributor can be set to the known ideal figure when it is being re-tuned at a later stage. If you get your engine tested and set up correctly, make sure that you know what the total ignition advance is. Having the wrong amount of ignition advance is one of the biggest causes of poor engine performance. Note that permanently marking the crankshaft damper with optimum degree settings is the best option for easy repeatable adjustments.

If you are not using a distributor and are able to programme the ignition curve then, if your engine has a little bit too much compression for the fuel you're using, you can retard the ignition at maximum torque a sufficient amount to stop the knock or 'pinking'/'pinging' and allow it to increase again as revs rise and the charge density reduces.

Caution! – All of the above values apply **only** if the engine is not over-compressed (CR to high) for the octane rating of the fuel actually being used. Running an engine with too much compression for the RON/MON octane rating of the fuel is folly. You're always better to have a more modest amount of compression and be able to keep the accelerator pedal hard down under all circumstances without the fear of pre-ignition. You can increase the fuelling to stop the 'pinking'/'pinging', but you'll be losing power by doing so. The fuel octane can be increased if your engine has a bit too much compression by using something like Millers CVL or TetraBOOST mixed with unleaded fuel (class rules permitting) or, if you're in the USA, use high octane unleaded.

Don't underestimate the beneficial effects of 'good fuel'. Engines which have a compression ratio that is a bit too high for the RON/MON octane rating don't go as well as they should. If, for example, you are using a certain octane fuel in your engine and you think that the compression ratio might be a bit high for it, drain the fuel and try some higher octane fuel instead. If the engine goes better then it's very likely that its compression ratio is too high, if there is no difference, then the fuel you have been using is satisfactory.

J.E. Developments
(John Eales)
The Rover V8 engine builder

Cubic Capacity (cc) of available engine sizes

	\multicolumn{5}{c}{Bore/mm}				
Stroke/mm	**88.9**	**90.0**	**94.0**	**94.5**	**96.0**
63.0			3497.7		
71.1	3531.6	3619.6	3948.5	3990.6	4118.3
77.0			4274.9	4320.5	
80.0			4441.5	4488.8	
79.4					4597.7
82.0			4552.5	4601.1	4748.3
86.3			4794.6	4845.7	5000.8
91.5			5079.9	5134.1	5298.4

- Large stock of Rover V8 parts
- Dry sump systems
- Downdraught and side inlet manifolds
- Sump baffles
- Small diameter flywheel and starter motor
- Forged steel adjustable rocker assemblies
- Hewland adaptor plate/bell housing
- Bell housing for T5, Getrag, etc
- Balancing
- Forged steel conrods
- Forged pistons for most capacities at 89.4mm, 90mm, 94mm, 94.5mm, and 96mm
- New cross bolted 3.5 and 3.9 blocks available
- Cross drilled crankshafts at 63mm, 71.12mm, 77mm, 80mm, 82mm, 86.36mm, 90mm and 91.5mm

Claybrooke Mill
Frolesworth Lane
Claybrooke Magna
Nr. Lutterworth
Leicestershire
LE17 5DB

Tel: 01455 202909
email: john@ealesxx.fsnet.co.uk
web: www.rover-v8.com

Index

28cc type cylinder heads 20, 54, 55

ACL (pistons) 47, 103, 104, 122
Adjustable length pushrods 74, 118
Adjustable oil pressure unit 61
Aftermarket 180 degree type inlet
    manifolds 163
Aftermarket 360 degree type inlet
    manifolds 163-165
Anti-pump-up hydraulic lifters 79
AP Racing (clutches) 202
ARP studs & nuts 37-39

Balancing 118, 119
Bearings 100
Block cracking 23
Block 'fretting' 33-36
Block registers 15-21
Block wall thickness 23-26
Blocks (38A type) 1 8-23
Bore wear 47, 48
Bosch Motronic (engine
    management) 187
Buick 10, 11, 17, 51, 56, 60, 61, 65,
    81, 90, 103, 127, 128, 132, 134,
    161-164

Camshaft bearings 39, 40
Camshaft/lifter problems 80, 81
Camshaft skew gears 61
Camshaft thrust bolt 43, 44
Cast pistons 45
Catalytic converters 188
Cloyes timing chains 40
Clutches 201, 202
Competition cams 74
Condensers 69
Connecting rods 110-112
CO/Lambda reading 204-208
Cracked blocks 24-33
Crankcase ventilation 150
Crankshaft dampers 36
Crankshaft snouts 18-22, 95, 96
Crankshaft snout key-ways 19-22
Cross bolted main cap blocks 36
Cylinder blocks 14-50
Cylinder block identification 14-23
    Type 1 15, 16
    Type 2 16
    Type 3 16, 17
    Type 4 17, 18
    Type 5 & 6 18
    Type 7 20-22

    Type 8 20-22
Cylinder bore preparation 48-50
Cylinder bore wall finish 48-50
Cylinder bore wear 48
Cylinder heads 82-84
Crane Cams 74, 76, 117
Connecting rods 110
Crankshafts 109, 110
Crossover exhaust systems 194

Dart inlet manifold 132
Distributors 57, 58, 62-70, 119
Distributor advance springs 63, 64
Distributor rates of advance (change
    them) 63, 64
Dual valve springs 51
Duplex timing chain sets 41

Eaton camshaft bearing installation
    tool 40
Edelbrock 180 degree type inlet
    manifold 132, 163-165
Engine balance 92-94, 118, 119
Engine block number/letter codes
    14
Engine capacities 112

Engine component clearances 50
Eutectic type pistons 47, 126
Exhaust pipe diameter sizes 193
Exhaust system configurations 121, 189-194

Firing order 161
Fitting liners 44, 45
Flanged liners 26-29
Flywheels 201, 202
Forged pistons 47
Forged steel rocker arms 116, 117
Four barrel carburettor type inlet manifolds 161-165
Four into one type exhaust manifolds 190-192
Four into two into one type exhaust manifolds 192-194
Front covers 57-61
Fuel 120
Fuel pressure 150

Gear-driven oil pumps 60
Gear drives (camshaft) 127
GEMS 8 (engine management) 57, 59, 60, 172, 182-188
'Group A' hydraulic camshafts 81
GT-40 type exhaust systems 194

Harcourt 360 degree type inlet manifold 164
High rise 180 degree inlet manifolds 162, 163
Holbay 90
Holley carburettors 156-160
    accelerator pump adjustment 156, 157
    adjustment tips 158, 159
    air cleaners 159
    automatic chokes 156
    cool air induction 160
    float levels 156
    fuel filters 160
    fuel pumps 160
    heat shielding 159, 160
    metering blocks 157-159
    two barrel carburettor to four barrel inlet manifold adapter 164

two barrel carburettors 164
390-CFM basic setting 156
390-CFM idle adjustment 156, 157
390-CFM mechanical secondary ('double pumper') 158
HSE cooling problems 29-32
Huffaker 360 degree inlet manifold, 132, 161, 164, 165
Hydraulic lifter preload 73, 79
Hydraulic lifters 79, 80
Hypereutectic pistons 45, 126
Hypoeutectic pistons 45, 126

Iceberg crankshafts 12
Induction systems 119
'Interim' blocks 18, 20-23, 25, 42, 43
Iskenderian 74, 76, 79, 80, 88, 90
Iskenderian anti-pump-up hydraulic lifters 79, 80

J.E. Developments 29, 39, 44, 50, 69, 74, 87, 94, 99, 104, 108-121, 136, 140, 142, 146, 147, 150, 151, 201
John McCormack 13

K-Line camshaft bearing installation tool 40
K-Line valve guide inserts 84-86, 137
Kenne Bell 97, 99
Kent Cams 44, 86, 88, 89, 90, 91
Keyways 19-22
Kwik-Way 84

L-Jetronic 4CU 166-178
L-Jetronic-twin plenum 178, 179
L-Jetronic 14CUX 58, 170-172, 180-182
L-Jetronic 13CU & 14CU 179, 180
Lambda/%CO readings 151-153, 206-208
Large bore blocks 17, 22-26
Large main bearing blocks 20-22
Leyland P76 12, 13, 16, 53, 54, 161
Long gear oil pumps 60

Loose liners 30, 31
Low rise 180 degree inlet manifolds 162
Lubrication 95-107
Lucas distributors 57-59, 62-70, 119
Lucas fuel injection systems 166-188
Lucas 'hot wire' injections 58
Lumentition 62

Main bearing cap studs & nuts 37-39
Main bearing caps 15-18, 20-24, 33-39
Main bearing tunnel distortion 37, 38
Main cap/block 'fretting' 33-36
Mallory coils 65
Mallory distributors 65-67
Mechanical advance (ignition) 63
Mixtures (fuel) 204-208
Modified standard type cylinder heads 136, 137, 140-142, 146, 147
Modular pushrods 74, 117, 118
Morse chain 40, 41
Mufflers 191-193

Offenhauser 161
Oldsmobile 10-12, 65, 90, 132, 161, 162, 164
Optimum fuel mixtures 120, 121
Outrigger end pillars (rocker shafts) 75
Oversized liners for 3.5 litre blocks 44, 45

P5 & P6 engines 51, 52
P76 engine 12, 13, 16, 53, 54, 161
Piper Cams 40, 44, 81-83, 85, 86, 88, 89, 91
Pistons 45-47, 111, 112
Piston rings 48-50
Plateau honing 48-50
Pontiac 10
Pushrods 74-76, 117, 118

Quick reference guide to block identification 23

Racing camshafts 112, 115, 116
Racing engine cylinder heads 51-53, 112-114, 140-142, 146, 147
Recommended cylinder head fixing 50
Regrinding standard camshafts 78, 79
Repairing cracked blocks 31, 32
Repco 11, 13, 122
Resurfacing cylinder heads 140
Reusing lifters 80
Rocker shaft end pillars 75, 116, 118
Rocker shaft geometry 71-73
Rocker shaft height 72
Roller rockers 73, 117
Rolling road tuning 203-208

Sealing exhaust manifolds to cylinder heads 194
Serpentine drive belt 60
Service blocks 22, 23
Setting roller rocker arm shaft heights 73
Sig Erson 88, 90
Silencers 191-193
Short gear oil pumps 61
Shortening standard pushrods 74
Small bore blocks 14-17, 22, 23
Small main bearing blocks 15-20, 22
Spark plug lead positions 69

Spark plug leads 69
Standard camshaft drive chain 40, 41
Standard exhaust manifolds 189, 190
Standard piston range 45
Standard rocker arms 71-76
Standard rocker arm geometry 71, 72
Standard rocker arm rpm limits 75, 76
Static ignition advance 63
Steel rocker arms (Federal Mogul) 75, 76, 117
Stretch bolts 19, 20
Studs & nuts 39, 50
Studs & nuts for two bolt blocks (mains) 37-39
'Superlifters' (Iskenderian) 74
SU carburettors 148-155
    Choosing suitable needles 151-154
    Float levels/fuel levels 149
    Idle mixtures/adjustment 149
    Main jet height 149
    Modifying SU carburettors 151
    Ram pipes and air cleaners 150, 151
Syncronizing carburettors 149, 150

Teflon thrust bolt 43, 44, 81
Thin wall liners for 3.5 litre blocks 44, 45
Timing chains 41
Thrust plate 16-19

Traco 11, 12, 36
Traco-Oldsmobile 11, 12, 36
Tubular exhaust manifolds 190-194
Tufftrided valves 137
TVR 12, 133-135
Two bolt main cap block problems 32, 33

Unleaded fuel use cylinder heads 55, 137

Vacuum advance (ignition) 64
Valves 56, 112-114, 128-132
Valve seat recession 136, 137
Valve seat widths 138, 139
Valve springs 56, 79, 80, 82-87, 114, 115
Valve spring retainers 56, 79, 82-87, 115, 116
Vandervell engine bearings 104

Water loss problem 29-33
Water pumps 60
Water temperatures 29-31, 34, 36-38

Wildcat Engineering 10, 26-29, 44, 50, 61, 74, 104, 122-135, 164
Wildcat Engineering 360 degree inlet manifold 164
Wildcat flanged linered blocks 26-29

Yella-Terra roller rockers 117